By definition, the informal economy is hard to stud[y] countries. This excellent book uses state-of-the-art available data to measure and analyze informality in advanced, emerging market and developing economies. In particular, it explores the business cycles in the informal sector in 160 countries over the past 30 years; the study is the first one to show that cycles in the formal economy cause those in the informal economy. Contrary to the widespread stereotype that the informal sector is a buffer that helps to mitigate recessions in the formal sector, the informal sector's output moves in sync with the formal one, and informal employment does not increase during recessions. This book also produces the first analysis of the role of informality during the COVID-19 pandemic. Informal economic activity is concentrated in labor-intensive service sectors and thus is especially vulnerable to social distancing and lockdowns. A rigorous, relevant, and highly timely must-read for development scholars and policy makers.

Sergei Guriev
Professor of Economics, Sciences Po, and
former Chief Economist, European Bank for Reconstruction and Development

Significant data gaps have previously limited our ability to thoroughly study the informal economy until now. The authors construct a novel and comprehensive data set on informality, which allows them to unpack the complexity of the informal sector and its interaction with the formal sector. This timely book provides an invaluable knowledge resource for researchers and practitioners alike through an approach that balances rigorous quantitative and qualitative methods. The resulting policy recommendations offer compelling pathways for policy makers looking to address some of the main obstacles to formalization of the economies and to accelerate economic development in the postpandemic world.

Brahima Sangafowa Coulibaly
Vice President, Global Economy and Development
The Brookings Institution

This highly informative and timely book compiles various measures of the informal economy in a comprehensive global data set. Its analysis of informality's most important correlates provides important insights and policy implications, written in highly accessible prose. Franziska Ohnsorge and Shu Yu have edited an authoritative source of reference for everyone interested in the informal economy. The questions raised in this book, and the answers given, make it essential reading for academics and policy makers alike.

Axel Dreher
Professor of International and Development Politics
Heidelberg University, Germany

Informal economic activity has long been recognized as an important phenomenon in developing economies, one that poses a broad range of potentially serious policy challenges for both social and material well-being in those countries. Yet, for all the attention that various aspects of the informality phenomenon have received, there is no single comprehensive treatment of the topic that simultaneously considers the challenges of measuring informality, the identification of its causes in diverse settings, its specific social and economic consequences, and the range of context-specific policy measures that can potentially be adopted to address those consequences. Drawing on a comprehensive data set covering a wide range of countries and time periods, this book fills that gap. I expect it to serve as a springboard for a more systematic and widespread integration of the problem of informality into development economics.

Peter Montiel
Fairleigh S. Dickinson, Jr. '41 Professor of Economics
Williams College

The COVID-19 crisis has exacerbated development challenges for many emerging market and developing economies, including as a result of disproportionate impacts on informal economic activity and therefore women, youth, and lower-skilled workers. *The Long Shadow of Informality* provides important insights as to the extent, impact, and policy challenges posed by informality. By deepening our understanding of a key constraint to development this book can help guide appropriately tailored and comprehensive policy responses required to avoid a great divergence in economic prospects both within and between countries.

Ceyla Pazarbasioglu
Director of the Strategy, Policy and Review Department
International Monetary Fund

By its very nature, informality is hard to measure and even harder to address with policies. This book provides the most comprehensive treatment to date, combining different estimation methods; covering every developing region in the world; and spanning growth, business cycles, and sectoral issues. Being wide-ranging, the book will elicit debate on various topics. Thanks to this book, those debates can be based on solid empirical foundations.

Shanta Devarajan
Professor of the Practice of International Development
Georgetown University

The Long Shadow
of Informality

The Long Shadow of Informality

Challenges and Policies

Edited by
Franziska Ohnsorge and Shu Yu

Summary of Contents

Contents

Boxes

Figures

Tables

Foreword

In emerging market and developing economies (EMDEs), far too many people and small enterprises operate outside the line of sight of governments—in a zone where little help is available to them in an emergency such as the COVID-19 (coronavirus) crisis. This "informal" sector constitutes more than 70 percent of total employment in these countries and roughly one-third of output.

Policy makers have long had good reasons to worry about this sector: Its participants are vulnerable even under normal conditions. Informal businesses rely heavily on family members and moneylenders for working capital, leaving them exposed to sudden income disruptions. These enterprises constitute 72 percent of firms in the services sector. Informal workers are predominantly women and usually young and low-skilled. When they lose their jobs or suffer severe income losses, they often have no recourse to social safety nets.

COVID-19 has heightened the need for prompt and comprehensive action. The pandemic increased global poverty for the first time in decades—and it hit informal firms and informally employed workers particularly hard: they struggled to adjust to lockdowns and the shift to business connected over the internet. Data on this matter may not be fully available for some time, but the damage to households and firms in the informal sector poses a significant threat—to the global economic recovery and to long-term efforts to achieve green, resilient, and inclusive development.

Widespread informality hampers development progress in a variety of ways. It is broadly associated with weaker economic outcomes. Countries with larger informal sectors have lower per capita incomes, greater poverty, less financial development, and weaker growth in output, investment, and productivity. Gross domestic product (GDP) per capita in countries with above-average informality tends to be just one-quarter to one-third the GDP per capita of countries with below-average informality.

Moreover, informality curbs government revenues, constraining governments' ability to provide services, conduct countercyclical policies, service debt, or implement crisis-response measures. Measured as a percentage of GDP, government revenues in EMDEs with above-average informality were 5 to 12 percentage points lower than those of EMDEs with below-average informality between 2000 and 2018. Not surprisingly, higher informality was also associated with lower public spending on education and health, contributing to the slower accumulation of human capital.

Yet the record shows informality *can* be tackled in EMDEs. In fact, it had been on a declining trend for decades before the onset of COVID-19. Between 1990 and 2018, on average, informality fell by about 7 percentage points of GDP to 32 percent of GDP. The decline partly reflected policy reforms: Over the past three decades, many EMDE governments implemented a wide range of policy reforms either to increase the benefits of formal-sector participation or to reduce the costs of such activities. These included tax reforms, reforms to increase access to finance, and stronger governance.

The key, however, is to recognize informality as a phenomenon that reflects broad-based underdevelopment—rather than a challenge that can be considered in isolation. For that reason, measures to address informality need to be equally broad-based.

This book offers the first detailed road map to cope with informality for policy makers in developing countries. Above all, it underscores the need for an encompassing approach. A comprehensive policy package tailored to country circumstances offers the greatest chance of success. Depending on country circumstances, such a package should include the following components:

- *Improvements in macroeconomic policies, governance, and business climates.* In the past three decades, EMDEs have made progress in reducing tax burdens, improving governance and regulatory quality, and enhancing access to finance, education, and public services. These actions haved helped reduce the extent of informality, but additional reforms are needed to make further progress.

- *Streamlined tax regulation and administration and improved public service delivery.* Policies aimed at invigorating private sector activity—such as measures to increase labor market flexibility and streamlining regulatory frameworks for firm start-up—have also been associated with declines in informality.

- *Attention to unintended consequences of policy reforms.* For instance, trade liberalization that raised competition in the tradable sector has been associated with greater informality in the short run—unless it is accompanied by measures that increase labor market flexibility.

- *Acceleration of financial sector development.* Such development has been associated with declining informality—because it reduces the average cost of access to external financing and creates incentives for firms to invest in higher-productivity projects and join the formal sector.

- *Campaigns to expand public awareness.* Reductions in informality have tended to be greater for reforms that have been accompanied by business development and training programs, public awareness campaigns, and stronger enforcement.

Rebuilding the global economy in the aftermath of COVID-19 will mean mobilizing every available reserve of productive power to generate green, resilient, and inclusive development. That effort must begin now—and it cannot succeed without full consideration of the challenges of the informal sector.

Mari Pangestu
Managing Director of Development Policy and Partnerships
The World Bank

Acknowledgments

This book is a product of the Prospects Group in the Equitable Growth, Finance and Institutions Vice Presidency at the World Bank. The project was managed by Franziska Ohnsorge and Shu Yu, under the general guidance of M. Ayhan Kose. Ayhan's constant support, thorough and carefully considered feedback, analytical insights, and dedication to the success of this book immeasurably raised the quality of the book.

The core team underlying the project included Salvatore Capasso, Ceyhun Elgin, Sergiy Kasyanenko, Yoki Okawa, Cedric Okou, and Dana Vorisek. The book reflects their original insights, analytical depth, and painstakingly careful work. The chapter on regional dimensions of informality was prepared by Gene Kindberg-Hanlon, Wee Chian Koh, Yoki Okawa, Temel Taskin, Ekaterine T. Vashakmadze, Dana Vorisek, and Lei Sandy Ye, who brought their extensive regional knowledge to the subject.

Many colleagues in the Prospects Group provided detailed comments and feedback during various stages of the project, including Carlos Arteta, Sinem Kilic Celik, Justin Damien Guenette, Jongrim Ha, Gene Kindberg-Hanlon, Patrick Alexander Kirby, Peter Stephen Oliver Nagle, Cedric Okou, Franz Ulrich Ruch, Naotaka Sugawara, Temel Taskin, Dana Vorisek, and Collette Mari Wheeler.

This book is built upon the foundation of chapter 3 of the 2019 January *Global Economic Prospects* report. The early work benefited from invaluable discussions with Shanta Devarajan, Pinelopi Goldberg, Ceyla Pazarbasioglu, William Maloney, and Norman Loayza. The team also received helpful comments and suggestions from James Brumby, Anna Custer, Mark Andrew Dutz, Margaret Grosh, Truman Packard, and Marijn Verhoeven. In addition, many World Bank Group colleagues provided extensive feedback at different stages of the project, including during the institutionwide review of our work.

The book benefited from constructive comments and feedback received during both preparation and production stages. The team is grateful to scholars who provided extensive comments on chapter drafts: Salvatore Capasso, Ugo Panizza, and Gabriel Ulyssea. The team is grateful as well to many World Bank colleagues who provided comments on the drafts during a final review process, including Mohammad Amin, Kevin Carey, Ergys Islamaj, Gerard Kambou, and Guillermo Javier Vuletin. The team benefited greatly from consultations and discussion with Mariam Dolidze, Andreja Marusic, Evgenij Najdov, Hulya Ulku, and Gabriel Zaourak. The team owes a particular debt of gratitude to Graham Hacche, who painstakingly edited all the chapters.

The team is also thankful to the organizers and participants at various seminars and conferences held in 2019-20, who provided valuable early feedback on various chapters of the book: Bank of England, De Nederlandsche Bank, European Central Bank, European Bank for Reconstruction and Development, Organisation for Economic Co-operation and Development, European Commission, ETH Zurich, Heidelberg University, the 7th International Monetary Fund Statistical Forum, the 2019 Fall Midwest Macroeconomic Meetings, and the 2020 Congress of the European Economic Association.

Zhuo Chen, Hrisyana Doytchinova, Maria Hazel Macadangdang, Jinxin Wu, Lorez Qehaja, Arika Kayastha, Shijie Shi, and Xinyue Wang provided outstanding research assistance. Yiruo Li, Zhuo Chen, Shituo Sun, Jinxin Wu, and Liwei Liu helped compile the database in the early stages of the project. Thanks also to Roberto Crotti and Margareta Drzeniek, who shared valuable data with us.

The team is indebted to colleagues who supported us throughout the production process: Maria Hazel Macadangdang for guiding us through the steps from beginning to completion of the book, Adriana Maximiliano for designing and typesetting, and Graeme B. Littler for editorial and website support. Abdennour Azeddine provided excellent technology support. The team also appreciates the great support from many colleagues in the External and Corporate Communications Vice Presidency of the World Bank, including Alejandra Viveros, Joseph Rebello, and Torie Smith, and colleagues from the Sustainable Development Goals Fund team, including Juliana Knapp and Lisa Maria Castro.

The Prospects Group gratefully acknowledges financial support from the World Bank Group Partnership Fund for the Sustainable Development Goals (SDG Fund) and the Research Support Budget overseen by the Research Committee of the Development Economics Vice-Presidency.

Authors

Salvatore Capasso, Professor of Economic Policy, University of Naples Parthenope and ISMed-CNR

Ceyhun Elgin, Professor of Economics, Boğaziçi University

Sergiy Kasyanenko, Economist, World Bank

Gene Kindberg-Hanlon, Economist, World Bank

Wee Chian Koh, former Economist, World Bank

M. Ayhan Kose, Director, World Bank

Franziska Ohnsorge, Practice Manager, World Bank

Yoki Okawa, Economist, World Bank

Cedric Okou, Economist, World Bank

Temel Taskin, Economist, World Bank

Ekaterine T. Vashakmadze, Senior Economist, World Bank

Dana Vorisek, Senior Economist, World Bank

Lei Sandy Ye, former Economist, World Bank

Shu Yu, Economist, World Bank

Executive Summary

Informal activity is widespread in emerging market and developing economies (EMDEs). In EMDEs, informal economic activity, on average, accounts for about one-third of output and more than two-thirds of employment (chapter 2). The phenomenon extends across all EMDE regions.

Widespread informality has long been associated with a whole host of development challenges (chapter 4). Most prominently, more widespread informality has been associated with significantly poorer governance and greater lags in achieving every dimension of the Sustainable Development Goals. Countries with larger informal sectors tend to have less access to finance for the private sector, lower labor productivity, slower physical and human capital accumulation, and smaller fiscal resources. Informality is associated with higher income inequality and poverty and less progress toward the Sustainable Development Goals.

Informal firms are, on average, less productive than formal ones because they tend to employ more low-skilled workers; have more restricted access to funding, services, and markets; and lack economies of scale. Informal workers tend to be paid less than formal workers, in part because they are lower-skilled. Female and young workers make up a disproportionate share of workers in the informal sector.

Pervasive informality is particularly pernicious at the current juncture. In the severe global recession caused by the COVID-19 (coronavirus) pandemic, the informal sector has been hit hard by the lockdowns and changes in consumer behavior triggered by the pandemic. Informal firms account for almost three-quarters of firms in the services sector, compared with one-third of firms in the manufacturing sector. With low incomes and little savings to fall back on, informal workers struggle to comply with lockdowns, and government support programs often cannot reach them.

Going forward, widespread informality may hold back the recovery to a green, inclusive, and resilient development path. Countries with high informality struggle to muster the fiscal resources to support economic activity, to implement effective monetary policy in a shallow financial system, and to generate informal-sector income growth or formal-sector employment in a recovery.

Government revenues in EMDEs with above-median informality are about 5-12 percentage points of gross domestic product (GDP) below those in other EMDEs, and so are their expenditures. The lack of fiscal resources constrains governments' ability to develop fiscal support packages that can help bring the pandemic under control and generate a robust recovery. Indeed, in 2020 -21, EMDEs with above-median informality implemented discretionary fiscal support packages that were only three-quarters the size of those in EMDEs with below-median informality.

In countries with widespread informality, shallow financial systems limit the reach and effectiveness of monetary policy. In EMDEs with above-median informality, domestic credit to the private sector is only one-third of GDP— significantly less than in other EMDEs where it is more than one-half of GDP—and many firms do not rely on the formal financial system at all. For example, in EMDEs with above-median informality, only 19 percent of firms can access bank financing for their investment needs, significantly lower than the 29 percent of firms in other EMDEs.

If history is any guide, large informal sectors will dampen the recovery. Historically, informal-economy output and, hence, incomes have fluctuated with formal-economy output, but they have done so less than proportionately (chapter 3). For every 1-percentage-point increase in formal-economy output, informal-economy output has risen only by 0.4-0.8 percentage point over the following year. While this muted co-movement dampened past recessions, it also held back past recoveries.

Moreover, informal employment historically has been largely unresponsive to formal-economy business cycles. This suggests that workers do not easily switch between formal and informal employment; instead, once they are informally employed, they tend to expand or curtail their working hours with the business cycle. It also suggests that whatever increase in informal employment the COVID-19 pandemic has induced—and we will not have the data to know for sure for many months—may not be unwound in the recovery from the pandemic.

This book offers a wide menu of policy options to address these challenges associated with informality. Improved access to education, markets, and finance can help informal workers and firms become sufficiently productive to move to the formal sector. Labor productivity in EMDEs with above-median informality is less than a third of the level in other EMDEs. This in part reflects low human capital: in EMDEs with above-median informality, the average number of years of schooling amounts to 5-6 years—1-3 years less than in other EMDEs.

In addition, improved governance and business climates and streamlined— but well-enforced—regulations can lower the cost of operating formally and increase the cost of operating informally. In these dimensions, EMDEs with high informality clearly lag those with low informality. For example, the average score on bureaucracy quality in EMDEs with above-median informality is one-third lower than in other EMDEs.

Policy measures that help to lower informality also spur growth more broadly. To protect vulnerable groups, they may need to be accompanied by stronger basic social safety nets (chapter 6).

These options are most likely to be effective when they follow two principles:

First, reform packages need to be comprehensive. Over the past several decades, many EMDE governments implemented policies at the microeconomic level and found that the implications for informality were more benign when these reforms were implemented in a supportive institutional and macroeconomic environment. For instance, trade liberalization programs that raised real wages and reduced firms' profitability in the tradable sector were associated with greater informality in the short term—unless they were accompanied by higher labor market flexibility and a more skilled labor force.

Second, reform packages need to be tailored to country circumstances, informed by the drivers of—and challenges posed by—informality and carefully tailored to country circumstances. In Sub-Saharan Africa, South Asia, and the Middle East and North African economies that are not part of the Gulf Cooperation Council, for example, general education and training programs to raise human capital could be prioritized (chapter 5). In Latin America and the Caribbean, reducing particularly high tax and regulatory costs to businesses could incentivize firms to join the formal sector. In Europe and Central Asia, improving government effectiveness and reducing corruption could be policy priorities.

Abbreviations

AEs	advanced economies
ATM	automated teller machine
BMA	Bayesian model averaging
COVID-19	coronavirus disease 2019
DGE	dynamic general equilibrium
EAP	East Asia and Pacific
ECA	Europe and Central Asia
EMDEs	emerging market and developing economies
EU	European Union
FD	financial development
FE	fixed effects
FEMP	formal employment
GCC	Gulf Cooperation Council
GDP	gross domestic product
GNI	gross national income
GVC	global value chain
HP	Hodrick-Prescott (filter)
ICRG	International Country Risk Guide
ICT	information and communication technology
IDB	Inter-American Development Bank
IE	informal economy
ILO	International Labour Organization
IMF	International Monetary Fund
IVs	instrumental variables
LAC	Latin America and the Caribbean
LICs	low-income countries
LSMS	Living Standards Measurement Study
MIMIC	multiple indicators multiple causes (model)
MNA	Middle East and North Africa
MRA	meta-regression analysis
OECD	Organisation for Economic Co-operation and Development
PIPs	posterior inclusion probabilities
PPP	purchasing power parity
PWT	Penn World Table

R&D	research and development
SAR	South Asia Region
SD	standard deviation
SDGs	Sustainable Development Goals
SEM	structural equation model
SEMP	self-employment
SMEs	small and medium enterprises
SSA	Sub-Saharan Africa
TLI	Tucker Lewis Index
VAT	value added tax
WDI	World Development Indicators
WEF	World Economic Forum
WGI	Worldwide Governance Indicators
WVS	World Values Survey

The current crisis is a sharp contrast from the recession of 2008. . . .
This time, the economic downturn is broader, much deeper, and has
hit informal sector workers and the poor, especially women and
children, harder than those with higher incomes or assets.

David Malpass (2020)
President
World Bank Group

CHAPTER 1
Overview

Motivation

By now, the economic damage of the COVID-19 (coronavirus) pandemic has been extensively documented. The pandemic and associated containment measures plunged the global economy into a severe contraction. Global output shrank by more than 4 percent in 2020, with output in emerging market and developing economies (EMDEs) contracting by about 3 percent, the group's first annual contraction in more than 60 years (World Bank 2021). Over the past century and a half, the pandemic-driven global recession was the deepest since the Second World War and featured the largest fraction of economies with declines in per capita output since at least 1870 (World Bank 2020a). The decline in per capita incomes during the pandemic has pushed millions of people into extreme poverty since the beginning of the pandemic.

While the pandemic has been simply devastating, its impact has been particularly severe on the informal sector (World Bank 2020a). With a prominent presence in the services sector, informal workers were more likely to lose their jobs or suffer severe income losses during lockdowns (Balde, Boly, and Avenyo 2020; Schotte et al. 2021). A large informal sector is also associated with poorer access for many to public health and sanitation facilities, making it harder to contain the spread of the pandemic (World Bank 2020a). Informal workers are largely excluded from formal social safety nets and have low incomes and limited buffers such as savings or access to government support programs.

Informality has been associated with broader development challenges since long before the pandemic (World Bank 2019). In EMDEs, the informal sector accounts for about a third of gross domestic product (GDP) and more than 70 percent of employment (of which self-employment is more than a half; figure 1.1). Regardless of the nature and causes of informality, countries with larger informal sectors tend to have less access to finance for the private sector, lower labor productivity, slower physical and human capital accumulation, and smaller fiscal resources (Docquier, Müller, and Naval 2017; La Porta and Shleifer 2014). Informality is also associated with higher income inequality and poverty and less progress toward the Sustainable Development Goals (SDGs; Chong and Gradstein 2007; Loayza, Servén, and Sugawara 2010). The informal sector is, on average, less productive than the formal sector because it tends to employ more low-skilled workers; have more restricted access to funding, services, and markets; and lack economies of scale (Amaral and Quintin 2006; Loayza 2018).

Note: This chapter was prepared by Franziska Ohnsorge and Shu Yu. Research assistance was provided by Hrisyana Doytchinova and Maria Hazel Macadangdang.

FIGURE 1.1 Informality: Main features

The informal sector accounts for about a third of GDP and more than 70 percent of employment (of which self-employment is more than a half) in EMDEs. A large informal sector is often associated with lack of development and weak governance as well as greater poverty and income inequality.

A. Share of informal output and self-employment

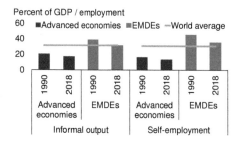

B. Informality: Output and employment shares, and perceptions

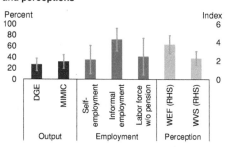

C. Informality by EMDE region

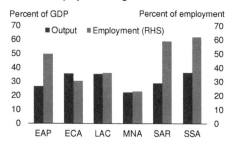

D. Per capita incomes and informality

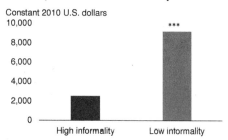

E. Informality, poverty, and income inequality

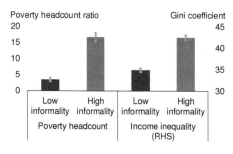

F. Governance in EMDEs with high and low output informality

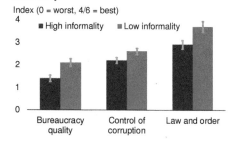

Sources: International Country Risk Guide (ICRG); International Labour Organization; World Bank (World Development Indicators); World Economic Forum; World Values Survey.

Note: EAP = East Asia and Pacific; ECA = Europe and Central Asia; EMDEs = emerging market and developing economies; DGE = dynamic general equilibrium model estimates in percent of official GDP; LAC = Latin America and the Caribbean; Labor force w/o pension = the share of labor force without pension; MIMIC = multiple indicators multiple causes model estimates in percent of GDP; MNA = Middle East and North Africa; RHS = right-hand side; SAR = South Asia; SSA = Sub-Saharan Africa; WVS = World Values Survey estimates (1 to 10; a higher value means that cheating on taxes is more justifiable); WEF = World Economic Forum estimates (1 to 7; 7 = most informal).

A. Unweighted averages. Self-employment shares with missing value interpolated in EMDEs for earlier years and filled using the latest available observation in recent years. They are proxies for informal employment. World averages between 1990 and 2018 are in orange.

B. Unweighted averages for latest available year. Whiskers are +/– 1 standard deviation. Measures are grouped into output informality, employment informality, and perception-based informality. Data on informal employment are for EMDEs.

C. Bars show simple average shares of DGE-based informal output (in blue; self-employment shares in red) for 1990-2018 .

*D. GDP per capita in constant 2010 U.S. dollars. Unweighted average for EMDEs with above-median ("High informality") and below-median share of (DGE-based) output informality ("Low informality"). *** = statistically significant difference at the 10 percent level.*

E-F. Bars are unweighted average for EMDEs with above-median ("High informality") and below-median share of (DGE-based) output informality ("Low informality") for 1990-2018. Poverty headcount measures the percent of population living on $1.90 a day or less (2011 purchasing power parity). Whiskers are 90 percent confidence intervals.

Realizing the growth potential of the resources employed by the informal sector is a pressing matter as EMDEs rebound from the current recession. Policy actions can unleash the growth potential of the informal sector's resources by promoting their transfer to the formal sector, and providing better public services and social safety nets to protect vulnerable groups who remain in the informal sector. These policy interventions are even more important now because the pandemic is expected to leave long-lasting scars on the global economy, including less physical capital because of lower investment, erosion of the human capital of the unemployed, and a weakening of global trade and supply linkages (World Bank 2020a). These effects may well lower the levels and growth rates of potential output and labor productivity over a long period.

Against this backdrop, this book presents the first comprehensive study of informality—of its extent, evolution, and consequences, and of the policy options to address its challenges. The book makes several contributions to an already-large literature.

Comprehensive assessment. The book brings together a wide range of topics related to the informal economy, ranging from measurement issues to policy options. In contrast, earlier work typically examines only one of the dimensions covered in this book, such as the advantages and drawbacks of existing informality measures, the cyclical features of the informal sector, the developmental implications of informality, or examples of policy impacts.[1]

Regional emphasis. The book brings a regional dimension to the discussion of informality in EMDEs (chapter 5). Existing studies often group all countries together (Medina and Schneider 2018, 2019) or focus on a few specific regions or countries (Loayza, Servén, and Suguwara 2010; Perry et al. 2007). To allow comparisons across all six EMDE regions, the book utilizes a comprehensive data set that covers more than 120 EMDEs. In addition, the two chapters in Part II include only EMDEs in the analysis to avoid the results being driven by differences in the nature of informality between advanced economies and EMDEs.

Analysis of the implications of COVID-19. The book provides an analysis of the impact of COVID-19 in EMDEs with pervasive informality (chapter 2). This links the features of the informal sector with the health and economic consequences of COVID-19. It also highlights the policy challenges arising from informality when EMDEs have been facing the consequences of the deepest global recession since the Second World War.

Multiple approaches. The book uses a wide range of approaches and synthesizes findings based on multiple measures of informality. The literature on informality has mostly relied on either survey-based estimates of informality or model-based estimates

---

[1] See Medina and Schneider (2018) and Schneider, Buehn, and Montenegro (2010) for discussions of the advantages and drawbacks of informality measures. See Bosch, Goni, and Maloney (2007); Fiess, Fugazza, and Maloney (2010); and Loayza and Rigolini (2011) for the cyclical features of the informal sector. See La Porta and Shleifer (2014), Loayza (2016), and Loayza, Servén, and Suguwara (2010) for the developmental implications of informality. See Dix-Carneiro et al. (2021) and Ulyssea (2020) for examples of policy impacts.

and examined informality in terms of either output or employment.[2] The book examines three dimensions of informality—output, employment, and perceived level of informality—and uses a combination of informality measures to overcome the limitation of each measure (chapter 2). In addition, various empirical strategies are employed to address the specific questions posed in different chapters. The study is the first to conduct a Bayesian model averaging (BMA) estimation—designed to capture model uncertainty—to identify robust correlates of informality, and a meta-analysis of published empirical studies to estimate the wage gap between formal and informal workers (chapter 4).

For the purposes of this study, informality is defined as market-based legal production of goods and services that is hidden from public authorities for monetary, regulatory, or institutional reasons (Schneider, Buehn, and Montenegro 2010).[3] Output informality is proxied by estimates based on a dynamic general equilibrium model, in percent of GDP, and employment informality is proxied by self-employment in percent of total employment, unless otherwise specified (chapter 2).

Key findings and policy messages

Using a comprehensive database of multiple informality measures, this book examines the main characteristics of the informal economy, discusses its developmental implications, and presents a range of policy options to address issues associated with it.

Features of informal activity

Informality is associated with underdevelopment more broadly (La Porta and Shleifer 2014). Whereas the informal economy accounts for one-fifth of GDP and 16 percent of employment in advanced economies, it accounts for, on average, one-third of GDP and 70 percent of employment in EMDEs (of which self-employment accounts for more than a half; see chapter 2). Both informal output and employment have declined since 1990, especially in EMDEs. Thus, on average in EMDEs, the share of informal output in GDP fell by about 7 percentage points (to 32 percent), and the share of self-employment in total employment declined by about 10 percentage points (to 36 percent) over 1990-2018. These declines were broad-based.

There is wide heterogeneity in informal activity among EMDEs and EMDE regions. For example, in 2018, in terms of output, the informal economy ranged from around 10 percent of GDP to 68 percent of GDP; in terms of employment, self-employment

---

[2] Studies like Fajnzylber, Maloney, and Montes-Rojas (2011) and Amin (2021) relied on survey-based estimates, whereas studies like Dreher and Schneider (2010) and Elgin, Elveren, and Bourgeois (2020) utilized model-based estimates. Bajada (2003), Dell'Anno (2008), and Giles (1997) examined output informality, whereas studies like Fiess, Fugazza, and Maloney (2010) and Loayza and Rigolini (2011) examined employment informality.

[3] The definition and classification of informality are context-specific. See chapter 2 for various other definitions.

ranged from near zero to 96 percent of total employment. On average among the EMDE regions, the informal economy's output share is highest in Sub-Saharan Africa (SSA), Europe and Central Asia (ECA), and Latin America and the Caribbean (LAC). The share of self-employment, however, is highest in SSA, South Asia (SAR), and East Asia and Pacific (EAP; chapter 5). Although all EMDE regions have witnessed declines in informality between 1990 and 2018, declines in output informality have been largest in EAP and SAR whereas declines in employment informality have been largest in the Middle East and North Africa (MNA) and SSA. In ECA, employment informality has remained broadly unchanged, whereas in LAC it has risen.

The pandemic's toll in EMDEs with widespread informality

COVID-19 has taken a particularly heavy toll on participants in the informal sector. Several features of the informal sector cause its participants to suffer more severe economic losses than their formal counterparts during lockdowns while limiting effective government support to informal workers and firms.

Characteristics of informal workers. Workers in the informal sector tend to be lower-skilled and lower-paid, with less access to finance and social safety nets, than workers in the formal sector (Loayza 2018; Perry et al. 2007). They often live and work in crowded conditions and conduct all transactions in cash—factors that promote the spread of disease (Chodorow-Reich et al. 2020; Surico and Galeotti 2020). The absence of social safety nets makes informal workers less able to afford to adhere to social distancing requirements, which undermines policy efforts to contain the spread of COVID-19 (Loayza and Pennings 2020). In EMDEs with the most pervasive informality, people are more likely to be driven into poverty if they have to make direct out-of-pocket payments for health care emergencies.

Characteristics of informal firms. Informal firms tend to be labor-intensive and more prevalent in the services sector. Such firms have been particularly hard-hit by measures to curtail social interactions (see Benjamin and Mbaye 2012; Panizza 2020; Surico and Galeotti 2020). In EMDE service sectors, about 72 percent of firms are informal, compared with 33 percent in manufacturing sectors (Amin, Ohnsorge, and Okou 2019). Informal firms rely on internal funds, making them especially vulnerable to cashflow disruptions caused by mitigation and other control measures (Farazi 2014).

Broader development challenges. A larger informal economy is associated with weaker economic, fiscal, institutional, and development outcomes. GDP per capita in countries with above-median informality is about one-quarter that of countries with below-median informality. EMDEs with more informality lack adequate public health systems, access to clean water, and handwashing facilities. Government capacity to mount an effective policy response to pandemics is more limited (box 2.1). In addition, in countries with widespread informality, governments have limited resources and few administrative structures in place to effectively deliver well-targeted relief to those most in need (Muralidharan, Niehaus, and Sukhtankar 2016).

Development challenges associated with informality

EMDEs with pervasive informality face a wide range of development challenges (chapter 4). Countries with larger informal sectors have lower per capita incomes, greater poverty, less developed financial sectors, and weaker growth in output, investment, and productivity. People living in EMDEs with more widespread informality suffer from greater prevalence of hunger, poorer health and education, and greater gender inequality. Informal firms are less productive than their formal counterparts, and informal workers are paid less than their formal counterparts because of their lack of work experience and education.

Policy challenges associated with informality

Underdevelopment. More pervasive informality is associated with significantly lower government revenues and expenditures, less effective institutions, more burdensome tax and regulatory regimes, and weaker governance (chapters 4 and 6). Weaknesses in governance and revenue collection constrain the provision of public services, contributing to poorer development outcomes and poorer access to, and lower-quality, infrastructure. Limited fiscal resources constrain the government's ability to provide social safety nets during recessions, as exemplified during COVID-19, and to use policy measures to smooth business cycles.

Cyclical features of the informal economy. Additional challenges are posed by the behavior of informal economic activity through business cycles. Although informal employment remains broadly stable through business cycles in the formal economy, informal output is mildly procyclical, responding positively, although less than proportionately, to formal-economy output swings (chapter 3). As a result, the informal sector appears to dampen output losses during downturns—but also seems to moderate output gains during upturns and to lessen the impact of macroeconomic stabilization policies.

Tackling informality

The decline in informality over the past three decades has been accompanied by improvements in policy climates in EMDEs. Most EMDEs have reduced tax burdens; enhanced access to finance, education, and public services; and improved governance and regulatory quality. Meanwhile, some policy measures have sometimes had unintended consequences. A coherent reform strategy calls for well-integrated reforms that complement each other and address the complexity of informality.

Need for comprehensive reform packages. Many EMDE governments implemented policies at the microeconomic level and found that the implications for informality were more benign when these reforms were implemented in a supportive institutional and macroeconomic environment. For instance, trade liberalization programs that raised real wages and reduced firms' profitability in the tradable sector were associated with greater informality in the short term—unless they were accompanied by higher labor market flexibility and a more skilled labor force (chapter 6).

Need for tailored reform packages. Country experiences suggest the need for a comprehensive development strategy that is informed by the drivers of, and challenges posed by, informality and carefully tailored to country circumstances. Each reform component requires a diagnosis of the country's current situation, followed by specific reforms to address the main weaknesses associated with and underlying sources of informality. In SSA, SAR, and the MNA economies that are not members of the Gulf Cooperation Council, for example, general education and training programs to raise human capital could be prioritized (chapter 5). In LAC, reducing particularly high tax and regulatory costs to businesses could incentivize firms to join the formal sector. In ECA, improving government effectiveness and reducing corruption could be policy priorities.

The success of implementation also depends on careful monitoring of potential unintended consequences and a supportive macroeconomic, political, and institutional environment. The latter ensures the political and fiscal viability of the implementation and reduces the transition costs for workers moving from the informal sector to the formal sector.

Policies that seek to improve fiscal operations, such as through strengthened tax administration or streamlined tax regulations, can be associated with lowering informality in some economies. Separately, policies that aim at invigorating private sector activity and productivity and leveling the playfield for all workers and firms, particularly measures to make the labor market more flexible, the regulatory framework more adaptable, and governance more effective, can lower informality or improve the working conditions in the informal sector. Finally, supportive macroeconomic and social policies (such as enhancing public service and social protection) can ease the implementation of these reforms and facilitate a smoother transition from the informal sector to the formal sector.

These policy measures can help lower informality while also spurring growth more broadly. They need to be accompanied by strengthening the basic social safety nets to preserve incomes of vulnerable groups. Disruptions to formal activity from interventions to lower informality could be mitigated by reforms to increase labor and product market flexibility.

Synopsis

The remainder of this introduction summarizes the main messages of each chapter. For each chapter, the main questions, contributions to the literature, and analytical findings are presented. These summaries are followed by a brief discussion of future research directions.

Part I: Characteristics of the Informal Economy

Part I examines the evolution of informality, as well as its main correlates. Chapter 2 documents the main features of, and trends in, informality over the past three decades, with an emphasis on EMDEs. Chapter 3 explores the cyclical features of informality.

Chapter 2. Understanding the Informal Economy: Concepts and Trends

By its nature, informality is difficult to observe and measure. Chapter 2 introduces a comprehensive database of informality measures and describes the evolution of informality across EMDEs. In these economies, on average, informal-economy output accounts for about one-third of GDP and informal employment constitutes about 70 percent of total employment (of which self-employment accounts for more than one-half). In some countries in SSA, informal employment accounts for more than 90 percent of total employment and informal output for as much as 62 percent of official GDP (ILO 2018).

Against this backdrop, this chapter reviews conceptual and measurement issues regarding the informal economy and documents its main features across countries and over time. Specifically, it addresses the following questions:

- How is the informal economy defined?

- How has informality evolved?

- What are the features of the informal economy?

Contributions. The chapter makes the following contributions to the literature. First, it compiles a comprehensive database of measures of informality developed in the literature, with a focus on measures that have broad cross-country and long historical coverage. The resulting database combines 12 cross-country databases and data provided by almost 90 national statistical agencies.[4] Second, the chapter presents two applications of this database. It distills stylized facts about the informal economy, such as its size and evolution over time, using a wide range of informality measures, and tests the consistency of these stylized facts across these measures. In addition, the chapter documents the cyclical behavior of the informal economy, such as the duration and amplitude of its recessions and recoveries.

Main findings. First, the chapter presents a careful analysis of the advantages and drawbacks of existing informality measures. Most of the macroeconomic literature on informality has relied solely on either survey-based or model-based estimates. Survey-based measures can cover many dimensions of the informal economy, but they suffer from poor country and year coverage (especially for EMDEs), reporting bias, and lack of consistency in survey methods.[5] Indirect, model-based measures of informal output stand out in their potentially comprehensive country and year coverage and their

---

[4] Official GDP statistics often make an adjustment for informal activity. However, the magnitude of such adjustments is rarely specified. In a survey in 2008, national statistical agencies for about 40 mostly advanced economies or economies in transition reported adjusting their official GDP statistics by amounts ranging from 0.8 to 31.6 percent for activity in the non-observed economy, which is a broader concept than the informal economy (United Nations 2008). For all reporting economies, the adjustments were well below those suggested by the measures of informality presented in this study.

[5] Survey-based informality measures are based on income data from surveys or audits that differ from incomes declared for tax purposes (Binelli and Attanasio 2010; McCaig and Pavcnik 2015) or earnings from firm surveys (Almeida and Carneiro 2012; Putnins and Sauka 2015).

consistent economic meaning, but they rely on strong assumptions. The chapter highlights the circumstances in which the various individual informality measures could be particularly helpful. This adds to earlier literature that has focused on the limitations of a narrow range of estimation methods.

Second, the chapter argues that the combination of direct, survey-based indicators with indirect, model-based estimates can overcome the limitations of each. Informal employment measures tend to cover either the number of hours worked per day in informal employment ("intensity" of participation in informal employment) or, regardless of the number of hours worked per day, the presence of informal employment ("extent" of participation; Meghir, Narita, and Robin 2015). Because the extent of participation in the informal economy and its intensity may evolve differently, informal production may move asynchronously with informal employment.[6] Thus measures of informal output are an important complement to measures of informal employment.

Third, the chapter distills the main features of the informal economy and its evolution over time. Three different dimensions of informality are identified in the chapter: output, employment, and perception. Cross-country rankings of informal output and employment are typically consistent. Both output and employment measures of informality have trended downward since 1990 and have shown some cyclicality (figure 1.2). In contrast, perception-based measures have tended to be highly stable over time and could, therefore, be more appropriate for cross-country comparisons.

Fourth, the chapter is the first study that documents the cyclical features of the informal sector in both advanced economies and EMDEs. Cyclical features of informal economy output do not differ statistically significantly from those of formal economy output. Like the formal economy, the informal economy undergoes larger output movements over the business cycle in EMDEs than in advanced economies. Steeper recessions and stronger recoveries in EMDEs contribute to greater output volatility, as shown in previous studies (Aguiar and Gopinath 2007). Meanwhile, unlike formal employment, which contracts significantly in advanced economies during formal economy recessions, informal employment in both advanced economies and EMDEs appears largely acyclical during informal output business cycles. This may reflect wage movements or changes in intensity (measured as number of hours worked per day) in labor markets, which may bear the brunt of adjustment during business cycles (Guriev, Speciale, and Tuccio 2019; Meghir, Narita, and Robin 2015).

Chapter 3. Growing Apart or Moving Together? Synchronization of Informal- and Formal-Economy Business Cycles

Chapter 3 investigates the role of the informal economy as a potential dampener of business cycles that policy makers need to take into account when deciding on

---

[6] For example, during a recession, labor may move from the formal sector to the informal sector and raise participation in the informal economy (Loayza and Rigolini 2011). However, because of the fall in demand, the intensity of participation, captured by the number of hours worked in informal employment, may remain the same or even drop, and informal output may decline.

FIGURE 1.2 Informality: Extent and evolution

Informality is more pervasive in EMDEs than in advanced economies. Although there remains wide cross-country heterogeneity in informality among EMDEs, informality has generally declined over the past three decades.

A. Informal share of output

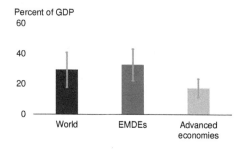

B. Informal share of employment

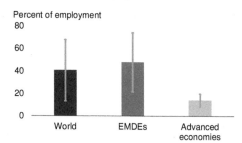

C. Informal share of output, 1990-2018

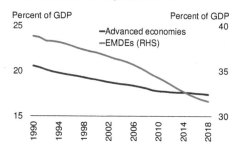

D. Informal share of employment, 1990-2018

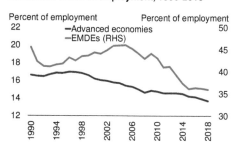

E. Informality: Output and employment shares, and perceptions

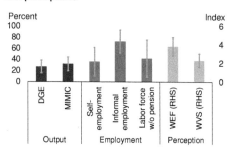

F. EMDEs with downward trend in informality, 1990-2018

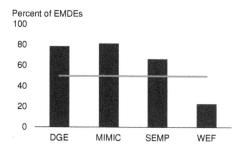

Source: World Bank.

Note: See chapter 2 for details on data definitions. Output informality is measured by dynamic general equilibrium (DGE) model estimates on informal output in percent of official GDP. In B and D, Informal employment is proxied by self-employment (SEMP) in percent of total employment. EMDEs = emerging market and developing economies; Labor force w/o pension = the share of labor force without pension; MIMIC = multiple indicators multiple causes model estimates on informal output in percent of GDP; RHS = right-hand side; WEF = World Economic Forum estimates (1 to 7; 7 = most informal); WVS = World Values Survey estimates.

A.B. Bars show simple group averages (world, advanced economies, and EMDEs) over the period 2010-18; -1 and +1 standard deviations shown in orange whiskers.

B.D. Missing data for self-employment in percent of total employment are interpolated in EMDEs for earlier years and filled using the latest available observation in recent years.

C-D. Lines show simple group averages.

E. Unweighted averages for latest available year. -1 and +1 standard deviations shown in orange whiskers. Measures are grouped into output informality, employment informality, and perception-based informality.

F. Based on country-specific linear regressions of the share of informality by each of the four measures of informality with a sufficiently long time-dimension. Bars show the share of EMDEs for which the time trend is statistically significantly negative (at least at 10 percent level). Orange line indicates 50 percent.

countercyclical macroeconomic policies. If the informal economy expands while the formal economy contracts, it may support household incomes and consumer demand during economic downturns and serve as a safety net for the economy (Loayza and Rigolini 2011). If the informal economy expands during expansions in the formal economy, it could function as an auxiliary "growth engine" during economic expansions (Chen 2005; Dell'Anno 2008; Meagher 2013).

In theory, the cyclical relationship between informal and formal sectors is ambiguous.[7] Some theoretical models have shown that the informal economy may absorb a larger share of workers as jobs become scarce in the formal sector during economic downturns (Bosch, Goni, and Maloney 2007; Dix-Carneiro et al. 2021; Loayza and Rigolini 2011). Such behavior by the informal sector could facilitate economic recovery—by providing a potential supply of labor to the formal sector and preventing the hysteresis costs on unemployment—if reentry into the formal sector is possible when the formal economy returns to expansion (Colombo, Onnis, and Tirelli 2016; IMF 2017).

In contrast, if informal firms provide services, as well as final and intermediate goods, to the formal sector, a positive correlation may emerge between formal and informal sector activity (Arvin-Rad, Basu, and Willumsen 2010; Lubell 1991). In addition, informal-economy income can support formal-economy demand (Docquier, Muller, and Naval 2017; Gibson 2005; Schneider 1998). In these circumstances, the informal economy would amplify macroeconomic fluctuations (Restrepo-Echavarria 2014; Roca, Moreno, and Sánchez 2001).

Empirical evidence on the behavior of the informal economy over the business cycle is also inconclusive. This has been attributed partly to different country characteristics and the roles of different economic shocks.

In light of these observations, this chapter addresses the following questions:

- What conclusions does the literature offer about the cyclical behavior of the informal economy?

- How synchronized are movements in informal and formal economies?

- Do fluctuations in formal economy output "cause" fluctuations in output or employment in the informal economy?

Contributions. The chapter makes three contributions to the literature. First, it is the first analysis of the cyclical linkages between formal and informal sectors using data for multiple measures of informality for a large set of economies—about 160 economies, comprising 36 advanced economies and about 124 EMDEs. It covers a long, recent period—1990-2018—and is the first study of the behavior of both output and

---

[7] Some early works suggested that the degree of cyclicality of the informal economy depends on the measure of informality used and country characteristics.

employment in the informal economy: previous studies focused on only one of these two variables. The comparison yields insights into the cyclicality of labor productivity.

Second, the chapter clarifies earlier studies by focusing on the size of the informal economy in absolute terms, rather than merely relative to the formal economy. Several earlier studies rested on examining the size of the informal economy relative to that of the formal economy, without explaining the underlying mechanism. For instance, when this ratio rises during recessions, it could reflect an expanding informal economy or an informal economy that shrinks less than the formal economy. Some previous studies have interpreted the rising ratio only as evidence for an expanding informal economy during recessions. The few previous studies of the procyclicality of informal output levels have been restricted to a small group of countries and study either solely output (Bajada 2003; Dell'Anno 2008; Giles 1997) or only employment (Fiess, Fugazza, and Maloney 2010).

Third, the chapter is the first to document a causal link from formal-economy developments to the informal economy by using an instrumental variables approach. This improves on existing studies that have tested for Granger causality between formal and informal economy within individual countries. The previous Granger causality tests help to determine whether one time series is useful in forecasting another. However, they do not test for "true causality" (as instrumental variable regressions do; Angrist and Pischke 2009), because omitted variables can generate spurious causality (Eichler 2009).

Main findings. The chapter reports two major results. First, informal-economy output moves in step with formal-economy output: informal-economy output movements are strongly positively correlated with formal-economy output movements. Hence, when earlier studies found that the share of the informal economy rose during formal-economy recessions, this rise reflected a slower absolute decline in informal than formal output rather than an absolute increase in informal activity (figure 1.3). In addition, this study finds that informal employment largely behaves "acyclically."

Second, in an instrumental variable estimation, this study shows that the direction of causality runs from the formal economy to the informal economy. Specifically, it documents a causal link from fluctuations in formal-economy output to fluctuations in informal-economy output. In terms of employment, such a causal link is not found: whereas informal output behaves procyclically, informal employment is not cyclical. The latter may indicate that informal labor markets do not adjust in terms of employment status during economic cycles but in terms of wages or working hours (Guriev, Speciale, and Tuccio 2019; Meghir, Narita, and Robin 2015).

Part II: Country and Regional Dimensions

Part II examines the features of informality across different economies and EMDE regions. Chapter 4 documents countries' economic and social characteristics that are associated with higher informality. Chapter 5 documents differences and similarities across EMDE regions.

FIGURE 1.3 **Formal- and informal-economy business cycles in EMDEs**

The shares of informal output and employment rise significantly above their long-term averages during downturns in the formal economy. Informal output levels fall less than formal output levels; informal employment remains broadly stable while formal employment falls. The reverse holds for formal economic upturns.

A. Informal shares of output and employment

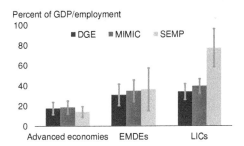

B. Changes in shares of informal economy during formal economy upturns and downturns

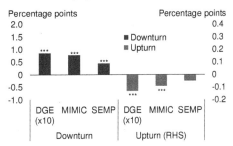

C. Output growth during formal economy upturns and downturns

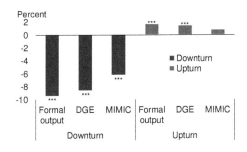

D. Employment growth during formal economy upturns and downturns

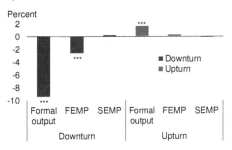

Sources: Penn World Table 9.1; World Bank.
Note: Data are for 1990-2018. DGE = dynamic general equilibrium model estimates; EMDEs = emerging market and developing economies; FEMP = formal employment; LICs = low-income countries; MIMIC = multiple indicators and multiple causes model estimates; RHS = right-hand side; SEMP = self-employment. "Downturn" refers to growth rates of official GDP below zero; "upturn" refers to growth rates of official GDP equal to or above zero. In B-D, *** indicates that the group average is significantly different from zero at the 10 percent level.
A. Bars show unweighted group averages for the latest year available, with the whiskers showing +/–1 standard deviation.
B. Shares of informal output (in percent of official GDP) and informal employment (in percent of total employment) are first-differenced and demeaned to capture detrended annual changes. Bars show unweighted group averages of detrended annual changes in shares of informal output/informal employment. Results for DGE-based estimates are shown in tenths (not percentage points).
C.D. Levels of output and employment in both formal and informal economies are logged, first-differenced, and demeaned to capture detrended annual growth rates. Bars show unweighted group averages of detrended annual growth rates.

Chapter 4. Lagging Behind: Informality and Development

Widespread informality is associated with a plethora of development challenges, as shown in chapter 4. Informal activity is widespread in EMDEs. Although informality is often considered a cause of development challenges, it is also a consequence of underdevelopment (see Fields 1975; Harris and Todaro 1970; Loayza 2016; Ulyssea 2020). EMDEs with more pervasive informality tend to be less developed, rely more on labor-intensive activities that employ unskilled and poorly paid workers, and have limited fiscal resources (World Bank 2019). Life expectancy, maternal mortality, and other human development indicators are, on average, lagging behind in EMDEs with more pervasive informality. Access to public services, such as electricity provision, that are essential to economic development, is limited.

A large informal sector weakens policy effectiveness and the government's ability to generate fiscal revenues (see Dabla-Norris, Gradstein, and Inchauste 2008; Joshi, Prichard, and Heady 2014; Ordóñez 2014; World Bank 2019). Government revenues in EMDEs with above-median informality are 5-12 percentage points of GDP below those with below-median informality (chapter 6). Limited fiscal resources constrain governments' ability to offer adequate coverage of social protection programs, provide broad access to public sector services, smooth business cycles, and close the productivity gap between the formal and informal sectors (Schneider, Buehn, and Montenegro 2010; World Bank 2020a). In turn, the limited access to public services further discourages firms and workers from engaging with the government, resulting in more participation in the informal sector (Loayza 2018; Perry et al. 2007).

EMDEs with widespread informality score particularly poorly on indicators of development. Many development outcomes are captured and quantified in measures of progress toward the SDGs. In 2020, EMDEs with above-median informality, on average, ranked around 110 out of 166 in overall SDG achievement, which is significantly worse than EMDEs with below-median informality (figure 1.4). About one quarter (26 percent) of the population of EMDEs with above-median informality lived in extreme poverty, much more than the 7 percent of the population in the EMDEs with below-median informality. In countries with greater informality, income inequality was higher, in part reflecting the wage gap between formal and informal workers and less progressive tax policies (Chong and Gradstein 2007; World Bank 2019; box 4.1).

Against this backdrop, chapter 4 addresses the following questions:

- What are the development challenges associated with the informal economy?

- What are the correlates of widespread informality?

- What are the correlates of changes in the informal sector over time?

Contributions. The chapter makes the following contributions to the literature on informality. First, it provides a systematic and comprehensive overview of developmental challenges facing countries with large informal sectors, highlighting their association with a wide range of development weaknesses and shortfalls from the SDGs. Previous studies have focused on the economic or institutional correlates of informality—such as per capita income (for instance, La Porta and Shleifer 2014; Loayza, Servén, and Sugawara 2010) or control of corruption (for instance, Choi and Thum 2005; Dreher and Schneider 2010)—and largely disregarded the linkages between informality and other aspects of sustainable development, ranging from life expectancy to lack of access to public infrastructure.

FIGURE 1.4 **Development challenges and informality**

EMDEs with widespread informality face a host of development challenges, ranging from extreme poverty to lack of public infrastructure. Those with more pervasive informality lag behind in achieving the SDGs.

A. SDG global index rank

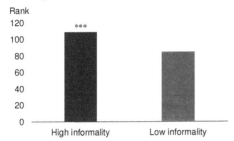

B. Extreme poverty headcount

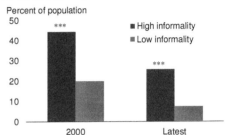

C. Wage premium for formal over informal employment

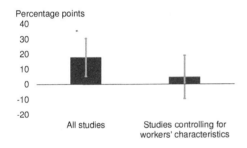

D. Differences in fiscal indicators between EMDEs with above-median and below-median output informality

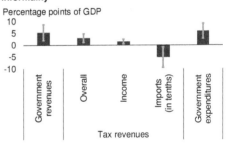

E. Quality of infrastructure

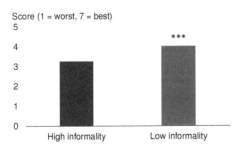

F. Probability of inclusion of variable group among explanatory variables of informality

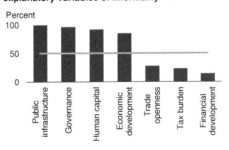

Sources: Sachs et al. 2018; Sachs et al. 2020; World Bank (World Development Indicators).

Note: EMDEs = emerging market and developing economies; DGE = dynamic general equilibrium model estimates in percent of official GDP; SDGs = Sustainable Development Goals; "High informality" ("Low informality") are EMDEs with above-median (below-median) DGE-based informal output measure over the period 1990-2018 (unless otherwise specified). *** indicates that group differences are significant at the 10 percent level.

A. Simple averages for 2020 for 132 EMDEs. A higher SDG global index rank indicates greater achievement of SDGs. Informality as measured by share of DGE output informality in GDP.

B. Simple averages for 155 EMDEs with "high informality" or "low informality." "Latest" refers to data from latest year available (2018 or earlier). Poverty headcount ratio is the percent of the population living on less than $1.90 a day at 2011 international prices.

C. The wage premium (shown in bars) is obtained from 18 empirical studies on the wage gap between formal and informal workers. The whiskers show the 90 percent confidence intervals. See box 4.1 for details.

D. Differences in percentage points of GDP between the average fiscal indicators among EMDEs with above-median and below-median informality are in bars. The whiskers show the 90 percent confidence intervals. All fiscal indicators and informality measures are 2000-18 averages for 74 EMDEs with populations above 3.5 million. (Several oil-exporting economies are dropped as outliers.)

E. Simple averages for the latest year available (Sachs et al. 2018).

F. Probability of including at least one variable from the group in the regression (posterior inclusion probability). The groups whose posterior inclusion probabilities exceed the prior probability of 50 percent (horizontal bar) can be regarded as most relevant.

Second, the chapter is the first published study to empirically and systematically document a broad range of correlates of informality in a large group of EMDEs, numbering about 130 countries. Previous studies have tended to focus on one dimension of informality, rely on a more limited range of correlates, or examine only the correlates of cross-country differences in informality without focusing on EMDEs (for instance, Medina and Schneider 2019; Oviedo, Thomas, and Karakurum-Özdemir 2009; Schneider, Buehn, and Montenegro 2010). To identify the robust correlates of informality, the chapter is also the first to use a BMA approach, which is designed to take account of model uncertainty (Fernandez, Ley, and Steel 2001).

Third, this chapter illustrates how informality can pose development challenges in EMDEs. First, it conducts the first extensive meta-analysis of studies that documented wage differences for workers in formal and informal sectors. Second, it utilizes a unique firm-level data set to show how the productivity gap between formal and informal firms in EMDEs can be narrowed by improvements in business climates.[8] Third, it empirically tests for the robustness of the relationship between declines in informality and poverty reduction (or income inequality).

Main findings. The chapter demonstrates that EMDEs with pervasive informality face a wide range of greater development challenges than other EMDEs. First, informality is associated with poor economic outcomes. Countries with larger informal sectors have lower per capita incomes, greater poverty, less financial development, and weaker growth in output, investment, and productivity. Informal firms are less productive than their formal counterparts (box 4.2).

Second, more pervasive informality is associated with significantly lower government revenues and expenditures, less effective policy institutions, more burdensome tax and regulatory regimes, and weaker governance. Weaknesses in governance and revenue collection constrain the provision of public services in EMDEs with more pervasive informality, contributing to poorer human development outcomes. People living in EMDEs with more widespread informality suffer from a greater prevalence of hunger, poorer health and education, and greater gender inequality. Countries with more widespread informality offer poorer access to, and lower-quality, infrastructure.

Third, the results from the BMA approach suggest that economic development, human capital, and governance are particularly robust correlates of output informality. That said, other correlates such as infrastructure, for instance, are also relevant.

Fourth, although informality is linked with a host of developmental challenges, formalization alone is unlikely to offer an effective path out of underdevelopment. For instance, although declines in informality were associated with poverty reduction, they

---

[8] Existing studies, such as Meghir, Narita, and Robin (2015) and Ulyssea (2020), show the productivity gap between formal and informal firms in individual countries.

were not systematically linked with declining income inequality (box 4.3). This may reflect the fact that informality itself is a symptom of underdevelopment, in line with the meta-analysis of the literature that finds that the wage penalty largely reflects the characteristics of informal workers (box 4.1).

Chapter 5. Informality in Emerging Market and Developing Economies: Regional Dimensions

Chapter 5 explores regional differences in informal activity in EMDE regions and their implications for policies. Before the COVID-19 pandemic, informality was falling on average in EMDEs over two decades, although the pace of decline varied widely across EMDE regions. The correlates of informality also vary across regions, shaped by distinctive regional cultures and histories, as well as economic, social, and policy structures.

This chapter addresses the following questions:

- How has informality evolved over the past two decades in each EMDE region?

- What are the correlates of informality in each region?

- What policy options are available to address the challenges associated with informality in each region?

Contributions. The chapter makes the following contributions to the literature. First, the chapter brings a regional perspective to the existing literature on informality in EMDEs. Past studies either grouped all countries together or focused on one or a few countries or a specific region. The chapter distills commonalities among EMDEs within each region and differences across regions. Second, the chapter brings together multiple strands of literature by investigating two key types of informality—output and employment informality—thus helping policy makers better understand the nature of informality in their respective regions. Previous studies typically examined either output informality or employment informality. Last, the chapter provides policy recommendations that are tailored to region-specific needs and conditions. Former studies tend to have a broad overview of all relevant policies without applying them to regional context.

Main findings. First, the chapter documents large differences in the evolution of informality across regions. Output informality is highest in ECA, LAC, and SSA, whereas employment informality is highest in EAP, SAR, and SSA (figure 1.5). Output informality declined most in EAP and SAR between the 1990s and the 2010s, while employment informality fell most in MNA, SAR, and SSA. Despite declines in output informality, and consistent with slower productivity growth in the informal than the formal sector, employment informality remained broadly unchanged in EAP, ECA, and LAC between 1990-99 and 2010-18.

FIGURE 1.5 Informality in EMDE regions

Informality is pervasive across all EMDE regions. Although the share of informal output in GDP has fallen over time, its incidence remains high in the regions with the lowest per capita incomes.

A. EMDE regions' shares of world output and employment

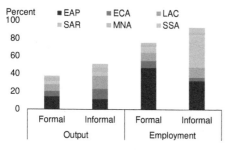

B. Output and employment informality by region

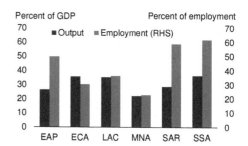

C. Output informality by region

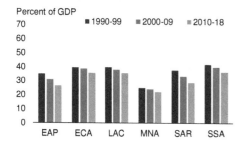

D. Employment informality by region

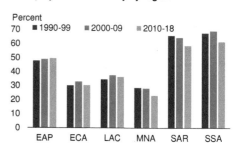

E. GDP per capita and output informality

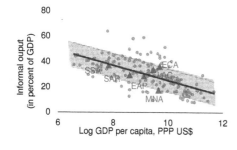

F. GDP per capita and employment informality

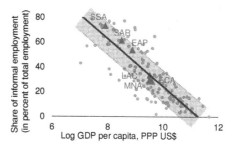

Sources: International Labour Organization; World Bank.

Note: Output informality is proxied by the estimates using a dynamic general equilibrium (DGE) model in percent of official GDP. Employment informality is the share of self-employment in total employment. EAP = East Asia and Pacific; ECA = Europe and Central Asia; LAC = Latin America and the Caribbean; MNA = Middle East and North Africa; PPP = purchasing power parity; RHS = right-hand side; SAR = South Asia; SSA = Sub-Saharan Africa.

A. DGE-based estimates of informal output in each region as a proportion of total estimated informal GDP. Estimates are based on economies' shares of output and employment averaged over the period 2010-18.

B. Blue bars show the simple average share of informal output as estimated by DGE model during 2010-18. Red bars show the simple average informal employment rate (proxied by self-employment rate) during 2010-18.

C.D. Bars are simple averages for corresponding regions and time periods.

E.F. Gray markers show unweighted average log GDP (2011 PPP $) relative to informal output and employment, with the fitted line shown in blue and the corresponding +1 and -1 standard errors shown in shaded gray areas. Red markers show median GDP per capita and median informal output (E) and employment (F) in EMDE regions. Data are for 2010-18.

Second, a mix of cross-regional, intraregional, and country-specific factors is associated with informality in EMDEs. Key correlates of high informality include low human capital, large agricultural sectors, and poor business climates. But there are also important region-specific factors, such as insufficient social protection coverage, trade liberalization, and economic disruptions due to armed conflict. Reflecting regional as well as national differences in informality, balanced policy mixes tailored to country circumstances are required to set the right conditions for informality to fall.

Part III: Policies

Part III examines the policy options available to address the challenges posed by informality. In particular, chapter 6 offers a menu of policy options to address both short-term and long-term challenges, and flags unintended consequences experienced in past policy experiments.

Chapter 6. Tackling Informality: Policy Options

Chapter 6 documents the challenges that informality poses for macroeconomic policies and explores policy options to address these challenges. Over the past three decades, many EMDE governments have implemented a wide range of policy reforms that may have helped to reduce informality (Jessen and Kluve 2021). These reforms have often been implemented to either increase the benefits of formal-sector participation or reduce the costs of formal activity.

Both corporate and personal income tax rates in EMDEs have been reduced by about one-third between the early 1990s and 2019 (Végh and Vuletin 2015). Time spent on paying taxes was also cut by about one-third in EMDEs between 2006 and 2020. Value added taxes, which can lower tax burdens through a refund on input taxes, had been adopted in 71 EMDEs by 2020 (World Bank 2020b). Access to financial services has broadened, with access to automatic teller machines (ATMs) per 100,000 adults and the share of the population with an account at a financial institution both increasing by more than 50 percent between 2010 and 2018. Over the same period, one-third to two-thirds of EMDEs improved their governance and institutional quality.

Policy reforms often had more benign effects on informality when they were implemented in a supportive institutional and macroeconomic environment. For instance, trade liberalization programs were often associated with greater informality in the short term—unless they were accompanied by greater labor market flexibility and an upgrading of skills in the labor force (Goldberg and Pavcnik 2003; McCaig and Pavcnik 2015; World Bank 2019).

The untapped potential of informal sectors, if harnessed to boost income growth and resilience, can help build back better from the severe global recession of 2020. Against this background, the chapter addresses the following questions:

- Which fiscal measures can help reduce informality?

- Which other policies can help reduce informality?

- What should be the elements of a comprehensive policy package to tackle informality?

Contributions. The chapter makes the following contributions to the literature. First, it offers a systematic review of policies that could affect informality, ranging from fiscal policies to labor market regulations and policies to encourage financial development. It covers both policies that are intentionally designed to encourage formalization and ones that could incidentally affect the informal sector.

Second, the chapter is the first attempt to comprehensively examine the link between financial development and informality both theoretically and empirically (box 6.1). It reviews the literature identifying the channels through which limited financial development can discourage formalization. It uses both descriptive statistics and regression approaches to show that informality is associated with lack of financial development, and that improvements in access to finance are associated with declining informality.

Third, the chapter describes novel empirical estimates of the cumulative changes in informality following various policy changes, obtained using a local projection model. Policy-related variables examined include tax rates, access to credit by the private sector, labor market efficiency, governance, and regulatory quality. This is the first study to conduct such empirical analysis for a wide range of policies. It is also the first to examine the share of informality in both economic output and employment: earlier studies have tended to focus on either informal output, or informal employment, or informal firms (see Bosch, Goni-Pacchioni, and Maloney 2012; Fajnzylber, Maloney, and Montes-Rojas 2011; Ihrig and Moe 2004; Rocha, Ulyssea, and Rachter 2018).

Main findings. First, macroeconomic policies, governance, and business climates have become more conducive to lowering informality over the past three decades. In the past three decades, EMDEs have made progress in reducing tax burdens, improving governance and regulatory quality, and enhancing access to finance, education, and public services (figure 1.6).

Second, policies that seek to streamline tax regulation, strengthen tax administration, and improve public service delivery have been associated with declines in informality. Separately, policies aimed at invigorating private sector activity broadly, such as measures to increase labor market flexibility, streamline regulatory frameworks for firm start-up, expand access to finance, and improve governance have also been associated with declines in informality.

Third, policy measures can have unintended consequences. For instance, trade liberalization that raised competition in the tradable sector was sometimes associated with greater informality in the short run, unless accompanied by measures that increase labor market flexibility. Also, reductions in informality have tended to be greater for

FIGURE 1.6 **Policies to address challenges of informality**

Governments have implemented a wide range of reforms that could affect informality.

A. Reforms in advanced economies and EMDEs

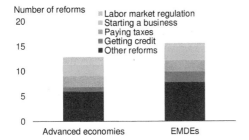

B. Reforms across EMDE regions

C. Reforms over time

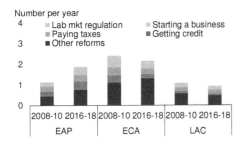

D. Reforms over time (continued)

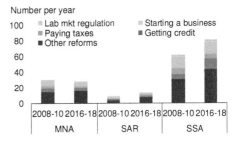

E. Economies with improvement in control of corruption

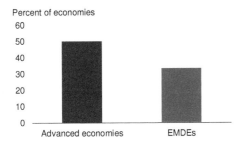

F. Economies with improvement in the ease of doing business

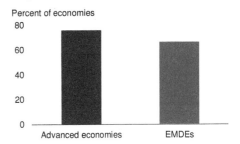

Sources: *International Country Risk Guide*; World Bank (*Doing Business*).

Note: See Doing Business database for reform details. EAP = East Asia and Pacific; ECA = Europe and Central Asia; EMDEs = emerging market and developing economies; LAC = Latin America and the Caribbean; MNA = Middle East and North Africa; SAR = South Asia; SSA = Sub-Saharan Africa.

A.B. The number of policy reforms for an average country over the period 2008-18 that are regarded as "improvements" (according to components of the ease of doing business index) or "neutral" (with regard to "labor market regulation").

C.D. For an average country, the average number of policy reforms per year that have been implemented during 2008-10 in comparison to the annual average number of reforms conducted during 2016-18 (shown in bars).

E.F. Bars show the shares of economies with improved control of corruption (E; the ease of doing business in F) between 2010 and 2018.

reforms accompanied by business development and training programs, public awareness campaigns, and stronger enforcement.

Fourth, financial development has been associated with declining informality (box 6.1). It reduces the average costs of access to external financing and incentivizes firms to invest in higher-productivity projects and to join the formal sector. Over the past three decades, increased access to financial services and increased credit availability have been followed by declining informality.

Fifth, a comprehensive policy package tailored to country circumstances offers the greatest chance of success in reducing informality. A combination of measures to strengthen economic development, boost productivity in both formal and informal sectors, streamline regulations, and ensure effective enforcement can address multiple sources of informality. The relative priorities will depend on the country-specific features of informality.

Future research directions

The study suggests several avenues for future research.

Concepts and measurement. Despite the richness of the informality database detailed in chapter 2, the limitations and weaknesses of existing measures remain. Future research could improve the quality of these measures and explore new approaches to better capture the extent of informality in EMDEs. Chapter 2 distills the main features of informal-economy business cycles but does not look into the factors and policies that could trigger cyclical turning points. Further analysis in this direction would be valuable.

Cyclical behavior of the informal economy. Chapter 3 focuses on how informal output and employment behave over the business cycle and points to several promising areas for future research. First, the cyclical behavior of other features of the informal economy could be examined. For example, if greater flexibility of wages or hours worked is indeed what makes informal employment acyclical despite procyclical informal output, informal wages or hours should be particularly procyclical, and evidence of this would be useful. Second, the channels through which formal-economy business cycles affect the informal economy could be further explored and quantified. This includes the degree of interconnectedness between formal and informal firms. Third, the impact of the pandemic on the informal sector and the effectiveness of policy responses should be studied further.

Consequences of informality for development. Chapter 4 establishes the link between informality and a range of symptoms of underdevelopment. However, it does not demonstrate a causal linkage between informality and various development outcomes. Future research could aim to uncover, for at least some of these correlates, the degree to which informality *causes* underdevelopment. Second, because of data limitations, some variables, such as access to paved roads and bank account ownership, that are relevant to informality are not included in the empirical analysis. Future studies can improve upon the work reported here by incorporating those variables. Third, future research could explore asymmetries in the challenges posed by informality. There may be interactions between country circumstances and worker or firm characteristics that can mitigate some of the challenges posed by informality. For firms, some of these interactions were explored in box 4.2, but other important interactions may yet come to light in future research.

Regional perspectives of informality. The varied nature of informality in EMDEs requires different policy mixes appropriate to each country's circumstances. Drawing on the discussion of policy options for different regions in chapter 5, future research could look into options that could be considered for implementation at a regional level. This could, in particular, include an examination of promising new areas such as digitalization.

Policy options. A few policy areas remain underexplored in the literature. First, although digitalization is a recent development, it holds great potential for both informal-economy participants and policy makers. Chapter 6 does not touch upon the practical perspectives of realizing the potential of digitalization in EMDEs with pervasive informality, and this could be an area for future research. Little is known about the impact of digitalization of government services or private economic activity on the informal economy. Second, past studies have focused on the impact of policies on formalization without looking into their effects on vulnerable groups active in the informal economy. Future studies could examine policies that can better protect these groups and prevent informal participants from being tipped into poverty by negative shocks such as COVID-19.

References

Aguiar, M., and G. Gopinath. 2007. "Emerging Market Business Cycles: The Cycle Is the Trend." *Journal of Political Economy* 115 (1): 69-102.

Almeida, R., and P. Carneiro. 2012. "Enforcement of Labor Regulation and Informality." *American Economic Journal: Applied Economics* 4 (3): 64-89.

Amaral, P., and E. Quintin. 2006. "A Competitive Model of the Informal Sector." *Journal of Monetary Economics* 53 (7): 1541-53.

Amin, M. 2021. "Does Competition from Informal Firms Hurt Job Creation by Formal Firms? Evidence Using Firm-Level Survey Data." Policy Research Working Paper 9515, World Bank, Washington, DC.

Amin, M., F. Ohnsorge, and C. Okou. 2019. "Casting a Shadow: Productivity of Formal Firms and Informality." Policy Research Working Paper 8945, World Bank, Washington, DC.

Angrist, J. D., and J.-S. Pischke. 2009. *Mostly Harmless Econometrics: An Empiricist's Companion.* Princeton University Press: Princeton, NJ.

Arvin-Rad, H., A. K. Basu, and M. Willumsen. 2010. "Economic Reform, Informal-Formal Sector Linkages and Intervention in the Informal Sector in Developing Countries: A Paradox." *International Review of Economics and Finance* 19 (4): 662-70.

Bajada, C. 2003. "Business Cycle Properties of the Legitimate and Underground Economy in Australia." *Economic Record* 79 (247): 397-411.

Balde, R., M. Boly, and E. Avenyo. 2020. "Labour Market Effects of COVID-19 in Sub-Saharan Africa: An Informality Lens from Burkina Faso, Mali and Senegal." UNU-MERIT Working Paper 2020-022, United Nations University–Maastricht Economic and Social Research Institute on Innovation and Technology, Maastricht, Netherlands.

Benjamin, N., and A. Mbaye. 2012. *The Informal Sector in Francophone Africa: Firm Size, Productivity, and Institutions.* Africa Development Forum. Washington, DC: World Bank.

Binelli, C., and O. Attanasio. 2010. "Mexico in the 1990s: The Main Cross-Sectional Facts." *Review of Economic Dynamics* 13 (1) : 238-264.

Bosch, M., E. Goni, and W. Maloney. 2007. "The Determinants of Rising Informality in Brazil: Evidence from Gross Worker Flows." Policy Research Working Paper 4347, World Bank, Washington, DC.

Bosch, M., E. Goñi-Pacchioni, and W. Maloney. 2012. "Trade Liberalization, Labor Reforms and Formal-Informal Employment Dynamics." *Labour Economics* 19 (5): 653-67.

Chen, M. 2005. "Rethinking the Informal Economy: Linkages with the Formal Economy and the Formal Regulatory Environment." Working Paper 25-10, United Nations University—World Institute for Development Economics Research, Helsinki, Finland.

Chodorow-Reich, G., G. Gopinath, P. Mishra, and A. Naraynan. 2020. "Cash and the Economy: Evidence from India's Demonetization." *Quarterly Journal of Economics* 135 (1): 57-103.

Choi, J. P., and M. Thum. 2005. "Corruption and the Shadow Economy." *International Economic Review* 46 (3): 817-36.

Chong, A., and M. Gradstein. 2007. "Inequality and Informality." *Journal of Public Economics* 91(1-2): 159-79.

Colombo, E., L. Onnis, and P. Tirelli, 2016. "Shadow Economies at Times of Banking Crises: Empirics and Theory." *Journal of Banking & Finance* 62 (C): 180-90.

Dabla-Norris, E., M. Gradstein, and G. Inchauste. 2008. "What Causes Firms to Hide Output?" *Journal of Development Economics* 85 (1-2): 1-27.

Dell'Anno, R. 2008. "What Is the Relationship between Unofficial and Official Economy? An Analysis in Latin American Countries." *European Journal of Economics, Finance and Administrative Sciences* 12: 185-203.

Dix-Carneiro, R., P. Goldberg, C. Meghir, and G. Ulyssea. 2021. "Trade and Informality in the Presence of Labor Market Frictions and Regulations." Working Paper 28391, National Bureau of Economic Research, Cambridge, MA.

Docquier, F., T. Müller, and J. Naval. 2017. "Informality and Long-Run Growth." *The Scandinavian Journal of Economics* 119 (4): 1040-85.

Dreher, A., and F. Schneider. 2010. "Corruption and the Shadow Economy: An Empirical Analysis." *Public Choice* 144: 215-38.

Eichler, M. 2009. "Causal Inference from Multivariate Time Series: What Can Be Learned from Granger Causality." In *Logic, Methodology and Philosophy of Science,* edited by C. Glymour, W. Wang, and D. Westerstahl. Proceedings of the 13th International Congress. London: College Publications.

Elgin, C., A. Elveren, and J. Bourgeois. 2020. "Informality, Inequality and Profit Rate." *Applied Economics Letters.* 1-4. https://doi.org/10.1080/13504851.2020.1795065.

Fajnzylber, P., W. Maloney, and G. Montes-Rojas. 2011. "Does Formality Improve Micro-Firm Performance? Evidence from the Brazilian SIMPLES Program." *Journal of Development Economics* 94 (2): 262-76.

Farazi, S. 2014. "Informal Firms and Financial Inclusion: Status and Determinants." Policy Research Working Paper 6778, World Bank, Washington, DC.

Fernandez, C., E. Ley, and M. Steel. 2001. "Model Uncertainty in Cross-Country Growth Regressions." *Journal of Applied Econometrics* 16 (5): 563-76.

Fields, G. S. 1975. "Rural-Urban Migration, Urban Unemployment and Underemployment, and Job-Search Activity in LDCs." *Journal of Development Economics* 2 (2): 165-87.

Fiess, N., M. Fugazza, and W. Maloney. 2010. "Informal Self-Employment and Macroeconomic Fluctuations." *Journal of Development Economics* 91 (2): 211-26.

Gibson, B. 2005. "The Transition to a Globalized Economy: Poverty, Human Capital and the Informal Sector in a Structuralist CGE Model." *Journal of Development Economics* 78 (1): 60-94.

Giles, D. 1997. "Causality between the Measured and Underground Economies in New Zealand." *Applied Economics Letters* 4 (1): 63-7.

Goldberg, P. K., and N. Pavcnik. 2003. "The Response of the Informal Sector to Trade Liberalization." *Journal of Development Economics* 72 (2): 463-96.

Guriev, S., B. Speciale, and M. Tuccio. 2019. "How Do Regulated and Unregulated Labor Markets Respond to Shocks? Evidence from Immigrants during the Great Recession." *Journal of Law, Economics, and Organization* 35 (1): 37-76.

Harris, J. R., and M. P. Todaro. 1970. "Migration, Unemployment, and Development: A Two Sector Analysis." *American Economic Review* 60 (1): 126-42.

Ihrig, J., and K. S. Moe. 2004. "Lurking in the Shadows: The Informal Sector and Government Policy." *Journal of Development Economics* 73 (2): 541-57.

ILO (International Labour Organization). 2018. *Informal Economy.* Geneva: International Labour Office. https://www.ilo.org/ilostat-files/Documents/description_IFL_EN.pdf.

IMF (International Monetary Fund). 2017. *Regional Economic Outlook: Restarting the Growth Engine.* Washington, DC: International Monetary Fund.

Jessen, J., and J. Kluve. 2021. "The Effectiveness of Interventions to Reduce Informality in Low-and Middle-Income Countries." *World Development* 138 (February): 1-19.

Joshi, A., W. Prichard, and C. Heady. 2014. "Taxing the Informal Economy: The Current State of Knowledge and Agendas for Future Research." *Journal of Development Studies* 50 (10): 1325-47.

La Porta, R., and A. Shleifer. 2014. "Informality and Development." *Journal of Economic Perspectives* 28 (3): 109-26.

Loayza, N. 2016. "Informality in the Process of Development and Growth." *The World Economy* 39 (12): 1856-916.

Loayza, N. 2018. "Informality: Why Is It So Widespread and How Can It Be Reduced?" Research & Policy Brief 20, World Bank, Kuala Lumpur, Malaysia.

Loayza, N., and S. Pennings. 2020. "Macroeconomic Policy in the Time of COVID-19: A Primer for Developing Countries." Research & Policy Brief 28, World Bank, Kuala Lumpur, Malaysia.

Loayza, N., and J. Rigolini. 2011. "Informal Employment: Safety Net or Growth Engine?" *World Development* 39 (9): 1503-15.

Loayza, N., L. Servén, and N. Sugawara. 2010. "Informality in Latin America and the Caribbean." In *Business Regulation and Economic Performance*, edited by N. Loayza and L. Servén. Washington, DC: World Bank.

Lubell, H. 1991. *The Informal Sector in the 1980s and 1990s*. Paris: Organisation for Economic Co-operation and Development.

McCaig, B., and N. Pavcnik. 2015. "Informal Employment in a Growing and Globalizing Low-Income Country." *American Economic Review* 105 (5): 545-50.

Meagher, K. 2013. "Unlocking the Informal Economy: A Literature Review on Linkages between Formal and Informal Economies in Developing Countries." WIEGO Working Paper 27, Women in Informal Employment: Globalizing and Organizing, Cambridge, MA.

Medina, M., and F. Schneider. 2018. "Shadow Economies around the World: What Did We Learn over the Last 20 Years?" IMF Working Paper 18/17, International Monetary Fund, Washington, DC.

Medina, M., and F. Schneider. 2019. "Shedding Light on the Shadow Economy: A Global Database and the Interaction with the Official One." CESifo Working Paper 7981, CESifo Group, Munich.

Meghir, C., R. Narita, and J. Robin. 2015. "Wages and Informality in Developing Countries." *American Economic Review* 105 (4): 1509-46.

Muralidharan, K., P. Niehaus, and S. Sukhtankar. 2016. "Building State Capacity: Evidence from Biometric Smartcards in India." *American Economic Review* 106 (10): 2895-929.

Ordóñez, J. 2014. "Tax Collection, the Informal Sector, and Productivity." *Review of Economic Dynamics* 17 (2): 262-86.

Oviedo, A., M. Thomas, and K. Karakurum-Özdemir. 2009. "Economic Informality: Causes, Costs, and Policies —A Literature Survey." Working Paper 167, World Bank, Washington, DC.

Panizza, U. 2020. "Europe's Ground Zero." In *Mitigating the COVID Economic Crisis: Act Fast and Do Whatever It Takes*, edited by R. Baldwin and B. Weder di Mauro, 151-66. Center for Economic Policy and Research. Washington, DC: CEPR Press.

Perry, G. E., W. F. Maloney, O. S. Arias, P. Fajnzylber, A. D. Mason, and J. Saavedra-Chanduvi. 2007. *Informality: Exit and Exclusion*. Washington, DC: World Bank.

Putnins, T., and A. Sauka. 2015. "Measuring the Shadow Economy Using Company Managers." *Journal of Comparative Economics* 43 (2): 471-90.

Restrepo-Echavarria, P. 2014. "Macroeconomic Volatility: The Role of the Informal Economy." *European Economic Review* 70 (August): 454-69.

Roca, J., C. Moreno, and J. Sánchez. 2001. "Underground Economy and Aggregate Fluctuations." *Spanish Economic Review* 3 (1): 41-53.

Rocha, R., G. Ulyssea, and R. Rachter. 2018. "Do Lower Taxes Reduce Informality? Evidence from Brazil." *Journal of Development Economics* 134 (September): 28-49.

Sachs, J., G. Schmidt-Traub, C. Kroll, G. Lafortune, and G. Fuller. 2018. *SDG Index and Dashboards Report 2018.* New York: Bertelsmann Stiftung and Sustainable Development Solutions Network (SDSN).

Sachs, J.D., G. Schmidt-Traub, C. Kroll, G. Lafortune, G. Fuller, and F. Woelm. 2020. *Sustainable Development Report 2020: The Sustainable Development Goals and COVID-19.* Cambridge, UK: Cambridge University Press.

Schneider, F. 1998. "Further Empirical Results of the Size of the Shadow Economy of 17 OECD Countries over Time." Discussion Paper, Department of Economics, University of Linz.

Schneider, F., A. Buehn, and C. E. Montenegro. 2010. "Shadow Economies All over the World: New Estimates for 162 Countries from 1999 to 2007." Policy Research Working Paper 5356, World Bank, Washington, DC.

Schotte, S., M. Danquah, R. D. Osei, K. Sen, and UNU-WIDER. 2021. "The Labour Market Impact of COVID-19 Lockdowns: Evidence from Ghana." Working Paper 21-27, United Nations University—World Institute for Development Economics Research, Helsinki, Finland.

Surico, P., and A. Galeotti. 2020. "The Economics of a Pandemic: The Case of COVID-19." European Research Council, Brussels, and Wheeler Institute, London. https://sites.google.com/site/paolosurico/covid-19.

Ulyssea, G. 2020. "Informality: Causes and Consequences for Development." *Annual Review of Economics* 12 (1): 525-46.

United Nations. 2008. *Non-observed Economy in National Accounts: Survey of Country of Practices.* New York; Geneva: United Nations.

Végh, C. A., and G. Vuletin. 2015. "How Is Tax Policy Conducted over the Business Cycle?" *American Economic Journal: Economic Policy* 7 (3): 327-70.

World Bank. 2019. *Global Economic Prospects: Darkening Skies.* January. Washington, DC: World Bank.

World Bank. 2020a. *Global Economic Prospects.* June. Washington, DC: World Bank.

World Bank. 2020b. *Doing Business.* Washington DC: World Bank.

World Bank. 2021. *Global Economic Prospects.* January. Washington, DC: World Bank.

It is better to be vaguely right than exactly wrong.

Carveth Read (1898)
Philosopher and logician

Not everything that can be counted counts,
and not everything that counts can be counted.

William Bruce Cameron (1963)
Sociologist

PART I

Characteristics of the Informal Economy

CHAPTER 2

Understanding the Informal Economy: Concepts and Trends

By its nature, informal economic activity—referred to in this study simply as "informality"—is difficult to observe systematically and to measure. This chapter introduces a comprehensive database of informality measures. This database shows that informality remains pervasive in emerging market and developing economies, notwithstanding a declining trend over the past three decades. Like the formal economy, the informal economy undergoes business cycles, which resemble those in the formal economy. Informal-economy output fluctuations tend to be more pronounced in emerging market and developing economies than in advanced economies, whereas employment fluctuations are more limited and do not differ significantly between the two groups.

Introduction

The livelihoods of the poor in emerging market and developing economies (EMDEs) often depend on informal economic activity. In these economies, informal-economy output on average accounts for about one-third of gross domestic product (GDP) and informal employment constitutes about 70 percent of total employment (of which self-employment accounts for more than one-half; figure 2.1). In some economies in Sub-Saharan Africa (SSA), informal employment accounts for more than 90 percent of total employment and informal output for as much as 62 percent of official GDP (World Bank 2019).

Depending on country circumstances and worker characteristics, workers may choose informal employment for a wide range of reasons. Thus informal workers range from agricultural day laborers to self-employed firm owners with a few employees.

A large informal sector has tended to be associated with unfavorable macroeconomic and development outcomes (figure 2.1; chapter 4). On average, economies with larger informal sectors have tended to have less access to finance for the private sector, lower productivity, slower physical and human capital accumulation, less educated workforces, and smaller fiscal resources (Docquier, Müller, and Naval 2017; La Porta and Shleifer 2014; World Bank 2019a). Some studies show that informality is associated with higher income inequality and poverty (Chong and Gradstein 2007; Loayza, Servén, and Sugawara 2010; Perry et al. 2007; Rosser, Rosser, and Ahmed 2000). Lower physical investment in the informal sector could reflect an unwillingness of informal firms to

Note: This chapter was prepared by Ceyhun Elgin, M. Ayhan Kose, Franziska Ohnsorge, and Shu Yu. Research assistance was provided by Zhuo Chen, Lorez Qehaja, and Xinyue Wang.

FIGURE 2.1 Informality: Magnitude, variety, and development challenges

The informal sector accounts for about a third of GDP and more than 70 percent of employment (of which self-employment accounts for more than one-half) in EMDEs. A large informal sector is often associated with lack of development and weak governance as well as greater poverty and income inequality. In some cases, informal workers voluntarily choose informal activity.

A. Shares of informal output and self-employment

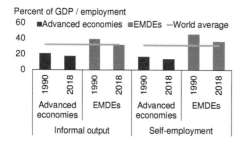

B. Informality: Output, employment, and perception

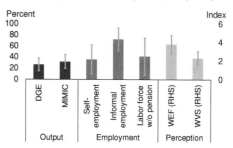

C. Informal output and development

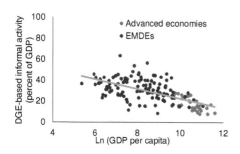

D. Brazil: Share of informal workers preferring informal over formal employment

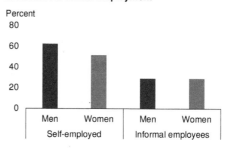

E. Informality, poverty, and income inequality

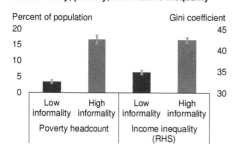

F. Governance in EMDEs, by informality

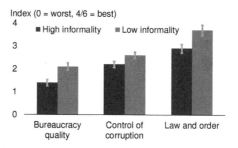

Sources: International Country Risk Guide (ICRG); International Labour Organization; Maloney 2004; World Bank (World Development Indicators; World Governance Indicators; World Values Survey); World Economic Forum.
Note: "High informality" ("Low informality") indicates economies with above- (below-) median informal output (using DGE-based estimates). DGE = dynamic general equilibrium model estimates of informal output in percent of official GDP; EMDEs = emerging market and developing economies; MIMIC = multiple indicators multiple causes model estimates of informal output in percent of GDP; RHS = right-hand side; WEF = World Economic Forum estimates; WVS = World Values Survey estimates.
A. Unweighted averages. Informal employment uses self-employment shares (in percent of total employment). Missing values are interpolated or filled using the latest available observations. World averages between 1990 and 2018 are in orange.
B. Unweighted averages for latest available year. Whiskers are +/–1 standard deviation. Measures are grouped into output informality, employment informality, and perception-based informality. Data on informal employment are for EMDEs. See table 2B.1A for details.
C. Latest available year (2018). Orange line shows fitted values. "Ln (GDP per capita)" is the logarithm of GDP per capita (in constant 2010 U.S. dollars).
D. The share of informal workers preferring informal over formal employment (Maloney 2004).
E. Data are for 1990-2018. Group means (bars) and 90 percent confidence intervals (whiskers) are shown for poverty headcount ratio (percent of population living on $1.90 a day at 2011 purchasing power parity) and Gini coefficients.
F. Data for 1990-2018 and EMDEs. Bars show unweighted averages of ICRG data; whiskers show 90 percent confidence intervals.

adopt technologies or larger scales of production that might make them visible to tax and other authorities (Dabla-Norris, Gradstein, and Inchauste 2008; Gandelman and Rasteletti 2017). The informal sector, on average, is characterized by lower productivity than the formal sector because it tends to employ less-skilled workers; use less capital; have restricted access to funding, services, and markets; and lack economies of scale (Amaral and Quintin 2006; Galiani and Weinschelbaum 2012; Loayza 2018). These long-term economic correlates of informality are explored in chapter 4.

Over the business cycle, informal employment can provide a safety net when the formal sector sheds jobs (Loayza and Rigolini 2011). But workers in the informal economy are largely excluded from the social security system and less protected against negative shocks than workers in the formal sector, which could amplify business cycles (box 2.1; chapter 3).

Against this backdrop, this chapter reviews conceptual and measurement issues regarding the informal economy and documents its main features across countries and over time. Specifically, it addresses the following questions:

- How is the informal economy defined?

- How has informality evolved?

- What are the features of the informal economy?

The chapter makes the following contributions to the literature. First, it introduces a comprehensive database of informality measures developed in the literature, with a focus on measures that have broad cross-country and long historical coverage. The resulting data set combines 12 cross-country databases and data provided by almost 90 national statistical agencies.[1] Second, the chapter presents two applications of this database. In a first step, it distills stylized facts about the informal economy, such as its size and evolution over time, using a wide range of informality measures, and tests the consistency of these stylized facts across these measures. In a second step, the chapter documents the cyclical features of the informal economy, such as the duration and amplitude of its recessions and recoveries.

The chapter presents several new findings. First, the chapter summarizes the advantages and drawbacks of existing informality measures. Most of the macroeconomic literature on informality has relied solely on either survey-based or model-based estimates. Survey-based measures can cover many dimensions of the informal economy, but they suffer

---

[1] Official GDP statistics often make an adjustment for informal activity. However, the magnitude of such adjustments is rarely specified. In a survey in 2008, national statistical agencies for about 40 mostly advanced economies or economies in transition reported adjusting their official GDP statistics by amounts ranging from 0.8 to 31.6 percent for activity in the non-observed economy, which is a broader concept than the informal economy (United Nations 2008). For all reporting economies, the adjustments were well below those suggested by the measures of informality presented in this chapter.

BOX 2.1 How does informality aggravate the impact of COVID-19?

COVID-19 (coronavirus) has taken an especially heavy humanitarian and economic toll on emerging market and developing economies (EMDEs) with large informal sectors. Large informal sectors make lockdowns and social distancing particularly challenging, thus reducing governments' ability to stem the spread of the virus. Informal workers tend to be employed in activities and locations where social distancing is difficult to implement. With few savings and lack of access to formal social benefits, many struggle to comply with government lockdown orders. Economies with large informal sectors are also associated with weak health care systems that can result in a larger number of fatal outcomes of infections. These vulnerabilities amplify the economic shock to livelihoods from COVID-19 and threaten to raise global extreme poverty. It is therefore critical to implement effective delivery channels for support to informal workers and firms. Unconditional support programs may be appropriate. Given their limited resources, low-income countries may require increased international funding for the effective implementation of such programs.

Informal activity is widespread in EMDEs (figure B2.1.1; World Bank 2019a). Large informal sectors are often associated with underdevelopment, with activity typically characterized by labor-intensive production, less educated and more poorly paid workers, limited access to financial and medical service, and poor or nonexistent coverage by social security. These features are likely to intensify the spread of COVID-19 among informal workers and worsen its adverse health and economic impacts (Nguimkeu and Okou 2020). Starting from a relatively lower level, confirmed COVID-19 cases have been rising rapidly in EMDEs with extensive informality since the end of March 2020, despite a lower level of testing.

Against this background, this box addresses the following questions:

- Which features of the informal economy can amplify or dampen the impact of the pandemic?

- How may widespread informality alter the impact of the pandemic?

- How do policies to mitigate the impact of the pandemic need to be tailored to the presence of large informal sectors?

Features of the informal economy

The informal economy has several features that tend to facilitate the spread of the pandemic. Other features worsen the economic impact of adverse shocks more generally.

Note: This box was prepared by Shu Yu.

BOX 2.1 How does informality aggravate the impact of COVID-19? (continued)

FIGURE B2.1.1 Informality in EMDEs

Informality is particularly prevalent in EMDEs. In Sub-Saharan Africa, Europe and Central Asia, and Latin America and the Caribbean, informal output averaged about 35 percent of GDP in 2010-18. Self-employment in Sub-Saharan Africa, South Asia, and East Asia and Pacific ranged from about 50 percent of employment to more than 60 percent. Confirmed COVID-19 cases have grown rapidly in EMDEs since the end of March 2020, with some concern about lack of testing in EMDEs with above-median informality.

A. Informality in EMDEs

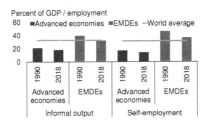

B. Informality across EMDE regions

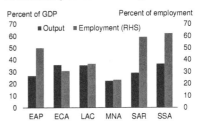

C. COVID-19 cases and the extent of informality

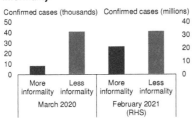

D. Informality and COVID-19 tests

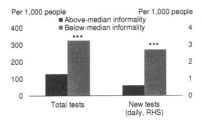

Sources: Haver Analytics; International Monetary Fund (Government Finance Statistics); *Our World in Data*; World Bank (World Development Indicators).

Note: In C-D, informality is measured by DGE informal output in percent of official GDP in 2018. DGE = dynamic general equilibrium model estimates of informal output in percent of official GDP; EAP = East Asia and Pacific; ECA = Europe and Central Asia; EMDEs = emerging market and developing economies; LAC = Latin America and the Caribbean; MNA = Middle East and North Africa; RHS = right-hand side; SAR = South Asia; SSA = Sub-Saharan Africa.

A. Simple averages. Informal employment uses self-employment shares with missing value interpolated in EMDEs for earlier years and filled using the latest available observation in recent years. World averages between 1990 and 2018 are orange.

B. Simple averages of informal output (DGE-based estimates) and employment estimate (share of self-employment) in each region during 2010-18.

C. Bars show the total number of confirmed COVID-19 cases (in thousands or millions) for EMDEs (excluding China) with less informality (that is, above group median) and EMDEs (excluding China) with less informality (that is, below group median) on March 24, 2020, and on February 12, 2021 (RHS).

D. Bars show the simple average number of COVID-19 tests per 1,000 people for EMDEs (excluding China) with less informality (that is, above group median) and EMDEs (excluding China) with less informality (that is, below group median) on February 12, 2021. The left two bars show the total number of COVID-19 tests done so far, and the right two bars show the daily number of COVID-19 tests performed. *** indicates that group averages are significantly different at the 10 percent level.

BOX 2.1 How does informality aggravate the impact of COVID-19? (continued)

Widespread informality in EMDEs. The informal sector, on average, accounts for about a third of official gross domestic product (GDP) and about 70 percent of total employment in EMDEs (of which self-employment accounts for more than one-half; figure B2.1.1; World Bank 2019a). Informal enterprises account for 8 out of every 10 enterprises in the world (ILO 2020a). The size of the informal economy varies widely across regions and countries. The share of informal output is highest in Sub-Saharan Africa (SSA), Europe and Central Asia (ECA), and Latin America and the Caribbean (LAC), averaging near 40 percent of GDP in those regions between 2010 and 2018. The share of self-employment, another measure of informality, is highest in SSA, South Asia (SAR), and East Asia and Pacific (EAP), ranging from 50 percent to 62 percent of total employment. In 2018, the informal economy accounted for more than 50 percent of GDP in Bolivia and Zimbabwe.[a] The sector accounted for about 90 percent of total employment in Mali, Mozambique, and India. In economies like Kenya, 8 out of 10 workers were self-employed.[b]

Characteristics of informal workers. Workers in the informal sector tend to be lower-skilled and lower-paid, with less access to finance and social safety nets than workers in the formal sector (Loayza 2018; Perry et al. 2007; World Bank 2019a). They often live and work in crowded conditions and conduct all transactions in cash—factors that facilitate the spread of disease (Chodorow-Reich et al. 2020; Surico and Galeotti 2020). Informal workers on average have incomes 19 percent lower than formal workers and have limited savings (figure B2.1.2; World Bank 2019a). In the one-third of EMDEs with the most pervasive informality, more than one-third of the population would be driven into poverty if they had to cover direct out-of-pocket payments for an unexpected health care emergency. On average, unemployment benefits are only available to a small fraction of the population (less than 4 percent) in EMDEs with above-median output informality between 1990 and 2018.

Characteristics of informal firms. Informal firms tend to be characterized by labor-intensive production and are more prevalent in the services sector (Benjamin and Mbaye 2012). These have been hard hit by measures to curtail social interactions (Surico and Galeotti 2020). In EMDE service sectors, about

---

a. Here, estimates based on the dynamic general equilibrium model are used to capture output in the informal sector. Estimates of informal output based on the multiple indicators and multiple causes model indicate that other economies also have informal output exceeding 50 percent of GDP.

b. Common employment measures of informality are ratios of *self-employment* and *informal employment* to total employment. The *self-employed* work on their own account, or with one or a few partners, or in a cooperative. *Informal employment* comprises all workers of the informal sector and informal workers outside the informal sector (World Bank 2019a).

BOX 2.1 How does informality aggravate the impact of COVID-19? (continued)

FIGURE B2.1.2 **Features of the informal sector**

Many informal workers are employed in the agricultural or services sectors, poorly paid, with limited access to social benefits, and at risk of impoverishing health spending.

A. Productivity in the informal sector

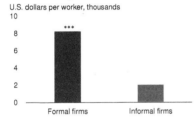

B. Agricultural sector

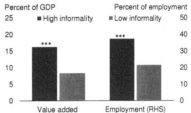

C. Risk of impoverishing expenditure for surgical care

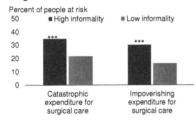

D. Social insurance

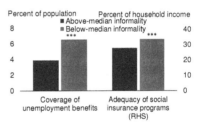

E. Informality in manufacturing and services

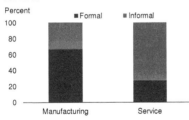

F. Wage premium for formal over informal employment

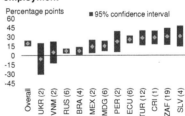

Sources: Amin, Ohnsorge, and Okou 2019; Program in Global Surgery and Social Change (PGSSC) at Harvard Medical School; World Bank (Enterprise Surveys, World Development Indicators).
Note: DGE = dynamic general equilibrium model estimates of informal output in percent of official GDP; EMDEs = emerging market and developing economies; RHS = right-hand side. *** indicates the group differences are not zero at 10 percent significance level.
A. Firm productivity is measured as sales per worker.
B.C. Bars are simple group mean for EMDEs. "High informality" is the highest one-third of EMDEs by DGE-based informal output and "low informality" is the lowest one-third over 2010-18.
D. Bars are simple group mean for EMDEs. "High informality" is the highest half of EMDEs by DGE-based informal output and "low informality" is the lowest half over 1990-2018. Adequacy of social insurance programs is measured in percent of total welfare of beneficiary households.
E. Data coverage as in Amin, Ohnsorge, and Okou (2019).
F. The wage premium is obtained from 18 empirical studies. See World Bank (2019a) for details. BRA = Brazil; CRI = Costa Rica; ECU = Ecuador; MEX = Mexico; MDG = Madagascar; PER = Peru; SLV = El Salvador; RUS = Russian Federation; TUR = Turkey; UKR = Ukraine; VNM = Vietnam; ZAF = South Africa. The number of studies or estimates for each country is shown in parenthesis; country means are calculated using a random-effects meta-analysis model.

BOX 2.1 How does informality aggravate the impact of COVID-19? (continued)

72 percent of firms are informal, compared with 33 percent in EMDE manufacturing sectors (see Amin, Ohnsorge, and Okou 2019 for sample coverage). Agricultural employment in EMDEs is roughly 90 percent informal. Epidemic-control measures have already disrupted access to markets and inputs and may also eventually threaten the food security of smallholder farmers (Cullen 2020; FAO 2020; ILO 2018b).

Broader development challenges. Economies with larger informal sectors are associated with weaker economic, fiscal, institutional, and developmental outcomes. GDP per capita in economies with above-median informality is about one-quarter that of economies with below-median informality (chapter 1). Health systems in EMDEs with more informality are relatively underdeveloped, and government capacity to mount an effective policy response to pandemics is limited.

- *Health and sanitation.* Although the populations of EMDEs with the most pervasive informality tend to be younger, they also tend to be less healthy, live in less sanitary conditions, and have access only to weak public health and medical systems (figure B2.1.3). [c] In the one-third of EMDEs with the most pervasive informality, sanitation facilities are accessible by only 36 percent of the population, and clean drinking water is available to only 54 percent of the population, compared to about 75 percent in the one-third where informality is least pervasive. Handwashing facilities are available for only 40 percent of the population in the former group. Access to medical care is also extremely limited in EMDEs with above-median informality, with only three-fourths the number of doctors and nurses per 1,000 people that the EMDEs with below-median informality have. In economies like Kenya and Malawi, thousands of people share access to only one or two intensive care unit beds (Murthy, Leligdowicz, and Adhikari 2015).

- *Government policy effectiveness.* Economies with pervasive informality are less likely to have the institutional and fiscal capacity to mount an effective policy response to the pandemic. Tax avoidance is prevalent in the informal sector, resulting in limited fiscal resources (Besley and Persson 2014). For example, government revenues and expenditures in the EMDEs with the most pervasive informality are 5-10 percentage points of GDP, on average, below

---

c. In the one-third of EMDEs with the most pervasive informality, life expectancy at birth is 66.2 years, compared with 71.4 years in the one-third with the least pervasive informality. In the one-third of EMDEs with the most pervasive informality, the numbers of deaths per 1,000 people caused by communicable diseases and maternal, prenatal, and nutrition conditions are about twice as high as in the one-third with the least pervasive informality.

BOX 2.1 How does informality aggravate the impact of COVID-19? *(continued)*

FIGURE B2.1.3 **Development challenges**

Pervasive informality is associated with short life expectancy, lack of access to medical resources, limited sanitation facilities, and other health system shortfalls. Economies with widespread informality have significantly lower government revenues and expenditures, substantially less effective governments, and greater corruption.

A. Life expectancy

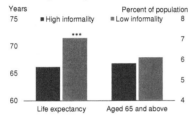

B. Access to medical resources

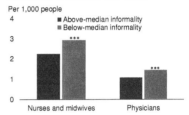

C. Access to water, sanitation, and hygiene facilities

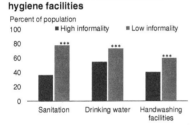

D. Mortality and disability-adjusted life years

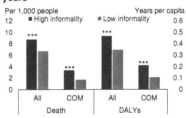

E. Government effectiveness

F. Fiscal indicators

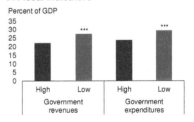

Sources: International Monetary Fund (Government Finance Statistics); *International Country Risk Guide* (ICRG); Program in Global Surgery and Social Change at Harvard Medical School; World Health Organization/United Nations Children's Fund Joint Monitoring Programme for Water Supply, Sanitation and Hygiene; World Health Organization; World Bank (World Development Indicators); World Bank 2019a.

Note: "High informality" is the highest one-third of EMDEs by DGE-based informal output and "low informality" is the lowest one-third over 2010-18. DALYs = disability-adjusted life years; DGE = dynamic general equilibrium estimates; EMDEs = emerging market and developing economies. *** indicates statistically significant group differences at 10 percent significance.

A.C. Simple group means for EMDEs with "high informality" and those with "low informality" over 2010-18.

B. Simple group means for EMDEs over 2010-18. "Above-median informality" are EMDEs with above-median informality by the share of DGE-based informal output. Two outliers, Belarus and Belize, are dropped.

D. Simple group means for EMDEs with "high informality" and those with "low informality" over 2010-18 (2016 for DALYs). DALYs refers to the number of healthy life years per person lost to diseases. "COM" indicates years lost to communicable diseases and maternal, prenatal, and nutrition conditions.

E. Simple group means for EMDEs with "high informality" and those with "low informality" over 2010-18. A higher value means better governance. "Bureaucracy quality" ranges from 0 to 4. The other measures range from 0 to 6.

F. Simple average fiscal indicators for EMDEs with "high" informality and those with "low" informality over 2000-18. Sample includes 69 EMDEs that have populations above 3.5 million people and that are not energy exporters.

**BOX 2.1 How does informality aggravate the impact of COVID-19?
(continued)**

those with the least pervasive informality (World Bank 2019a; figure
B2.1.3). In addition, governments are less effective, and corruption is more
rampant, in economies with more pervasive informality (Loayza, Oviedo,
and Servén 2006). Moreover, less than a quarter of informal firms use bank
accounts and about one-half of small informal firms identified lack of access
to finance as a major obstacle to their operations, which makes it difficult to
use the financial system to channel support to the informal economy (Farazi
2014; Schneider, Buehn, and Montenegro 2010). The rising availability of
digital payments—whether on mobile phones, cards, or online—provides an
alternative financial channel for governments to reach the informal sector.
However, it is doubtful whether sufficient cash-in and cash-out points are in
place to allow people using digital payments to deposit and withdraw cash
safely and reliably (World Bank 2017).[d] The lack of registration also makes it
a challenge to provide effective support to informal workers and firms via
official fiscal measures (such as tax deductions).

Impact of the COVID-19 outbreak

As a result of these features of the informal sector, the impact of COVID-19 is
likely to be worse in EMDEs with widespread informality. It can intensify the
pandemic's adverse health and economic consequences while weakening the
ameliorative effects of policies.

Health consequences. Health consequences of the pandemic are more adverse in
EMDEs with more pervasive informality. In these countries, lack of adequate
public health systems worsens the transmission of infectious disease. Access to
clean water and handwashing facilities is often difficult or unfeasible. Living
quarters and working environments are often overcrowded and insanitary. In
SSA, where informality is pervasive, 70 percent of city dwellers live in crowded
slums (World Bank 2019b). Lack of medical facilities and a generally less healthy
population can worsen the severity of infections and limit the ability to treat
those infected (Dahab et al. 2020). The absence of social safety nets means that
informal market participants are unable to afford to stay at home, or to adhere to
social distancing requirements, which undermines policy efforts to slow down the
spread of COVID-19 (Loayza and Pennings 2020).

Economic consequences. Lockdowns hit informal market participants in the
service sector, where informality is particularly common, especially hard (ILO
2020a; Panizza 2020). In SAR, about one of four households currently living in

---

d. These cash-in and cash-out points are often in the form of a bank agent, a mobile money agent, or an
automated teller machine (ATM; Klapper and Singer 2017).

BOX 2.1 How does informality aggravate the impact of COVID-19? (continued)

poverty is engaged in informal activities in the service or construction sectors, which have been significantly affected by closures and disruptions (World Bank 2020a). Women are overrepresented in sectors that are subject to high risks during the pandemic: 42 percent of women workers are in such sectors, compared to 32 percent of men (ILO 2020a). Also, about 80 percent of informal firms rely on internal funds and financing from family and moneylenders for working capital, making them especially vulnerable to the disruption to cashflows caused by mitigation and other control measures (Farazi 2014). Informal workers too have limited financial resources to buffer temporary income losses during the containment period, making them more likely to be pushed into poverty.[e] The health crisis also causes immediate revenue losses for firms, forcing them to temporarily or permanently close their businesses. This could trigger an unprecedented surge in unemployment and a potential expansion of the informal economy (ILO 2020b).

Past outbreaks, such as the Ebola epidemic in West Africa in 2014-15, provide a stark illustration of the vulnerability of smallholder farmers (World Bank 2015).[f] The agricultural sector has the highest share of informal employment—estimated at more than 90 percent (ILO 2018b). Farmers producing for the urban market may experience massive income losses because they are unable to sell their produce during the lockdowns (ILO 2020d).[g] Small informal firms play a critical role in the food supply chain and are likely to run into operational distress and insolvency due to logistical breakdowns during containment periods (FAO 2020; ILO 2020b; World Bank 2020b). Because they are among the poorest and most vulnerable groups of society, informal workers, especially farmers, may have reduced access to food in the event of sharp income losses.

In countries with widespread informality, governments typically have neither the resources nor the administrative structures in place to effectively deliver well-targeted relief to those most in need (Muralidharan, Niehaus, and Sukhtankar 2016). In a number of EMDEs with widespread informality, social benefit

e. For those without alternative income sources, lost labor income during the containment period could result in an increase in relative poverty for informal workers and their families of more than 21 percentage points in upper-middle-income countries and 56 percentage points in lower-middle-income countries (ILO 2020c). This could increase income inequality among workers (ILO 2020c).

f. In 2014-16, the Ebola outbreak was followed by an economic crisis in West Africa, triggered by massive health and social spending to cope with the outbreak and compounded by the almost simultaneous collapse in commodity prices (Cangul, Sdralevich, and Sian 2017; World Bank 2014).

g. Farmers may be increasingly affected by the health crisis if the virus spreads further into rural areas (ILO 2020a). In the case of India and Senegal, the inability of informal (or self-employed) workers to earn a living and gain access to health care has led to migration from urban to rural areas, which may cause the virus to spread further.

BOX 2.1 How does informality aggravate the impact of COVID-19? (continued)

systems, such as ration cards, are plagued by corruption that weakens their capacity to deliver support to the most vulnerable (Peisakhin and Pinto 2010; World Bank 2004).

Policy implications

Informality adds to the challenges of dealing with the COVID-19 pandemic. Fiscal resources need to be used to strengthen public health systems to prevent, contain, and treat the virus, and to support the livelihoods of participants in the informal economy during the outbreak. Because conventional measures—such as wage subsidies and tax relief—would hardly reach informal firms and workers, innovative emergency measures should be considered to deliver income support to informal workers, and credit support to informal firms (World Bank 2020b).[h] When managing the trade-off between coverage and costs, policy makers need to strive for a maximum reach to informal participants during the crisis, prioritizing temporary and reversable measures to minimize the longer-term fiscal burden. In some situations, however, the crisis has exposed gaps in a patchwork of social security facilities that should be filled, perhaps in the context of a thorough reform.

Expand social safety nets. The first line of response includes existing social protection and social assistance programs that could be quickly scaled up to provide immediate but temporary relief to families whose earnings have been adversely affected by the outbreak (World Bank 2020c, 2020d). Food aid, cash (or in-kind) transfers, and rent or utility bill waivers can be particularly effective in countries with pervasive informality, because they are easy to implement and have wide reach outside the formal sector (Özler 2020).[i]

Utilize flexible platforms and technologies to reach informal workers. Cash transfer and other support programs could utilize various existing registries and platforms that have wider coverage than banking or tax systems (Aker et al. 2016; Aron 2018). Such platforms should have sufficient coverage, provide possibilities to establish identities, and connect accounts with beneficiaries (World Bank 2020e). Examples include existing national social registries (for example, Brazil), new online platforms (Brazil and Thailand), new mobile payment devices

h. See World Bank (2020b) for details on the conventional measures. See ILO (2020b) for details on the importance of reducing the exposure of informal workers and their families to the virus and the risks of contagion while ensuring their access to health care.

i. Where conditional programs exist, waiving conditionality for a period could ensure wider coverage in the context of a health emergency (World Bank 2020c). See World Bank (2020e) for a summary of country examples.

BOX 2.1 **How does informality aggravate the impact of COVID-19?** *(continued)*

(Morocco), and databases in health (Morocco) and energy (El Salvador) sectors. Public transfers via mobile money have been shown to improve food security and assets as compared to manual cash transfers in the short term (Aker et al. 2016; Haushofer and Shapiro 2016).[j] "Big data" analyses and geographic (or age group or social group) targeting may help expand program coverage by identifying vulnerable groups that are not on any existing registry (Loayza and Pennings 2020; World Bank 2019a, 2020a, 2020e).

Facilitate access to finance for informal firms. To support informal firms, access to finance should be provided to help them stay in business, keep jobs, and maintain links to local and global value chains (World Bank 2020c, 2020f). Such support could be provided, potentially under government guarantees, by commercial banks, microfinance institutions, digital lending platforms, corporate supply chains, or other intermediaries. Easier access to credit, collateralization of existing properties, and online or mobile banking could help owners of informal firms to tap available financial resources, especially with the help of digital technologies.

Consider untargeted and unconditional programs when needed. Targeted programs reduce the risk that payments end up with those who do not need them, especially in the absence of effective targeting and delivery systems (Gentilini 2020; Loayza and Pennings 2020). In EMDEs where informality is pervasive and most of the population is either poor or near-poor, simple untargeted transfers may be better. Attempts to exclude the relatively few who are not in need would likely slow relief down and reduce the desired coverage of informal workers (Özler 2020). In practice, support programs that made formalization a condition of assistance have reduced the number of intended beneficiaries and have not offered net benefits to many informal enterprises (Campos, Goldstein, and McKenzie 2018). During the height of the pandemic and economic downturn, and the potentially weak recovery right afterward, the need is to quickly reach as many informal workers and firms as possible. To this end, in many EMDEs, unconditional support programs would be advisable. Given their limited resources, low-income countries may require international funding for the effective implementation of such programs.

---

j. Mobile money is a technology that allows people to receive, store, and spend money using a mobile phone. Cash-in and cash-out points—a bank agent, a mobile money agent, or an automated teller machine—should be provided to ensure the success of public transfers via digital platforms (World Bank 2017).

from poor country and year coverage (especially for EMDEs), reporting bias, and lack of consistency in survey methods.[2] Indirect, model-based measures of informal output stand out in their potentially comprehensive country and year coverage and their consistent economic meaning, but they rely on strong assumptions. The chapter highlights the circumstances in which the various individual informality measures could be particularly helpful. This adds to earlier work that has focused on the limitations of a confined number of estimation methods.

Second, the chapter argues that the combination of direct, survey-based indicators with indirect, model-based estimates can overcome the limitations of each. Informal employment measures tend to cover either the number of hours worked per day in informal employment ("intensity" of participation in informal employment) or, regardless of the number of hours worked per day, the presence of informal employment ("extent" of participation; Meghir, Narita, and Robin 2015). Because the extent of participation in the informal economy and its intensity may evolve differently, informal production may move asynchronously with informal employment.[3] Thus measures of informal output are an important complement to measures of informal employment.

Third, the chapter distills the main features of the informal economy and its evolution over time. Three different dimensions of informality are identified in the chapter: output, employment, and perception. Cross-country rankings of informal output and employment are typically consistent. Both output and employment measures of informality have trended downward since 1990 and have shown some cyclicality. In contrast, perception-based measures have tended to be highly stable over time and could, therefore, be more appropriate for cross-country comparisons.

Fourth, the chapter describes the first study to document the cyclical features of the informal sector in both advanced economies and EMDEs. Cyclical movements in informal economy output do not differ statistically significantly from those in formal economy output. Like the formal economy, the informal economy undergoes larger output movements over the business cycle in EMDEs than in advanced economies. Steeper recessions and stronger recoveries in EMDEs contribute to greater output volatility, as shown in previous studies (Aguiar and Gopinath 2007). Meanwhile, unlike formal employment, which contracts significantly in advanced economies during formal economy recessions, informal employment in both advanced economies and EMDEs appears largely acyclical during informal output business cycles. This may reflect wage movements or changes in intensity (measured as number of hours worked per day) in

---

[2] Survey-based informality measures are based on income data from surveys or audits that differ from incomes declared for tax purposes (Binelli and Attanasio 2010; McCaig and Pavcnik 2015) or earnings from firm surveys (Almeida and Carneiro 2012; Putnins and Sauka 2015).

[3] For example, during a recession, labor may move from the formal sector to the informal sector and raise participation in the informal economy (Loayza and Rigolini 2011). However, because of the fall in demand during a recession, the intensity of participation, captured by the number of hours worked in informal employment, may remain the same or even drop, reducing informal output.

labor markets, which may bear the brunt of adjustment during business cycles (Guriev, Speciale, and Tuccio 2019; Meghir, Narita, and Robin 2015).

The following section discusses how informality is defined and describes various measures of informality. Then, the chapter documents the main features of the informal economy across EMDE regions and the main similarities and differences across various measures of informality. Next, it documents informal-economy business cycles, followed by concluding remarks.

Definition of informality

Informality is typically defined as market-based and legal production of goods and services that is hidden from public authorities for monetary, regulatory, or institutional reasons (Schneider, Buehn, and Montenegro 2010). Monetary reasons include the avoidance of taxes and social security contributions, regulatory reasons include the avoidance of government bureaucracy or regulatory burdens, and institutional reasons include corruption, related often to the poor quality of political institutions and weak rule of law. These factors affect firms' and workers' decisions to participate in the formal sector (Perry et al. 2007; Ulyssea 2020). For the purposes of this book, the informal economy involves activities that, if recorded, would contribute to GDP, and does not cover illegal activities or household production (Medina and Schneider 2018; Schneider, Buehn, and Montenegro 2010). This section summarizes the definitions and classifications of informality used by previous studies.

Motivations for informal economic activity. The definition and classification of informality are highly context-specific. Similarly, the choice of informality measures will depend on the question being explored. The general definition referred to above encompasses many types of informal activities by workers and firms.

- *Exit versus exclusion.* Some workers and firms are "excluded" from the modern economy or from state benefit systems because of burdensome entry regulations and lack of human capital (de Soto 1989; Loayza, Oviedo, and Servén 2006; Perry et al. 2007). This type of informality is frequently associated with low productivity and with poorly paid and low-skilled employment (La Porta and Shleifer 2014; Loayza 2018). Other informal workers voluntarily "exit" the formal sector and choose informal activity for its flexibility, independence, and lower regulatory compliance burdens (figure 2.1; Blanchflower, Oswald, and Stutzer 2001; Falco and Haywood 2016; Günther and Launov 2012; Maloney 2004). Both "excluded" and "exiting" types of informality could coexist in an economy (Bosch and Maloney 2008, 2010; Lehmann and Pignatti 2007; Nordman, Rakotomanana, and Roubaud 2016).

- *Subsistence informality.* Other studies focus on "subsistence informality," which is pervasive in lower-income countries and characterized by low-skilled technology and the fact that, in the absence of such informal economic activity, the incomes of the workers involved would fall below subsistence levels (Docquier, Müller, and Naval 2017).

- *Evaders, avoiders, and outsiders.* Yet another group of studies classifies informal workers and firms into evaders, avoiders, and outsiders depending on their compliance with regulations and the regulations' applicability (Kanbur 2009; Kanbur and Keen 2015). Evaders are firms that are covered by regulations but do not comply, avoiders are firms that adjust to be outside the remit of regulations, outsiders are firms that are simply not covered by regulations.

- *Margins.* More recent studies distinguish different types of informality by the entities engaged in informal activity, without focusing on their motivation: firms that do not register their business (the extensive margin) or registered firms that hire workers "off the books" (the intensive margin; Ulyssea 2018, 2020).

Informal workers. Informal employment covers all workers in the informal sector and informal workers outside the informal sector (ILO 2018a; Perry et al. 2007). The former comprises all persons who were employed in at least one informal firm. The latter group consists of some self-employed and workers who are not employed in formal contractual arrangements or not subject to social security or employment benefits.[4] Some have defined informal employment more specifically as referring to workers who do not contribute to retirement pension schemes, which form part of social security (Loayza, Servén, and Sugawara 2010).

The most commonly used proxy for the relative size of informal employment is the share of self-employment in total employment, capturing workers who, working on their own account or with one or a few partners or in a cooperative, hold the type of jobs defined as "self-employment jobs" (annex 2A; ILO 1993; La Porta and Shleifer 2014). The other popular measure of informal employment comprises all workers in the informal sector (workers in at least one informal sector enterprise, irrespective of their status in employment and whether it was their main or a secondary job) together with informal workers outside the informal sector (the self-employed and employees holding informal jobs). For the remainder of the chapter, informal employment will be proxied by self-employment because data on informal employment are not available for advanced economies. The numbers throughout this chapter refer to the latest available years, unless otherwise specified.

Informal firms. Some studies use the following criteria to define an informal firm (ILO 2018a). First, it is not an incorporated enterprise that is a legal entity separate from its owners, with its own complete set of accounts, and it is not owned or controlled by one person or a few household members. Second, it is a market enterprise that sells its goods or services. Third, it falls into one of the following categories: it keeps the number of workers employed on a continuous basis and below a threshold determined by the state, it is not registered, or its workers are not registered. Other studies provide an alternative definition of degrees of firm informality on a continuum depending on size, registration,

---

[4] See the annex of Hussmanns (2003) for the overlap between informal employment and self-employment.

honesty of accounting, tax payments, mobility of workplace, and access to bank credit (Benjamin and Mbaye 2012; Mbaye, Benjamin, and Gueye 2017).

Database of informality measures

Reflecting the difficulty of measuring informality, researchers have developed a wide range of estimation methods to capture its scale. The database compiled for this study includes the 12 measures most commonly used in the literature. These can be categorized into two groups based on their estimation methods. The first group encompasses indirect model-based estimates of the relative size of informal output (that is, informal output in percent of official GDP). The second group encompasses direct measures gathered from surveys, such as labor force, household, firm, or opinion surveys. In the database, indirect and direct measures together cover up to 196 economies (36 advanced economies and 160 EMDEs) and for periods as long as 1950-2018 (table 2B.1A and table 2B.7).

This section describes the informality database and the limitations and advantages of each measure included in it. Indirect measures stand out for their broad country and long year coverage, but they suffer from their narrow focus on economic production and strong reliance on model specifications and assumptions. Direct measures capture more dimensions of informality and do not involve particular model specifications and assumptions, but they tend to have limited country and year coverage, making them less well suited to cross-country, time-series analyses. Indirect measures provide only a macro perspective on the extent of informality in an economy, whereas direct measures can also provide a micro perspective on how firms and workers behave in the informal sector.

Indirect estimates

Previous studies have used various indirect approaches to estimate the size of the informal sector, including the currency-demand approach (Ardizzi et al. 2014), the electricity-demand approach (Schneider and Enste 2000), the multiple indicators multiple causes (MIMIC) model (Schneider, Buehn, and Montenegro 2010), and the dynamic general equilibrium (DGE) model (Elgin and Oztunali 2012; Ihrig and Moe 2004; Orsi, Raggi, and Turino 2014). Among all indirect estimation methods, the MIMIC and DGE models stand out in terms of their long time series and broad country coverage. For this reason, the focus here is mainly on the use of MIMIC and DGE models to estimate the size of informal economic activity. To make the measures comparable with those in the literature, both DGE-based and MIMIC-based estimates are reported in percent of official GDP.

The MIMIC model. This is a type of structural equations model that can be used to estimate the relative size of informal economic activity. Two features of MIMIC are particularly important: first, it explicitly takes into account multiple possible causes of informal activity and captures multiple outcome indicators of it; and, second, it can readily be used to estimate informal activity across countries and over time. Other indirect approaches, like the currency-demand approach and the electricity-demand approach, condense all the features of informal activity across product and factor markets into just one indicator.[5] The informal sector, however, shows its effects in various markets, which can be captured better in a MIMIC model (Schneider, Buehn, and Montenegro 2010). The data on causes and indicators of informal activity identified in the literature are largely macroeconomic data in a panel setting and can be updated annually.

The limitations of the standard MIMIC model, used by Schneider, Buehn, and Montenegro (2010) and others, have been widely discussed in the literature (Feige 2016; Medina and Schneider 2018). The limitations include (1) the use of GDP (that is, GDP per capita and its growth rates) as both cause and indicator variables; (2) its reliance on another, independent study's base-year estimates of the informal economy to calibrate the size of the informal economy in percent of GDP; and (3) the sensitivity of the model's estimated coefficients to alternative model specifications and sample coverage.[6] These limitations can open the MIMIC estimates to charges of manipulation and misrepresentation (Breusch 2005).

The most cited MIMIC study, Schneider, Buehn, and Montenegro (2010), is replicated here to estimate the size of the informal sector in percent of official GDP. Six causes and three indicators are used in the estimation to capture the hypothesized relationships between the informal sector (the latent variable) and its causes and indicators (annex 2A). Once the relationships are identified and the parameters are estimated, the estimation results are used to calculate the MIMIC index, which gives the absolute values of the size of the informal sector after a benchmarking or calibration procedure. The estimates from the model specification that ensures maximum data coverage are used here (annex 2A). The MIMIC approach delivers a panel of estimates for 160 economies (36 advanced economies and 124 EMDEs) over the period 1993-2018.

The MIMIC estimates capture the combination of both employment and productivity in the informal sector, whereas measures of informal employment reflect only the level of employment in the informal sector. Despite the comprehensive country and long time-series coverage, MIMIC estimates do not fluctuate much over time, which makes the estimates less suited for time-series analyses (including the business cycle analysis below).

The DGE model. The DGE model considers how optimizing households will allocate labor between formal and informal economies in each period and how the allocation

---

[5] The electricity-demand and currency-demand approaches suffer from limited data availability and are subject to specific caveats. The electricity-demand model rests on the strong assumptions that all informal economic activity requires only the use of electricity, and the association between informal production and use of electricity is constant over time. The currency-demand approach rests on the assumption that transactions in the informal sector are paid in cash and that there is no informal sector in the base year (Ahumada, Alvaredo, and Canavesa 2007).

[6] Medina and Schneider (2018) try to overcome the limitation of using official GDP (which may capture part of the informal economy) by using night-light data to independently capture economic activity.

changes over time (Elgin and Oztunali 2012; Ihrig and Moe 2004). In comparison with other estimation methods, the DGE approach stands out in the comprehensive country and year coverage that it allows, its clear theoretical basis, and its applicability to policy experiments and projections (Loayza 2016).

The DGE approach has some limitations. First, it relies on strong assumptions about the functional form of activity in the informal and formal sector and about the relationship between formal and informal productivity (Orsi, Raggi, and Turino 2014; Schneider and Buehn 2016). Second, like the MIMIC approach, it requires base-year estimates of the informal economy from another independent study to calibrate the size of informal economy (Elgin and Oztunali 2012; Ihrig and Moe 2004). Third, a computable DGE model captures only some of the stylized facts of the informal sector. Data availability, especially for EMDEs, presents a challenge to matching DGE models with all aspects of informality.

Here, a deterministic DGE model proposed by Elgin and Oztunali (2012) is used to estimate the size of the informal sector. The model captures the essence of labor allocation between the formal and informal sectors and provides a mapping between the formal and informal economies in a dynamic setting. The model relies on two key equilibrium conditions for calibration and data construction processes (annex 2A). The two key equilibrium conditions are one that connects the formal and informal economies through labor allocation and another that captures intertemporal substitution. The model results in estimates of informal output in percent of official GDP for 158 economies (36 advanced economies and 122 EMDEs) over the period 1950-2018.

The DGE estimates reflect the levels of both employment and productivity in the informal sector and stand out in their broad country and long year coverage. The time variation of the DGE estimates is sufficient for time-series analysis, including the business cycle analysis in the following sections. But the time variation of the DGE estimates relies partially on strong assumptions. For instance, in Elgin and Oztunali (2012), the growth rate of productivity in the informal sector is assumed to be a function of the growth rates of capital and productivity in the formal sector.[7]

Survey-based estimates

Four existing informality measures are labor-related, of which three are related to employment and one to pension coverage. These measures are gathered mainly from labor force surveys but sometimes from household surveys.

Labor force surveys. Measures related to labor force surveys have the advantages of not relying on strong assumptions, having no need for base-year estimates for calibration,

---

[7] In the case of Elgin and Oztunali (2012), the heavy reliance of DGE estimates on assumptions and base-year estimates on the informal economy for calibration could be reduced by using other sources of information on the informal economy (survey-based estimates of informal employment).

and having sufficient time variation for time-series analysis. But they also have several limitations: the data are costly to gather, contributing to limited country and year coverage; survey methodologies may vary over time and across countries, limiting the comparability of the data; there are the typical drawbacks of survey-based data (such as sample bias); and employment measures cannot reflect other changes in the informal sector, such as in productivity and the number of working hours.

Despite the limitations, survey-based labor-related measures can provide useful guidance for the construction and use of indirect informality measures. Among all labor-related measures, self-employment stands out in its year and country coverage and sufficient time variation, making it suitable for time-series analysis and cross-country comparisons.[8] For labor-related questions (employment creation and destruction in the informal sector, or social security issues), labor-related measures are typically preferred.

The most frequently used measure is the share of self-employment in total employment (in the database used here labeled *SEMP*; La Porta and Shleifer 2014; Maloney 2004). As defined by the 1993 International Classification of Status in Employment, self-employed workers include four subcategories of jobs, as classified in the World Bank's World Development Indicators (WDI) and by the International Labour Organization (ILO): employers, own-account workers, members of producers' cooperatives, and contributing family workers.[9] Self-employed workers are those who, working on their own account (own-account workers or employers) or with one or a few partners or in a cooperative, hold "self-employment jobs" as defined above. These are jobs for which the remuneration is directly dependent upon the profits derived from the goods and services produced.

Two other measures are informal employment and employment outside the formal sector.[10] These are usually expressed in percent of total employment (or nonagricultural employment) and refer to different aspects of informality.[11] Whereas employment outside the formal sector is an enterprise-based concept that includes persons employed

---

[8] ILO also produces model-based estimates that it uses to construct an internationally comparable data set on the share of self-employment in total employment (https://www.ilo.org/ilostat-files/Documents/TEM.pdf). Such model-based estimates largely rely on collected survey-based estimates but still could be sensitive to model specifications. Over the period 1990-2018, the pairwise correlation between survey-based estimates on self-employment shares and model-based estimates is 0.95. For the purpose of this book, survey-based estimates of self-employment shares are preferred.

[9] Self-employment largely overlaps with informal employment, but not all self-employed workers are in informal employment. For example, the owner of a formally registered firm is both self-employed and formally employed. Whereas contributing family workers are always classified as informal, workers who hold other types of "self-employment jobs" are classified as being in informal employment when their production units are informal sector enterprises or households. See 17th ICLS guidelines for details (https://www.ilo.org/public/libdoc/ilo/2013/480862.pdf).

[10] ILO presents detailed definitions of these two measures (ILO 2021a, b). Here, the harmonized series of these two measures, which allow for cross-country comparisons, are preferred, despite some remaining limitations (ILO 2021c).

[11] ILO reports these two measures both in percent of total employment and in percent of nonagricultural employment. Due to space limitations, the analysis here focuses on these two measures in percent of total employment, which are comparable with the self-employment measure.

by informal sector enterprises or in households, informal employment is a job-based concept and has a broader definition. Informal employment comprises all workers in the informal sector and informal workers outside the informal sector. Almost all persons employed in the informal sector are in informal employment. But not all informal employment is in the informal sector. For example, informal employment includes internships in the formal sector without contracts or pension contributions.

For a comprehensive data set on labor-related measures on informality, cross-country databases, provided by the WDI, ILO, and Organisation for Economic Co-operation and Development, are combined, with additional data gathered from various sources (annex 2A). The resulting data set on self-employment is a panel of 180 economies or regions over the period 1955-2018. The data set on informal employment covers 72 EMDEs from various years during 2000-18 whereas the data set on employment outside the formal sector contains 76 EMDEs from various years during 1999-2018. Data on informal employment and on employment outside the formal sector are obtained from ILO.

Data on pension coverage are gathered from various issues of the WDI (book version, reported until 2012). The measure is defined as the fraction of the labor force that contributes to a retirement pension scheme (Loayza, Servén, and Sugawara 2010). It yields a panel that covers 135 economies from 1990 to 2010. The measure is suitable for analyzing social security issues related to the informal economy.

Firm opinion surveys. Two data sets based on surveys of firms have outstanding coverage and data quality: the World Bank's Enterprise Surveys and the Executive Opinion Surveys conducted by the World Economic Forum (WEF). The World Bank Enterprise Surveys cover 140 economies over the period 2006-18 whereas the Executive Opinion Surveys cover 154 economies over the period 2008-18.[12]

Both surveys are answered by top managers and business owners, who can be expected to be familiar with the business climate in the country concerned. The surveys could reveal some dimensions of informality (for example, regarding the ease of doing business in the informal sector) that are not captured in the output or labor-related measures of informality. Similar to labor-related measures, measures from firm surveys also have the advantage of being independent of strong assumptions and base-year estimates for calibration.

There are two particular drawbacks of informality measures based on firm surveys. First, data from firm surveys tend to have limited year coverage. Second, because perceptions tend not to move much over time, these types of measures do not have much time

---

[12] Due to survey design changes, the data collected by the Executive Opinion Surveys over the period 2004-07 are not comparable with those for subsequent years. The World Bank also conducts Productivity and Investment Climate Surveys at the firm level. Although these surveys occasionally report measures of informality, they are obtained from various sources and use different methodologies.

variation. Both drawbacks limit their application in time-series analysis. Nonetheless, they shed light on the perceived extent of informality in a country and can provide useful guidance for constructing and validating indirect model estimates.

World Bank Enterprise Surveys compile responses on various topics (including informality) from face-to-face interviews with top managers and business owners in over 161,000 companies in 144 economies. The surveys yield the following measures of informality that have been used in the literature (La Porta and Shleifer 2014; World Bank 2019a): percent of firms competing against unregistered or informal firms (*WB1*), percent of firms formally registered when they started operations in the country (*WB2*), (average) number of years that firms operate without formal registration (*WB3*), and percent of firms identifying practices of competitors in the informal sector as a major constraint (*WB4*). Higher values of *WB1*, *WB3*, and *WB4* and a lower value of *WB2* indicate higher levels of informality. *WB1* and *WB4* also provide some insights into informal firms' competitiveness whereas *WB2* and *WB3* are considered indicative of constraints imposed by registration requirements.

In comparison to Enterprise Surveys, Executive Opinion Surveys provide a more balanced panel data set, making them more suitable for business cycle analysis. The WEF has been conducting Executive Opinion Surveys every year since 1979. As reported in the 2014 edition, over 13,000 executives in 144 economies were surveyed. From 2006, the survey has asked the question, "In your country, how much economic activity do you estimate to be undeclared or unregistered? (1 = Most economic activity is undeclared or unregistered; 7 = Most economic activity is declared or registered)." The average responses at the country-year level constitute a series of informality measures with a lower average indicating a relatively larger informal economy.

Household surveys. Household surveys may report perceptions of the extent of informality in an economy or opinions on informal economic activities. The World Values Surveys (WVS) stand out in terms of their extensive country and year coverage; others household surveys mainly focus on European economies.[13] The WVS asked whether respondents considered it justifiable to cheat on taxes, with the data averaged for five periods from 1981-84 to 2010-14. The responses could range from 1 (never justifiable) to 10 (always justifiable). In total, 317,750 respondents from 96 economies participated in the survey. The average responses at the country and year level are used as a measure for attitudes toward informality. A higher average at the country level implies that people find cheating on taxes more justifiable and thus consider informal activity more acceptable. It is regarded as an indirect measure of informality because a lack of tax morality is associated with a higher level of informality (Oviedo, Thomas, and Karakurum-Özdemir 2009).

---

[13] These surveys, which include the Eurobarometer Survey, European Values Survey, and the European Social Survey, are not used in this study because of their limited coverage of EMDEs. Details about other social surveys are shown in annex 2B (tables 2B.1A and 2B.9).

Comparison of statistical features across measures

For any economy, the various measures of informality will differ somewhat, both in the level of informality implied and in its variation over time. In general, MIMIC estimates indicate lower and less volatile informal sector activity than DGE estimates. This partly reflects the differences in the assumed underlying drivers of informality in the two approaches: MIMIC is based on slow-moving variables such as ones relating to institutional quality whereas DGE is based on more volatile variables such as employment, investment, and productivity. In EMDEs, the share of informal activity in GDP (by either measure) tends to be well below the share of self-employment in total employment, which may reflect lower labor productivity in the informal economy than the formal economy or some self-employed workers contributing to the formal economy (Loayza 2018).[14] Survey-based measures tend to be stable over decades, potentially reflecting a profound rigidity in perceptions.

Size and evolution of the informal economy

This section distills the empirical findings on the main features of the informal economy and its evolution over time. The informal economy is more prevalent in EMDEs than in advanced economies but is widely heterogeneous across countries and regions. Both output and employment measures of informality have trended downward since 1990. In contrast, survey-based measures relating to perceptions have tended to be highly stable, making them more appropriate for cross-country comparisons than for over-time analyses.

About one-third of activity. Globally, the informal economy accounted for 32-33 percent of GDP and 31 percent of employment over the period 1990-2018 (table 2B.1B). As shown in previous studies, a higher level of development, as measured by per capita income, is associated with lower informality, virtually regardless of the measure of informality, other than survey-based ones, or the year chosen (La Porta and Shleifer 2014). Thus informality tends to be considerably more pervasive in EMDEs than in advanced economies (figure 2.2): in advanced economies, it accounts for about 19 percent of GDP and 16 percent of employment, on average, whereas in EMDEs it accounts for 36-37 percent of GDP and 39 percent of employment.

Wide cross-country heterogeneity. There is wide heterogeneity in informal activity among EMDEs (figure 2.2). For example, the informal economy's share in GDP, depending on the measure used, ranged from about 10 percent to 68 percent; and the share of self-employment in total employment ranged from near zero to 96 percent.

---

[14] In this section and below, self-employment is used to proxy for informal employment as in La Porta and Shleifer (2014), unless otherwise specified. In the following sections, "in percent of GDP or output" is used as the equivalent of "in percent of official GDP" in the context of the share of informal output (both DGE-based and MIMIC-based estimates), and "in percent of employment" is used as the equivalent of "in percent of total employment."

FIGURE 2.2 **Informality and development**

Informality is more pervasive in EMDEs than in advanced economies, indicating a positive link between development and informality. But informality varies widely among EMDEs.

A. DGE-based informal activity

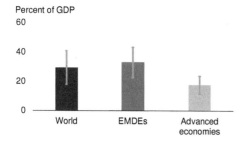

B. MIMIC-based informal activity

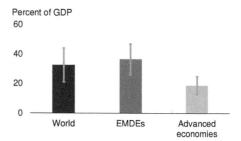

C. Self-employment

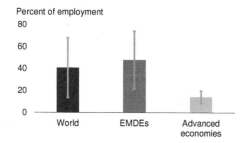

D. Labor force without pension

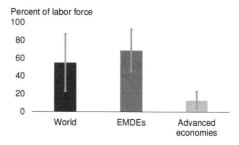

E. Perceived informal activity

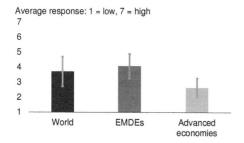

F. Attitudes to informality

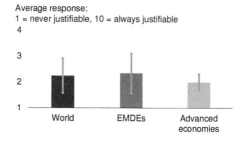

Sources: World Bank; World Economic Forum; World Values Survey.

Note: See table 2B.1A for details on data definitions. Simple group means for the period 2010-18 (2000-10 for D and F due to data availability) are shown in bars with their -1 and +1 standard deviation shown by orange whiskers. DGE = dynamic general equilibrium model estimates of informal output in percent of official GDP; EMDEs = emerging market and developing economies; MIMIC = multiple indicators multiple causes model estimates of informal output in percent of GDP.

C. Missing data for self-employment in percent of total employment are interpolated in EMDEs for earlier years and filled using the latest available observation in recent years.

D. "Labor force without pension" is in percent of labor force, averaged over 2000-10, given data availability.

E. World Economic Forum index of perceived informality is used.

F. Data from World Values Survey on the attitude toward cheating on taxes are used here and averaged over 2000-10, given data availability.

FIGURE 2.3 **Informality in EMDE regions**

Informality is common in all EMDE regions but takes different forms. On average, the share of informal output is highest in Sub-Saharan Africa, Europe and Central Asia, and Latin America and the Caribbean. The share of self-employment is highest in Sub-Saharan Africa, South Asia, and East Asia and Pacific.

A. DGE-based informal activity

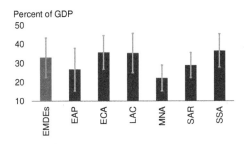

B. MIMIC-based informal activity

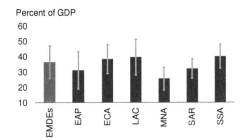

C. Self-employment

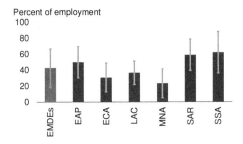

D. Labor force without pension

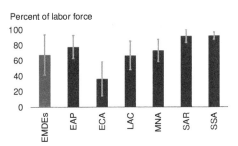

E. Perceived informal activity

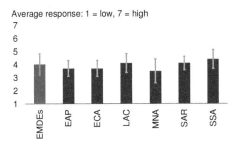

F. Shares of EMDE regions in world output and employment

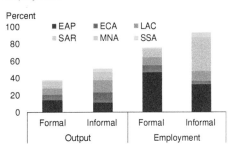

Sources: International Labour Organization; World Bank (World Development Indicators); World Economic Forum.

Note: Blue and red bars indicate group means for 2010-18 (2006-16 for D), with whiskers indicating +/-1 standard deviation. DGE = dynamic general equilibrium model estimates on informal output; EAP = East Asia and Pacific; ECA = Europe and Central Asia; EMDEs = emerging market and developing economies; LAC = Latin America and the Caribbean; MIMIC = multiple indicators multiple causes model estimates on informal output; MNA = Middle East and North Africa; SAR = South Asia; SSA = Sub-Saharan Africa.

C. Self-employment shares (in percent of total employment) are used here.

E. Perceived informal activity is proxied by World Economic Forum index, which ranges from "1 = Most economic activity is undeclared or unregistered" to "7 = Most economic activity is declared or registered." See table 2B.1A for details on data definitions.

F. The stacked bars show the formal and informal output (employment) in each EMDE region as a share of the world's total formal or informal output (employment) using data averaged from 2010-18. Formal output is proxied by official GDP, while DGE-based estimates are used to capture the level of informal output. Informal employment is proxied by self-employment, while formal employment is the difference between total employment and self-employment.

FIGURE 2.4 Evolution of informality in advanced economies and EMDEs, 1990-2018

The shares of informal employment and output have declined in both advanced economies and EMDEs since 1990, despite largely unchanged perceptions of the size of the informal sector.

A. DGE-based informal activity

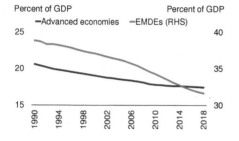

B. MIMIC-based informal activity

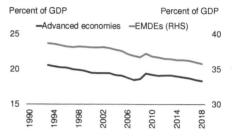

C. Self-employment

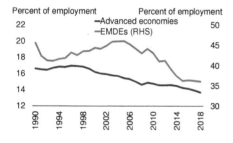

D. Perceived informal activity

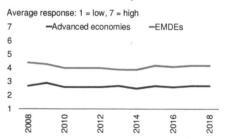

Source: World Bank; World Economic Forum.
Note: See table 2B.1A for details on data definitions. Group means are calculated for advanced economies (in blue) and emerging market and developing economies (EMDEs, in red). DGE = dynamic general equilibrium model; MIMIC = multiple indicators multiple causes model; RHS = right-hand side.
C. Informal employment is proxied by self-employment in percent of total employment. Missing data for self-employment are interpolated in EMDEs for earlier years and filled using the latest available observation in recent years.
D. World Economic Forum index of informality is used, which ranges from "1 = Most economic activity is undeclared or unregistered" to "7 = Most economic activity is declared or registered."

Widespread informality across all EMDE regions. Informality is common in all EMDE regions but takes different forms (World Bank 2012). On average, the informal economy's share of output is highest in SSA, Europe and Central Asia (ECA), and Latin America and the Caribbean (LAC). The share of self-employment, however, is highest in SSA, South Asia (SAR), and East Asia and Pacific (EAP; figure 2.3).

Declining employment and output informality over time. The shares of both informal output and employment have declined since 1990, especially in EMDEs (figure 2.4). Between 1990 and 2018, on average, the share of informal output in GDP fell by about 8 percentage points in EMDEs, to 31 percent, and by 3 percentage points in the advanced economies, to 17 percent. Over the same period, the average share of self-employment in total employment declined by about 3 percentage points in the advanced economies, to 14 percent, and by about 10 percentage points in EMDEs, to

36 percent. In EMDEs, the largest declines in the shares of informal output and employment occurred from the early 2000s, in a reversal of a decade of a rising share of informal employment and barely shrinking share of informal output.[15] In advanced economies, the largest declines in the share of informal employment occurred between the late 1990s and the global financial crisis of 2008-09; they have since partly reversed, amid anemic postcrisis growth (figure 2.4).

Broad-based declines. The declines in informality between 1990 and 2018 were broad-based, especially for output- and employment-based measures. Country-specific regressions of the shares of the informal economy in GDP and employment on a time trend were estimated to capture this secular decline (figure 2.5). In 69 (*SEMP*) to 100 (*DGE*) percent of advanced economies (depending on the measure) and 54 (*SEMP*) to 81 (*MIMIC*) percent of EMDEs, statistically significant downward trends in the share of the informal economy in GDP (or employment) were found. The trend decline in the share of informal output suggests that economic growth may be associated with more rapidly rising labor productivity in the formal economy than in the informal economy. As economies grow, formal-sector productivity growth may benefit from greater technological improvements and availability of capital than can be accessed by the informal sector (Amaral and Quintin 2006). In only a few cases did output and employment informality move in different directions. Noticeable drops in the share of informal output were associated with only moderate falls in the share of informal employment in some EMDEs, and even with increases in the share of informal employment in others (see chapter 5 for detailed discussion).

Stable perceptions of informality over time. Perceptions of informality appear to have changed much more slowly than actual informal output and employment.[16] In the majority of advanced economies and EMDEs, perceptions of the scale of informality—as measured by the WEF and WVS indexes—have not declined significantly since 1990. There are, however, a few exceptions. This often coincided with rapid GDP growth and reductions in the shares of both informal output and employment.

Consistency among the various measures of informality

The various measures of informality refer to three distinct aspects of it: output (DGE and MIMIC estimates), employment (for example, self-employment and workers without pensions), and perception (for example, the WEF and WVS surveys). This section explores the consistency among the various measures of informality.

---

[15] The persistence of high levels of informality in EMDEs in the early 1990s in part reflects the expanding informal sector in Eastern and Central European economies during their economic transition (Kaufmann and Kaliberda 1996). By construction, slow-moving indicators for institutional quality in MIMIC estimates dampen these estimates' movements over time.

[16] Guiso, Sapienza, and Zingales (2009) demonstrate that perceptions of trustworthiness are largely historically determined with limited time variance.

FIGURE 2.5 Downward trends in informality, 1990-2018

Informality declined in both advanced economies and EMDEs during 1990-2018. The share of informal output dropped in all EMDE regions, but by most in East Asia and Pacific, Latin America and the Caribbean, and South Asia.

A. Changes in informality: Income groups

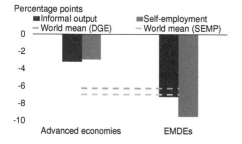

B. Changes in informality: EMDE regions

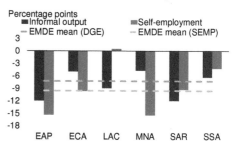

C. Advanced economies with downward trends in informality

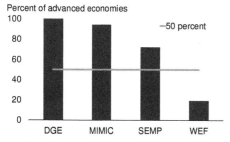

D. EMDEs with downward trends in informality

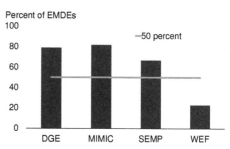

Source: World Bank; World Economic Forum.

Note: Data are for the period 1990-2018. DGE = dynamic general equilibrium model; EAP = East Asia and Pacific; ECA = Europe and Central Asia; EMDEs = emerging market and developing economies; LAC = Latin America and the Caribbean; MIMIC = multiple indicators multiple causes model; MNA = Middle East and North Africa; SAR = South Asia; SEMP = self-employment in percent of total employment; SSA = Sub-Saharan Africa; WEF = World Economic Forum estimates.

A. The bars indicate the simple group means for advanced economies and EMDEs, with the red bars for self-employment (in percent of total employment) and blue bars for DGE-based informal output (in percent of official GDP). Lines show world averages.

B. The bars indicate the simple group means for EMDE regions, with red bars for self-employment (in percent of total employment) and blue bars for DGE-based informal output (in percent of official GDP). Lines show EMDE averages.

C.D. Data for the period 1990-2018. Based on country-specific linear regressions of the share of informality on each of the four measures of informality with a sufficiently long time dimension. Figures show the share of advanced economies (C) and EMDEs (D) for which the time trend is statistically significantly negative (at least at the 10 percent level). In D, missing values for self-employment are interpolated. Horizontal line indicates 50 percent.

Correlations in cross-country rankings: Output and employment. The various measures for informality are generally positively correlated with each other, with the correlations within each block (output, employment, perception) being stronger than correlations between blocks (table 2B.2). The cross-country rank correlation between the two model-based estimates of informal output is close to 1 and significantly different from zero at the 1 percent level. In addition, the rank correlations between DGE estimates and both employment measures and some perception measures are also positive and significant (figure 2.6). The correlations among the various measures of informal employment range from 0.20 to 0.94 and are mostly significant at the 10

FIGURE 2.6 **Consistency among various informality measures**

The various measures for informality are generally positively correlated with each other, with the correlations within each block (output, employment, perception) being stronger than correlations between blocks.

A. Correlations between DGE estimates and other informality estimates

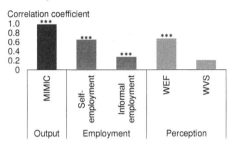

B. Correlations between self-employment and other informality measures

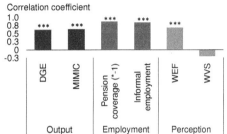

C. Correlations between self-employment and other labor-related informality measures

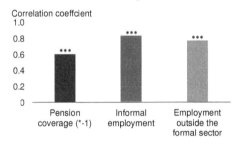

D. Correlations between WEF index and other perception-related informality measures

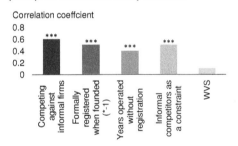

E. Coincidence of signs of first differences: DGE estimates and other informality estimates

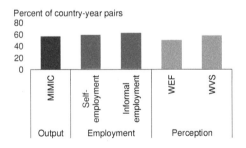

F. Coincidence of signs of first differences: Self-employment estimates and other informality estimates

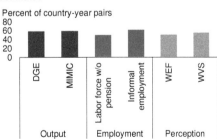

Sources: World Bank (Enterprise Surveys); World Economic Forum; World Values Survey.
Note: Data for the period 1990-2018. Pension coverage is in percent of labor force, while informal employment and employment outside the formal sector are in percent of total employment. WVS asks whether cheating on taxes is justifiable (1 is "never justifiable" and 0 is "always justifiable") and reports average responses at the country-year level. A higher level indicates a country is more tolerant of informality. WEF asks, "In your country, how much economic activity do you estimate to be undeclared or unregistered? (1 = Most economic activity is undeclared or unregistered; 7 = Most economic activity is declared or registered)," and reports average responses at the country-year level. Here, the average responses have been reordered to make "7 = most economic activity is undeclared or unregistered" and "1 = most economic activity is declared or registered" such that a higher score indicates more informality (see also tables 2B.1 and 2B.2). DGE = dynamic general equilibrium model; MIMIC = multiple indicators and multiple causes model; SEMP = self-employment in percent of total employment; WEF = World Economic Forum estimates; WVS = World Values Survey.
A.-D. Medians of rank correlations of data across countries within each year. All survey-based measures are interpolated. *** indicates significance at 10 percent level. The responses from World Bank Enterprise Surveys are shown in D (see table 2B.3 for details).
E.F. Shares of country-year pairs where first differences of DGE estimates (E) or self-employment (F) coincide with first differences of other informality estimates. Survey-based estimates are interpolated to fill gaps in data series.

percent level. On average, the correlation between an estimate of informal output and employment-based measures is above 0.60 and significant at the 1 percent level.

Correlations in cross-country rankings: Perceptions. Perception-based estimates of informality tend to be more correlated with each other than with estimates of informal output or employment. The WVS is an exception: it tends to be uncorrelated or little correlated with all other measures, including perception-based ones. This suggests that a large informal sector reflects more than citizens' weak tax morality, which WVS purports to capture. Among the perception-based measures, the WEF, which purports to capture perceptions of the extent of informal economic activities, is the one most correlated with the other measures, both output-based (about 0.70) and employment-based (about 0.5-0.7 with the share of labor force without pension and self-employment as a share of total employment).

Correlation in direction of movements over time. To examine the consistency of movements over time among various measures, the coincidence of the directions of movements in different variables is checked by looking at the shares of country pairs in which first differences in two measures have the same sign (figure 2.6; table 2B.3).[17] This is the case in about 50 percent of all the country pairs—and highest, at 82 percent of country-year pairs, for informal employment and employment outside the formal sector. The directions of changes in output measures and employment measures coincide in 55-65 percent of country-year pairs, suggesting that output measures capture important additional factors to employment measures, such as changes in labor productivity or intensity of work.

Cyclical features of the informal economy

Like formal economies, informal economies feature business cycles, which share some features with those in the formal economy: they are stronger in EMDEs than in advanced economies, and they feature downturns and recoveries with similar speeds. That said, they are not fully synchronized with business cycles in the formal economy. This section distills the main cyclical features of the informal economy. Building on this section, chapter 3 explores the links between formal and informal business cycles in greater detail and their implications for macroeconomic policy.

Volatility of formal and informal economies

Employment and output volatility. The business cycles of formal and informal economies are not entirely synchronous (as discussed in detail in chapter 3). Employment growth in the informal sector is slightly, but statistically significantly, negatively correlated with employment growth in the formal sector (-0.2 percent). As a

---

[17] As a robustness check, the pairwise correlations of first-differenced informality measures over time for each country are calculated, with their medians computed across countries. The results are in line with table 2B.3. Whereas significant and positive correlations are observed among pension coverage, informal employment, and employment outside the formal sector, no significant correlations between informal employment (or perception) measures and informal output measures are found.

FIGURE 2.7 **Volatility of formal and informal economies, 1990-2018**

Formal and informal output and employment are significantly more volatile in EMDEs than in advanced economies, possibly reflecting larger shocks to, or less resilience to shocks in, EMDEs.

A. Volatility of formal and informal output

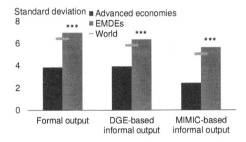

B. Volatility of formal and informal employment

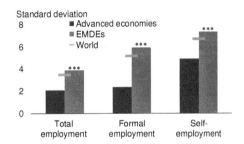

Source: World Bank.
Note: Data are for the period 1990-2018. Formal output is captured by official GDP, while informal output uses DGE-based or MIMIC-based estimates. "Total employment" is the sum of formal employment and self-employment. Volatility shows the standard deviations of the concerning variables' annual growth rates. *** indicates significant differences at 5 percent level between advanced economies and emerging market and developing economies (EMDEs). DGE = dynamic general equilibrium model; MIMIC = multiple indicators and multiple causes model.

result, formal or informal employment alone is more volatile than total employment (the sum of formal and informal employment).[18]

Volatility in EMDEs and in advanced economies. Formal and informal output and employment are significantly more volatile in EMDEs than in advanced economies, possibly reflecting larger shocks, or lesser resilience to shocks, in EMDEs (figure 2.7; table 2B.4; Aguiar and Gopinath 2007; Neumeyer and Perri 2005; Restrepo-Echavarria 2014).[19] In addition, in both EMDEs and advanced economies, self-employment is somewhat more volatile than formal employment (that is, total employment excluding self-employment), perhaps reflecting greater rigidity in the formal labor market (Djankov and Ramalho 2009).

Informal-economy business cycles

Dating informal business cycles. Formal and informal business cycles were identified using the commonly used algorithm of Harding and Pagan (2002). Business cycle turning points are years in which output peaks or troughs. When there are several peaks or troughs within a five-year interval, the deepest trough or steepest peak was used. A recession is defined as the period from peak to trough, whereas an expansion is the converse, the period from trough to peak. A recovery, the early part of an expansion, is

---

[18] This supports earlier findings that the informal sector may help stabilize total employment over business cycles (Fernández and Meza 2015; Loayza and Rigolini 2011).

[19] Detailed results on the volatility of formal and informal economies are presented in table 2B.4.

defined as the period during which output rebounds from the trough to its prerecession peak. The main characteristics of the recession and recovery phases, including duration, amplitude, and slope, are defined as in Claessens, Kose, and Terrones (2012; annex 2A). Here employment was logged and detrended.

The results are in line with earlier studies (Bajada 2003; Birinçi and Elgin 2013) of informal business cycle recessions and expansions in advanced economies.[20] In contrast to these studies, however, the main focus here is on recessions and recoveries. Because recoveries are the early parts of expansions, they reflect more of an economy's short-term cyclical movements rather than its long-term growth path.

Output movements through informal-economy business cycles. Neither recessions nor recoveries in the informal economy differ statistically significantly from those in the formal economy (figure 2.8; tables 2B.5A and 2B.5B). The duration of both formal- and informal-economy recoveries was slightly longer than formal- and informal-economy recessions in EMDEs but not in advanced economies.[21] The speed of recessions resembled that of recoveries in both formal and informal economies. As for formal economies, informal-economy recessions were steeper and informal economy recoveries were stronger in EMDEs than in advanced economies. As a result, output and employment in EMDEs tended to be more volatile than in advanced economies—a feature well documented in the literature (Aguiar and Gopinath 2007). One of the reasons could be the tendency for fiscal policy to be procyclical in EMDEs, exacerbating the underlying business cycle (Frankel, Végh, and Vuletin 2013).

- *Recessions.* The average DGE-based informal economy recession lasted 1.5 years, with a GDP contraction, on average, of 3.5 percent per year, 5.2 percent from peak to trough, and 5.7 percent cumulatively—broadly in line with formal economy recessions.[22] Both formal-economy and informal-economy recessions were significantly shallower in advanced economies than in EMDEs.

- *Recoveries.* On average, output in both formal and informal economies took about 2 years to return to it prerecession peak, expanding by 2-6 percent in the first year and by 2-5 percent per year during the entire recovery phase.[23] Like formal-economy recoveries, informal-economy recoveries were significantly shallower in advanced economies than in EMDEs.

---

[20] A comparison between findings here and former studies will be provided upon request.

[21] The differences in durations between recessions and recoveries are not significant for EMDEs when using MIMIC-based estimates.

[22] The recessions of MIMIC-based informal output are slightly shallower and more prolonged than those of formal output and DGE-based informal output (tables 2B.5A and 2B.5B). The slightly shallower recessions of MIMIC-based informal output could be due to the slow-moving institutional measures embedded in MIMIC's estimation methods (for example, government effectiveness).

[23] MIMIC-based informal recoveries were significantly shorter, occurred less frequently, and were less pronounced than DGE-based informal recoveries and formal recoveries.

FIGURE 2.8 Cyclical features of formal and informal business cycles

In most cases, informal-economy recessions and recoveries do not differ statistically significantly from formal-economy recessions and recoveries. Meanwhile, both formal- and informal-economy recessions and recoveries are less pronounced in advanced economies than in EMDEs.

A. Recessions in formal output

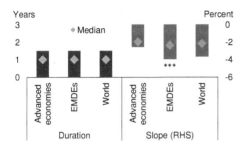

B. Recoveries in formal output

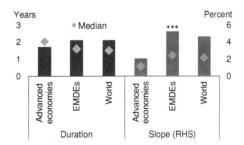

C. Recessions in DGE-based informal output

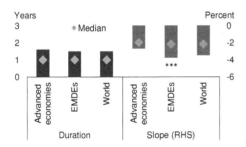

D. Recoveries in DGE-based informal output

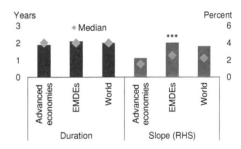

E. Recessions in MIMIC-based informal output

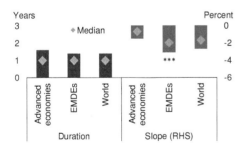

F. Recoveries in MIMIC-based informal output

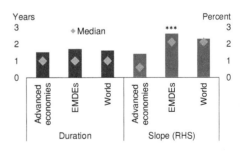

Source: World Bank.
Note: Data for recession (recovery) episodes starting and ending in the period 1990-2018. Business cycle turning points determined on the basis of formal and informal GDP levels (that is, official GDP statistics for formal output, and DGE and MIMIC estimates for informal output) using the algorithm of Harding and Pagan (2002). Recession is defined as the phase from peak to trough, while recovery is defined as the phase from the trough in output to its peak level before the recession (Claessens, Kose, and Terrones 2012). "Duration" captures the period from peak to trough for a recession, and the period it takes for output to return to its pretrough peak for a recovery. "Slope," which measures the speed of a given cyclical phase, is defined as the ratio of amplitude over duration for a recession phase and the ratio of the change from the trough to the last peak divided by the duration for a recovery phase. DGE = dynamic general equilibrium model; EMDEs = emerging market and developing economies; MIMIC = multiple indicators multiple causes model; RHS = right-hand side.
A.-F. Bars show simple group means and diamonds show group medians. *** indicates that differences between advanced economies and EMDEs are significant at the 10 percent level.

FIGURE 2.9 Employment changes during formal and informal business cycles

Total and formal employment contracted significantly during formal economy recessions in advanced economies but remained largely stable during those in EMDEs. Self-employment in both advanced economies and EMDEs did not change significantly in either recessions or recoveries. The lack of response was found in cycles in both formal and informal economies.

A. Changes in total employment during formal business cycles

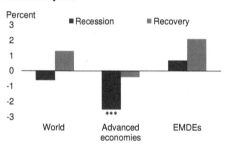

B. Changes in formal employment during formal business cycles

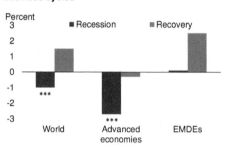

C. Changes in self-employment during formal business cycles

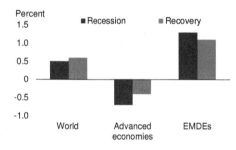

D. Changes in self-employment during informal business cycles

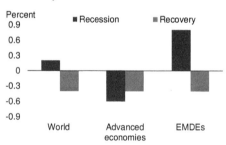

Source: World Bank.
Note: Data for the period 1990-2018. Business cycle turning points determined on the basis of formal and informal GDP levels (that is, official GDP statistics for formal output and DGE-based estimates for informal output) using the algorithm of Harding and Pagan (2002). Recession is defined as the phase from peak to trough, while recovery is defined as the phase from the trough in output to its peak level before the recession (Claessens, Kose, and Terrones 2012). DGE = dynamic general equilibrium model; EMDEs = emerging market and developing economies.
A.-D. Bars show simple group means of overall changes in employment during business cycle phases. *** indicates that numbers significantly differ from zero at 10 percent significance level. EMDEs with poor statistical capacity and three outliers (Democratic Republic of Congo, Gabon, and Zimbabwe) were dropped.

Informal employment during informal-economy business cycles. Informal employment, proxied by self-employment, in both advanced economies and EMDEs was broadly stable in informal recessions as well as recoveries. This finding applies to both formal and informal economy business cycles (figure 2.9; table 2B.6A). This may be because wage movements or changes in work intensity (measured as number of hours worked per day) bore the brunt of the adjustment in labor markets during business cycles (Guriev, Speciale, and Tuccio 2019; Meghir, Narita, and Robin 2015).

Formal and total employment during formal-economy business cycles. Total and formal employment in advanced economies behaved significantly differently from both types of employment in EMDEs during formal economy recessions and recoveries (tables 2B.6A and 2B.6B). Both total and formal employment contracted significantly (by 2.5 and 2.7 percent, respectively) in advanced economies during formal economy recessions, whereas neither total nor formal employment fell significantly in EMDEs. Employment changes during formal-economy recoveries were insignificant in both advanced economies and EMDEs. The lack of significant responses in employment during formal economy recoveries suggests delayed responses in the labor market and the emergence of "jobless" recoveries in recent decades (Farber 2012; Hall 2005; Shimer 2010, 2012).

Conclusion

The compilation of a comprehensive database of model-based and survey-based estimates of informal economic activity provides a rich set of measures available for cross-country analysis and a more limited set of measures available for time-series or panel analysis. Among all the measures, DGE-based estimates and survey-based estimates of self-employment stand out in their cross-country and year coverage. In contrast, survey-based measures of perceptions tend to be highly stable over time and, therefore, are mainly useful for cross-country comparisons. Last, for cross-country analyses of narrowly defined questions, measures from labor, firm, and household surveys may be more suitable, especially when surveys are done consistently.

Two applications of the constructed database are illustrated in this chapter. First, using the widest possible range of measures, the chapter illustrates the broad-based and steady decline in the shares of informal output and employment since 1990. Three somewhat distinct aspects of informality are identified: output, employment, and perceptions. Cross-country rankings of informal output or employment are typically consistent with each other although varying over time.

Second, the chapter documents that informal economies experience business cycles just as formal economies do. Like formal-economy output cycles, informal-economy output cycles tend to be shallower in advanced economies than in EMDEs. Informal employment tends to behave acyclically in EMDEs and advanced economies, largely invariant to both output recessions and recoveries. In contrast to distinct cyclical movements in informal output, perceptions of the scale of informality shown by surveys are highly persistent.

Several possible areas for further research are worth noting. First, the limitations and weaknesses of all existing measures of informality remain, despite the richness of the database described here. More work is needed to improve the quality of existing measures and to explore new approaches to better capture the extent of informality in EMDEs. Second, the chapter distills the main features of informal-economy business cycles. It does not look into the factors and policies that could affect informal-economy business cycles. Further analyses in this direction would be valuable.

ANNEX 2A Estimation methodologies

This annex describes the estimation methodologies used to construct the concerning informality measures. A detailed data description is listed in table 2B.7.

The MIMIC model

To estimate the size of the informal sector in percent of official GDP with the MIMIC model, this study closely follows Schneider, Buehn, and Montenegro (2010) and includes six causes and three indicators used in their study.[24] The six cause variables used are (1) size of government (general government final consumption expenditure as a percent of GDP, from United Nations data spliced with WDI); (2) share of direct taxation (direct taxes in percent of overall taxation, from WDI); (3) fiscal freedom index from Heritage Foundation; (4) business freedom index from Heritage Foundation; (5) unemployment rate and GDP per capita to capture the state of the economy (from WDI, and GDP per capita spliced with World Economic Outlook database [WEO]); and (6) government effectiveness (Worldwide Governance Indicators). The three indicator variables include (1) growth rate of GDP per capita (from WDI, spliced with WEO); (2) the labor force participation rate (people over age 15 economically active in percent of population; from WDI, spliced with Haver Analytics); and (3) currency as a ratio of M0 (currency outside the banks) over M1 (International Monetary Fund International Financial Statistics and Haver Analytics).

The estimation results are shown in table 2B.8. The model specification that ensures maximum data coverage, which is shown in column (5) of table 2B.8, is used to generate the MIMIC index of the share of informal output relative to official GDP ($\tilde{\eta}_t$). Then an additional benchmarking procedure is carried out where t is converted into absolute values of the informal sector ($\hat{\eta}_t$) using the following equation:[25]

$$\hat{\eta}_t = \frac{\tilde{\eta}_t}{\tilde{\eta}_{2000}}\eta^*_{2000}, \qquad (2A.1)$$

where t denotes year, $\tilde{\eta}_{2000}$ is the value of the estimated index in the base year 2000, and η^*_{2000} is the exogenous estimate (base value) of the shadow economies in 2000. Whereas the estimates ($\tilde{\eta}_t$) determine the movement of the absolute values of the informal sector over time, the base values η^*_{2000} decide the rankings of the countries' informal sector within the sample in year 2000. The base values η^*_{2000} are taken from Schneider (2007) or, for another 10 economies, from Schneider, Buehn, and Montenegro (2010).

The DGE model

In the model of Elgin and Oztunali (2012), an infinitely lived representative household is endowed with K_0 units of productive capital and a total of $H_t > 0$ units of time. The

---

[24] MIMIC is a type of structural equation model (SEM). The estimation of a SEM with latent variables can be done by means of LISREL (used by Schneider, Buehn, and Montenegro 2010), SPSS, and Stata. Here, Stata is used.

[25] Calibration is performed separately for each country. Following Schneider, Buehn, and Montenegro (2010), the MIMIC index has been adjusted to the positive range by adding a positive constant.

household has access to two productive technologies, denoted formal and informal, and maximizes its lifetime utility by solving the following optimization problem:

$$\{C_t, I_t, K_{t+1}N_{It}, N_{Ft}\}_{t=0}^{\infty} \overset{\max}{\sum_{t=0}^{\infty}} \beta^t U(C_t)$$

$$s.t. \ \ C_t + I_t = (1 - \tau_t)A_{Ft}K_t^{\alpha}N_{Ft}^{1-\alpha} + A_{It}N_{It}^{\gamma} \qquad (2A.2)$$

$$K_{t+1} = I_t + (1 - \delta)K_t \qquad (2A.3)$$

$$N_{It} + N_{Ft} = H_t \qquad (2A.4)$$

$\beta < 1$ is a discount factor and the instantaneous utility function $U(.)$ is strictly increasing and strictly concave. Equation (2A.2) defines the household's resource feasibility constraint: the sum of consumption C_t and investment I_t should equal the amount produced using the formal and informal technologies. The right-hand side of equation (2A.2) shows that the formal technology (A_{Ft}) follows a standard Cobb-Douglas specification and is exclusive to the formal sector. K_t is the household's capital stock while N_{Ft} is the number of hours the household devotes to the formal sector. τ_t captures the tax rate imposed on formal output. Informal output depends on the number of hours the household devotes to the informal sector, N_{It}, and its technology, A_{It}.[26]

The rest of the household's problem is standard: Equation (2A.3) specifies the law of motion for capital, where $\delta \in [0; 1]$ is the depreciation rate. Equation (2A.4) is the household's time constraint. In this simple model, the government's policy τ_t is assumed to be exogenously given and the tax revenue is assumed to be used to finance an exogenous stream of government spending, G_t. Then, given the government policy variable tax burden, $\{\tau_t\}$, a competitive equilibrium of the two-sector model is a set of sequences $\{C_t, \ I_t, \ K_{t+1}, \ N_{Ft}, \ G_t\}_{t=0}^{\infty}$ that maximize the expected utility from consumption, which is $\sum_{t=0}^{\infty}\beta^t U(C_t)$.

The model provides a mapping between the formal economy and informal economy in a dynamic setting. The two key equilibrium conditions are the equilibrium condition that connects the formal and informal economy through labor allocation and the equilibrium condition that captures the intertemporal substitution. The calibration and data construction processes rely on these two conditions to estimate the ratio, $\frac{Y_{It}}{Y_{Ft}}$, which can be further expressed as $\frac{A_{It}N_{It}^{\gamma}}{A_{Ft}K_t^{\alpha}N_{Ft}^{1-\alpha}}$.

The calibration follows Elgin and Oztunali (2012) and takes parameter values suggested by the earlier literature (for example, Ihrig and Moe 2004).[27] α is assumed to be equal to 0.36, and γ takes the value of 0.425. Data are gathered from Penn World Table 9.1 for

---

[26] The model also assumes no cost for hiding income, that the government cannot enforce payment of taxes, and that the household will attempt to hide any income received from the informal sector.

[27] Elgin and Oztunali (2012) are not using the model to do a full calibration exercise (where each equilibrium condition is satisfied for every period). Because only two of the equilibrium conditions are utilized, stationarity of empirical data for calibration is a lesser concern. Their approach is followed here.

capital stock (K_t), private consumption (C_t), formal employment (N_{Ft}), depreciation rates (δ, country averages), and tax rates (τ_t). By matching the productivity in the informal sector to the informal-economy size in 2007 of the series reported in Schneider, Buehn, and Montenegro (2010) and assuming that A_{It} grows at the average growth rate of K_t and A_{Ft},[28] the DGE estimates are computed for 158 economies over the period 1950-2018.

The estimation results are qualitatively robust to different model specifications like using alternative values for δ, α, γ, or adding a labor-leisure choice or a tax enforcement parameter to informal sector income. See Elgin and Oztunali (2012) for details.

Labor-related measures of Informality

Several cross-country databases report the survey-based estimates on the share of self-employment in total employment:[29] (1) the 2016 WDI (World Bank 2016), which cover 175 economies from 1980 (mainly from 1990s) to 2014; (2) the ILO (2016), which covers 109 economies from 1997 to 2014; and (3) the Organisation for Economic Co-operation and Development (OECD; updated in 2016, 2018, and 2020), which covers 34 OECD countries from 1955 to 2018. When regarding employment outside the formal sector and informal employment, ILO compiled statistics for up to 76 middle- and low-income countries for 1999-2018.

For a comprehensive data set on labor-related measures on informality, we combine the cross-country databases, provided by WDI, ILO, and OECD, and gather additional data from the national statistical bureaus (offices), Haver Analytics, the disclosed Living Standards Measurement Studies (LSMS, World Bank), and spliced data from the Inter-American Development Bank (IDB) and Eurostat to fill some gaps in years. Data priority is first given to cross-country databases (WDI, ILO, and OECD) and then national statistical bureaus (offices), Haver Analytics, and LSMS, followed by estimates obtained from previous studies, IDB and Eurostat. IDB reports the share of self-employment in total employment of the 15-to-64-year-old group for 19 Latin American economies between 1990 and 2018, while Eurostat reports the same measure for 29 European Union (EU) economies and 5 non-EU economies for the period 1983-2018. By focusing on employment of the 15-to-64-year-old group, their data are systematically lower than those from other cross-country databases. The final step adds 105 more observations to the sample (3 percent of the full sample).

The national statistical bureaus (offices) that provided data or were contacted are Angola, Argentina, Azerbaijan, The Bahamas, Bahrain, Belarus, Belize, Benin, Bhutan,

---

[28] This assumption implies that growth in the formal sector can spill over to the informal sector via capital accumulation and technological diffusion.

[29] Both ILO and WDI only report model-based estimates from 2018 onward, which may suffer from caveats such as strong economic assumptions and reliance on other studies' independent estimates to do the benchmarking. Due to the issues related with model-based estimates, historical WDI and ILO reports are collected to obtain survey-based estimates. The model-based estimates from ILO and WDI were used to update the share of self-employment when no other source of information is available.

Bosnia and Herzegovina, Botswana, Brunei Darussalam, Bulgaria, Burkina Faso, Burundi, Cabo Verde, Cambodia, Cameroon, Central African Republic, Chad, China, Comoros, Croatia, Cyprus, Democratic Republic of Congo, Republic of Congo, Arab Republic of Egypt, Equatorial Guinea, Eritrea, Eswatini, Ethiopia, Fiji, Gabon, The Gambia, Georgia, Ghana, Guinea, Guinea-Bissau, Guyana, Haiti, Islamic Republic of Iran, Jamaica, Jordan, Kenya, Kuwait, Kyrgyz Republic, Lao People's Democratic Republic, Latvia, Lebanon, Libya, Lithuania, Malawi, Maldives, Malta, Mauritania, Moldova, Morocco, Mozambique, Myanmar, Nepal, Niger, Nigeria, North Macedonia, Oman, Papua New Guinea, Qatar, Romania, Rwanda, Saudi Arabia, Senegal, Sierra Leone, Singapore, Solomon Islands, Sudan, Suriname, Syrian Arab Republic, Tajikistan, Tanzania, Togo, Trinidad and Tobago, Tunisia, United Arab Emirates, República Bolivariana de Venezuela, Vietnam, and Republic of Yemen.

Dating informal business cycles

Identifying turning points. Bry and Boschan's (1971) algorithm is applied to date the business cycles of formal and informal sectors, following Berge and Jordà (2011); Claessens, Kose, and Terrones (2012); and Harding and Pagan (2002). Peaks (troughs) are defined as occurring at time t whenever $\{\Delta y_t > (<)0, \Delta y_{t+1} < (>)0\}$. As the censoring rule, if there are additional peaks (troughs) within a five-year period around a peak, the one with the deepest contraction/expansion is picked. When calculating characteristics of business cycles, the closest peaks (troughs) before troughs (peaks) are used when there are several peaks (troughs) in a row.

Characteristics of business cycle phases. The main characteristics of the recession and recovery phases, including duration, amplitude, and slope, are defined as in Claessens, Kose, and Terrones (2012):

- The *duration* captures, for a recession, the period from peak to trough and, for a recovery, the period it takes for output to return to its pretrough peak.

- The *amplitude* of a recession measures the change in output from a peak to the next trough. The amplitude of a recovery measures the change in output during the first year of an expansion, which is the period between a trough and its following peak.

- The *slope* measures the speed of a given cyclical phase. It is defined as the ratio of amplitude over duration for a recession phase and the ratio of the change from the trough to the last peak divided by the duration for a recovery phase.

For recessions only, another widely used measure, cumulative loss, is calculated. It captures the overall cost of a recession. The cumulative loss is defined as the difference between the sum of annual changes in output and half of the amplitude during a recession.

ANNEX 2B Tables

TABLE 2B.1A Summary statistics

Estimation method		Aspect		Measures	# of obs	# of econ.	Time period	Mean	Median	Min	Max
Indirect		Output (a)		DGE (percent of GDP)	4,540	158	1990-2018	31.8	31.6	8.0	67.7
				MIMIC (percent of GDP)	4,150	160	1993-2018	33.3	33.5	8.1	69.3
	Labor force surveys	Employment		Pension coverage (percent of labor force)	359	135	1990-2010	44.4	36.0	1.1	99.0
				Self-employment (percent of total employment)	2,711	179	1990-2018	31.0	25.8	0.0	95.5
				Informal employment (percent of total employment)	369	72	2000-18	64.7	67.9	18.9	99.7
				Employment outside the formal sector (percent of total emp.)	386	76	1999-2018	55.4	56.4	9.8	95.7
Direct (survey-based)	Firm surveys	Perception	(a)	WEF (1-7; 7 = most informal)	1,548	154	2008-18	3.7	3.8	1.4	6.6
				WB: Percent of firms competing against informal firms	248	140	2006-18	55.7	57.4	7.2	95.2
			Firms	WB: Percent of firms formally registered when founded	233	138	2006-18	89.0	91.3	29.1	100.0
				WB: Number of years operated without registration	233	138	2006-18	0.7	0.5	0.0	6.8
				WB: Percent of firms that found competitors in the informal sector as a constraint	249	139	2006-18	30.0	29.2	0.0	76.0
	Household surveys		(b)	WVS: Cheating on taxes (justifiable)	200	94	1994-2010	2.3	2.1	1.0	4.7

Sources: World Bank; World Bank (Enterprise Surveys); World Economic Forum; World Values Survey.

Note: Data for the period 1990-2018 (except where indicated). World Values Survey (WVS) asks whether cheating on taxes is justifiable (1 is "never justifiable" and 10 is "always justifiable") and reports average responses at the country-year level, with a higher level suggesting that the country is more tolerant toward the informal sector. World Economic Forum (WEF) asks, "In your country, how much economic activity do you estimate to be undeclared or unregistered? (1 = Most economic activity is undeclared or unregistered; 7 = Most economic activity is declared or registered)" and reports average responses at the country-year level. Here, the average responses have been reordered to make "7 = Most economic activity is undeclared or unregistered; 1 = Most economic activity is declared or registered," where a higher level suggests a larger informal sector in the country. WB shows the results for World Bank Enterprise Surveys. (a) stands for "Output" and (b) stands for "Opinions/Tax Morality." Because the data on self-employment for Equatorial Guinea are only for year 1983, the data on self-employment are available for 179 economies (instead of 180 economies) here. DGE = dynamic general equilibrium model estimates of informal output in percent of official GDP; MIMIC = multiple indicators multiple causes model estimates on informal output in percent of GDP.

TABLE 2B.1B Summary statistics by country groupings

	World		AEs		EMDEs	
	Mean	Median	Mean	Median	Mean	Median
Output						
DGE (percent of GDP)	31.8	31.6	18.7	17.2	35.7	36.0
MIMIC (percent of GDP)	33.3	33.5	19.3	18.2	37.3	36.8
Employment						
Pension coverage (percent of labor force)	44.4	36.0	86.5	90.0	30.5	24.0
Self-employment (percent of total employment)	31.0	25.8	15.7	13.9	39.4	37.1
Informal employment (percent of total employment)	64.7	67.9			64.7	67.9
Employment outside the formal sector (percent of total employment)	55.4	56.4			55.4	56.4
Perception						
WEF (1-7; 7 = most informal)	3.7	3.8	2.7	2.6	4.1	4.2
WB: Percent of firms competing against informal firms	55.7	57.4	35.8	35.0	57.0	59.7
WB: Percent of firms formally registered when founded	89.0	91.3	98.1	98.4	88.4	91.0
WB: Number of years operated without registration	0.8	0.5	0.2	0.1	0.8	0.6
WB: Percent of firms that found competitors in the informal sector as a constraint	30.0	29.2	18.1	17.7	30.7	29.9
WVS: Cheating on taxes (justifiable)	2.3	2.1	2.2	2.1	2.3	2.1

Sources: World Economic Forum; World Bank; World Bank (Enterprise Surveys); World Values Survey.

Note: Data for the period 1990-2018. World Values Survey (WVS) asks whether cheating on taxes is justifiable (1 is "never justifiable" and 10 is "always justifiable") and reports average responses at the country-year level, with a higher level suggesting that the country is more tolerant toward the informal sector. World Economic Forum (WEF) asks, "In your country, how much economic activity do you estimate to be undeclared or unregistered? (1 = Most economic activity is undeclared or unregistered; 7 = Most economic activity is declared or registered)" and reports average responses at the country-year level. Here, the average responses have been reordered to make "7 = Most economic activity is undeclared or unregistered; 1 = Most economic activity is declared or registered" where a higher level suggests a larger informal sector in the country. WB shows the results for World Bank Enterprise Surveys. Detailed information is listed in table 2B.1A. Country groupings follow the method used by World Bank (2020g). AEs = advanced economies; DGE = dynamic general equilibrium model estimates of informal output in percent of official GDP; EMDEs = emerging market and developing economies; MIMIC = multiple indicators multiple causes model estimates on informal output in percent of GDP.

TABLE 2B.2 **Spearman rank correlations (across countries within individual years)**

	DGE	MIMIC	PENSION	SEMP	IF_EMP	EMP_NF	WEF	WB1	WB2	WB3	WB4	WVS
Output												
DGE (percent of GDP)	1											
MIMIC (percent of GDP)	0.98***	1										
Employment												
Pension coverage (percent of labor force)	-0.60***	-0.60***										
Self-employment (percent of total employment)	0.64***	0.62***	-0.86***	1								
Informal employment (percent of total employment)	0.27*	0.31**	-0.86***	0.83***	1							
Employment outside the formal sector (percent of total emp.)	0.20	0.25	-0.60	0.77***	0.94***	1						
Perception												
WEF (1-7; 7 = most informal)	0.67***	0.70***	-0.47***	0.68***	0.54***	0.50***	1					
WB: Percent of firms competing against informal firms	0.40***	0.40***	-0.07	0.33***	0.38*	0.36	0.56***	1				
WB: Percent of firms formally registered when founded	-0.28**	-0.29**	0.67***	-0.54***	-0.53***	-0.57***	-0.54***	-0.60***	1			
WB: Number of years operated without registration	0.28**	0.28**	-0.30	0.40***	0.23	0.31*	0.41***	0.38***	-0.72***	1		
WB: Percent of firms that found competitors in the informal sector as a constraint	0.40***	0.33***	0.08	0.19*	0.28	0.32*	0.51***	0.77***	-0.36***	0.26*	1	
WVS: Cheating on taxes (justifiable)	0.20	0.27*	0.31*	-0.21	-0.2	-0.26	0.11	-0.21	0.33	-0.12	-0.21	1

Sources: World Economic Forum; World Bank; World Bank (Enterprise Surveys); World Values Survey.

Note: Data for the period 1990-2018. Medians of rank correlation of data across countries within each year. All survey-based measures are interpolated. World Values Survey (WVS) asks whether cheating on taxes is justifiable (1 is "never justifiable" and 10 is "always justifiable") and reports average responses at the country-year level, with a higher level suggesting that the country is more tolerant toward the informal sector. World Economic Forum (WEF) asks, "In your country, how much economic activity do you estimate to be undeclared or unregistered? (1 = Most economic activity is undeclared or unregistered; 7 = Most economic activity is declared or registered)" and reports average responses at the country-year level. Here, the average responses have been reordered to make "7 = Most economic activity is undeclared or unregistered; 1 = Most economic activity is declared or registered" where a higher level suggests a larger informal sector in the country. "WB" here stands for "World Bank. Enterprise Surveys." Detailed information is listed in table 2B.1A. ***, **, * denote significance at the 1, 5, and 10 percent significance levels. DGE = dynamic general equilibrium model estimates of informal output in percent of official GDP; MIMIC = multiple indicators multiple causes model estimates on informal output in percent of GDP. PENSION = pension coverage in percent of labor force. SEMP=self-employment in percent of total employment. IF_EMP = informal employment in percent of total employment. EMP_NF = employment outside the formal sector in percent of total employment.

TABLE 2B.3 **Coincidence of signs of first-differences**

	DGE	MIMIC	w/o PENSION	SEMP	INF_EMP	EMP_NF	WEF	WVS
DGE	100							
MIMIC	56.9	100						
Labor force without pension	53.2	53.5	100					
Self-employment	59.1	58.1	50.0	100				
Informal employment	61.9	59.4	51.4	61.3	100			
Employment outside the formal sector	64.5	57.8	55.0	63.7	82.4	100		
WEF (1-7; 7 = most informal)	50.3	56.2	50.0	50.3	57.9	54.5	100	
WVS: Cheating on taxes (justifiable)	57.8	55.9	42.3	55.1	47.4	50.0	51.1	100

Source: World Bank.
Note: Data for the period 1990-2018. Shares of country-year pairs in which the first difference in the two measures has the same sign are shown. Survey-based estimates are interpolated to fill the gaps in data series. DGE is benchmarked to Schneider, Buehn, and Montenegro (2010). World Values Survey (WVS) asks whether cheating on taxes is justifiable (1 is "never justifiable" and 10 is "always justifiable") and reports average responses at the country-year level, with a higher level suggesting that the country is more tolerant toward the informal sector. World Economic Forum (WEF) asks, "In your country, how much economic activity do you estimate to be undeclared or unregistered? (1 = Most economic activity is undeclared or unregistered; 7 = Most economic activity is declared or registered)" and reports average responses at the country-year level. Here, the average responses have been reordered to make "7 = Most economic activity is undeclared or unregistered; 1 = Most economic activity is declared or registered" where a higher level suggests a larger informal sector in the country. WB shows the results for World Bank Enterprise Surveys. Detailed information is listed in table 2B.1A. DGE = dynamic general equilibrium model estimates of informal output in percent of official GDP; MIMIC = multiple indicators multiple causes model estimates on informal output in percent of GDP. w/o PENSION = the share of labor force without pension (that is, 100 minus pension coverage in percent of labor force). SEMP = self-employment in percent of total employment. IF_EMP = informal employment in percent of total employment. EMP_NF = employment outside the formal sector in percent of total employment.

TABLE 2B.4 **Volatility of formal and informal economies**

	Output		
	(1)	(2)	(3)
	Formal output	DGE-based informal output	MIMIC-based informal output
World	6.42	5.83***	5.04***
AEs	3.82^	3.89^	2.42^***
EMDEs	6.92	6.27***	5.55***
	Employment		
	(4)	(5)	(6)
	Total employment	Formal employment	Self-employment
World	3.46	5.16***	6.69***
AEs	2.05^	2.34^***	4.88^***
EMDEs	3.84	5.90***	7.31***

Source: World Bank.
Note: Data are for the period 1990-2018. Formal output is captured by official GDP, while informal output uses DGE- or MIMIC-based estimates. Total employment is the sum of formal employment and self-employment. Volatility shows the standard deviations (SDs) of the concerning variables' annual growth rates. *** implies significant differences at 1 percent level in the SDs of the annual growth rates of formal output and those of informal output in columns (1)-(3) (in the SDs of the annual growth rates of total employment and those of formal/self-employment in columns (4)-(6)). The shaded areas indicate that the SDs of the annual growth rates of DGE-based informal output (formal employment) significantly differ from those of MIMIC-based informal output (self-employment). AEs = advanced economies; DGE = dynamic general equilibrium model; EMDEs = emerging market and developing economies; MIMIC = multiple indicators multiple causes model. ^ indicates significant differences at 5 percent level between AEs and EMDEs.

TABLE 2B.5A Cyclical features of recessions in formal and informal economies

	# of observations	Formal output			
		Duration (years)	Amplitude (percent)	Cumulative loss (percent)	Slope (percent)
World	307	1.5	-5.6	-6.5	-3.7
		[1.0]	[-3.1]	[-1.8]	[-2.2]
AEs	72	1.5	-4.0*	-4.0	-2.6**
		[1.0]	[-2.4]**	[-1.4]*	[-2.0]
EMDEs	235	1.5	-6.0	-7.3	-4.0
		[1.0]	[-3.1]	[-2.0]	[-2.4]

	# of observations	DGE-based informal output			
		Duration (years)	Amplitude (percent)	Cumulative loss (percent)	Slope (percent)
World	336	1.5	-5.2	-5.7	-3.5
		[1.0]	[-2.9]	[-1.8]	[-2.2]
AEs	87	1.6	-4.2	-4.8	-2.7**
		[1.0]**	[-2.7]	[-1.6]	[-2.0]
EMDEs	249	1.5	-5.6	-6.1	-3.8
		[1.0]	[-3.2]	[-1.9]	[-2.2]

	# of observations	MIMIC-based informal output			
		Duration (years)	Amplitude (percent)	Cumulative loss (percent)	Slope (percent)
World	155	1.4	-4.2	-5.6	-2.7
		[1.0]	[-2.1]	[-1.1]	[-1.7]
AEs	44	1.6	-2.7*	-3.1	-1.5***
		[1.0]	[-0.7]**	[-0.4]***	[-0.7]***
EMDEs	111	1.4	-4.7	-6.4	-3.1
		[1.0]	[-2.4]	[-1.3]	[-2.0]

Source: World Bank.

Note: Data for recession episodes starting and ending in the period 1990-2018. Business cycle turning points determined based on formal and informal GDP levels (that is, official GDP statistics for formal output, DGE- and MIMIC-based estimates for informal output) using the algorithm of Harding and Pagan (2002). Recession is defined as the phase from peak to trough while its corresponding "Duration," "Amplitude," "Cumulative loss," and "Slope" are defined as in Claessens, Kose, and Terrones (2012). All statistics correspond to sample means. Medians are in brackets. AEs = advanced economies; DGE = dynamic general equilibrium model; EMDEs = emerging market and developing economies; MIMIC = multiple indicators multiple causes model. Asterisks refer to the significant differences in means (or medians) between AEs and EMDEs. ***, **, * denote significance at the 1, 5, and 10 percent significance levels. Differences between informal and formal economies that are significant at 10 percent level are highlighted in shaded gray.

TABLE 2B.5B Cyclical features of recoveries in formal and informal economies

	# of observations	Formal output		
		Duration (years)	Amplitude (percent)	Slope (percent)
World	194	2.1	5.4	4.6
		[1.5]	[3.3]	[2.1]
AEs	37	1.7	2.7**	2.0*
		[2.0]	[2.3]**	[1.1]**
EMDEs	157	2.1	6.1	5.2
		[1.6]	[3.6]	[2.4]
	# of observations	DGE-based informal output		
		Duration (years)	Amplitude (percent)	Slope (percent)
World	236	2.0	4.1	3.6
		[2.0]	[3.1]	[2.2]
AEs	58	1.9	2.4***	2.2**
		[2.0]	[1.8]***	[1.5]***
EMDEs	178	2.1	4.7	4.0
		[2.0]	[3.7]	[2.5]
	# of observations	MIMIC-based informal output		
		Duration (years)	Amplitude (percent)	Slope (percent)
World	87	1.6	3.5	2.3
		[1.0]	[3.0]	[2.1]
AEs	22	1.5	1.9***	1.4*
		[1.0]	[1.7]***	[0.6]***
EMDEs	65	1.7	4.1	2.6
		[1.0]	[3.4]	[2.1]

Source: World Bank.
Note: Data for recovery episodes starting and ending in 1990-2018. Business cycle turning points determined based on formal and informal GDP levels (that is, official GDP statistics for formal output, DGE-based and MIMIC-based estimates for informal output) using the algorithm of Harding and Pagan (2002). Recovery is defined as the time it takes for output to rebound from the trough to the peak level before the recession while its corresponding "Duration," "Amplitude," and "Slope," are defined as in Claessens, Kose, and Terrones (2012). All statistics correspond to sample means. Medians are in brackets. AEs = advanced economies; DGE = dynamic general equilibrium model; EMDEs = emerging market and developing economies; MIMIC = multiple indicators multiple causes model. Asterisks refer to the significant differences in means (or medians) between AEs and EMDEs. ***, **, * denote significance at the 1, 5, and 10 percent significance levels. Differences between informal and formal economies that are significant at 10 percent level are highlighted in shaded gray.

TABLE 2B.6A Informal employment during formal and informal business cycles

	Formal output		DGE-based informal output		MIMIC-based informal output	
	Recession	Recovery	Recession	Recovery	Recession	Recovery
World	0.5	0.6	0.2	-0.4	-0.7	0.9
	[1.1]	[0.3]	[0.7]	[0.2]	[0.5]	[0.1]
AEs	-0.7	-0.4	-0.6	-0.4	-1.3	-0.3
	[-0.2]**	[0.03]	[-0.3]*	[-0.1]	[-1.1]**	[0.4]
EMDEs	1.3	1.1	0.8	-0.4	-0.3	1.5
	[2.1]	[0.9]	[1.2]	[0.2]	[1.4]	[-0.9]

Source: World Bank.
Note: Data for the period 1990-2018. Business cycle turning points determined based on formal and informal GDP levels (that is, official GDP statistics for formal output, DGE and MIMIC estimates for informal output) using the algorithm of Harding and Pagan (2002). Recession is defined as the phase from peak to trough while recovery is defined as the time it takes for output to rebound from the trough to the peak level before the recession (Claessens, Kose, and Terrones 2012). Expansion is defined as the period from trough to next peak (Claessens, Kose, and Terrones 2012). All statistics correspond to the sample means of the overall percentage changes in self-employment over the corresponding business cycle phases. Medians are in brackets. EMDEs with poor statistical capacity and three outliers (Democratic Republic of Congo, Gabon, and Zimbabwe) were dropped. Shaded cells represent numbers that significantly differ from zero. AEs = advanced economies; DGE = dynamic general equilibrium model; EMDEs = emerging market and developing economies; MIMIC = multiple indicators multiple causes model. Asterisks refer to the significant differences in means (or medians) between AEs and EMDEs. ***, **, * denote significance at the 1, 5, and 10 percent significance levels.

TABLE 2B.6B Formal and total employment during formal business cycles

	Total employment		Formal employment	
	Recession	Recovery	Recession	Recovery
World	-0.6	1.3	-1.0	1.5
	[-0.3]	[0.6]	[-1.0]	[0.6]
AEs	-2.5***	-0.4**	-2.7***	-0.3**
	[-1.4]***	[-0.5]***	[-1.6]	[-0.3]***
EMDEs	0.7	2.1	0.1	2.5
	[1.2]	[1.6]	[-0.0]	[2.1]

Source: World Bank.
Note: Data for the period 1990-2018. Formal employment is proxied by total employment excluding self-employment. Business cycle turning points determined based on official GDP statistics for formal output using the algorithm of Harding and Pagan (2002). Recession is defined as the phase from peak to trough while recovery is defined as the time it takes for output to rebound from the trough to the peak level before the recession (Claessens, Kose, and Terrones 2012). All statistics correspond to the sample means of the overall percentage changes in total (formal) employment over the corresponding business cycle phases. EMDEs with poor statistical capacity and three outliers (Democratic Republic of Congo, Gabon, and Zimbabwe) were dropped. Medians are in brackets. Shaded cells represent numbers that significantly differ from zero. AEs = advanced economies; DGE = dynamic general equilibrium model; EMDEs = emerging market and developing economies; MIMIC = multiple indicators multiple causes model. Asterisks refer to the significant differences in means (or medians) between AEs and EMDEs. ***, **, * denote significance at the 1, 5, and 10 percent significance levels.

TABLE 2B.7 Summary of data coverage

Data	Method	Sources	Measure	# of Ctry	Period	Setup
MIMIC-based informal output	Indirect estimates (MIMIC)	Original calculations	Size of the informal sector as a percentage of official GDP estimated using the model of Schneider, Buehn, and Montenegro (2010).	160	1993-2018	Balanced panel
DGE-based informal output	Indirect estimates (DGE)	Original calculations	Size of the informal economy as a percentage of official GDP estimated using the approach of Elgin and Oztunali (2012).	158	1950-2018	Balanced panel
Share of self-employment	Labor force survey and household survey	WDI, ILO, OECD, National Statistical Offices, Eurostat, IDB, Haver Analytics, and LSMS	The share of self-employment in total employment (survey-based estimates).	180	1955-2018	Unbalanced panel
Share of informal employment	Labor force survey and household survey	ILO	The share of informal employment in percent of total employment (harmonized)	72	2000-18	Repeated cross-sections
Share of employment outside the formal sector	Labor force survey and household survey	ILO	The share of employment outside the formal sector in percent of total employment (harmonized).	76	1999-2018	Unbalanced panel
Pension coverage	Labor force survey and household survey	WDI	The fraction of the labor force that contributes to a retirement pension scheme.	135	1990-2010	Unbalanced panel
World Bank Enterprises Surveys	Firm survey	World Bank Enterprise Surveys	Four measures on informality: percent of firms competing against unregistered or informal firms, percent of firms formally registered when they started operations in the country, (average) number of years a firm operated without formal registration, and percent of firms identifying practices of competitors in the informal sector as a major constraint.	140	2006-18	Repeated cross-sections

TABLE 2B.7 Summary of data coverage (continued)

Data	Method	Sources	Measure	# of Econ.	Period	Setup
World Economic Forum (Executive Opinion Survey)	Firm survey	World Economic Forum	The extent of informal economy based on the question: "In your country, how much economic activity do you estimate to be undeclared or unregistered? (1 = Most economic activity is undeclared or unregistered; 7 = Most economic activity is declared or registered)."	154	2008-18	Balanced panel
Informal Market Index (Heritage Foundation)	Firm survey	Heritage Foundation	The subjective perceptions of general compliance with the law, with particular emphasis on the role played by official corruption. The index ranges from 1 to 5 with higher values indicating more informal market activity.	165	1995-2005	Balanced panel
Non-observed activities (percent of GDP)	National account approach	United Nations (2008)	Non-observed activities (percent of GDP).	44	Various years	Cross-sections
The Eurobarometer Survey: Indirect measure of the informal economy	Household surveys and social opinion surveys	The Eurobarometer Survey	Interviewers ask respondents whether he/she has purchased goods or serviced embodied undeclared work or supplied labor in the informal economy. The survey also includes information on whether the respondents receive all or part of their regular salary or the remuneration for extra work or overtime hours as cash-in-hand and without declaring it to tax or social security authorities. Finally, the survey shows whether respondents find informal economic activities acceptable.	27	2007 and 2013	Repeated cross-sections
World Values Survey: Tax morale	Household surveys and social opinion surveys	World Values Survey	Interviewers ask whether respondents can justify cheating on taxes. Detailed descriptions are reported in table 2B.9.	94	1981-84, 1994-98, 1999-2004, 2005-09, 2010-14	Repeated cross-sections
European Values Survey: Tax morale	Household surveys and social opinion surveys	European Values Survey	Interviewers ask whether it is justifiable for the respondents or their compatriots to cheat on taxes or pay cash to avoid taxes.	16-47	1981, 1990, 1999, and 2008	Repeated cross-sections
European Social Survey: Indirect measure of the informal economy	Household surveys and social opinion surveys	European Social Survey	Interviewers ask whether respondents paid cash for goods or services with no receipt so as to avoid VAT or taxes over the past five years and whether respondents have a written employment contract.	24	Every two years from 2004-14	Repeated cross-sections

Source: World Bank.

Note: IDB = Inter-American Development Bank; ILO = International Labour Organization; LSMS = Living Standards Measurement Survey; WDI = World Development Indicators.

TABLE 2B.8 **MIMIC model estimation results, 1993-2018**

	(1)	(2)	(3)	(4)	(5)
	88 EMDEs	98 EMDEs	120 economies	151 economies	160 economies
Size of government	0.134***	0.144***	0.149***	0.161***	0.152***
	(0.024)	(0.020)	(0.022)	(0.018)	(0.018)
Share of direct taxation	0.016		0.013		
	(0.025)		(0.020)		
Business freedom	0.047**	0.029	0.050**		
	(0.022)	(0.018)	(0.022)		
Fiscal freedom	0.008	-0.018	-0.038		
	(0.024)	(0.019)	(0.023)		
Unemployment rate	0.077***	0.104***	0.059***	0.073***	0.071***
	(0.024)	(0.019)	(0.021)	(0.018)	(0.018)
GDP per capita	-0.311***	-0.239***	-0.348***	-0.327***	-0.334***
	(0.034)	(0.026)	(0.029)	(0.021)	(0.021)
Government effectiveness			-0.070***	-0.059***	-0.060***
			(0.019)	(0.017)	(0.017)
Growth rate of GDP per capita	-0.679***	-0.738***	-0.421***	-0.312***	-0.298***
	(0.119)	(0.105)	(0.079)	(0.060)	(0.060)
Labor force participation rate	-0.297***	-0.222***		-0.194***	-0.166***
	(0.089)	(0.084)		(0.053)	(0.052)
Growth rate of labor force			-0.100		
			(0.066)		
Currency (M0/M1)	1.000	1.000	1.000	1.000	1.000
	(0.000)	(0.000)	(0.000)	(0.000)	(0.000)
Statistical tests					
RMSEA	0.066	0.054	0.073	0.081	0.082
p(RMSEA<=0.05)	0.027	0.268	0.000	0.000	0.000
Chi^2	77.975	61.510	147.337	147.305	154.978
(p-val)	(0.000)	(0.000)	(0.000)	(0.000)	(0.000)
AIC	30360.170	37812.139	46480.999	48963.901	50399.970
BIC	30437.337	37888.618	46568.955	49040.351	50476.798
CFI	0.755	0.827	0.733	0.781	0.773
TLI	0.572	0.689	0.543	0.589	0.574
SRMR	0.034	0.029	0.043	0.042	0.043
CD	0.602	0.930	0.975	1	1
Observations	1,267	1,742	1,803	2,646	2,724

Source: World Bank.

Note: Data sources for variables used in the model are listed in annex 2A. See Elgin et al. (2021) for details. Following the MIMIC models' identification rule, the currency (M0/M1) variable is fixed to an a priori value. The currency variable shows the level of money (cash) in circulation. AIC = Akaike's information criterion; BIC = Bayesian information criterion; CD = coefficient of determination; CFI = comparative fit index; MIMIC = multiple indicators multiple causes model; RMSEA = root mean square error of approximation; TLI = Tucker Lewis index; SRMR = standardized root mean square residual. These are goodness-of-fit statistics. Absolute z-statistics in parentheses. ***, **, * denote significance at the 1, 5, and 10 percent significance levels. All variables are used as their standardized deviations from the mean.

TABLE 2B.9 **World Values Survey**

Survey	Coverage
World Values Survey (WVS)	Questions: "Justifiable: cheating on taxes" 1 is "never justifiable" and 10 is "always justifiable"
WVS 1981-84	9 economies: Argentina; Australia; Finland; Japan; Korea, Rep.; Mexico; South Africa; Sweden; United States.
WVS 1989-93	16 economies: Argentina; Brazil; Belarus; Chile; China; India; Japan; Korea, Rep.; Mexico; Nigeria; Poland; Russian Federation; South Africa; Spain; Switzerland; Turkey.
WVS 1994-99	52 economies, including Albania; Argentina; Armenia; Australia; Azerbaijan; Bangladesh; Bosnia and Herzegovina; Belarus; Bulgaria; Chile; China; Colombia; Croatia; Czech Republic; Dominican Republic; El Salvador; Estonia; Finland; Georgia; Hungary; India; Japan; Korea, Rep.; Latvia; Lithuania; Mexico; Moldova; Montenegro; New Zealand; Nigeria; North Macedonia; Norway; Peru; Philippines; Poland; Puerto Rico; Romania; Russian Federation; Serbia; Slovak Republic; Slovenia; South Africa; Spain; Sweden; Switzerland; Ukraine; United States; Uruguay.
WVS 2000-04	37 economies, including Albania; Algeria; Argentina; Bangladesh; Bosnia and Herzegovina; Canada; Chile; China; Egypt, Arab Rep.; India; Indonesia; Iran, Islamic Rep.; Japan; Jordan; Korea, Rep.; Kyrgyz Republic; Mexico; Moldova; Montenegro; Morocco; Nigeria; North Macedonia; Pakistan; Peru; Philippines; Puerto Rico; Serbia; Singapore; South Africa, Spain; Tanzania; Uganda; United States; Vietnam; Zimbabwe.
WVS 2005-09	56 economies, including Andorra; Argentina; Australia; Brazil; Bulgaria; Burkina Faso; Canada; Chile; China; Colombia; Cyprus; Egypt, Arab Rep.; Ethiopia; Finland; France; Georgia; Germany; Ghana; Guatemala; Hungary; India; Indonesia; Iran, Islamic Rep.; Italy; Japan; Jordan; Korea, Rep.; Malaysia; Mali; Mexico; Moldova; Morocco; Netherlands; New Zealand; Norway; Poland; Romania; Russian Federation; Rwanda; Serbia; Slovenia; South Africa; Spain; Sweden; Switzerland; Thailand; Trinidad and Tobago; Turkey; Ukraine; United Kingdom; United States; Uruguay; Vietnam; Zambia.
WVS 2010-14	57 economies, including Algeria; Argentina; Armenia; Australia; Azerbaijan; Brazil; Belarus; Chile; China; Colombia; Cyprus; Ecuador; Egypt, Arab Rep.; Estonia; Georgia; Ghana; India; Iraq; Japan; Kazakhstan; Jordan; Korea, Rep.; Kuwait; Kyrgyz Republic; Lebanon; Libya; Malaysia; Mexico; Morocco; Netherlands; New Zealand; Nigeria; Pakistan; Peru; Philippines; Poland; Romania; Russian Federation; Rwanda; Singapore; Slovenia; South Africa; Spain; Sweden; Thailand; Trinidad and Tobago; Tunisia; Turkey; Ukraine; United States; Uruguay, Uzbekistan; West Bank and Gaza; Yemen, Rep.; Zimbabwe.

Sources: World Bank; World Values Survey.
Note: See World Values Survey, European Values Survey, and European Social Survey for details.

References

Aguiar, M., and G. Gopinath. 2007. "Emerging Market Business Cycles: The Cycle Is the Trend." *Journal of Political Economy* 115 (1): 69-102.

Ahumada, H., F. Alvaredo, and A. Canavesa. 2007. "The Monetary Method and the Size of the Shadow Economy: A Critical Assessment." *Review of Income and Wealth* 53 (2): 363-71.

Aker, J., R. Boumnijel, A. McClelland, and N. Tierney. 2016. "Payment Mechanisms and Antipoverty Programs: Evidence from a Mobile Money Cash Transfer Experiment in Niger." *Economic Development and Cultural Change* 65 (1): 1-37.

Almeida, R., and P. Carneiro. 2012. "Enforcement of Labor Regulation and Informality." *American Economic Journal: Applied Economics* 4 (3): 64-89.

Amaral, P. S., and E. Quintin. 2006. "A Competitive Model of the Informal Sector." *Journal of Monetary Economics* 53 (7): 1541-53.

Amin, M., F. Ohnsorge, and C. Okou. 2019. "Casting a Shadow: Productivity of Formal Firms and Informality." Policy Research Working Paper 8945, World Bank, Washington, DC.

Ardizzi, G., C. Petraglia, M. Piacenza, and G. Turati. 2014. "Measuring The Underground Economy with The Currency Demand Approach: A Reinterpretation of The Methodology, with An Application to Italy." *Review of Income and Wealth* 60 (4): 747-72.

Aron, J. 2018. "Mobile Money and the Economy: A Review of the Evidence." *The World Bank Research Observer* 33 (2): 135-88.

Bajada, C. 2003. "Business Cycle Properties of The Legitimate and Underground Economy in Australia." *Economic Record* 79 (247): 397-411.

Benjamin, N., and A. A. Mbaye. 2012. *The Informal Sector in Francophone Africa: Firm Size, Productivity, and Institutions.* Washington, DC: World Bank.

Berge, T., and Ò. Jordà. 2011. "Evaluating the Classification of Economic Activity into Recessions and Expansions." *American Economic Journal: Macroeconomics* 3 (2): 246-77.

Besley, T., and T. Persson. 2014. "Why Do Developing Countries Tax So Little?" *Journal of Economic Perspectives* 28 (4): 99-120.

Binelli, C., and O. Attanasio. 2010. "Mexico in the 1990s: The Main Cross-Sectional Facts." *Review of Economic Dynamics* 13 (1) : 238-264.

Birinçi, S., and C. Elgin. 2013. "Shadow Economy over the Business Cycle: How Do Formal and Informal Cycles Interact?" Unpublished manuscript.

Blanchflower, D. G, A. Oswald, and A. Stutzer. 2001. "Latent Entrepreneurship across Nations." *European Economic Review* 45 (4): 680-91.

Bosch, M., and W. Maloney. 2008. "Cyclical Movements in Unemployment and Informality in Developing Countries." Policy Research Working Paper 4648, World Bank, Washington, DC.

Bosch, M., and W. Maloney. 2010. "Comparative Analysis of Labor Market Dynamics Using Markov Processes: An Application to Informality." *Labour Economics* 17 (4): 621-31.

Breusch, T. 2005. "Estimating The Underground Economy, Using MIMIC Models." Working Paper, National University of Australia, Canberra.

Bry, G., and C. Boschan.1971. *Cyclical Analysis of Time Series: Selected Procedures and Computer Programs*. Cambridge, MA: National Bureau of Economic Research.

Campos, F., M. Goldstein, M., and D. Mckenzie. 2018. "How Should the Government Bring Small Firms into the Formal System? Experimental Evidence from Malawi." Policy Research Working Paper 8601, World Bank, Washington, DC.

Cangul, M., C. Sdralevich, and I. Sian. 2017. "Beating Back Ebola." *Finance & Development*, June, International Monetary Fund, Washington, DC.

Chodorow-Reich, G., G. Gopinath, P. Mishra, and A. Naraynan. 2020. "Cash and the Economy: Evidence from India's Demonetization." *Quarterly Journal of Economics* 135 (1): 57-103.

Chong, A., and M. Gradstein. 2007. "Inequality and Informality." *Journal of Public Economics* 91(1-2): 159-179.

Claessens, S., M. A. Kose, and M. E. Terrones. 2012. "How Do Business and Financial Cycles Interact?" *Journal of International Economics* 87 (1): 178-90.

Cullen, M. 2020. "A Battle Plan for Ensuring Global Food Supplies during the COVID-19 Crisis." Food and Agriculture Organization of United Nations. http://www.fao.org/news/story/en/item/1268059/icode.

Dabla-Norris, E., M. Gradstein, and G. Inchauste. 2008. "What Causes Firms to Hide Output?" *Journal of Development Economics* 85 (1-2): 1-27.

Dahab, M., K. van Zandvoort, S. Flasche, A. Warsame, P. Spiegel, R. Waldman, and F. Checchi. 2020. "COVID-19 Control in Low-Income Settings and Displaced Populations: What Can Realistically Be Done?" London School of Hygiene and Tropical Medicine, London. https://www.lshtm.ac.uk/newsevents/news/2020/covid-19-control-low-income-settings-and-displaced-populations-what-can.

De Soto, H. 1989. *The Other Path: The Invisible Revolution in the Third World.* New York: Harper & Row.

Djankov, S., and R. Ramalho. 2009. "Employment Laws in Developing Countries." *Journal of Comparative Economics* 37 (1): 3-13.

Docquier, F., T. Müller, and J. Naval. 2017. "Informality and Long-Run Growth." *The Scandinavian Journal of Economics* 119 (4): 1040-85.

Elgin, C, A. Kose, F. Ohnsorge, and S. Yu. 2021. "Understanding Informality." CEPR Discussion Paper DP16497, Centre for Economic Policy Research, London.

Elgin, C., and O. Oztunali. 2012. "Shadow Economies around the World: Model Based Estimates." Working Paper No. 2012/05, Bogazici University, Department of Economics, Istanbul.

Falco, P., and L. Haywood. 2016. "Entrepreneurship versus Joblessness: Explaining the Rise in Self-Employment." *Journal of Development Economics* 118 (January): 245-65.

FAO (Food and Agriculture Organization of the United Nations). 2020. "Q&A: COVID-19 Pandemic—Impact on Food and Agriculture." Food Agriculture Organization of the United Nations, Rome. http://www.fao.org/2019-ncov/q-and-a/en/.

Farazi, S. 2014. "Informal Firms and Financial Inclusion: Status and Determinants." Policy Research Working Paper 6778, World Bank, Washington, DC.

Farber, H. 2012. "Unemployment in the Great Recession: Did the Housing Market Crisis Prevent the Unemployed from Moving to Take Jobs?" *American Economic Review* 102 (3): 520-25.

Feige, E. L. 2016. "Reflections on the Meaning and Measurement of Unobserved Economies: What Do We Really Know about the 'Shadow Economy'?" *Journal of Tax Administration* 2 (1): 1-37.

Fernández, A., and F. Meza. 2015. "Informal Employment and Business Cycles in Emerging Economies: The Case of Mexico." *Review of Economic Dynamics* 18 (2): 381-405.

Frankel, J., C. Végh, and G. Vuletin. 2013. "On Graduation from Fiscal Procyclicality." *Journal of Development Economics* 100 (1): 32-47.

Galiani, S., and F. Weinschelbaum. 2012. "Modeling Informality Formally: Households and Firms." *Economic Inquiry* 50 (3): 821-38.

Gandelman, N., and A. Rasteletti. 2017. "Credit Constraints, Sector Informality and Firm Investments: Evidence from a Panel of Uruguayan Firms." *Journal of Applied Economics* 20 (2): 351-72.

Gentilini, U. 2020. "5 Lessons for Using Universal Basic Income during a Pandemic." *Future Development* (blog), Brookings Institution, March 13, 2020. https://www.brookings.edu/blog/future-development/2020/03/13/5-lessons-for-using-universal-basic-income-during-a- pandemic.

Guiso, L., P. Sapienza, and L. Zingales. 2009. "Cultural Biases in Economic Exchange?" *The Quarterly Journal of Economics* 124 (3): 1095-131.

Günther, I., and A. Launov. 2012. "Informal Employment in Developing Countries: Opportunity or Last Resort?" *Journal of Development Economics* 97 (1): 88-98.

Guriev, S., B. Speciale, and M. Tuccio. 2019. "How Do Regulated and Unregulated Labor Markets Respond to Shocks? Evidence from Immigrants during the Great Recession." *The Journal of Law, Economics, and Organization* 35 (1): 37-76.

Hall, R. 2005. "Employment Fluctuations with Equilibrium Wage Stickiness." *American Economic Review* 95 (1): 50-65.

Harding, D., and A. Pagan. 2002. "Dissecting the Cycle: A Methodological Investigation." *Journal of Monetary Economics* 49 (2): 365-81.

Haushofer, J., and J. Shapiro. 2016. "The Short-Term Impact of Unconditional Cash Transfers to the Poor: Experimental Evidence from Kenya." *Quarterly Journal of Economics* 131 (4): 1973-2042.

Hussmanns, R. 2003. *Defining and Measuring Informal Employment*. Geneva: International Labour Office. https://www.ilo.org/public/english/bureau/stat/download/papers/meas.pdf.

Ihrig, J., and K. S. Moe. 2004. "Lurking in The Shadows: The Informal Sector and Government Policy." *Journal of Development Economics* 73 (2): 541-57.

ILO (International Labour Organization). 1993. *Resolution concerning the International Classification of Status in Employment (ICSE), adopted by the Fifteenth International Conference of Labour Statisticians.* Geneva: International Labour Office. http://www.ilo.ch/wcmsp5/groups/public/---dgreports/---stat/documents/normativeinstrument/wcms_087562.pdf.

ILO (International Labour Organization). 2016. *ILO-Stat.* Geneva: International Labour Office. https://ilostat.ilo.org/.

ILO (International Labour Organization). 2018a. *Informal Economy.* Geneva: International Labour Office. https://www.ilo.org/ilostat-files/Documents/description_IFL_EN.pdf.

ILO (International Labour Organization). 2018b. *Women and Men in the Informal Economy: A Statistical Picture.* Geneva: International Labour Office.

ILO (International Labour Organization). 2020a. "ILO Monitor: COVID-19 and the World of Work." Second edition. International Labour Office, Geneva.

ILO (International Labour Organization). 2020b. "COVID-19 Crisis and the Informal Economy: Immediate Responses and Policy Challenges." *ILO Brief*. International Labour Office, Geneva.

ILO (International Labour Organization). 2020c. "ILO Monitor: COVID-19 and the World of Work." Third edition. International Labour Office, Geneva.

ILO (International Labour Organization). 2020d. "Rapid Assessment of the Impact of COVID-19 on Enterprises and Workers in the Informal Economy in Developing and Emerging Countries: Guidelines." International Labour Office, Geneva.

ILO (International Labour Organization). 2021a. ILOSTAT. Accessed on April 23, 2021. https://ilostat.ilo.org/.

ILO (International Labour Organization). 2021b. "Informal Economy." ILOSTAT. https://www.ilo.org/ilostat-files/Documents/description_IFL_EN.pdf.

ILO (International Labour Organization). 2021c. "Indicator Description: Informality." ILOSTAT. https://ilostat.ilo.org/resources/concepts-and-definitions/description-informality/

Kanbur, R. 2009. "Conceptualizing Informality: Regulation and Enforcement." IZA Discussion Paper 4186, IZA-Institute of Labor Economics, Bonn, Germany.

Kanbur, R., and M. Keen. 2015. "Rethinking Informality." *Voxeu* (blog), June 15, 2015. https://voxeu.org/article/rethinking-informality.

Kaufmann, D., and A. Kaliberda. 1996. "Integrating the Unofficial Economy into the Dynamics of Post-Socialist Economies: A Framework of Analysis and Evidence." Policy Research Working Paper 1691, World Bank, Washington DC.

Klapper, L., and D. Singer. 2017. "The Opportunities and Challenges of Digitizing Government-to-Person Payments." *World Bank Research Observer* 32 (2): 211-26.

La Porta, R., and A. Shleifer. 2014. "Informality and Development." *Journal of Economic Perspectives* 28 (3): 109-26.

Lehmann, H., and N. Pignatti. 2007. "Informal Employment Relationships and Labor Market Segmentation in Transition Economies: Evidence from Ukraine." IZA Discussion Paper 3269, IZA-Institute of Labor Economics, Bonn, Germany.

Loayza, N. 2016. "Informality in the Process of Development and Growth." *World Economy* 39 (12): 1856-916.

Loayza, N. 2018. "Informality: Why Is It So Widespread and How Can It Be Reduced?" Research & Policy Brief 20, World Bank, Kuala Lumpur.

Loayza, N., A. M. Oviedo, and L. Servén. 2006, "The Impact of Regulation on Growth and Informality—Cross-Country Evidence." In *Linking the Formal and Informal Economy*, edited by B. Guha-Khasnobis, R. Kanbur and E. Ostrom. New York: Oxford University Press.

Loayza, N., and S. Pennings. 2020. "Macroeconomic Policy in the Time of Covid-19: A Primer for Developing Countries." Research & Policy Brief 28, World Bank, Kuala Lumpur.

Loayza, N., and J. Rigolini. 2011. "Informal Employment: Safety Net or Growth Engine?" *World Development* 39 (9): 1503-15.

Loayza, N., L. Servén, and N. Sugawara. 2010. "Informality in Latin America and the Caribbean." In *Business Regulation and Economic Performance*, edited by N. Loayza and L. Servén. Washington, DC: World Bank.

Maloney, W. F. 2004. "Informality Revisited." *World Development* 32 (7): 1159-78.

Mbaye, A., N. Benjamin, and F. Gueye. 2017. "The Interplay between Formal and Informal Firms and Its Implications on Jobs in Francophone Africa: Case Studies of Senegal and Benin." In *The Informal Economy in Global Perspective* edited by A. Polese, C. C. Williams, I. O. Horodnic, and P. Bejakovic. Basingstoke, UK: Palgrave Macmillan.

McCaig, B., and N. Pavcnik. 2015. "Informal Employment in a Growing and Globalizing Low-Income Country." *American Economic Review* 105 (5): 545-50.

Medina, M., and F. Schneider. 2018. "Shadow Economies around the World: What Did We Learn over the Last 20 Years?" IMF Working Paper 18/17, International Monetary Fund, Washington, DC.

Meghir, C., R. Narita, and J. Robin. 2015. "Wages and Informality in Developing Countries." *American Economic Review* 105 (4): 1509-46.

Muralidharan, K., P. Niehaus, and S. Sukhtankar. 2016. "Building State Capacity: Evidence from Biometric Smartcards in India." *American Economic Review* 106 (10): 2895-929.

Murthy, S., A. Leligdowicz, and N. Adhikari. 2015. "Intensive Care Unit Capacity in Low-Income Countries: A Systematic Review." *PloS ONE* 10 (1): e0116949.

Neumeyer, P. A., and Perri, F., 2005. "Business Cycles in Emerging Economies: The Role of Interest Rates." *Journal of Monetary Economics* 52 (2): 345-80.

Nguimkeu, P., and C. Okou. 2020. "A Tale of Africa Today: Balancing the Lives and Livelihoods of Informal Workers during the COVID-19 Pandemic." Africa Knowledge in Time Policy Brief, World Bank, Washington, DC.

Nordman, C., F. Rakotomanana, and F. Roubaud. 2016. "Informal versus Formal: A Panel Data Analysis of Earnings Gaps in Madagascar." *World Development* 86 (October): 1-17.

OECD (Organisation for Economic Co-operation and Development). 2016. *OECD Labor Force Statistics*. OECD: Paris.

OECD (Organisation for Economic Co-operation and Development). 2018. *OECD Labor Force Statistics*. OECD: Paris.

OECD (Organisation for Economic Co-operation and Development). 2020. *OECD Labor Force Statistics*. OECD: Paris.

Orsi, R., D. Raggi, and F. Turino. 2014. "Size, Trend, and Policy Implications of the Underground Economy." *Review of Economic Dynamics* 17 (3): 417-36.

Oviedo, A., M. Thomas, and K. Karakurum-Özdemir. 2009. "Economic Informality: Causes, Costs, and Policies—A Literature Survey." Working Paper 167, World Bank, Washington, DC.

Özler, B. 2020. "What Can Low-income Countries Do to Provide Relief for the Poor and the Vulnerable during the COVID-19 Pandemic?" *Development Impact* (blog), World Bank, March 19, 2020. https://blogs.worldbank.org/impactevaluations/what-can-low-income-countries-do-provide-relief-poor-and-vulnerable-during-covid.

Panizza, U. 2020. "Europe's Ground Zero." In *Mitigating the COVID Economic Crisis: Act Fast and Do Whatever It Takes*, edited by R. Baldwin and B. Weder di Mauro, 151-66. Center for Economic Policy and Research. Washington, DC: CEPR Press.

Peisakhin, L., and P., Pinto. 2010. "Is Transparency an Effective Anti-Corruption Strategy? Evidence from a Field Experiment in India." *Regulation and Governance* 4 (3): 261-80.

Perry, G. E., W. F. Maloney, O. S. Arias, P. Fajnzylber, A. D. Mason, and J. Saavedra-Chanduvi. 2007. *Informality: Exit and Exclusion*. Washington, DC: World Bank.

Putnins, T., and A. Sauka. 2015. "Measuring the Shadow Economy Using Company Managers." *Journal of Comparative Economics* 43 (2): 471-90.

Restrepo-Echavarria, P. 2014. "Macroeconomic Volatility: The Role of The Informal Economy." *European Economic Review* 70: 454-9.

Rosser, J., M. Rosser, and E. Ahmed. 2000. "Income Inequality and the Informal Economy in Transition Economies." *Journal of Comparative Economics* 28 (1): 156-71.

Schneider, F. 2007. "Shadow Economies and Corruption All over the World: New Estimates for 145 Countries." *Economics: The Open-Access, Open Assessment E-Journal* 1(2007-9): 1-66.

Schneider, F., and A. Buehn. 2016. "Estimating the Size of the Shadow Economy: Methods, Problems and Open Questions." IZA Discussion Paper 9820, IZA-Institute of Labor Economics, Bonn, Germany.

Schneider, F., A. Buehn, and C. E. Montenegro. 2010. "Shadow Economies All over the World: New Estimates for 162 Countries from 1999 to 2007." Policy Research Working Paper 5356, World Bank, Washington, DC.

Schneider, F., and D. Enste. 2000. "Shadow Economies: Size, Causes, and Consequences." *Journal of Economic Literature* 38 (1): 77-114.

Shimer, R. 2010. *Labor Markets and Business Cycles*. Princeton, NJ: Princeton University Press.

Shimer, R. 2012. "Wage Rigidities and Jobless Recoveries." *Journal Monetary Economics* 59 (Supplement): S65-S77.

Surico, P., and A. Galeotti. 2020. "The Economics of a Pandemic: The Case of COVID-19." European Research Council, Brussels, and Wheeler Institute, London. https://sites.google.com/site/paolosurico/covid-19.

Ulyssea, G. 2018. "Firms, Informality, and Development: Theory and Evidence from Brazil." *American Economic Review* 108 (8): 2015-47.

Ulyssea, G. 2020. "Informality: Causes and Consequences for Development." *Annual Reviews of Economics* 12: 525-46.

United Nations. 2008. *Non-observed Economy in National Accounts: Survey of Country Practices*. New York: United Nations.

World Bank. 2004. *World Development Report 2004: Making Services Work for Poor People*. Washington, DC: World Bank.

World Bank. 2012. *Jobs—World Development Report 2013*. Washington, DC: World Bank.

World Bank. 2014. *The Economic Impact of the 2014 Ebola Epidemic: Short- and Medium-Term Estimates for West Africa*. Washington, DC: World Bank.

World Bank. 2015. "The Socio-Economic Impacts of Ebola in Liberia: Results from a High Frequency Cell Phone Survey Round 5." World Bank, Washington, DC.

World Bank. 2016. *World Development Indicators 2016*. Washington, DC: World Bank.

World Bank. 2017. *The Global Findex Database 2017: Measuring Financial Inclusion and the Fintech Revolution*. Washington, DC: World Bank.

World Bank. 2019a. *Global Economic Prospects: Darkening Skies*. January. Washington, DC: World Bank.

World Bank. 2019b. *Africa's Pulse: An Analysis of Issues Shaping Africa's Economic Future*. Fall. Washington, DC: World Bank.

World Bank. 2020a. *South Asia Economic Focus: The Cursed Blessing of Public Banks*. Spring. Washington, DC: World Bank.

World Bank. 2020b. *Africa's Pulse: An Analysis of Issues Shaping Africa's Economic Future*. Spring. Washington DC: World Bank.

World Bank. 2020c. *World Bank East Asia and Pacific Economic Update: East Asia and Pacific in the Time of COVID-19*. April. Washington, DC: World Bank.

World Bank. 2020d. *Semiannual Report of the Latin America Region: The Economy in the Time of COVID-19*. April. World Bank, Washington, DC.

World Bank. 2020e. "Social Protection and Jobs Responses to COVID-19: A Real-Time Review of Country Measures." World Bank, Washington, DC.

World Bank. 2020f. "Assessing the Impact and Policy Responses in Support of Private-Sector Firms in the Context of the COVID-19 Pandemic." World Bank, Washington, DC.

World Bank. 2020g. *Global Economic Prospects*. June. Washington, DC: World Bank.

World Economic Forum. 2008-2018. *Executive Opinion Surveys*. Geneva: World Economic Forum. https://reports.weforum.org/.

World Values Survey (database). Accessed May 5, 2021. https://www.worldvaluessurvey.org/wvs.jsp.

CHAPTER 3

Growing Apart or Moving Together?
Synchronization of Informal- and Formal-Economy Business Cycles

Given its relative large size and the potential to dampen formal-economy business cycles, the informal economy needs to be factored into macroeconomic policy decisions. This chapter provides empirical evidence that informal output moves in the same direction as formal output, but in a more muted manner, with the direction of causality running from the formal economy to the informal economy. Informal employment, in contrast, does not co-move with the formal economy. Hence, the informal sector can provide a short-term buffer to formal-economy labor market disruptions even if, in the long run, it can act as a poverty trap. Policies that aim to curtail informal employment therefore need to be complemented with interventions that provide other buffers to short-term adverse shocks.

Introduction

In an average emerging market and developing economy (EMDE), the informal sector accounts for about one-third of gross domestic product (GDP), compared with about 18 percent of GDP in advanced economies (figure 3.1). Its large size makes the informal economy a potential amplifier or dampener of business cycles that policy makers need to take into account when deciding on countercyclical macroeconomic policies. If the informal economy expands while the formal economy contracts, it may support household incomes and consumer demand during economic downturns and serve as a safety net (Loayza and Rigolini 2011). If the informal economy behaves procyclically (that is, grows during expansions in the formal economy), it could function as an auxiliary "growth engine" during economic expansions (Chen 2005; Dell'Anno 2008; Meagher 2013).

In theory, the cyclical relationship between informal and formal sectors is ambiguous.[1] Some theoretical models have shown that the informal economy may absorb a larger share of workers as jobs become scarce in the formal sector during economic downturns (Bosch, Goni, and Maloney 2007; Dix-Carneiro et al. 2021; Loayza and Rigolini 2011). Such behavior by the informal sector could facilitate economic recovery—by providing a potential supply of labor to the formal sector and preventing the hysteresis costs on unemployment—if reentry into the formal sector is possible when the formal economy returns to expansion (Colombo, Onnis, and Tirelli 2016; IMF 2017).

Note: This chapter was prepared by Ceyhun Elgin, M. Ayhan Kose, Franziska Ohnsorge, and Shu Yu. Research assistance was provided by Hrisyana Doytchinova and Maria Hazel Macadangdang.

[1] Some early research suggested that the degree of cyclicality of the informal economy depends on the measure of informality used and country characteristics.

FIGURE 3.1 **Formal- and informal-economy business cycles**

Informal economic activity may amplify or dampen formal-economy business cycles. In EMDEs, the shares of informal output and informal employment rise significantly above their long-term averages during formal-economy downturns, even though informal output growth falls significantly below its long-term average. Informal employment growth remains around its long-term average during both upturns and downturns in the formal economy.

A. Share of informal economy

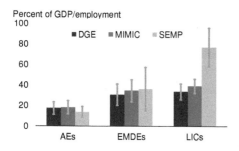

B. Changes in shares of informal economy during formal economy upturns and downturns in EMDEs

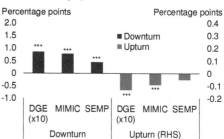

C. Output growth during formal economy upturns and downturns in EMDEs

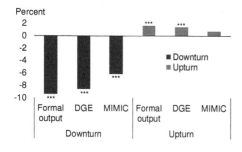

D. Employment growth during formal economy upturns and downturns in EMDEs

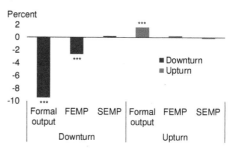

Sources: Penn World Table 9.1; World Bank.
Note: Data are for 1990-2018. AEs = advanced economies; DGE = dynamic general equilibrium model estimates; EMDEs = emerging market and developing economies; FEMP = formal employment; LICs = low-income countries; MIMIC = multiple indicators and multiple causes model estimates; RHS = right-hand side; SEMP = self-employment. "Downturn" refers to growth rates of official GDP below zero, while "upturn"
refers to growth rates of official GDP equal to or above zero. In B-D, *** indicates that the group average is significantly different from zero at the 10 percent level.
A. Bars show unweighted group averages for the latest year available, with the whiskers showing one standard deviation.
B. Shares of informal output (in percent of official GDP) and informal employment (in percent of total employment) are first-differenced and demeaned to capture detrended annual changes. Bars show unweighted group averages of detrended annual changes in shares of informal output/informal employment. Results for DGE-based estimates are shown in tenths.
C.D. Levels of output and employment in both formal and informal economies are logged, first-differenced and demeaned to capture detrended annual growth rates. Bars show unweighted group averages of detrended annual growth rates of output/employment levels.

In contrast, if informal firms provide services, as well as final and intermediate goods, to the formal sector, formal and informal sectors move in tandem. In addition, informal-economy income can support formal-economy demand. In these circumstances, the informal economy would amplify macroeconomic fluctuations.[2]

---

[2] For cyclical linkages between the formal sector and informal sector, see Arvin-Rad, Basu, and Willumson (2010); Docquier, Müller, and Naval (2017); Gibson (2005); Lubell (1991); Restrepo-Echavarria (2014); Roca, Moreno, and Sánchez (2001); and Schneider (1998).

Empirical evidence on the behavior of the informal economy over the business cycle is also inconclusive. This has been attributed partly to different country characteristics and the roles of different economic shocks.

After presenting a brief review of the literature on the cyclical behavior of the informal economy, this chapter addresses the following questions:

- How synchronized are movements in informal and formal economies?

- Do fluctuations in formal economy output "cause" fluctuations in output or employment in the informal economy?

Contributions. The chapter makes three contributions to the literature. First, it is the first analysis of the cyclical relationships between formal and informal sectors using data for multiple measures of informality for a large set of economies—about 160 economies, comprising 36 advanced economies and about 120 EMDEs. It covers a long, recent period—1990-2018—and is the first study of the behavior of both output and employment in the informal economy because previous studies have focused on either one or the other of these two variables. The comparison yields valuable insights into the cyclicality of labor productivity.

Second, the chapter focuses on the absolute size of the informal economy whereas earlier studies examined the informal economy only in relation to the formal economy. This allows for a more precise understanding of cyclical dynamics. Earlier studies examined the size of the informal economy relative to that of the formal economy without explaining the underlying mechanism. For instance, when the relative size of the informal sector rises during recessions, it could reflect an expanding informal economy or an informal economy that shrinks less than the formal economy. Some previous studies have interpreted the rising ratio as evidence for an expanding informal economy during recessions. The few previous studies of the procyclicality of informal output levels have been restricted to a small group of countries and study either solely output (Bajada 2003; Dell'Anno 2008; Giles 1997) or solely employment (Fiess, Fugazza, and Maloney 2010).

Third, the chapter is the first to document a causal linkage from formal-economy cyclical developments to the informal economy by using an instrumental variables approach. This improves on existing studies that have tested for basic Granger causality between formal and informal economies within individual countries. The previous Granger causality tests help to determine whether one time series is useful in forecasting another. However, they do not test for "true" causality as instrumental-variable regressions are able to identify (Angrist and Pischke 2009), because omitted variables can generate spurious causality (Eichler 2009).

Main findings. The chapter reports two major results. First, informal-economy output moves in step with formal output: informal-economy output movements are strongly positively correlated with formal-economy output movements. Hence, when earlier studies found that the share of the informal economy rose during formal-economy recessions, this reflected a slower absolute decline in informal output than in formal output rather than an absolute increase in informal activity. In addition, this chapter finds that informal employment largely behaves "acyclically."

Second, in an instrumental variable estimation, the study shows that the direction of causality runs from the formal economy to the informal economy. Specifically, it documents a causal linkage from fluctuations in formal-economy output to fluctuations in informal-economy output. In terms of employment, such a causal linkage is not found: whereas informal output behaves procyclically, informal employment behaves acyclically. The latter may indicate that informal labor markets do not adjust in terms of employment status during economic cycles but in terms of wages or working hours (Guriev, Speciale, and Tuccio 2016; Meghir, Narita, and Robin 2015).

The rest of the chapter is organized as follows. First, the chapter summarizes past studies of the co-movement between formal and informal business cycles, followed by a section on the data and methodologies. The chapter then presents evidence on the co-movement of formal and informal economies. The chapter further provides new estimates of the causal relationship between formal and informal economy business cycles and discusses potential explanations for the cyclical behavior of the informal economy. Finally, it concludes with a discussion of policy implications and directions for future research.

Literature review: Linkages between formal and informal sectors

The literature on the cyclical behavior of the informal economy offers mixed conclusions. Studies focusing on the share of the informal economy in total output or employment tend to find countercyclical behavior whereas studies focusing on output or employment levels tend to find procyclical behavior. The theoretical literature suggests that the nature and degree of cyclicality will depend on the type of shocks causing business cycle fluctuations and on the presence of labor market rigidities. This section summarizes that literature.[3]

Informal economy as a countercyclical safety net

The informal sector can serve as a buffer and safety net for the poor if it absorbs labor during recessions. This can facilitate an economic recovery provided that reentry into the formal sector is possible when the formal economy returns to expansion (Colombo, Onnis, and Tirelli 2016; IMF 2017; Loayza and Rigolini 2011).

---

[3] Several recent studies argue that pervasive informality may influence the measured cyclicality of the formal economy. For example, models with a large and poorly measured informal sector can generate excess volatility of formal consumption relative to formal output—a common feature of business cycles in many EMDEs (Horvath 2018; Restrepo-Echavarria 2014).

Macroeconomic evidence. Macroeconomic studies suggest that the informal economy can behave "countercyclically" in the sense that the share of informal employment rises during business cycle downturns. For example, one study reported that, on average in 54 economies during 1984-2008, a 1-standard-deviation slowdown in GDP per capita growth (that is a slowdown of 3 percentage points a year) was associated with a short-run increase in the share of self-employment in the total labor force by 1.2 percentage points, although with considerable cross-country heterogeneity (Loayza and Rigolini 2011).

In one study, the correlation between informal employment and official GDP has been estimated as modestly negative (about -0.3), whereas the correlation between formal employment and formal output was strongly positive (Fernández and Meza 2015). A study that used electricity consumption as a proxy for total economic activity found that the informal economy expanded following banking crises in 48 economies over the 1984-2005 period (Colombo, Onnis, and Tirelli 2016). Several studies have found that, during economic downturns, the share of informal output tended to increase (Busato and Chiarini 2004; Elgin 2012; Kaufmann and Kaliberda 1996).

More procyclical fiscal policy in less developed economies with weaker institutions may contribute to the countercyclicality of informal activity. Fiscal policy tends to be more procyclical in countries with higher informality (Çiçek and Elgin 2011). In particular, procyclical fiscal consolidation during recessions, including through higher taxes, may encourage more informal employment and output.

Microeconomic evidence. Work-flow data for Brazilian metropolitan labor markets between 1983 and 2002 showed that the informal sector was able to absorb more labor during economic downturns as jobs became scarcer in the formal sector (Bosch, Goni, and Maloney 2007). The share of formal employment fell as formal-economy output contracted, in part because the rate at which workers found formal jobs plummeted while the rate at which they found informal jobs remained broadly stable (Bosch and Esteban-Pretel 2012).

Informal economy as a procyclical engine of growth

Because informal firms provide services, as well as final and intermediate goods to the formal sector, a positive correlation between formal and informal sector activity may emerge. In addition, informal-economy income can support formal-economy demand.[4]

Macroeconomic evidence. In studies focusing on absolute output levels rather than the share of the informal economy, movements in informal-economy output have been

---

[4] For linkages between the two sectors, see Arvin-Rad, Basu, and Willumsen (2010); Lubell (1991); and Moreno-Monroy, Pieters, and Erumban (2014). For links focusing on income support, see Docquier, Müller, and Naval (2017); Eilat and Zinnes (2002); Gibson (2005); Kanbur (2017); Schneider (1998); and World Bank (2014). Although the relationship between formal and informal sectors may be symbiotic in the short run, in the long run pervasive informality may create poverty traps and stymie economic development.

found to be positively correlated with movements in formal-economy output in Australia, Canada, New Zealand, and a group of 19 Latin American economies (Bajada 2003; Dell'Anno 2008; Giles 1997; Tedds and Giles 2000). In a group of developing countries, episodes during which relative demand or productivity shocks expanded the nontradable sector (as opposed to the tradable sector) were associated with higher informal employment (hence, procyclicality; Fiess, Fugazza, and Maloney 2010). In Brazil and Mexico, higher separation rates from informal jobs and a large drop of the formal job finding rate may induce labor outflows from the informal sector during recessions (Bosch and Maloney 2008). A theoretical model establishes procyclical informal-formal sector linkages when formal firms subcontract labor-intensive stages of production to the informal sector (Arvin-Rad, Basu, and Willumsen 2010).

Microeconomic evidence. In firm-level data for India, formal and informal sector employment have been found to be positively correlated, in part because subcontracting by formal-sector firms to informal firms contributes to job creation in the informal sector (Moreno-Monroy, Pieters, and Erumban 2014).[5] An examination of data from Indian manufacturing firms showed that the gross value added of several predominantly informal industries was positively correlated with that of the formal sector as well as with foreign direct investment. This may be indicative of technological spillovers to both formal and informal sectors (Beladi, Dutta, and Kar 2016).

Factors influencing the cyclicality of the informal economy

Some studies have sought to reconcile the mixed evidence by pointing to country characteristics that would generate different degrees of procyclicality. Others have pointed to different kinds of shocks that would lead to different types of cyclical linkages.

Cross-country heterogeneity. There is considerable cross-country heterogeneity in the degree of procyclicality of informal employment. It has been found to be higher when informality was greater (Loayza and Rigolini 2011), when informal employment was more common (Shapiro 2014), or when there were stronger informal-formal sector linkages such as through subcontracting (Mbaye, Benjamin, and Gueye 2017; Moreno-Monroy, Pieters, and Erumban 2014).

Sources of shocks causing business cycles. The informal economy can move procyclically or countercyclically, depending on the sectoral origin of the shocks that generate business cycles in the presence of wage rigidities, especially in the formal sector (Fiess, Fugazza, and Maloney 2010; Leyva and Urrutia 2018). Positive relative demand or productivity shocks to the nontradable sector, especially services, where the share of informal employment tends to be higher could increase informal employment,

---

[5] In an earlier study focusing on two European countries, it was found that at least two-thirds of the income earned in the informal economy was immediately spent in the formal economy, providing a considerable stimulus for it (Schneider 1998).

generating procyclicality in informal employment, especially when combined with wage rigidities in the formal sector.[6] Conversely, in the presence of wage rigidities, a negative shock to the tradable sector would expand informal (nontradables) employment and thus appear as countercyclical.

Data and methodology

This chapter relies on the database discussed in the previous chapter. It applies a battery of statistical tests used, first, to establish the co-movement between formal output and measures of informal activity and, second, to analyze the direction of causality.

Data. This chapter uses the two model-based estimates of informal output—the multiple indicators multiple causes (MIMIC) estimates and the dynamic general equilibrium (DGE) estimates (chapter 2).[7] Annual MIMIC estimates are available for 160 economies (including 36 advanced economies) for 1993-2018. Annual DGE estimates are available for 158 economies (including 36 advanced economies) for 1990-2018. These measures of informal output are complemented with self-employment as a proxy indicator of informal employment (La Porta and Shleifer 2014). Annual data on shares of self-employment are available for 179 economies (including 36 advanced economies) between 1990 and 2018. All measures of informal activity are defined in levels of output or levels of employment, rather than as shares of total activity or employment as is standard practice in the business cycle literature (for example, Claessens, Kose, and Terrones 2012; Fernández and Meza 2015). Data for formal output are from the Penn World Table 9.1 and the World Development Indicators (WDI) (in 2011 U.S. dollars; data from Penn World Table 9.1 were expanded using WDI). The Hodrick-Prescott (HP) filter is used to detrend the time series with the smoothing parameter set to 100. All exercises rely on detrended logarithms of these levels. The findings are robust to using annual growth of formal and informal output and employment or to using the Baxter-King filter to detrend series.

Methodologies. To quantify the co-movement of formal output with the various measures of informality, the chapter employs a wide range of measures, including correlation, factor models, coincidence of turning points and business cycle phases, and probit regression models (Claessens, Kose, and Terrones 2012; Kose, Prasad, and Terrones 2003; Restrepo-Echevarria 2014). Some methodological details are presented in annex 3B. As a second step, the chapter uses a two-stage least squares instrumental variable approach to estimate the direction of causality between formal output and measures of informal activity. Specifically, formal-economy output is instrumented using government consumption, export growth, and trade-to-GDP ratios. The methodology is described in greater detail in annex 3C.

---

[6] See chapter 4 for a discussion about sectoral distribution in the informal economy. Informality tends to be higher in labor-intensive service sectors, which are largely nontradable.

[7] The correlation of the DGE measure does not occur by construction (see annex 3A for details).

FIGURE 3.2 Correlations of informal output with formal output

Informal-economy output is highly and positively correlated with formal-economy output, both contemporaneously and in lagged terms. Formal employment is also positively and significantly correlated with formal-economy output, whereas informal employment is largely uncorrelated with formal-economy output in EMDEs.

A. Correlation between formal output and informal output (DGE-based estimates)

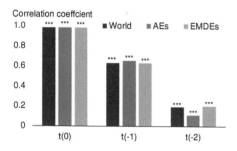

B. Correlation between formal output and informal output (MIMIC-based estimates)

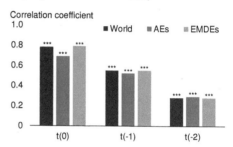

C. Correlation between formal output and formal employment

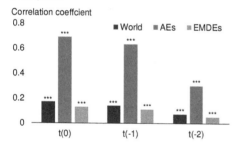

D. Correlation between formal output and informal employment

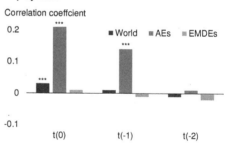

Sources: Penn World Table 9.1; World Bank.
Note: Data are for 1990-2018. AEs = advanced economies; DGE = dynamic general equilibrium model estimates; EMDEs = emerging market and developing economies; MIMIC = multiple indicators multiple causes model estimates. *** denotes 10 percent significance.
A.-D. Each bars shows the correlation between the cyclical components of formal-economy output (in logs, of year t(-2), t(-1) and t(0)) and the cyclical components of informal-economy output (A, B; in logs), formal employment (that is, total employment excl. self-employment in logs; in C) and informal employment proxied by self-employment (in logs; in D; in logs) of year t(0).

Synchronization of formal and informal business cycles

A battery of statistical exercises suggests that informal output is strongly positively correlated with formal output; hence, it behaves in a procyclical manner. In contrast, informal employment is largely unrelated to formal output movements; hence, it behaves in an acyclical manner.

Correlations. Contemporaneously, informal-economy output movements are highly and statistically significantly correlated with formal-economy output movements (figure 3.2). Formal employment is also positively and statistically significantly correlated with

FIGURE 3.3 Co-movement between formal and informal business cycles

A common factor explains about 40 percent of variance in formal-economy output. It also explains 40 percent of variance of informal-economy output when based on DGE estimates, and 24 percent using MIMIC estimates. However, it explains only about 10 percent or less of movements in formal employment and informal employment.

A. Share of variance in formal output and informal output explained by a common factor

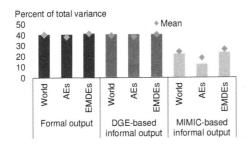

B. Share of variance in formal output and formal and informal employment explained by a common factor

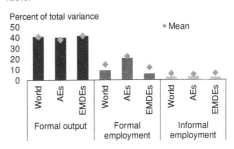

Sources: Penn World Table 9.1; World Bank.
Note: Data are for 1990-2018. All data series are transformed into cyclical components and standardized before the estimations. Formal employment is proxied by total employment excluding self-employment. Informal employment is proxied by self-employment. AEs = advanced economies; DGE = dynamic general equilibrium model estimates; EMDEs = emerging market and developing economies; MIMIC = multiple indicators multiple causes model estimates.
A.B. Bars show the median (diamond for mean) fractions of variance explained by the common dynamic factor in each group. The results here are obtained from estimating dynamic common factor model, as in Stock and Watson (2011), for each country in the sample (see annex 3B for details). AR(1) process for the common dynamic factor is used, as suggested by the estimation results.

formal-economy output, although considerably less strongly, particularly in EMDEs, whereas informal employment is largely uncorrelated with formal-economy output, again particularly in EMDEs. Lag correlations are considerably smaller than contemporaneous correlations, suggesting that informal output responds to formal-economy output fluctuations within a year.[8]

Common factor approach. For each country, a common factor is extracted from informal- and formal-sector output as well as informal and formal employment, in a dynamic factor model (annex 3B; Kose, Prasad, and Terrones 2003). The results are broadly in line with the correlations discussed above. On average, the common factor explains about 40 percent of the variance in both formal-economy output and DGE-based informal-economy output (figure 3.3). It explains somewhat less (24 percent) of the variance in MIMIC-based informal-economy output, in part because MIMIC estimates tend to be more stable than DGE estimates as a result of the reliance of the former measure on slow-moving country characteristics such as economic and business freedom indexes. The common factor also explains a modest fraction of movements in formal employment, especially in advanced economies. In contrast, informal employment does not appear to share a common factor with formal employment or with informal- or formal-economy output in either advanced economies or EMDEs.

---

[8] In EMDEs, however, lag correlations are statistically indistinguishable from contemporaneous correlations.

FIGURE 3.4 Coincidence of formal and informal business cycles

In more than 90 percent of country-year pairs, formal and informal output are in the same business cycle phase. This coincidence of business cycle phases is less pronounced for employment than for output, with informal employment being in the same phase as formal output in about a half of country-year pairs.

A. Coincidence of business cycle phases: Formal and informal output

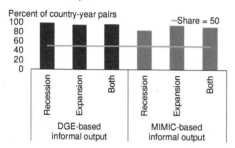

B. Coincidence of business cycle phases: Formal output and employment

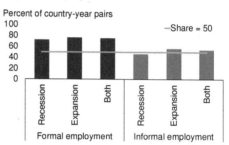

C. Coincidence of business cycle turning points: Formal and informal output

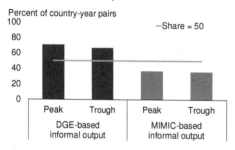

D. Coincidence of business cycle turning points: Formal output and employment

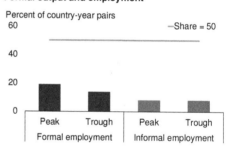

Sources: Penn World Table 9.1; World Bank.
Note: Data are for 1990-2018. Business phases and turning points are identified as in chapter 2. Recessions are the periods from peak to trough whereas expansions are the periods from trough to peak (Claessens, Kose, and Terrones 2012). Trough and peaks are identified as in chapter 2, where the Bry and Boschan (1971) method is used to identify turning points. Formal employment is proxied by total employment excluding self-employment. Informal employment is proxied by self-employment. DGE = dynamic general equilibrium model estimates; MIMIC = multiple indicators multiple causes model estimates.
A.B. Bars show the percent of country-year pairs where formal output and informal output (in A; formal or informality employment in B) are in the same business cycle phases (that is, both are in recession, or in expansions, or in either cases, labeled as "both").
C.D. Bars show the share of formal peaks (or troughs) that happen to be informal peaks (or troughs).

Coherence in business cycle phases and turning points. Formal and informal sectors typically share the same business cycle phases (figure 3.4). In more than 90 percent of country-year pairs, formal and informal output are in the same business cycle phase. This coincidence of business cycle phases is considerably less pronounced for employment than for output. Formal employment and formal output share the same business cycle phases in 75 percent of all country-year pairs, whereas informal employment is in the same phase as formal output in 54 percent of country-year pairs. Similarly, between 30 and 70 percent (using MIMIC or DGE, respectively) of turning points (peak or trough) of formal output business cycles coincide with turning points of informal output business cycles, whereas informal employment turning points coincide about 10 percent of the time with formal-economy output turning points.

Econometric approaches. A probit regression is used to estimate the probability of the informal economy being in recession at the same time that the formal economy is (annex 3B). Indeed, the probability of informal output being in recession is statistically significantly higher when formal output is in a recession, even after controlling for country and year fixed effects as well as investment and credit growth (figure 3.5). On average, the probability of informal output being in recession is higher by about 25 percentage points when formal output is in recession than when formal output is not in recession.[9] Similar results pertain to the probability of a new recession starting in the informal sector when the formal economy is in recession. Again, this contrasts with the finding that the probability of informal employment declining is little affected by a formal-economy contraction.

Causal linkages between formal- and informal-economy business cycles

The results described in the previous section suggest a strong correlation between formal and informal economies. Some previous studies reported strong evidence of Granger causality running from the formal economy to the informal economy in individual countries, and mild evidence of reverse causality in some cases (Bajada 2003; Giles 1997; Giles, Tedds, and Werkneh 2002). However, Granger causality does not establish "true" causality, and ignoring reverse causality could lead to biased estimation results (Angrist and Pischke 2009). Hence, the chapter employs a novel approach with an instrumental variables estimation to test for the direction of causality. The results based on this approach suggest that formal-economy output fluctuations "truly" cause informal-economy output fluctuations.

Econometric approach. Formal-economy output is instrumented using government spending and two trade-related variables: the cyclical components of the terms of trade and real exports (annex 3C). Being largely concentrated in the nontradable sector, the informal economy is unlikely to be highly influenced directly by movements in trade-related variables. In addition, government spending is typically restricted, by legislation and regulation, from purchasing goods and services from the informal economy. Therefore, movements in trade-related variables and changes in government consumption can be interpreted as exogenous instruments that directly affect the formal economy without directly influencing the informal economy.

Results. The regression results confirm that formal-economy output fluctuations in the previous year, as instrumented by lagged trade-related terms and government consumption, "cause" fluctuations in the informal economy in the following year. On average, a 1 percent increase in formal-economy output "causes" a 0.4-0.8 percent expansion in the following year in informal-economy output and formal employment.

---

[9] Probabilities for the global sample need not be near the average of the advanced economy and EMDE sample because of different year fixed effects.

FIGURE 3.5 **Probability of a recession**

Informal output and formal employment are more likely to be in (or moving toward) a recession when formal output is in a recession. However, the same does not hold for informal employment.

A. Impact of formal output recession on probability of informal output recession

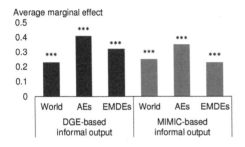

B. Impact of formal output recession on probability of employment recession

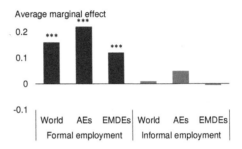

C. Impact of formal output recession on probability of starting an informal output recession

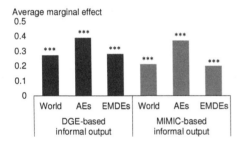

D. Impact of formal output recession on probability of starting an employment recession

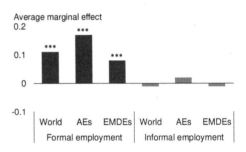

Source: World Bank.

Note: Data are for 1990-2018. Average marginal effects are shown in bars. Recessions are the periods from peak to trough, whereas expansions are the periods from trough to peak (Claessens, Kose, and Terrones 2012). Troughs and peaks are identified as in chapter 2, where the Bry and Boschan 1971 method is used to identify turning points. Formal employment is proxied by total employment excluding self-employment. Informal employment is proxied by self-employment. AEs = advanced economies; DGE = dynamic general equilibrium model estimates; EMDEs = emerging market and developing economies; MIMIC = multiple indicators multiple causes model estimates. *** denotes 10 percent significance.

A.B. Bars show regression results from the following probit model: $Pr(ISREC_{it} + 1) = \phi(\alpha + \beta FS_{it} + \theta X_{it} + \pi_i + \mu_t + \epsilon_{it})$, where $ISREC_{it}$ is a dummy variable that equals one when the informal sector in country i and year t is in recession, and zero otherwise. FS_{it} is a dummy representing recession in the formal economy, and X_{it} is a vector of control variables (including the annual growth rates of real investment and domestic credit to the private sector; Penn World Table 9.1 and 2020 World Development Indicators). All regressions include country dummies (π_i) and year dummies (μ_t). See annex 3B for details.

C.D. Bars show regression results from the probit model with the same form as in A and B. Here $ISREC_{it}$ is a dummy variable that equals one when the informal sector in country i and year t is in the start of a recession, and zero otherwise. See annex 3B for details.

This impact does not differ materially between advanced economies and EMDEs. In contrast, such formal-economy output fluctuations do not cause significant fluctuations in informal employment, especially in EMDEs (figure 3.6).

Robustness tests. These results are robust to several alternative specifications. Instrumenting only with either trade-related variables or government consumption yields similar results. In addition, the results are robust to using system generalized methods of moments (GMM) estimation to address potential endogeneity; to specifying the dependent variable in terms of the share of the informal economy in the total

FIGURE 3.6 **Impact of formal output fluctuations on the informal sector**

A 1 percent increase in formal economy output raises informal output and formal employment by 0.4-0.8 percent one year later, but does not affect informal employment significantly.

A. Impact of formal output fluctuations on informal output

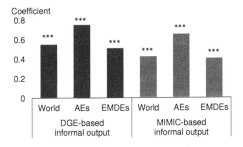

B. Impact of formal output fluctuations on employment

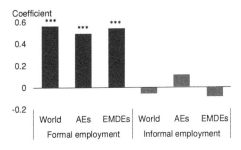

Source: World Bank.
Note: Data are for 1990-2018. See annex 3C for details. Government consumption and trade-related terms (proxied by terms of trade and exports) are included as instrumental variables (IVs) to explain the variation in formal output (proxied by official GDP). Formal employment is proxied by total employment excluding self-employment. Informal employment is proxied by self-employment.
AEs = advanced economies; DGE = dynamic general equilibrium model estimates; EMDEs = emerging market and developing economies; MIMIC = multiple indicators multiple causes model estimates. *** denotes 10 percent significance.
A. Bars show estimated coefficients when DGE- or MIMIC-based estimates are used as the dependent variable.
B. Bars show estimated coefficients when formal employment or informal employment (defined as self-employment) are used as the dependent variable.

economy (annex 3C); and to using an alternative variant of the DGE measures to test for robustness to different modeling assumptions in the construction of the DGE estimates (annex 3D).

Explaining the cyclicality of the informal sector

The previous sections have established that informal-economy output and formal employment behave "procyclically" in the sense of responding to formal-economy output fluctuations significantly and positively. Meanwhile, informal employment acts "acyclically" in the sense of not significantly and systematically responding to formal-economy output fluctuations. This accounts for the rising share of informal employment during formal-economy recessions documented by studies like Loayza and Rigolini (2011).

There are at least two possible reasons explaining why informal employment behaves acyclically. First, informal employment may respond to different shocks from informal output and formal employment, or it may respond differently to the same shocks. As an example of the latter, the informal labor market, being more flexible than the formal sector, may respond by reducing hours worked per person or by lowering wages, rather than by reducing the number of employed.[10] A second possible reason is that, although

---

[10] For discussions of these arguments, see Guriev, Speciale, and Tuccio (2016); Loayza and Rigolini (2011); Maloney (2004); and Meghir, Narita, and Robin (2015).

job separation rates rise during recessions in both formal and informal sectors, the rate at which workers find formal jobs plummets whereas that at which they find informal jobs remains broadly stable (Bosch and Esteban-Pretel 2012; Bosch, Goni, and Maloney 2007).

Conclusion

This chapter presents a wide variety of approaches that document the strong co-movement of informal-economy output with formal-economy output, caused by movements in formal output, but the lack of such co-movement for informal employment. This suggests that, although output in the informal economy behaves procyclically and, therefore, may amplify aggregate output fluctuations (for example, Ferreira Tiryaki 2008; Roca, Moreno, and Sánchez 2001), the unresponsiveness of informal employment to the business cycle may provide a buffer for household incomes by ensuring continuity of employment in the informal economy.

The resilience of informal employment in the face of business cycle swings, juxtaposed with the weaker development levels associated with informality (discussed in chapter 4), suggests a trade-off. In the short run, informal employment can provide a safety net during business cycles; in the long term, however, the informal sector can exacerbate poverty and stymie development (Docquier, Müller, and Naval 2017). Policy measures that—deliberately or inadvertently—reduce informality and thus benefit longer-term development and poverty reduction could, therefore, usefully be accompanied by a strengthening of official social safety nets to protect vulnerable population groups from the short-term costs of the loss of the unofficial safety net provided by the informal sector. The necessity of strengthening the resilience of the informal sector is particularly relevant in the context of the COVID-19-induced recession (box 2.1).

Also, if co-movement between formal and informal output reflects synergies, such as through subcontracting, policy measures aimed at curtailing informal activity could disrupt formal activity. These effects could be mitigated if measures that reduce informality were accompanied by greater labor and product market flexibility in the formal sector that facilitates the absorption of informal participants (World Bank 2019).

Directions for future research. The results reported in this chapter point to several promising areas for future research. First, the cyclical behavior of other features of the informal economy could usefully be examined. For example, if greater flexibility of wages or hours worked is what ensures acyclical behavior of informal employment despite procyclical informal output, then informal wages or hours of employment should be particularly procyclical. It would be useful to establish whether this is the case. Second, the channels through which formal-economy business cycles affect the informal economy could be further explored and quantified. This includes the degree of interconnectedness between formal and informal firms.

ANNEX 3A Theory behind the cyclicality of the DGE-based estimates

The production function for official GDP is assumed to have the following form:

$$Y_{Ft} = A_{Ft} K_t^{\alpha} N_{Ft}^{1-\alpha} \tag{3A.1}$$

where Y_{Ft} is output in the formal sector in year t, A_{Ft} is total factor productivity in the formal sector in year t, K_t is the capital stock available in year t, and N_{Ft} is employment in the formal sector in year t.

The production function for informal output is assumed to have the following form:

$$Y_{It} = A_{It} N_{It}^{\gamma}, \tag{3A.2}$$

where Y_{It} is output in the informal sector in year t, A_{It} is labor productivity in the informal sector, and N_{It} is employment in the informal sector. As assumed in Elgin and Oztunali (2012), $\dot{A}_{It} = (\dot{K}_t + \dot{A}_{Ft})/2$ and N_{It} is a function of A_{Ft} and K_t. To simplify the discussion, it is assumed that $A_{It} = (A_{Ft} + K_t)/2 + c$, where c is a constant. N_{It} has the following form: [11]

$$N_{It} = \left\{ \frac{\gamma A_{It}}{(1-\tau_t)(1-\alpha)A_{Ft}} \left[\frac{\frac{1}{\beta}-1+\delta}{\alpha(1-\tau_t)A_{Ft}} \right]^{\frac{\alpha}{1-\alpha}} \right\}^{\frac{1}{1-\gamma}} \tag{3A.3}$$

Because A_{It} and N_{It} are functions of A_{Ft} and K_t, Y_{It} can be expressed as a function of A_{Ft} and K_t. The co-movement between Y_{It} and Y_{Ft} can be driven only by shocks in A_{Ft} and K_t. Assuming that shocks in N_{Ft} are not related to shocks in K_t or in A_{Ft}, because $\frac{\partial Y_{Ft}}{\partial K_{Ft}} > 0$ and $\frac{\partial Y_{Ft}}{\partial A_{Ft}} > 0$, the positive correlation between Y_{Ft} and Y_{It} could be driven by construction if $\frac{\partial Y_{It}}{\partial A_{Ft}} > 0$ and $\frac{\partial Y_{It}}{\partial K_{Ft}} > 0$. Therefore, the values of $\frac{\partial Y_{It}}{\partial A_{Ft}}$ and $\frac{\partial Y_{It}}{\partial K_{Ft}}$ will be discussed below.

First, $\frac{\partial Y_{It}}{\partial K_t} = N_{It}^{\gamma} \frac{\partial A_{It}}{\partial K_t} + A_{It} * \gamma N_{It}^{\gamma-1} * \frac{\partial N_{It}}{\partial K_t}$, where $\frac{\partial N_{It}}{\partial K_t} > 0$ and $\frac{\partial A_{It}}{\partial K_t} = \frac{1}{2} > 0$.

Hence, $\frac{\partial Y_{It}}{\partial K_t} > 0$.

Second, it is easy to derive that

$$\frac{\partial Y_{It}}{\partial A_{Ft}} = N_{It}^{\gamma} \frac{\partial A_{It}}{\partial A_{Ft}} + A_{It} * \gamma N_{It}^{\gamma-1} * \frac{\partial N_{It}}{\partial A_{Ft}} = N_{It}^{\gamma} \left(\frac{1}{2} + \gamma * \frac{A_{It}}{N_{It}} * \frac{\partial N_{It}}{\partial A_{Ft}} \right)$$

---

[11] See Elgin and Oztunali (2012) for the definitions of the parameters used here.

where

$$\frac{\partial N_{It}}{\partial A_{Ft}} = \Omega * A_{It}^{\frac{\gamma}{1-\gamma}} (A_{Ft})^{-\frac{1}{(1-\alpha)(1-\gamma)}} * \frac{1}{1-\gamma} * \left[\frac{1}{2} - \frac{1}{1-\alpha} * \frac{A_{It}}{A_{Ft}} \right]$$

and

$$\Omega = \left\{ \frac{\gamma}{(1-\tau_t)(1-\alpha)} \left[\frac{\frac{1}{\beta}-1+\delta}{\alpha(1-\tau_t)} \right]^{\frac{\alpha}{1-\alpha}} \right\}^{\frac{1}{1-\gamma}}.$$

Since $\alpha = 0.36$ and $A_{It} = (A_{Ft} + K_t)/2 + c$, $\frac{1}{2} - \frac{1}{(1-\alpha)} * \frac{A_{It}}{A_{Ft}} < 0$ and $\frac{\partial N_{It}}{\partial A_{Ft}} < 0$.

This yields $\frac{\partial Y_{It}}{\partial A_{Ft}} = N_{It}^{\gamma} * \left[\frac{1}{2} + \frac{\gamma}{1-\gamma} * \left(\frac{1}{2} - \frac{1}{(1-\alpha)} * \frac{A_{It}}{A_{Ft}} \right) \right]$.

Hence, if $\frac{A_{It}}{A_{Ft}}$ falls below $\frac{1-\alpha}{2\gamma} \approx 0.75$, $\frac{\partial Y_{It}}{\partial A_{Ft}}$ turns from positive to negative.

Because the co-movement between Y_{It} and Y_{Ft} is largely driven by the assumption that $\dot{A}_{It} = (\dot{K}_t + \dot{A}_{Ft})/2$, the DGE model is reestimated by benchmarking N_{It} to survey-based self-employment in annex 3D as a robustness check. This gives the estimates of A_{It} and subsequently Y_{It} without replying on specific assumptions. The regression results for instrumental variables two-stage least squares (IV-2SLS) models using DGE estimates benchmarked to self-employment are largely in line with those shown in the main text.

ANNEX 3B Model specifications for measuring co-movement among informality measures

Dynamic common factor model

The dynamic common factor model has the following form (Stock and Watson 2011):

$$Y_t = \beta f_t + \varepsilon_t ; f_t = \varnothing (L) f_{t-1} + \mu_t , \qquad (3B.1)$$

where Y_t is a vector of variables that contains official GDP, DGE-based and MIMIC-based informal output estimates, formal employment, and informal employment. f_t is the dynamic common factor, which follows an autoregressive (AR(1)) process. ε_t and μ_t are error terms that are independently and identically distributed (i.d.d.). The dynamic common factor model is estimated for each country. Robustness tests for longer lags indicate that the coefficients for additional lags of the common factor are insignificant. All data series are detrended and standardized before estimation. Additional results are available upon request.

Probit model

The probit model has the following form:

$$Pr\ (ISREC_{it} = 1) = \phi(\alpha + \beta FS_{it} + \boldsymbol{\theta X_{it}} + \pi_i + \mu_t + \epsilon_{it}),$$

where $ISREC_{it}$ is a dummy variable that equals one when the informal sector in country i and year t is in recession, and zero otherwise. FS_{it} is a dummy representing recession in the formal economy, and $\boldsymbol{X_{it}}$ is a vector of control variables. Following Elgin and Oztunali (2012 and 2014), $\boldsymbol{X_{it}}$ includes the annual growth rates of real investment (Penn World Table [PWT] 9.1) and domestic credit to the private sector obtained from WDI. All regressions include country dummies (π_i) and year dummies (μ_t) to control for macro trends across countries in a certain year and factors that are country specific. For probit model on the start of informal recessions, $ISREC_{it}$ is a dummy variable that equals one when the informal sector in country i and year t is in the start of a recession, and zero otherwise. Recessions are identified as in chapter 2, where the algorithm in Bry and Boschan (1971) is used to identify peaks and troughs of business cycles and recessions are defined as the period from peak to trough (Claessens, Kose, and Terrones 2012).

ANNEX 3C Causal linkages between formal- and informal- economy business cycles

The following instrumental variables that affect formal-economy output but do not directly influence informal-economy output are considered: movements in trade-related variables and changes in government consumption. Being concentrated in the nontradable sector (Fiess, Fugazza, and Maloney 2010), the informal economy is unlikely to be influenced by movements in trade-related variables directly. In addition, government consumption includes all government current expenditures for purchases of goods and services (including compensation of employees), without covering transfers such as social benefits, subsidies, and so on. Governments are typically restricted, by legislation and regulation, from purchasing goods and services directly from the informal economy. As governments purchase goods and services from the formal economy, changes in government consumption lead to fluctuations in the formal economy without affecting the informal economy directly. Therefore, movements in trade-related variables and changes in government consumption can be interpreted as exogenous instruments that directly affect the formal economy without directly influencing the informal economy.

Data on movements in trade-related variables and changes in government consumption are obtained from the WDI. Trade-related variables include terms of trade and exports of goods and services (at constant 2010 U.S. dollars). Government consumption captures general government final consumption expenditure (at constant 2010 U.S. dollars). These measures—as well as all the output and employment measures—are transformed into cyclical components as deviations from the HP-filtered trend with a smoothing parameter of 100. To further make sure that the causal direction runs only from the formal economy to the informal economy, cyclical movements in formal GDP are lagged in the following regressions. The results are robust to using annual growth rates of these variables and when cyclical movements in formal GDP are not lagged.

The IV-2SLS regression model has the following form:

$$FS_{it-1} = \alpha_1 + \beta_1 IV_{it-1} + \theta\mathbf{X_{it}} + \pi_i + \mu_t + \epsilon_{it} \qquad \text{(3C.1: 1st stage)}$$

$$IS_{it} = \alpha_0 + \beta_0 \widehat{FS_{it-1}} + \theta\mathbf{X_{it}} + \pi_i + \mu_t + \epsilon_{it} \qquad \text{(3C.1: 2nd stage)}$$

In the first stage, the lagged cyclical component of formal-economy output (FS_{it-1}) is the dependent variable, whereas the lagged trade-related variables and government consumption in country i (IV_{it-1}) are the explanatory variables. The regression results of the first stage are used to obtain the estimated cyclical component of formal economy output $\widehat{FS_{it-1}}$, which is used as the explanatory variable in the second stage. $\widehat{FS_{it-1}}$ is used to explain the cyclical components of informal-economy output or informal employment (IS_{it}) in year t. The coefficient estimate β measures the magnitude and direction of the impact of fluctuations in the formal business cycle on the informal economy. In both stages, a vector of control variables ($\mathbf{X_{it}}$), country fixed effects (π_i), and year fixed effects (μ_t) are controlled for. The vector of control variables ($\mathbf{X_{it}}$) includes the growth rates of domestic credit to the private sector and real investment. These control variables are included because they influence the fluctuations in both formal and informal economies (for example, Elgin and Oztunali, 2014; Ferreira Tiyaki 2008; La Porta and Shleifer 2014). Data for investment are provided by PWT 9.1, updated with data from WDI, and credit data are obtained from WDI. Detailed baseline estimation results are shown in table 3C.1.

Movements in trade-related terms and changes in government consumption are jointly used as instruments for formal-economy output fluctuations. To remove the potential endogeneity of government consumption in the case of MIMIC, results are also obtained using trade-related instrumental variables (terms of trade and export growth) only (figure 3C.1).

Several robustness exercises are carried out. First, a system GMM model is carried out to address potential endogeneity bias. The results are strongly in line with baseline findings and results from fixed-effect models, where a 1 percent rise in formal economy output significantly increases output in the informal sector in the following year by 0.4-0.8 percent but has no significant response from informal employment (figure 3C.2). Second, an alternative variant of the DGE measures, detailed in methodological annex 3D, is used to test for robustness to different modeling assumptions in the construction of the DGE estimates. The results show that, on average, informal output expands significantly by 0.5-0.8 percent, especially in EMDEs, when formal-economy output rises by 1 percent in the previous year. Third, the same set of empirical analyses are applied to the shares of the informal economy in output and employment to ensure consistency with previous estimates in the literature. Both correlation and IV-2SLS regression analyses are carried out here. As expected, both shares of informal output and shares of informal employment are found to be significantly negatively correlated with formal-economy output, whereas shares of formal employment are positively correlated (figure 3C.3). The

FIGURE 3C.1 Impact of formal output fluctuations on the informal sector: Alternative instrumental variables

Results from using alternative sets of instrumental variables, such as trade-related variables or government consumption alone, confirm baseline results that expansion in formal-economy output significantly leads to a rise in informal output in the following year, while having no significant impact on informal employment.

A. Impact of formal output fluctuations on informal output: Trade-related variables

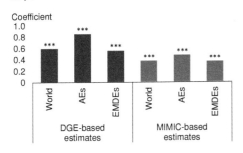

B. Impact of formal output fluctuations on employment: Trade-related variables

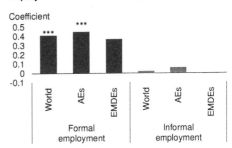

C. Impact of formal output fluctuations on informal output: Government consumption

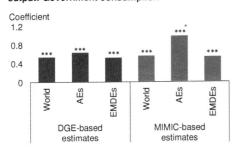

D. Impact of formal output fluctuations on employment: Government consumption

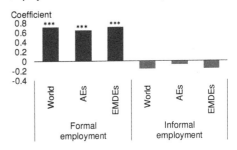

Source: World Bank.
Note: Data are for 1990-2018. Trade-related variables (proxied by terms of trade and export) are used as the instrumental variable to explain the variation in formal output (proxied by official GDP) in A and B, whereas government consumption is used as the instrumental variable in C and D. See annex 3C for details. Formal employment is proxied by total employment excluding self-employment. Informal employment is proxied by self-employment. AEs = advanced economies; DGE = dynamic general equilibrium model estimates; EMDEs = emerging market and developing economies; MIMIC = multiple indicators multiple causes model estimates. *** denotes 10 percent significance.
A.C. Bars show estimated coefficients when DGE- or MIMIC-based estimates are used as the dependent variable.
B.D. Bars show estimated coefficients when formal employment or informal employment (defined as self-employment) are used as the dependent variable.

regression results show that the share of informal output contracts significantly by 0.1-0.4 percentage point of GDP, on average, when formal-economy output expands by 1 percent in the previous year (figure 3C.4).

FIGURE 3C.2 Impact of formal output fluctuations on the informal sector: Additional robustness checks

Robustness checks, such as ones using a fixed-effect estimator and a system GMM estimator, confirm formal findings that rises in formal-economy output significantly increase output in the informal sector in the following year while having no significant impact on informal employment, especially in EMDEs.

A. Impact of formal output fluctuations on informal output (DGE-based estimates)

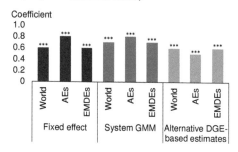

B. Impact of formal output fluctuations on informal output (MIMIC-based estimates)

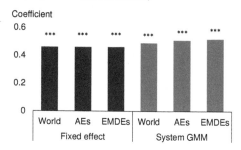

C. Impact of formal output fluctuations on formal employment

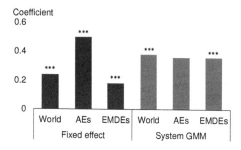

D. Impact of formal output fluctuations on informal employment

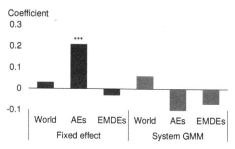

Source: World Bank.

Note: Data are for 1990-2018. Formal employment is proxied by total employment excluding self-employment. Informal employment is proxied by self-employment. AEs = advanced economies; DGE = dynamic general equilibrium model estimates; EMDEs = emerging market and developing economies; GMM = generalized method of moments; HP = Hodrick-Prescott (filter); MIMIC = multiple indicators multiple causes model estimates. *** denotes 10 percent significance.

A-D. Bars show the estimated coefficients for the lagged cyclical component of official GDP. "Fixed effects" show results for the fixed-effect model, where the dependent variable is the cyclical component of informal output or employment derived using the HP filter, and the variable of interest is the lagged cyclical component of official GDP (HP filtered). Country fixed effects and year dummies are used here. "System GMM" shows regression results from system GMM estimators with informal output, formal employment and informal employment being the dependent variables and lagged official GDP being the explanatory variable. See annex 3D for details on "alternative DGE-based estiamtes." All dependent variables and official GDP are cyclical components (in logs) obtained using the HP filter. Control variables, such as the growth rates of domestic credit to private sector and real investment, are included in both models.

FIGURE 3C.3 Correlations of informal output with formal output: Shares of informal output and employment

Both shares of informal output and shares of informal employment are negatively correlated with formal-economy output, whereas shares of formal employment are positively correlated.

A. Correlation between formal output and informal output shares (DGE-based estimates)

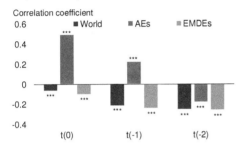

B. Correlation between formal output and informal output shares (MIMIC-based estimates)

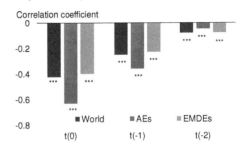

C. Correlation between formal output and formal employment shares

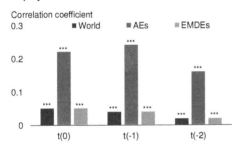

D. Correlation between formal output and informal employment shares

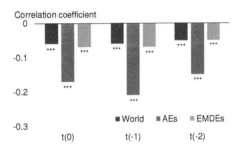

Sources: Penn World Table 9.1; World Bank.
Note: Data are for 1990-2018. Formal employment is proxied by total employment excluding self-employment. Informal employment is proxied by self-employment. AEs = advanced economies; DGE = dynamic general equilibrium model estimates; EMDEs = emerging market and developing economies; MIMIC = multiple indicators multiple causes model estimates. *** denotes 10 percent significance.
A-B. Bars show the correlations between the cyclical components of formal-economy output (in logs) in year t(-2), t(-1) and t(0), respectively, and the cyclical components of informal output shares in year t(0). Both DGE-based and MIMIC-bases estimates on informal ouput are in percent of official GDP.
C-D. Bars show the correlations between the cyclical components of formal-economy output (in logs) in year t(-2), t(-1) and t(0), respectively, and the cyclical components of employment shares in year t(0). Formal employment (in C) is proxied by total employment excluding self-employment and expressed in percent of total employment. Informal employment (in D) is proxied by self-employment in percent of total employment.

FIGURE 3C.4 Impact of formal output fluctuations on shares of output and employment in the informal sector

During formal-economy recessions, formal-economy output shrinks slightly more than informal-economy output, raising the share of informal-economy output in percent of official GDP. Meanwhile, formal employment shrinks and informal employment remains largely stable.

A. Impact of formal output fluctuations on informal output: Full set

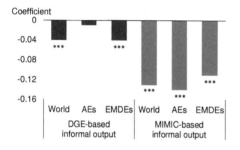

B. Impact of formal output fluctuations on employment: Full set

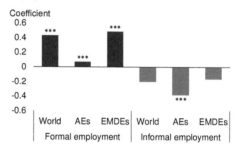

C. Impact of formal output fluctuations on informal output: Trade-related variables

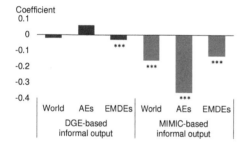

D. Impact of formal output fluctuations on employment: Trade-related variables

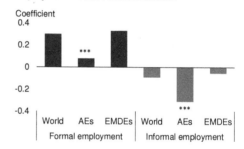

Source: World Bank.

Note: Data are for 1990-2018. See annex 3C for details. Formal employment is proxied by total employment excluding self-employment. Informal employment is proxied by self-employment. "Full set" are models where both government consumption and trade-related variables (proxied by terms of trade and export) are included as instrumental variables (IVs) to explain the variation in formal output (proxied by official GDP). "Trade-related variables" are models where only trade-related variables are used as IVs. AEs = advanced economies; DGE = dynamic general equilibrium model estimates; EMDEs = emerging market and developing economies; MIMIC = multiple indicators multiple causes model estimates. *** denotes 10 percent significance.

A.C. Bars show estimated coefficients when DGE- (MIMIC)-based estimates (in percent of official GDP) are used as the dependent variable.

B.D. Bars show estimated coefficients when formal employment (informal employment proxied by self-employment; in percent of total employment) is used as the dependent variable.

TABLE 3C.1 IV-2SLS regression: Baseline results

	Informal output (DGE)			Informal output (MIMIC)			Formal employment			Informal employment		
	(1)	(2)	(3)	(4)	(5)	(6)	(7)	(8)	(9)	(10)	(11)	(12)
	Full	AE	EMDE	Full	AE	EMDE	Full	AE	EMDE	Full	AE	EMDE
2nd stage dependent variable: Informal output/employment												
Official GDP	0.55***	0.75***	0.51***	0.42***	0.65***	0.40***	0.56***	0.49***	0.54**	-0.06	0.11	-0.09
	(0.05)	(0.07)	(0.05)	(0.04)	(0.05)	(0.05)	(0.25)	(0.09)	(0.30)	(0.16)	(0.14)	(0.20)
With controls	Yes	Yes	Yes	Yes	Yes	Yes	Yes	Yes	Yes	Yes	Yes	Yes
Country dummy	Yes	Yes	Yes	Yes	Yes	Yes	Yes	Yes	Yes	Yes	Yes	Yes
Year dummy	Yes	Yes	Yes	Yes	Yes	Yes	Yes	Yes	Yes	Yes	Yes	Yes
Kleibergen-Paap rk LM stat	29.81***	14.10***	24.44***	30.58***	13.99***	25.00***	36.25***	14.01***	29.10***	36.25***	14.01***	29.10***
Cragg-Donald Wald F stat	192.96	100.52	141.77	203.31	102.65	148.74	228.24	99.56	155.95	228.24	99.56	155.95
Observations	2,947	637	2,310	2,847	629	2,218	2,263	626	1,635	2,263	626	1,635
R-squared	0.50	0.79	0.47	0.37	0.62	0.35	0.05	0.60	0.04	0.03	0.10	0.04
1st stage dependent variable: Official GDP												
Terms of trade	0.09***	0.45***	0.08***	0.09***	0.46***	0.09***	0.13***	0.46***	0.11***	0.13***	0.46***	0.11***
	(0.03)	(0.11)	(0.03)	(0.03)	(0.11)	(0.03)	(0.03)	(0.11)	(0.03)	(0.03)	(0.11)	(0.03)
Exports	0.13**	0.07	0.12*	0.15**	0.07	0.13*	0.23***	0.06	0.22***	0.23***	0.06	0.22***
	(0.07)	(0.15)	(0.07)	(0.07)	(0.15)	(0.07)	(0.07)	(0.15)	(0.08)	(0.07)	(0.15)	(0.08)
Government consumption	0.14***	0.24***	0.13***	0.14***	0.24***	0.14***	0.16***	0.23***	0.15***	0.16***	0.23***	0.15***
	(0.02)	(0.04)	(0.03)	(0.02)	(0.04)	(0.03)	(0.02)	(0.04)	(0.02)	(0.02)	(0.04)	(0.02)
With controls	Yes	Yes	Yes	Yes	Yes	Yes	Yes	Yes	Yes	Yes	Yes	Yes
Country dummy	Yes	Yes	Yes	Yes	Yes	Yes	Yes	Yes	Yes	Yes	Yes	Yes
Year dummy	Yes	Yes	Yes	Yes	Yes	Yes	Yes	Yes	Yes	Yes	Yes	Yes
F-stats	17.06***	26.57***	13.78**	16.84***	26.89***	13.53**	24.39***	26.36***	19.01***	24.39***	26.36***	19.01***
Obs	2,947	637	2,310	2,847	629	2,218	2,263	626	1,635	2,263	626	1,635

Source: World Bank.

Note: First-stage F-stat show whether the concerning variable is a weak instrumental variable (IV), with a higher value suggesting a stronger IV. The equation is exactly identified. Kleibergen-Paap rk LM statistic shows the results for underidentification test, where a rejection shows the instrument is relevant. Significant Cragg-Donald Wald F statistic also shows that the used instrument is strong. Formal employment is total employment (excl. self-employment). Informal employment is proxied by self-employment. All dependent variables, official GDP, export and government consumption (in logs) obtained using the HP filter. Terms of trade is cyclical component (in percent of trend) obtained using the HP filter. Official GDP, government consumption, terms of trade and export are lagged to deal with the endogeneity issue. The control variables include the growth rates of domestic credit to private sector and real investment. See annex 3C for details. Full sample with period over 1990-2018 is used here. AE = advanced economy; EMDE = emerging market and developing economy; HP = Hodrick-Prescott (filter); IV-2SLS = two-stage least squares instrumental variable. Robust standard errors in parentheses. *** p < 0.01, ** p < 0.05, * p < 0.10.

ANNEX 3D Calibrating DGE estimates using survey-based self-employment data

As shown in Elgin and Oztunali (2012), the employment in the informal sector, N_{It} has the following form:

$$N_{It} = \left\{ \frac{\gamma A_{It}}{(1-\tau_t)(1-\alpha)A_{Ft}} \left[\frac{\frac{1}{\beta}-1+\delta}{\alpha(1-\tau_t)A_{Ft}} \right]^{\frac{\alpha}{1-\alpha}} \right\}^{\frac{1}{1-\gamma}} \quad (3D.1)$$

After transforming equation (3D.1), A_{It} can be expressed as follows:

$$A_{It} = \frac{N_{It}^{1-\gamma}(1-\tau_t)(1-\alpha)A_{Ft}}{\gamma \left[\frac{\frac{1}{\beta}-1+\delta}{\alpha(1-\tau_t)A_{Ft}} \right]^{\frac{\alpha}{1-\alpha}}} \quad (3D.2)$$

Following Fiess, Fugazza, and Maloney (2010) and Loayza and Rigolini (2011), data on self-employment, as shown in chapter 2, are used as estimates for N_{It} and to calculate A_{It} using equation (3D.2). Following the earlier literature, α is assumed to be equal to 0.36, and δ takes the country average of the depreciation rates reported in PWT 9.1 (expanded using WDI). Following Ihrig and Moe (2004), γ takes the value 0.425. Capital stock (K_t) and formal employment (N_{Ft}) are obtained from PWT 9.1. Assuming a balanced budget for the government, τ_t is obtained as the share of government spending in GDP reported in PWT 9.1 (expanded using WDI).

Rewriting the production function of the informal sector (Y_{It}) using equation (3D.2), Y_{It} is a function of A_{Ft} and N_{It}:

$$Y_{It} = N_{It} * \frac{(1-\tau_t)(1-\alpha)}{\gamma \left[\frac{\frac{1}{\beta}-1+\delta}{\alpha(1-\tau_t)} \right]^{\frac{\alpha}{1-\alpha}}} * (A_{Ft})^{\frac{1}{1-\alpha}}, \quad (3D.3)$$

which gives $\frac{\partial Y_{It}}{\partial A_{Ft}} > 0$. Because $\frac{\partial Y_{Ft}}{\partial A_{Ft}} > 0$, it is possible that the DGE estimates will move procyclically in the presence of large shocks in formal productivity when other types of shocks are absent. However, when other types of shocks also occur at the same time, Y_{It} may not move procyclically. For instance, if N_{It} and N_{Ft} experienced shocks in different directions at the same time, Y_{It} might move countercyclically in the absence of other types of shocks.

References

Angrist, J. D., and J.-S. Pischke. 2009. *Mostly Harmless Econometrics: An Empiricist's Companion.* Princeton University Press: Princeton, NJ.

Arvin-Rad, H., A. K. Basu, and M. Willumsen. 2010. "Economic Reform, Informal-Formal Sector Linkages and Intervention in the Informal Sector in Developing Countries: A Paradox." *International Review of Economics & Finance* 19 (4): 662-70.

Bajada, C. 2003. "Business Cycle Properties of the Legitimate and Underground Economy in Australia." *Economic Record* 79 (247): 397-411.

Beladi, H., M. Dutta, and S. Kar. 2016. "FDI and Business Internationalization of the Unorganized Sector: Evidence from Indian Manufacturing." *World Development* 83: 340-49.

Bosch, M., and J. Esteban-Pretel. 2012. "Job Creation and Job Destruction in the Presence of Informal Markets." *Journal of Development Economics* 98 (2): 270-86.

Bosch, M., E. Goni, and W. Maloney. 2007. "The Determinants of Rising Informality in Brazil: Evidence from Gross Worker Flows." Policy Research Working Paper 4347, World Bank, Washington, DC.

Bosch, M., and W. F. Maloney. 2008. "Cyclical Movements in Unemployment and Informality in Developing Countries." Policy Research Working Paper 4648, World Bank, Washington, DC.

Bry, G., and C. Boschan. 1971. *Cyclical Analysis of Time Series: Selected Procedures and Computer Programs.* New York: National Bureau of Economic Research.

Busato, F., and B. Chiarini. 2004. "Market and Underground Activities in a Two-Sector Dynamic Equilibrium Model." *Economic Theory* 23 (4): 831-61.

Chen, M. 2005. "Rethinking the Informal Economy: Linkages with the Formal Economy and the Formal Regulatory Environment." UNU-WIDER Working Paper 2005/10, United Nations University World Institute for Development Economics Research, Helsinki.

Çiçek, D., and C. Elgin. 2011. "Cyclicality of Fiscal Policy and the Shadow Economy." *Empirical Economics* 41 (3): 725-37.

Claessens, S., A. Kose, and M. Terrones. 2012. "How Do Business and Financial Cycles Interact?" *Journal of International Economics* 87 (1): 178-90.

Colombo, E., L. Onnis, and P. Tirelli. 2016. "Shadow Economies at Times of Banking Crises: Empirics and Theory." *Journal of Banking & Finance* 62 (C): 180-90.

Dell'Anno, R. 2008. "What Is the Relationship between Unofficial and Official Economy? An Analysis in Latin American Countries." *European Journal of Economics, Finance and Administrative Sciences* 12: 185-203.

Dix-Carneiro, R., P. Goldberg, C. Meghir, and G. Ulyssea. 2021. "Trade and Informality in the Presence of Labor Market Frictions and Regulations." NBER Working Paper 28391, National Bureau of Economic Research, Cambridge, MA.

Docquier, F., T. Müller, and J. Naval. 2017. "Informality and Long-Run Growth." *Scandinavian Journal of Economics* 119 (4): 1040-85.

Eichler, M. 2009. "Causal Inference from Multivariate Time Series: What Can Be Learned from Granger Causality." In *Logic, Methodology and Philosophy of Science: Proceedings of the 13th International Congress,* edited by C. Glymour, W. Wang, and D. Westerstahl. London: College Publications.

Eilat, Y., and C. Zinnes. 2002. "The Shadow Economy in Transition Countries: Friend or Foe? A Policy Perspective." *World Development* 30 (7): 1233-54.

Elgin, C. 2012. "Cyclicality of Shadow Economy." *Economic Papers* 31 (4): 478-90.

Elgin, C., and O. Oztunali. 2012. "Shadow Economies around the World: Model Based Estimates." Working Paper 2012/05, Department of Economics, Bogazici University.

Elgin, C., and O. Oztunali. 2014. "Institutions, Informal Economy, and Economic Development." *Emerging Markets Finance and Trade* 50 (4): 117-34.

Fernández, A., and F. Meza, 2015. "Informal Employment and Business Cycles in Emerging Economies: The Case of Mexico." *Review of Economic Dynamics* 18 (2): 381-405.

Ferreira Tiryaki, G. 2008. "The Informal Economy and Business Cycles." *Journal of Applied Economics* 11 (1): 91-117.

Fiess, N., M. Fugazza, and W. Maloney, 2010. "Informal Self-Employment and Macroeconomic Fluctuations." *Journal of Development Economics* 91 (2): 211-26.

Gibson, B. 2005. "The Transition to a Globalized Economy: Poverty, Human Capital and the Informal Sector in a Structuralist CGE Model." *Journal of Development Economics* 78 (1): 60-94.

Giles, D. 1997. "Causality between the Measured and Underground Economies in New Zealand." *Applied Economics Letters* 4 (1): 63-7.

Giles, D., L. Tedds, and G. Werkneh. 2002. "The Canadian Underground and Measured Economies: Granger Causality Results." *Applied Economics* 34 (18): 2347-52.

Guriev, S., B. Speciale, and M. Tuccio. 2016. "How Do Regulated and Unregulated Labor Markets Respond to Shocks? Evidence from Immigrants during the Great Recession." CEPR Working Paper DP11403, Centre for Economic Policy Research, Washington, DC.

Horvath, J. 2018. "Business Cycles, Informal Economy, and Interest Rates in Emerging Countries." *Journal of Macroeconomics* 55 (March): 96-116.

Ihrig, J., and K. S. Moe. 2004. "Lurking in the Shadows: The Informal Sector and Government Policy." *Journal of Development Economics* 73 (2): 541-57.

IMF (International Monetary Fund). 2017. *Regional Economic Outlook (Sub-Saharan Africa): Restarting the Growth Engine.* Washington, DC: International Monetary Fund.

Kaufmann, D., and A. Kaliberda.1996. "Integrating the Unofficial Economy into the Dynamics of Post-Socialist Economies: A Framework of Analysis and Evidence." Policy Research Working Paper 1691, World Bank, Washington, DC.

Kanbur, R. 2017. "Informality: Causes, Consequences and Policy Responses." *Review of Development Economics* 21 (4): 939-61.

Kose, M. A., E. Prasad, and M. Terrones. 2003. "How Does Globalization Affect the Synchronization of Business Cycles?" *AEA Papers and Proceedings* 93 (2): 57-62.

La Porta, R., and A. Shleifer. 2014. "Informality and Development." *Journal of Economic Perspectives* 28 (3): 109-26.

Leyva, G., and C. Urrutia. 2018. "Informality, Labor Regulation, and the Business Cycle." Banco de Mexico Working Papers 2018-19, Mexico City.

Loayza, N., and J. Rigolini. 2011. "Informal Employment: Safety Net or Growth Engine?" *World Development* 39 (9): 1503-15.

Lubell, H. 1991. *The Informal Sector in the 1980s and 1990s.* Paris: Organisation for Economic Co-operation and Development.

Maloney, W. 2004. "Informality Revisited." *World Development* 32 (7): 1159-78.

Mbaye, A. A., N. Benjamin, and F. Gueye. 2017. "The Interplay between Formal and Informal Firms and Its Implications on Jobs in Francophone Africa: Case Studies of Senegal and Benin." In *The Informal Economy in Global Perspective: Varieties of Governance,* edited by A. Polese, C. C. Williams, I. A. Horodnic, and P. Bejakovic. London: Palgrave Macmillan.

Meagher, K. 2013. "Unlocking the Informal Economy: A Literature Review on Linkages between Formal and Informal Economies in Developing Countries." WIEGO Working Paper 27, Women in Informal Employment: Globalization and Organization, Manchester, England.

Meghir, C., R. Narita, and J.-M. Robin. 2015. "Wages and Informality in Developing Countries." *American Economic Review* 105 (4): 1509-46.

Moreno-Monroy, A., J. Pieters, and A. Erumban. 2014. "Formal Sector Subcontracting and Informal Sector Employment in Indian Manufacturing." *IZA Journal of Labor & Development* 3 (22).

Restrepo-Echavarria, P. 2014. "Macroeconomic Volatility: The Role of the Informal Economy." *European Economic Review* 70 (August): 454-69.

Roca, J., C. Moreno, and J. Sánchez. 2001. "Underground Economy and Aggregate Fluctuations." *Spanish Economic Review* 3 (1): 41-53.

Schneider, F. 1998. "Further Empirical Results of the Size of the Shadow Economy of 17 OECD Countries over Time." Discussion Paper. Linz, Austria: Department of Economics, University of Linz.

Shapiro, A. F. 2014. "Self-employment and Business Cycle Persistence: Does the Composition of Employment Matter for Economic Recoveries?" *Journal of Economic Dynamics and Control* 46 (September): 200-18.

Stock, J. H., and M. Watson. 2011. "Dynamic Factor Models." In *Oxford Handbook of Economic Forecasting,* edited by M. P. Clements and D. F. Hendry. Oxford, UK: Oxford University Press.

Tedds, L., and D. Giles, 2000. "Modelling the Underground Economies in Canada and New Zealand: A Comparative Analysis." Econometrics Working Papers 0003, Department of Economics, University of Victoria.

World Bank. 2014. *World Development Report 2014: Risks and Opportunities.* Washington, DC: World Bank.

World Bank. 2019. *Global Economic Prospects: Darkening Skies.* January. Washington, DC: World Bank.

If there are costs to becoming legal, there are also bound to be costs to remaining outside the law.

Hernando de Soto (2001)
Economist

In developing countries, informal firms account for up to half of economic activity. They provide livelihood for billions of people. Yet their role in economic development remains controversial.

Rafael La Porta and Andrei Shleifer (2014)
Professor of Economics, Brown University
Professor of Economics, Harvard University

PART II

Country and Regional Dimensions

CHAPTER 4
Lagging Behind: Informality and Development

Informality is associated with a wide range of development challenges. Emerging market and developing economies with greater informality have significantly lower per capita incomes and greater poverty, less developed financial markets, weaker governance and public service provision, poorer human development outcomes, and more limited access to public infrastructure. This wide range of correlates suggests that any policies to address informality need to be embedded in a broader development agenda.

Introduction

Informal activity is widespread in emerging market and developing economies (EMDEs). Although informality is often considered a cause of development challenges, informality itself is also a consequence of underdevelopment.[1] EMDEs with more pervasive informality tend to be less developed, rely more on labor-intensive activities that employ unskilled and poorly paid workers, and have limited fiscal resources (World Bank 2019). Life expectancy, maternal mortality, and other human development indicators are, on average, lagging behind in EMDEs with more pervasive informality. Access to public services, such as electricity provision, that are essential to economic development, is limited.

A large informal sector weakens policy effectiveness and the government's ability to generate fiscal revenues.[2] Government revenues in EMDEs with above-median informality are 5-12 percentage points of gross domestic product (GDP) below those with below-median informality (World Bank 2019). Limited fiscal resources constrain governments' ability to offer adequate coverage of social protection programs, provide broad access to public sector services, smooth business cycles, and close the productivity gap between the formal and informal sectors (Schneider, Buehn, and Montenegro 2010; World Bank 2020a). In turn, the limited access to public services further discourages firms and workers from engaging with the government, resulting in more participation in the informal sector (Loayza 2018; Perry et al. 2007).

Note: This chapter was prepared by Franziska Ohnsorge, Yoki Okawa, and Shu Yu. Research assistance was provided by Lorez Qehaja, Arika Kayastha, and Jinxin Wu.

[1] For the links between informality and economic development, see, for instance, Fields (1975), Harris and Todaro (1970), and Loayza (2016). Ulyssea (2020) provides a recent review on informality, its causes, and its consequences for development.

[2] Past studies, such as Dabla-Norris, Gradstein, and Inchauste (2008), Joshi, Prichard, and Heady (2014), and Ordóñez (2014), showed the links between informality and taxation. World Bank (2019) further demonstrated the implication of informality on tax revenue composition.

FIGURE 4.1 Development challenges and informality

EMDEs with more pervasive informality face severe development challenges, ranging from extreme poverty to lack of public infrastructure, and lag behind in progress toward the SDGs.

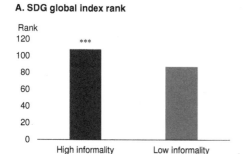

A. SDG global index rank

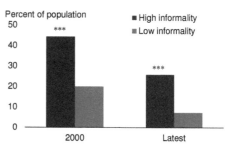

B. Extreme poverty headcount

Sources: Sachs et al. (2020); World Bank (World Development Indicators).

Note: "High informality" ("Low informality") are EMDEs with an above-median (below-median) DGE-based informal output measure over the period 1990-2018. DGE = dynamic general equilibrium model estimates in percent of GDP; EMDEs = emerging market and developing economies; SDGs = Sustainable Development Goals. Results are robust to regressions using quartile dummies (table 4D.14). Based on 132 EMDEs (A) or 155 EMDEs (B). *** indicates that group differences are significant at the 10 percent level.

A. Bars show group averages for the latest year available (that is, 2020). SDG global index rank provides the economy's rank regarding SDG achievement, with a high value suggesting lack of SDG achievement.

B. Bars show group averages for EMDEs with "high informality" and "low informality" in 2000 and the latest year available. Poverty headcount ratio at $1.90 a day is the percentage of the population living on less than $1.90 a day at 2011 international prices.

EMDEs with widespread informality score particularly poorly on indicators of development. Many development outcomes are captured and quantified in measures of progress toward the Sustainable Development Goals (SDGs). There are 17 SDGs, each with multiple underlying targets and associated data indicators, to be achieved by 2030. They add specificity to the broad objectives of ending poverty, protecting the planet, and ensuring shared prosperity (Vorisek and Yu 2020). They were adopted in 2015 as a key component of the 2030 Agenda for Sustainable Development. They include goals related to human development, such as an end to poverty, zero hunger, reduced inequality, high-quality education, and good health care services, and also infrastructure-related goals, such as access to clean water, sanitation, and affordable clean energy. Despite recent improvements, progress toward the SDGs has been uneven.

In 2020, EMDEs with above-median informality, on average, ranked about 110 out of 166 in overall SDG achievement, which is significantly worse than EMDEs with below-median informality (figure 4.1).[3] In 2018, 26 percent of the population of EMDEs with above-median informality lived in extreme poverty, much more than the 7 percent of the population in EMDEs with below-median informality. In countries with greater informality, income inequality was higher, in part reflecting the wage gap between

---

[3] Unless otherwise specified, informality refers to estimates of informal output based on dynamic general equilibrium (DGE) modeling in percent of official GDP. Results pertaining to employment informality, proxied by self-employment in percent of total employment, are shown in table 4D.12 and table 4D.15.

formal and informal workers and less progressive tax policies (box 4.1; Chong and Gradstein 2007; World Bank 2019).

It would take substantial additional financial resources to meet the SDGs by 2030, even if those resources were accompanied by big strides in policy improvements (UN SDSN 2019; Vorisek and Yu 2020). The World Bank estimates that low- and middle-income countries face additional investment needs of $1.5 trillion-2.7 trillion per year between 2015 and 2030 to meet infrastructure-related SDGs alone (Rozenberg and Fay 2019). The International Monetary Fund estimates that additional spending of about $1.3 trillion per year during 2019-30 is required to make meaningful progress toward infrastructure-related SDGs in EMDEs, and another $1.3 trillion for SDGs related to human development (Gaspar et al. 2019). The United Nations estimates that an additional $400 billion per year is needed in lower-income developing countries between 2019 and 2030, mainly for social protection, health, education, and climate change mitigation and adaptation (UN SDSN 2019).

Against this backdrop, this chapter addresses the following questions:

• What are the development challenges associated with the informal economy?

• What are the correlates of widespread informality?

• What are the correlates of changes in the informal sector over time?

Contributions. The chapter makes the following contributions to the literature on informality. First, it provides a systematic and comprehensive overview of developmental challenges facing countries with large informal sectors, highlighting their association with a wide range of development weaknesses and shortfalls from the SDGs.[4] Previous studies have focused on the economic or institutional correlates of informality—such as per capita income (for instance, La Porta and Shleifer 2014; Loayza, Servén, and Sugawara 2010) or control of corruption (for instance, Choi and Thum 2005; Dreher and Schneider 2010)—and largely disregarded the linkages between informality and other aspects of sustainable development, ranging from life expectancy to lack of access to public infrastructure.

Second, the chapter is the first published study to empirically and systematically examine a broad range of correlates of informality in a large group of EMDEs, numbering about 130. Previous studies have tended to focus on one dimension of informality, rely on a more limited range of correlates, and examine only the correlates of cross-country differences in informality without focusing on EMDEs. To identify the robust correlates of informality, the chapter is also the first to use a Bayesian model averaging (BMA)

---

[4] Several studies, such as Medina and Schneider (2018), Oviedo, Thomas, and Karakurum-Özdemir (2009), and Schneider, Buehn, and Montenegro (2010), provide surveys on various correlates of inforamlity, including development weaknesses.

BOX 4.1 Informality and wage inequality

An extensive literature has documented the wage penalty for workers in the informal economy compared to their peers in the formal economy. Estimates of this penalty, however, vary substantially across countries. A comprehensive review of the relevant empirical studies suggests that the wage penalty largely reflects the characteristics of workers who self-select into informal activities.

Worldwide, 2 billion people, or more than 60 percent of all workers aged 15 and over, have informal jobs (ILO 2018a). Informality is often associated with lower wages than the formal sector. If these lower wages reflect a wage penalty for informality that is independent of worker characteristics, policies that encourage the movement of workers to the formal sector might be a powerful remedy for income inequality and poverty. If, however, the wage differential largely reflects the characteristics of the workers employed in the informal sector, moving workers to the formal sector would be unlikely to achieve such gains.

Persistent informality frequently overlaps with poverty because many working poor remain employed in the informal sector (ILO 2018b; box 4.3). Lower wages in the informal sector can result from different worker characteristics, possibly reflecting comparative advantage, or reflect nonwage benefits that might accrue to work in the informal sector (Heckman and Li 2003; Maloney 2004). Wage differences may also reflect subjective well-being or job satisfaction of workers in the formal and informal sectors, with informal jobs offering more flexibility and independence (see, for example, Blanchflower, Oswald, and Stutzer 2001; Falco et al. 2011; Sanfey and Teksoz 2007). Alternatively, wage differentials could stem from rigidities and other factors that create a wedge in wages between similar workers in informal and formal employment (Harris and Todaro 1970).

This box sifts through a large body of empirical evidence on informal wage differentials to explore the following questions:

• What factors can create wage differentials between formal and informal sectors?

• How large is the wage gap between formal and informal jobs?

• What accounts for the wage gap between formal and informal jobs?

A comprehensive review of empirical models, identification strategies, estimation methods, and data sources delivers mixed results. Some studies detect a substantial formal wage premium over informal employment; other estimates, however, do not find a significant wage gap after controlling for individual and firm-specific characteristics. In light of these different findings, a meta-regression

Note: This box was prepared by Sergiy Kasyanenko.

BOX 4.1 Informality and wage inequality *(continued)*

analysis (MRA) is used to aggregate multistudy estimates of the formal wage premium and obtain a quantitative assessment of the sources of cross-study variation in research outcomes.

Causes of wage differentials

Wage differentials between formal and informal employment reflect a confluence of worker-, job- and country-specific characteristics. Broadly speaking, differentials can reflect inefficiencies caused by labor market frictions or self-selection of workers into their most productive employment—with diametrically opposed policy implications.

Segmented labor markets. Lower informal wages may result from workers being rationed out of better-paying formal jobs. For example, García and Badillo (2018) find that formal job rationing may affect over 60 percent of the workers in the informal sector of Colombia. Rigidities in the formal job market induced by, for example, labor regulations, unions, tax laws, and labor regulations or efficiency wages may restrict competitive access to formal jobs. This creates a wedge in wages between formal and informal employment for workers of equal productivity (Harris and Todaro 1970). Formal wage premiums may also reflect better job matches in formal activities, particularly in denser and larger urban areas (Matano, Obaco, and Royuela 2020).

Self-selection into informal employment. A wage differential can also arise because of worker preferences. Workers may self-select into informal employment, either because of desirable nonwage benefits or amenities attached to informal jobs or because they have a comparative advantage—that is typically unobserved in research studies—in informal sector activities (Heckman and Li 2003; Maloney 2004). A worker may stay at a lower-paying informal job simply because the opportunity cost of forgone wages in the formal sector does not offset nonmonetary benefits of informal employment, such as greater autonomy and more flexible working hours relative to a formal, salaried job.

Characteristics of informal workers. In emerging market and developing economies (EMDEs), self-employed workers constitute the core of informal employment; they typically lack registration at the national level, do not contribute to social security, and are not entitled to paid annual or sick leave.[a] However, not all informal workers are self-employed, and the informal sector itself may be divided into tiers such as informal self-employed entrepreneurs or

---

a. According to ILO (2018b), nearly 90 percent of all own-account workers—the largest component of self-employed in EMDEs—are in the informal sector, accounting for over 45 percent of all informal jobs.

BOX 4.1 Informality and wage inequality *(continued)*

professional workers and informal nonprofessional employees.[b] In EMDEs, about half of informal workers are nonprofessional self-employed workers—who migrate to formal employment as per capita incomes grow—and the majority of the remainder are informal employees (Gindling, Mossaad, and Newhouse 2016). Depending on the restrictiveness of regulations and the quality of education systems, the composition of informal employment varies across countries and EMDE regions. For example, contributing family members (predominantly women) and the self-employed are the majority of informal workers in developing Asia and Africa, where public education systems can be rudimentary, whereas informal employees and employers dominate the informal sector in Europe and Central Asia and in Latin America where tax and business regulations can be burdensome (ILO 2018b).

Interpreting the literature

Selection of studies. The representative sample of studies on informality and wage inequality used here follows the selection guidelines in Stanley et al. (2013) and is broadly similar to criteria applied by van der Sluis, van Praag, and Vijverberg (2005). An initial search was conducted in the major English language repositories of academic articles and working papers.[c] A study was included in the database if it (1) provided a quantitative estimate of the informal-formal wage gap and a corresponding standard error or t-statistic; (2) used data from micro-level household or labor surveys to obtain these estimates; (3) analyzed an EMDE or group of EMDEs as defined by the World Bank classification; and (4) was published no earlier than 1990.[d] The resulting database included 18 studies with a total of 83 individual coefficient estimates covering 20 EMDEs (annex 4A, table 4D.1).

Definitions matter. Differences in estimates of the incidence of informal employment and the wage differentials between formal and informal workers in part reflect differences in data coverage and definitions of informal workers (see Hussmanns 2004; ILO 2013; Perry et al. 2007). Studies typically find that self-employed informal workers earn the same or more than formal workers, but employed informal workers earn less than formal workers (figure B4.1.1; Abraham

---

b. Several studies challeng the assumption that the informal sector is homogenous (Cunningham and Maloney 2001; Fields 1990, 2005). There are also empirical evidences for the existence of both competitive and segmented employment in the informal sectort (for instance, Günther and Launov 2006).

c. Covered online databases include EBSCO, EconLit, Google Scholar, JSTOR, International Monetary Fund Working Paper series, IZA Working Papers, the National Bureau of Economic Research (NBER), RePEc, Social Science Research Network (SSRN), and World Bank Policy Research Working Paper series.

d. Before 1990, reliable and comparable individual or household level survey data, used to estimate wage gaps between the formal and informal sectors, are very limited for developing countries.

BOX 4.1 Informality and wage inequality _(continued)_

2019).[e] In EMDEs with more restrictive business regulations, however, self-employment may be associated with a higher wage penalty because less favorable business climates may deter more productive workers, particularly women, from transitioning to nonprofessional self-employment (Gindling, Mossaad, and Newhouse 2020).

Methodology matters. Empirical research on the wage differential between informal and formal workers has largely relied on estimating "Mincerian" wage regressions conditional on the observed characteristics of workers, although more recent studies have used quantile regressions to assess sector wage gaps along the wage distribution.[f] Such cross-sectional wage regressions are biased when workers' unobserved characteristics affect both their occupational choice and wages. For example, several studies find workers transitioning from the formal sector into the informal sector after spending several years accumulating experience and knowledge in the formal sector (Gong, van Soest, and Villagomez 2004; Maloney 2004). Hence, studies that rely on panel data to control for time-invariant unobserved worker characteristics find smaller informal-formal wage differentials.[g] Similarly, semiparametric matching models, such as propensity score matching and difference-in-difference estimators that are immune to the misspecification of the wage regressions, find modest or insignificant wage differentials between formal and informal jobs (Pratap and Quintin 2006).

Empirical estimates of wage differentials

Wage differentials. The estimates of the wage differential between informal and formal workers in the 18 studies selected here range from a formal sector wage penalty of 50 percent in Tajikistan (Huber and Rahimov 2014) to a formal sector wage premium of 113 percent in South Africa (El Badaoui, Strobl, and Walsh 2008) with a median formal wage premium of about 18 percent.[h] On average,

---

e. Arias and Khamis (2008) find no significant differences between the earnings of formal salaried workers and the self-employed, while informal salaried employment carries significant earnings penalties. Similar results are shown in Kahyalar et al. (2018), Lehmann and Pignatti (2007), Maloney (1999), and Nguye, Nordman, and Roubaud (2013).

f. Quantile estimations are conducted in studies, such as Bargain and Kwenda (2014), Lehmann and Zaiceva (2013), and Tansel and Kan (2012), to gauge the wage gap along the wage distribution.

g. Smaller wage gaps between formal and informal workers are found in studies, such as Botelho and Ponczek (2011), Cho and Cho (2011), El Badaoui, Strobl, and Walsh (2008), Tansel, Keskin, and Ozdemir (2020), where time-invariant unobserved worker characteristics are controlled for in a panel setting.

h. A formal-sector wage premium indicates that formal-sector wages exceed those in the informal sector, whereas a formal sector wage penalty indicates formal-sector wages are below informal-sector wages. Huber and Rahimov (2014) attribute a large formal wage penalty in Tajikistan to self-selection and find no evidence of labor market segmentation. Meanwhile, El Badaoui, Strobl, and Walsh (2008) find that a formal wage premium in South Africa disappears once they controlled for unobserved worker characteristics.

BOX 4.1 **Informality and wage inequality** *(continued)*

FIGURE B4.1.1 **EMDEs: Estimates of informal-formal wage gaps**

Estimates of informal-formal wage gaps vary considerably across countries and definitions of informality. Countries in Latin America and the Caribbean and Sub-Saharan Africa tend to exhibit both a higher incidence of informality and a larger wage premium in the formal sector.

A. EMDEs: Informal-formal wage gaps

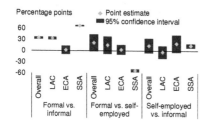

B. Informal-formal wage gaps: Meta-analysis

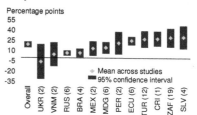

C. Informal-formal wage gaps

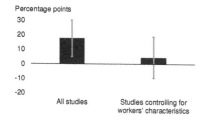

D. Informal-formal wage gap and income inequality by EMDE region

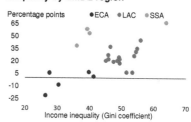

Sources: Gindling, Mossaad, and Newhouse (2016); World Bank.

Note: A positive wage gap indicates a penalty for working informally—a lower wage for informal workers than for comparable formal workers. A negative wage gap indicates a premium for working informally—a higher wage for informal workers than for comparable formal workers. Wage gap between wage employees in the informal and formal sectors is displayed on the vertical axis. EAP = East Asia and Pacific; ECA = Europe and Central Asia; EMDE = emerging market and developing economy; LAC = Latin America and the Caribbean; MNA = Middle East and North Africa; SAR = South Asia; SSA = Sub-Saharan Africa.

A. Formal vs. informal = a wage gap between wage employees in the formal and informal sectors; Formal vs. self-employed = a wage gap between workers with formal jobs and self-employed workers; Self-employed vs. informal = a wage gap between self-employed workers and wage employees in the informal sector.

B. BRA = Brazil; CRI = Costa Rica; ECU = Ecuador; MDG = Madagascar; MEX = Mexico; PER = Peru; RUS = Russian Federation; SLV = El Salvador; TUR = Turkey; UKR = Ukraine; VNM = Vietnam; ZAF = South Africa. The number of studies or estimates for each economy is shown in parenthesis; economy means are calculated using a random-effects meta-analysis model.

C. The wage premium (shown in bars) is obtained from 18 empirical studies of the wage gap between formal and informal workers. The whiskers show the 90 percent confidence intervals. See box 4.1 for details.

D. Income inequality is measured as Gini coefficient provided by the World Bank's World Development Indicators.

BOX 4.1 Informality and wage inequality (continued)

the random-effects meta-analysis estimate of the wage premium in the formal sector obtained from pooling all studies is 19 percent (figure B4.1.1 and table 4D.2).[i]

Explaining wage differentials. The wage premium largely disappears in studies using worker fixed effects, which are controlling for unobserved characteristics of workers.[j] It turns into a statistically insignificant 8 percent penalty in studies that compared wages of self-employed informal workers with formal-sector employees.[k] Informal employment tends to be associated with low levels of education and a U-shaped age profile and is more prevalent in rural areas, where there are fewer job alternatives in the formal sector (Gasparini and Tornarolli 2007; Hazans 2011).[l] In general, low productivity attributes of workers in the informal sector may limit their earnings potential in comparable formal jobs.

Country characteristics. Even after controlling for study and sample-specific attributes, most of the cross-study variation in the estimates of the wage differential remains unexplained. That said, wage premiums tend to be higher where informality is more widespread (figure B4.1.1). Differentials are particularly wide in Latin America and the Caribbean and Sub-Saharan Africa but are below average in Europe and Central Asia and South Asia (figure B4.1.1). Overall, the data do not offer strong evidence of a significant relationship between the size of the formal sector wage premium and the level of development or the quality of institutions.

Conclusion

Despite years of declining poverty, many working poor remain employed in the informal sector where they face significantly lower wages than workers in the formal economy. Estimates of the formal sector wage premium vary widely but, in the meta-analysis of the 18 studies conducted here, amount to just under 20 percent of informal wages. However, among studies controlling for worker characteristics, there is no statistically significant evidence of a formal sector wage premium.

---

i. See annex 4A for technical details.

j. In the regression in annex 4A, the informal-formal wage gap for studies using fixed worker effects is estimated as the sum of the coefficients for μ and *FE*, tested for joint significance: the test statistic $F(1,76) = 0.41$ indicates that the null hypothesis of a zero sum of two coefficients cannot be rejected at any conventional significance level.

k. In the regression in annex 4A, the wage premium for self-employed is estimated as the sum of the coefficients for μ and *Self-employed*, tested for joint significance: the test statistic $F(1,76) = 0.33$ indicates that the null hypothesis of a zero sum of two coefficients cannot be rejected at any conventional significance level.

l. Younger and older workers are typically less productive, whereas older retired workers may be choosing informal employment to supplement their social security benefits.

BOX 4.1 Informality and wage inequality *(continued)*

This suggests that any formal-informal wage differential is largely a reflection of the characteristics of the types of workers who self-select into informal and formal employment. Workers in the informal sector tend to be less-skilled, younger or older, and more agricultural than workers in the formal sector. This points to the need for policies to lift these workers' human capital and, thus, allow them to switch into productive formal employment.

---

approach, which is designed to take account of model uncertainty (Fernandez, Ley, and Steel 2001).

Third, in three boxes, this chapter illustrates how informality can pose developmental challenges to EMDEs. Box 4.1 conducts the first extensive meta-analysis of studies that document wage differences for workers in formal and informal sectors. Box 4.2 utilizes a unique firm-level data set to show how the productivity gap between formal and informal firms in EMDEs can be narrowed by improvements in business climates.[5] Box 4.3 empirically tests whether there is a strong relationship between declines in informality and poverty reduction (or income inequality).

Main findings. The chapter demonstrates that EMDEs with pervasive informality face a wider range of greater development challenges than other EMDEs. First, informality is associated with poor economic outcomes. Countries with larger informal sectors have lower per capita incomes, greater poverty, less financial development, and weaker growth in output, investment and productivity. Informal firms are less productive than their formal counterparts (box 4.2).

Second, more pervasive informality is associated with significantly lower government revenues and expenditures, less effective policy institutions, more burdensome tax and regulatory regimes, and weaker governance. Weaknesses in governance and revenue collection constrain the provision of public services in EMDEs with more pervasive informality, contributing to poorer human development outcomes. People living in EMDEs with more widespread informality suffer from a greater prevalence of hunger, poorer health and education, and greater gender inequality. Countries with more widespread informality offer poorer access to, and lower-quality, infrastructure.

Third, the results from the BMA approach suggest that economic development, human capital, and governance are particularly robust correlates of informality. That said, other correlates such as infrastructure, for instance, are also relevant.

---

[5] Existing studies, such as Meghir, Narita, and Robin (2015) and Ulyssea (2018), explore the productivity gap between formal and informal firms in individual countries.

Fourth, although informality is linked to a host of developmental challenges, formalization alone is unlikely to offer an effective path out of underdevelopment. For instance, although declines in informality were associated with poverty reduction, they were not systematically linked to declining income inequality (box 4.3). This may reflect the fact that informality itself is a symptom of underdevelopment, in line with the meta-analysis of the literature that finds that the wage penalty largely reflects the characteristics of informal workers (box 4.1).

The following section summarizes the transmission mechanisms underlying the link between informality and development challenges. Here informality is regarded as both a cause and a consequence of underdevelopment: there are reasons to expect causation potentially to run in both directions. The subsequent sections examine the economic and institutional correlates of informality, followed by sections that describe the link between informality and various SDGs. The penultimate section summarizes the finding of the BMA approach, followed by a conclusion in the final section.

Links between informality and development challenges

EMDEs with widespread informality face relatively large development challenges. Informality may be linked with these challenges through several channels. For the purposes of the discussion here, informality refers to output informality, but the results are robust to using employment informality.

Low productivity, low incomes. Informal workers tend to be less skilled and lower paid than their formal counterparts (Loayza 2018; Perry et al. 2007; World Bank 2019). A meta-analysis of worker-level empirical studies shows that informal workers are, on average, paid 19 percent less than formal workers (figure 4.2; World Bank 2019). In part, this reflects lower productivity on account of lower skill and experience levels than formal workers have. The meta-analysis suggests that, when controlling for worker characteristics, the wage gap is no longer statistically significant (box 4.1).[6] In 2020, these features made participants in the informal sector particularly vulnerable during lockdowns associated with the COVID-19 pandemic (World Bank 2020a; box 2.1).

Similarly, informal firms tend to be small, lack funds, and operate in labor-intensive sectors, and, as a result, are less productive than formal firms (figure 4.2; Fajnzylber, Maloney, and Montes-Rojas 2011; Farazi 2014; McKenzie and Sakho 2010). They tend to invest less, possibly in an effort to avoid adopting technologies that would make them more visible to tax and other authorities (Dabla-Norris, Gradstein, and Inchauste 2008; Gandelman and Rasteletti 2017). For example, in about 11,600 firms that participated in Enterprise Surveys in 18 economies during 2007-14, the fraction of formal firms that

---

[6] This lower productivity may also account for the inability of the formal sector in cities to absorb rural migrants during the urbanization process (Fields 1975; Harris and Todaro 1970; Loayza 2016).

FIGURE 4.2 **Features of informal firms and workers**

Informal workers tend to be less well-paid and employed in the agricultural or services sectors. Informal firms are less productive than their formal-sector peers.

A. Wage premium for formal employment over informal employment

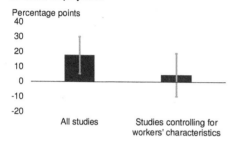

B. Labor productivity differential between firms in formal and informal sectors

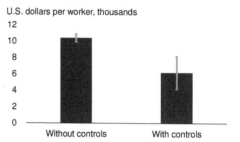

C. Sectoral distribution of informal firms

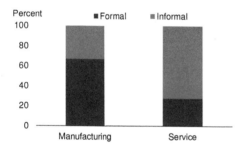

D. Agricultural sector and informality

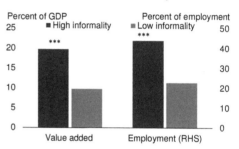

Sources: Amin, Ohnsorge, and Okou (2019); World Bank (Enterprise Surveys, World Development Indicators); World Bank.
A. The wage premium (shown in bars) is obtained from 18 empirical studies of the wage gap between formal and informal workers. The whiskers show the 90 percent confidence intervals. See box 4.1 for details.
B. Difference between labor productivity of formal and informal firms, without controlling for firm characteristics and with controlling for firm characteristics. Firm productivity is measured as sales per worker in 2009 U.S. dollars. Whiskers show the corresponding +/- 2 standard errors.
C. See Amin, Ohnsorge, and Okou (2019) for data coverage.
D. Bars are group means from the latest year available calculated for EMDEs with "high informality" (that is, above-median DGE-based informal output in percent of GDP) and those with "low informality" (EMDEs with below-median DGE-based informal output measure) over the period 1990-2018. DGE = dynamic general equilibrium model-based estimates; EMDEs = emerging market and developing economies; RHS = right-hand side. *** indicates group differences are not zero at 10 percent significance level.

invested was significantly higher than that of informal firms. Low productivity in the informal sector can also cast a shadow over formal firms: a sizeable informal sector that competes with the formal sector for low-skilled workers reduces the incentives to invest in human and physical capital and new technologies and slows growth in the long run (box 4.2; Amin, Ohnsorge, and Okou 2019; Distinguin, Rugemintwari, and Tacneng 2016; Docquier, Müller, and Naval 2017; Loayza 1996; Perry et al. 2007; Sarte 2000).

Sectoral distribution. Informal workers in EMDEs tend to be concentrated in the agricultural and services sectors (figure 4.2). Agricultural employment in EMDEs is about 90 percent informal. In EMDEs with above-median informality, the agricultural sector, on average, accounts for about 20 percent of GDP and for nearly 40 percent

BOX 4.2 Casting a shadow: Productivity in formal and informal firms

Labor productivity in the average informal firm in emerging market and developing economies (EMDEs) is only one-quarter of that of the average firm operating in the formal sector. Moreover, firms in the formal sector that face informal competition are, on average, only three-quarters as productive as those that do not. This suggests that competition from the informal sector can erode formal firms' market share and resources available to boost productivity as they shoulder the costs of regulatory compliance. More effective governance and stronger control of corruption can help mitigate these effects.

Introduction

The differential in labor productivity between formal and informal firms is well established in the literature (Loayza and Rigolini 2006; Oviedo 2009). However, there is mixed evidence on the impact of a large informal sector on formal firms' labor productivity.[a] Some studies suggest that the informal and formal sectors operate independently so that there are no productivity spillovers (La Porta and Shleifer 2014). Others report that competition from the informal sector may erode the profitability of firms in the formal sector, limiting their resources to enhance firm productivity. The aggregate effect varies with country characteristics (Amin and Okou 2020).

Against this backdrop, this box documents the productivity gap between formal and informal firms and their interactions. Specifically, it addresses the following questions:

- How large is the differential in labor productivity between formal and informal firms?

- To what extent are formal firms exposed to informal competition?

- How does informal competition affect the labor productivity of formal firms?

Productivity differential between formal and informal firms

Literature review. The literature documents that informal firms in EMDEs are less productive than formal firms, with labor productivity gaps ranging between 30 and 216 percent (La Porta and Shleifer 2008; Perry et al. 2007). The

---

Note: This box was prepared by Mohammad Amin and Cedric Okou. The box closely follows box 3.3 in the January 2019 *Global Economic Prospects* report.

a. Gonzalez and Lamanna (2007) show that formal firms affected by head-to-head competition with informal firms largely resemble them. Heredia et al. (2017) find a negative effect on the innovation performance of formal companies from the competition with informal firms. Mendi and Costamagna (2017) find an inverted-U relationship between propensity to innovate and competitive pressure from firms in the informal sector.

BOX 4.2 Casting a shadow: Productivity in formal and informal firms (continued)

productivity gap between informal and formal firms is attributed to more backward technologies in informal firms, their greater reliance on unskilled labor, their more limited economies of scale, and their more restricted access to services, markets, and funding.[b] Labor productivity has also been found to vary within the informal sector along different dimensions such as firm size and type of activity (Amin and Huang 2014; Amin and Islam 2015).

Methodology. In this box, the labor productivity gap between formal and informal firms is estimated using the World Bank's Enterprise Surveys data collected over the period 2007-14 for a cross-section of 4,036 informal firms and 7,558 formal firms in 18 EMDEs. Formal firms are those that register with the relevant authorities; unregistered firms belong to the informal sector. To estimate the productivity gap, a measure of labor productivity—log annual sales in 2009 U.S. dollars per worker—is regressed on a dummy variable that takes the value 1 for informal firms and 0 otherwise and a set of control variables capturing additional firm characteristics (employment size, time in business, location, sector, economy).[c]

Lower productivity in informal than formal firms. Virtually across the board, firm-level labor productivity is much lower in the informal sector than in the formal sector (table 4D.3).[d] The productivity differentials vary widely in this sample, from 48 (Côte d'Ivoire) to 93 percent (Argentina). On average across the whole sample, labor productivity in informal firms is only one-quarter of labor productivity in formal firms.

Drivers of productivity gap between informal and formal firms. Firm size, age, location in the capital city, and manager experience are associated with significantly larger productivity gaps between informal and formal sectors (figure B4.2.1; table 4D.4). Formal firms appear to be better equipped to reap productivity benefits from large size, advanced age, and urban location than informal firms.

- *Firm age.* As firms grow older, either they are sufficiently productive to survive or they disappear ("selection effect"; Brandt, Van Biesenbroeck, and Zhang 2012). In addition, learning from experience may have taught older firms lessons that deliver productivity gains ("learning effect"; Luttmer

---

b. The contributing factors to the productivity gap between informal and formal firms are found in studies, such as Amaral and Quintin (2006), Galiani and Weinschelbaum(2012), and Jovanovic (1982).

c. Commonly used revenue-based measures of productivity may conflate efficiency and price effects. Disentangling these effects, by using physical productivity measures, may shed new light on productivity patterns, especially at the firm level (Cusolito and Maloney 2018; Jones and Nordhaus 2008).

d. Exceptions are Cabo Verde and the Democratic Republic of Congo, possibly because of low productivity of formal firms.

BOX 4.2 Casting a shadow: Productivity in formal and informal firms *(continued)*

FIGURE B4.2.1 Labor productivity in informal firms

In EMDEs, labor productivity is significantly higher in informal firms that have managers with higher education and in those without any employees other than the owner. This labor productivity differential between formal and informal firms is particularly pronounced among larger and older firms that operate in the capital city and are led by experienced managers.

A. Labor productivity differential between different types of informal firms

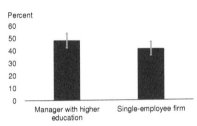

B. Average labor productivity differential between formal and informal firms

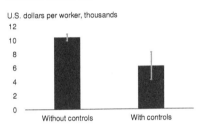

C. Labor productivity differential between formal and informal firms: By firm age and size

D. Labor productivity differential between formal and informal firms: By firm location and manager experience

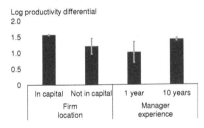

Source: World Bank.
Note: World Bank's Enterprise Surveys data for 135 countries (2008-18). Labor productivity is proxied by annual sales per worker in 2009 U.S. dollars. Whiskers show the corresponding +/- 2 standard errors.
A. Cross-country average of percent difference between labor productivity in the median informal firm with a manager with higher education or without any employees other than the owner, and the median informal firm with a manager without higher education or with more employees than the owner. Estimates from table 4D.3.
B. Difference between productivity of formal and informal firms, with and without controlling for other firm characteristics. Labor productivity in the average formal and average informal firm, controlling for firm characteristics (firm size and age, manufacturing sector activity, location in the capital city, and country fixed effects) as shown in column (1) in table 4D.4.
C.D. Difference in log of labor productivity between the average formal and average informal firm in each group, as estimated in coefficient estimates of table 4D.4. "Not in capital" stands for "not located in capital city"; "In capital" stands for "located in capital city."

BOX 4.2 Casting a shadow: Productivity in formal and informal firms (continued)

2007). These effects appear to be much more pronounced among formal firms than among informal firms. As a result, the productivity differential between formal and informal firms widens as the age of firms increases. Among 1-year-old firms, informal firms have about half the labor productivity of formal firms. Among 10-year-old firms, informal firms have less than one-quarter the labor productivity of formal firms.

- *Firm size.* Larger firms can reap economies of scale that raise their labor productivity compared to smaller firms. Again, in this sample, this effect appears to be stronger among formal firms than among informal firms. Among firms with 1 employee, informal firms have just under one-third the labor productivity of formal firms; among firms with 10 employees, informal firms have less than one-quarter the productivity of formal firms.

- *Firm location.* Capital cities are typically among countries' largest economic centers and so can offer agglomeration benefits, such as larger markets, better infrastructure to access markets and operate, a larger pool of workers, and greater technology spillovers (Duranton and Puga 2004; Rosenthal and Strange 2004). Again, formal firms appear to be better able to benefit from these locational advantages, though the difference is economically modest (although statistically significant). Among firms operating inside the capital city, informal firms' productivity is 31 percent that of similar formal firms; outside the capital city, informal firms' productivity is 30 percent that of similar formal firms.

- *Manager experience.* Managerial ability has been associated with higher labor productivity, through a variety of channels including hiring decisions and input choices (Fernandes 2008). Again, managerial experience appears to benefit formal firms' productivity more than informal firms' productivity. Among firms managed by managers with 1 year of experience, informal firms' labor productivity is just over one-third that of formal firms; among firms with managers with 10 years of experience, informal firms' labor productivity is less than one-quarter that of formal firms.

Productivity differentials across informal firms. Labor productivity also differs across different types of informal firms, although the characteristics that are associated with higher labor productivity in informal firms differ across countries.[e] In two-fifths of economies, informal firms having a manager with

---

e. Past studies on the productivy differentials across informal firms include Amin and Huang (2014), Amin and Islam (2015), de Mel, McKenzie, and Woodruff (2011), Deininger, Jin, and Sur (2007), Grimm, Knorringa, and Lay (2012), Haltiwanger, Lane, and Spletzer (1999), Islam (2018), and Maloney (2004).

BOX 4.2 Casting a shadow: Productivity in formal and informal firms (continued)

higher education or without any employees other than the owner are significantly more productive than other informal firms (column (1) in table 4D.4). Other informal firm characteristics, such as operating in the services sector or being a start-up, are accompanied by higher productivity in some countries but lower productivity in others.

Robustness tests. Labor productivity differentials between formal and informal firms remain significant when each control variable is included separately. They are also robust to including interaction terms of informality with firm characteristics that make "hiding" revenue more difficult, such as firm size, exporter status, location in the capital city or having reported fixed asset purchases (Amin and Okou 2020).

Productivity of formal firms amid high informality

Impact of informal competition on formal firms. The extent of competition between formal and informal firms depends partly on the reasons for the existence of the informal firms (Amin and Okou 2020). [f]

- *Informality as a survival strategy of unproductive firms.* Low-productivity firms may be forced into informal operations or, if they continue to operate formally, into employing informal workers because this may reduce their costs (Boly 2018; Ulyssea 2018). Operating in the informal sector or employing informal labor may, therefore, be a survival strategy for less-productive firms. "Surviving" informal firms are likely to operate in very different markets and sell different products than formal firms (La Porta and Shleifer 2014). Competition between informal and formal firms and its impact on formal firms may then be limited.

- *Informality as an evasion strategy of productive firms.* Some informal firms may be sufficiently productive to survive in the formal sector yet choose to remain informal to benefit from the cost advantages of noncompliance with (possibly excessive) taxes and regulations (de Mel, McKenzie, and Woodruff 2011; Maloney 2004). [g] Such informal firms could have untapped potential

---

f. This discussion assumes that firms are either formal or informal. In practice, the degree of informality can vary (Perry et al. 2007; Ulyssea 2018). Firms can operate fully informally, both in product markets and labor markets ("extensive margin). They sell their output informally and employ informal labor. Or firms can operate semiformally ("intensive margin"): they sell their output into formal product markets but employ, in part, informal labor, as observed in EMDEs and low-income countries.

g. Such circumstances are likely to be associated with an environment of weak regulatory and tax enforcement (Benjamin and Mbaye 2012; Dabla-Norris, Gradstein, and Inchauste 2008; Quintin 2008; Ulyssea 2010).

BOX 4.2 Casting a shadow: Productivity in formal and informal firms (continued)

for a productivity boost (de Soto 1989). At the same time, they can create aggressive competition with formal firms that do shoulder the additional cost of tax and regulatory compliance. Credit constraints tend to be higher for formal firms in sectors that host many informal firms (Distinguin, Rugemintwari, and Tacneng 2016). Such informal competition can reduce the profitability necessary for formal firms to invest in productivity-enhancing new technologies or to innovate, especially in a context of weak property rights enforcement. [h] Alternatively, this very competition could force formal firms to increase productivity or, for the lowest-productivity ones, to exit. [i]

Extent of informal-firm competition for formal firms. In the World Bank's nationally representative survey data for 75,137 formal (registered) firms in 135 economies between 2008 and 2018, about 55 percent of formal firms reported facing competition from informal firms. [j] The share of informal firms competing against formal firms was about 60 percent in EMDEs, 13 percentage points higher than in advanced economies. The level of competition varied widely across economies, ranging from about 7 percent in Bhutan to 95 percent in Uganda. Smaller firms were significantly more likely to be exposed to informal competition than larger firms, but there is little evidence of any other systematic difference between firms that were exposed and those that were not (figure B4.2.2).

Impact of informal competition on the productivity of formal firms

Methodology. Ordinary least squares regressions are used to estimate the difference in labor productivity between formal firms that compete against informal firms and those that do not. In the baseline specification, the dependent variable is again labor productivity measured by the (log of) annual sales per worker in 2009 U.S. dollars. The main explanatory variable is the informal competition indicator proxied by the proportion of other formal firms in a

---

h. This has been documented for Latin America countries, and for India, Panama, Poland, Portugal, Russian Federation, and Turkey. For evidence, see Allen and Schipper (2016); Capp, Elstrodt, and Jones (2005); Distinguin, Rugemintwari, and Tacneng (2016); Farrell (2004); Friesen and Wacker (2013); Gonzalez and Lamanna (2007); Heredia et al. (2017); Iriyama, Kishore, Talukda (2016); Perry et al. (2007); and Vargas (2015).

i. This was documented for the Arab Republic of Egypt. See Ali and Najman (2017); Melitz (2003); and Schipper (2020).

j. In the World Bank's Enterprise Surveys, formal firms are asked the following question: "Does this establishment compete against unregistered or informal firms?"

BOX 4.2 Casting a shadow: Productivity in formal and informal firms (*continued*)

FIGURE B4.2.2 **Formal firms facing informal competition**

A larger share of formal firms in EMDEs—about three-fifths—reported facing informal competition in 2008-18 than in advanced economies—about half. The degree of informal competition reported by formal firms was higher for smaller than for larger firms.

A. Formal firms reporting competition from informal firms: By country group

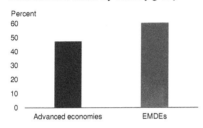

B. Formal firms reporting competition from informal firms: By firm size

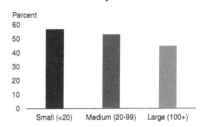

Source: World Bank (Enterprise Surveys).
Note: World Bank's Enterprise Surveys data for 135 economies (2008-18). Figures show the shares of formal firms. EMDEs = emerging market and developing economies.

subgroup that report facing competition from informal firms. Such a subgroup is defined as a group of firms of similar size and in the same region and sector.[k]

Productivity gap between formal firms with and without informal competition. Formal firms that face informal competition are, on average, 24 percent less productive than those that do not (figure B4.2.3; table 4D.5). After controlling for informal competition, formal firms in the manufacturing and retail industries have higher productivity than those in other services. Older, exporting, and foreign-owned formal firms also have higher productivity even if they face competition from informal firms.

Role of the business climate and development. Economic development and the business climate may substantially shape the productivity gap between formal

k. As a caveat, the informal competition faced by a specific firm may also be driven by its low productivity, thus generating endogeneity concerns. To address this possible endogeneity issue, the proportion of formal firms facing informal competition in a group of firms of similar size in the same region and sector (a "cell") is used rather than a firm dummy. A cell proportion should be much less correlated with the productivity of a specific firm, and therefore, should be more robust to endogeneity concerns.

BOX 4.2 Casting a shadow: Productivity in formal and informal firms (continued)

FIGURE B4.2.3 Labor productivity differential of formal firms with and without informal competition

On average, labor productivity in formal firms that face informal competition is only three-quarters of that of firms that do not face informal competition, after controlling for firm characteristics. Better business climates and governance and more advanced economic development can narrow this productivity differential.

A. Formal firms reporting competition from informal firms: By firm sector

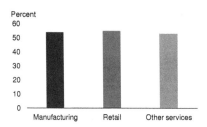

B. Labor productivity differential of formal firms with and without informal competition: By intensity

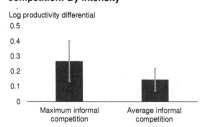

C. Labor productivity differential of formal firms with and without informal competition: By level of development

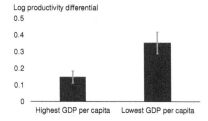

D. Labor productivity differential of formal firms with and without informal competition: By business climate indicator

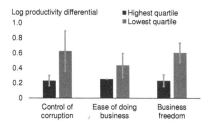

Sources: World Bank; World Bank (Enterprise Surveys).

A. Figures show the shares of formal firms.

B.-D. Based on coefficient estimates from table 4D.5. It shows the results from an ordinary least squares (OLS) regression with labor productivity as dependent variable, proxied by annual sales (in 2009 U.S. dollars) per worker. Sample of World Bank's Enterprise Surveys collected during 2007-14, including 4,036 informal firms and 7,558 formal firms in 18 countries. Whiskers show the corresponding +/- 2 standard errors.

B. Figure shows log productivity differential between formal firms facing informal competition and formal firms not facing informal competition. "Maximum informal competition" assumes that all firms in a cell face informal competition. "Average informal competition" assumes that 55 percent of firms in a cell face informal competition.

C.D. Figure shows log productivity differential between formal firms facing informal competition and formal firms not facing informal competition (conditional on development and institution). Assumes that 55 percent of firms in a cell face informal competition. Each bar shows average labor productivity of the median country in the top ("highest quartile") or bottom ("lowest quartile") quarter of countries in terms of GDP per capita (C), control of corruption (D), ease of doing business (D) or Business Freedom Index (D).

BOX 4.2 Casting a shadow: Productivity in formal and informal firms (continued)

firms that face informal competition and those that do not. This is captured in interaction terms between the share of similar formal firms reporting informal competition and indicators of development (the logarithm of per capita GDP), the quality of the business climate (proxied by the distance to the frontier in the World Bank *Doing Business* data set), the control of corruption as measured by the Worldwide Governance Indicators, and the Business Freedom Index of the Economic Freedom indicators (table 4D.5). Higher GDP per capita, better control of corruption, and a business environment that is freer and closer to best practices were all found to dampen the detrimental impact of informal competition on formal firm productivity (figure B4.2.3).

- *Development.* Two groups of economies in the sample were examined: those economies with per capita income in the highest quartile in the sample and those in the lowest quartile. In formal firms that face informal competition in the average economy in the highest quartile of per capita incomes, labor productivity is only 14 percentage points less than in formal firms that do not face such competition. In contrast, on average in economies in the lowest quartile of per capita incomes, labor productivity in formal firms facing informal competition is 30 percent less than in those firms that do not face such competition.

- *Control of corruption.* Again, two groups of economies were examined: those in the quartile of economies with the strongest control of corruption and those in the quartile with the weakest control of corruption. In economies with the strongest control of corruption, on average, labor productivity in formal firms that face informal competition is only 22 percentage points less than in formal firms that do not face such competition, whereas in the economies with the weakest control of corruption, this differential grows to 35 percent.

- *Ease of doing business.* Similarly, the labor productivity differential between formal firms that face informal competition and those that do not might halve (to 21 percent) if an economy like Angola (in the quartile of economies with the most difficult business climates) were to improve its business climate to the level of an economy like North Macedonia (among the economies with the most conducive business climates).

Robustness tests. The impact of informal competition on formal firm productivity is robust to alternative specifications. In particular, it is robust to controlling for characteristics that make the underreporting of output difficult (Amin and Okou 2020).

BOX 4.2 Casting a shadow: Productivity in formal and informal firms (continued)

Conclusion

The productivity gap between informal and formal firms is substantial in EMDEs, averaging 75 percent in a sample of 18 EMDEs during 2007-14. Competition from informal firms also appears to weigh on the productivity of exposed formal firms: the productivity of formal firms that compete with informal firms is only three-quarters that of formal firms that do not compete with informal firms, after controlling for other firm characteristics. Improvements in the business climate, and economic development more broadly, can mitigate some of these negative productivity spillovers from informal to formal firms.

---

of total employment—almost twice as much as in EMDEs with below-median informality. In addition, informal firms tend to be smaller, less productive, and concentrated in labor-intensive sectors, such as low-value-added services. In EMDE service sectors, about 72 percent of firms are informal, compared with 33 percent in manufacturing (World Bank 2020a).[7] Large productivity gaps exist between manufacturing, agricultural, and service sectors in EMDEs (Dieppe 2020).

Access to resources. In EMDEs with widespread informality, access to finance and public resources is limited. Informal firms struggle to access conventional banks because of lack of property rights, lack of documentation for assets, and inadequate financial statements (Bose, Capasso, and Wurm 2012; de Soto 1989). In the World Bank's Enterprise Surveys for 2010-18, on average, more than one-third of firms in EMDEs with above-median informality identified access to finance as a major constraint—9 percentage points higher than the average for EMDEs with below-median informality—and a need to resort to internal finance to fund investment (figure 4.3). On average, three out of four firms in EMDEs with above-median informality depend on internal finance for investment, and only one out of five firms can utilize bank funds to finance its investment needs. Poor access to public services and markets also discourages entrepreneurs from entering the formal sector (Oviedo, Thomas, and Karakurum-Özdemir 2009). In EMDEs with above-median employment informality, support for small and medium enterprises (SMEs), such as access to business infrastructure and physical infrastructure, is significantly poorer than in EMDEs with below-median employment informality.[8]

---

[7] As these economies grow richer, households tend to shift away from agricultural and informal sector goods (Saracoğlu 2008).

[8] Business infrastructure refers to the presence of property rights, commercial, accounting, and other legal and assessment services and institutions that support or promote SMEs.

FIGURE 4.3 **Access to finance and public services**

In EMDEs with more pervasive informality, access to external finance and public services is more limited, constraining productivity and entrepreneurship.

A. Firms' financing conditions and informality

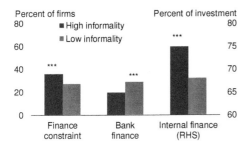

B. Financial development and informality

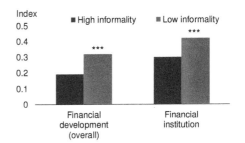

C. Household access to finance and informality

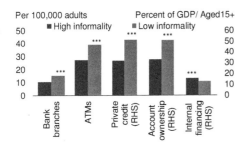

D. Entrepreneurial framework conditions and informality

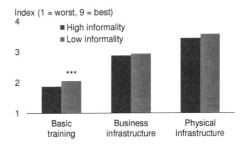

Sources: International Monetary Fund (Financial Development Index Database); World Bank (Enterprise Surveys, Global Financial Development Database, World Development Indicators).
Note: "High informality" ("Low informality") are emerging market and developing economies (EMDEs) with above-median (below-median) dynamic general equilibrium-based informal output measures. RHS = right-hand side. *** indicates group differences are not zero at 10 percent significance level.
A. Bars are group means for EMDEs over the period 2000-18. "Finance constraint" measures the percent of firms identifying access to finance as a major constraint. "Bank finance" measures the percent of firms using banks to finance investment. "Internal finance" measures the average proportion of investment financed internally.
B. Bars show simple averages for EMDEs over the period 2010-18. "Financial development (overall)" is the aggregate financial development index from the International Monetary Fund's Global Financial Development Database. It purports to measure the overall level of financial development, in both "financial institutions" and "financial markets." The latter refers to the accessibility, depth, and efficiency of an economy's stock and debt markets, which is less relevant for informal participants in EMDEs. The "Institutions" index measures how developed financial institutions are in terms of their depth (size and liquidity), accessibility (ability of individuals and companies to access financial services), and efficiency (ability of institutions to provide financial services at low cost and with sustainable revenues).
C. Bars are unweighted group averages for EMDEs over the period 2010-18. "Bank branches" measures the number of commercial bank branches per 100,000 adults. "ATMs" measures the number of automated teller machines (ATMs) per 100,000 adults. "Private credit" measures domestic credit to private sector in percent of GDP. "Account ownership" is the percentage of survey respondents (aged 15 and above) who report having an account (by themselves or together with someone else) at a bank or other financial institution, or report personally using a mobile money service in the past 12 months. "Internal financing" refers to the percentage of respondents (aged 15 and above) who report saving or setting aside any money in the past 12 months to start, operate, or expand a farm or business.
D. Bars are group means for EMDEs over the period 2000-18. The score is based on the Global Entrepreneurship Monitor's National Expert Survey. Ranging from 1 to 9, a higher score represents better perceived conditions. Basic training = extent to which training in creating or managing small and medium enterprises (SMEs) is incorporated within the education and training system at primary and secondary levels; Business infrastructure = presence of property rights that support or promote SMEs, including commercial, accounting, and other legal and assessment services and institutions; Physical infrastructure = ease of access to physical resources, communications, utilities, transportation, land, or space at a price that does not discriminate against SMEs. Outliers (Kuwait and Saudi Arabia) are not included.

FIGURE 4.4 **Access to social benefits**

Limited access to social protection programs makes informal workers more vulnerable during economic downturns.

A. Adequacy of social insurance programs

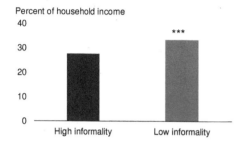

B. Coverage of unemployment benefits

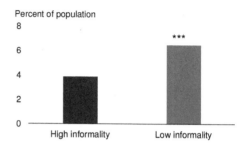

Source: World Bank (World Development Indicators).
A.B. Bars are group means calculated for emerging market and developing economies with "high informality" (above-median DGE-based informal output in percent of GDP) and those with "low informality" (with below-median DGE-based informal output measure) over the period 1990-2018. Adequacy of social insurance programs is measured in percent of total welfare of beneficiary households. *** indicates group differences are not zero at 10 percent significance level. DGE-based informal output is based on dynamic general equilibrium model estimates.

Social safety nets. In EMDEs, access to social security programs is often limited for informal workers (Medina and Schneider 2018; WIEGO 2019). As a result, in EMDEs with above-median output informality, only about 4 percent of the population is covered by social security programs such as unemployment insurance—about two-thirds of the level in EMDEs with below-median informality (figure 4.4). Without the ability to fall back on social safety nets and with limited personal savings, informal workers are vulnerable to adverse shocks, which can tip them into poverty. For example, in the one-third of EMDEs with the most pervasive informality, large health care expenses could impoverish more than one-third of households, which is 15 percentage points more than in the one-third of EMDEs with the least informality (box 2.1).

Distorted incentives. In weak institutional and regulatory environments, informal activity can perpetuate and deepen institutional weaknesses.[9] For example, high taxation and heavy-handed regulation will increase firms' incentives to avoid taxation and regulatory compliance by remaining informal.[10] Excessive labor regulations will encourage informal employment by increasing the cost of formal employment.[11] Corruption and rent-seeking bureaucracies will increase firms' incentives to avoid

---

[9] Conversely, access to productivity-enhancing public goods, such as electricity and the legal system, can raise the share of formal production (Mendicino and Prado 2014).

[10] Existing studies showing links between informality and high taxation and heavy-handed regulation include Amaral and Quintin (2006), Auriol and Walters (2005), D'Erasmo and Moscoso Boedo (2012), Dabla-Norris et al. (2018), Ihrig and Moe (2004), Kanbur (2017), Prado (2011), and Ulyssea (2018).

[11] Past studies, such as Loayza (2016), Oviedo, Thomas, and Karakurum-Özdemir (2009), and Rauch (1991), examined the link between informal employment and labor maket regulations.

interaction with the state by remaining informal (Choi and Thum 2005; Friedman et al. 2000; Sarte 2000).[12] Governments may strategically design and implement systems of poor governance to promote informality for the poor as an alternative redistributive strategy (Marjit, Mukherjee, and Kolmar 2006). But poor governance stymies development.

Lack of resilience against the COVID-19 pandemic. The COVID-19 pandemic has exacerbated these development challenges (box 2.1). The global recession caused by the pandemic hit firms and workers in the informal sector particularly hard. Lockdowns have had a particularly disruptive effect on services activities involving human interaction, where informal firms are common, and have thus hit informal employment particularly hard. Large-scale fiscal support implemented in 2020 primarily targeted formal workers and formal firms, with limited support for informal workers or firms (chapter 2; World Bank 2020a). The unprecedented surge in unemployment caused by the global lockdown after the pandemic disproportionally affected jobs in low-value-added services with a large presence of informal jobs (Al Masri, Flamini, and Toscani 2021). A portion of job losses in the service sector may be permanent (Autor and Reynolds 2020; Zenker and Kock 2020).

Informality and economic correlates

A large empirical literature has documented the links between informality and poor economic conditions. In particular, a large informal economy is associated with lower per capita incomes, greater poverty, less financial development, limited trade openness, and weaker output growth. These indicators differ significantly between EMDEs with high and low informality (figure 4.5).

Methodology. The next sections rely on a comprehensive literature review as well as several empirical approaches to identify and illustrate the main correlates of informality. The data are drawn from the database detailed in chapter 2 and include data for up to 160 EMDEs and 36 advanced economies for 1990-2018. First, a descriptive statistical approach is used. The sample of more than 122 EMDEs for 1990-2018 is split into those with above-median and below-median shares of informality by output (estimates based on dynamic general equilibrium [DGE] model) and by employment (proxied by self-employment shares, see table 4D.12; for other measures of informality, see table 4D.13). Average development outcomes for these two groups are then compared provided that differences between the two groups are statistically significant. In the following sections, results are obtained using output informality, unless otherwise specified. The findings are robust to using employment informality, to the use of alternative definitions of informality, or to using a regression that differentiates between quartiles of economies by informality (tables 4D.14-4D.15). These comparisons

---

[12] In turn, widespread informality incentivizes government officials to impose excessive regulations that confers on them the power to collect bribes in return for providing permits (Shleifer and Vishny 1993).

BOX 4.3 Informality, poverty, and income inequality

Economies with greater informality also feature more poverty and greater income inequality. The coincidence of informality, poverty, and income inequality partly reflects wage differentials between formal and informal employment and the presence in those emerging market and developing economies (EMDEs) where informality is more prevalent of weaker fiscal positions, social safety nets, and growth. Declines in informality have been associated with poverty reduction but not systematically with declines in income equality.

Introduction

Prevalence of informality is associated with persistent poverty and income inequality.[a] This may reflect higher wages for formal than informal workers and more limited income redistribution in EMDEs with widespread informality. Limited redistribution, in turn, in part reflects a lack of fiscal resources, inefficient or inadequate tax and social security systems, burdensome regulations and taxation, and relatively slow economic growth.[b] The association with inequality has been noted especially in poorer countries (Dell'Anno 2016; Elgin and Elveren 2019), other researchers have found an association with increases in income inequality (for instance, Mishra and Ray 2010; Rosser, Rosser, and Ahmed 2000).[c]

The COVID-19 (coronavirus) pandemic has led to an increase in global poverty for the first time in decades (World Bank 2020b, 2021). It has hit informal firms and informally employed workers particularly hard, in part because they struggled to adjust to digital operations and to access government support schemes (box 2.1; Yoshida, Narayan, and Wu 2020). Meanwhile, because of severe economic contractions in the formal sector, the share of informal activity is likely to have increased as a result of the pandemic.

Against this backdrop, this box explores and quantifies the relationships between informality and poverty and income inequality by addressing the following questions:

• How strong is the association between informality and poverty or income inequality?

Note: This box was prepared by Sergiy Kasyanenko.

a. For cross-country studies, see Devicienti, Groisman, and Poggi (2009); Fields and Pieters (2018); Gasparini and Tornaroli (2007); ILO (2018b); and World Bank (2019, 2020b).

b. For studies showing the potneital channels via which informality is linked with limited redistribution, see Besley and Persson (2014), Ordóñez (2014), Perry et al. (2007), and World Bank (2019, 2020b).

c. Country-level studies often find that higher informality is associated with greater income inequality (Amarante, Arim, and Yapor 2016; Ariza and Montes-Rojas 2017; Docquier and Iftikhar 2019).

BOX 4.3 Informality, poverty, and income inequality (*continued*)

- Which factors could account for the correlation between informality and poverty or income inequality?

- Is declining informality associated with reductions in poverty and inequality?

This box finds that more pervasive informality is associated with higher poverty and income inequality in EMDEs and that high preexisting informality may substantially slow subsequent poverty reduction and improvements in shared prosperity. Economies with high informality have slower output and labor productivity growth, holding back poverty reduction and income growth for low-income workers. Declines in informality turn out to be significantly associated with poverty reduction—but not with reductions in income inequality. The link between declining informality and poverty reduction is weaker in regions that started with above-average poverty levels, such as South Asia (SAR) and Sub-Saharan Africa (SSA).

This box contributes several new findings to the literature. It uses a large sample of EMDEs to quantify the correlation between changes in informality and changes in poverty and income inequality over time. The existing literature predominately focuses on country-level studies of poverty and informality.[d] Berdiev, Saunoris, and Schneider (2020) find a positive association between the *levels* of poverty and informality in a sample of over 100 countries. This box explores the links between *changes* in informality and poverty or inequality over time, as well as the associations between the levels of these variables. It shows that declines in poverty tend to follow declines in informality, although income inequality remains largely stable.

Cross-country patterns in informality, poverty, and income inequality

A large empirical and theoretical literature has documented the associations between informality and poverty and income inequality. This box updates and extends previous studies.

Methodology. The sample of 122 EMDEs for 1990-2018 is split into those with above-median and below-median shares of output informality. Output informality is measured by estimates of informal output based on dynamic general equilibrium (DGE) modeling in percent of official GDP. Average indicators of poverty and income inequality for these two groups are tested for statistically significant differences. Cross-economy regressions are estimated for

---

d. See Amuedo-Dorantes (2004), Canelas (2019), Devicienti, Groisman, and Poggi (2009), Kim (2005), and Nazier and Ramadan (2015).

BOX 4.3 Informality, poverty, and income inequality (continued)

the associations between informality and poverty or income inequality, controlling for the differences in overall development (proxied by real GDP per capita; table 4D.6). Similar regressions are also conducted for the relationships between the changes in poverty and income inequality over time and preexisting levels of informality (annex 4B).

Poverty and informality. On average between 1990 and 2018, more than one in four people in EMDEs with above-median informality lived below the international extreme poverty line of $1.90 per day (in 2011 U.S. dollars)—about five times as many as in EMDEs with below-median informality (figure B4.3.1). Workers in the informal sector face higher risks of impoverishment than their formal counterparts (Chen, Vanek, and Heintz 2006).

Income inequality and informality. Between 2009 and 2018, average consumption or income of the poorest 40 percent of the population in EMDEs with above-median informality amounted to about $4 per day (measured in 2011 purchasing power parity terms)—statistically significantly below the $5-6 per day average in EMDEs with below-median informality. Over the same period, income growth for the bottom 40 percent of the population outstripped average income growth by significantly more in EMDEs with below-median informality than in EMDEs with above-median informality. This suggests that progress in improving shared prosperity was more rapid in EMDEs with below-median informality than in those with above-median prosperity.

Channels of interaction

Several channels have been suggested for links between informality, poverty, and inequality: wage differentials between formal and informal workers; less redistributive and effective fiscal policies, including poorer coverage of social safety nets, in more informal economies; and slower economic growth in more informal economies (Besley and Persson 2014; Perry et al. 2007; World Bank 2019, 2020a).

Informality and fiscal indicators. Pervasive informality erodes the tax base and constrains governments' ability to provide public services, conduct countercyclical policies, service debt, and implement inequality-reducing redistributive measures (Besley and Persson 2014; Ordóñez 2014). Government revenues in EMDEs with above-median informality were 5-12 percentage points of GDP below those in EMDEs with below-median informality and were tilted toward trade taxes and away from income taxes (chapter 6). Higher informality was also associated with statistically significantly lower public spending on education and health, contributing to the slower accumulation of human capital and income convergence.

BOX 4.3 Informality, poverty, and income inequality (*continued*)

FIGURE B4.3.1 Informality and poverty and income inequality

More pervasive informality is associated with significantly more prevalent poverty and higher income inequality. A reduction in informality is positively associated with poverty alleviation, although the strength of this link varies across EMDE regions. The link between formalization and improvement in income inequality is largely missing.

A. Change in poverty by EMDE region

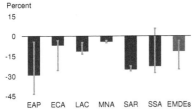

B. Change in output informality by EMDE region

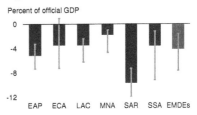

C. Extreme poverty above 5 percent across EMDE regions

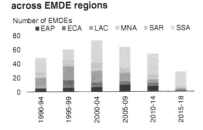

D. Output informality above 35 percent across EMDE regions

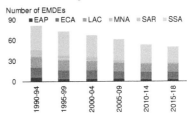

E. Output informality and poverty and income inequality

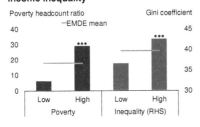

F. Elasticities of poverty and shared prosperity to output informality

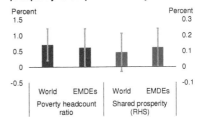

Source: World Bank (World Development Indicators).
Note: Data for the period 1990-2018. Informality is proxied by dynamic general equilibrium model-based estimates on informal output in percent of official GDP. Low/high informality indicates informality below/above median output informality. "Poverty" refers to income below the $1.90 per day poverty line. "Shared prosperity" refers to the income share of the bottom 40 percent of population. EAP = East Asia and Pacific; ECA = Europe and Central Asia; EMDEs = emerging market and developing economies; LAC = Latin America and the Caribbean; MNA = Middle East and North Africa; RHS = right-hand side; SAR = South Asia; SSA = Sub-Saharan Africa.
A.B. Median change from 1990-99 to 2010-18. Whiskers show 25-75 percentile range.
C.D. Based on average poverty/output informality during the period. Sample includes 122 EMDEs.
E. Averages over the period 1990-2018 for EMDEs with high and low informality. The EMDE averages are shown in orange lines. *** indicates group differences are significant (at least at 10 percent level).
F. Bars show coefficient estimates from regressions of changes in poverty (table 4D.7; and changes in shared prosperity in table 4D.8) on changes in output informality. A positive coefficient indicates that a decline in output informality reduces (increases) poverty (income inequality). Whiskers show 90 percent confidence intervals.

BOX 4.3 Informality, poverty, and income inequality (*continued*)

Greater reliance on indirect taxation in more informal economies made the tax system less progressive than systems based more on direct taxation. The reduction in income inequality due to taxes and transfers (that is, the difference between Gini coefficients before and after taxes and transfers) was about 6 Gini points on average in EMDEs with above-median output informality—statistically significantly less, by 13 Gini points, than in EMDEs with below-median output informality.

Informality and social safety nets. Limited government spending envelopes and poor spending efficiency also constrain the coverage of social protection programs (Dabla-Norris, Gradstein, and Inchauste 2008; Joshi, Prichard, and Heady 2014; Ordóñez 2014). During 1998-2018, only one-third of people in the poorest quintile of the population in EMDEs with above-median employment informality were covered by social protection and labor market programs—considerably less than the more than half in EMDEs with below-median employment informality. In EMDEs with above-median informality, the average daily transfer per capita (in purchasing power parity terms) was one-third less than in EMDEs with below-median informality.

In EMDEs with above-median informality, social protection and labor programs lowered the Gini coefficient by 2-4 points, significantly less than the 8-to-11-point reduction in EMDEs with below-median informality. Social protection and labor programs accounted for only about a 10th of poverty reduction in EMDEs with above-median informality during 2009-18, again significantly less than the one-quarter of poverty reduction in EMDEs with below-median informality.

Worker earnings differentials. A formal wage premium—systematically higher wages in the formal than informal sector—is a long-established finding in the literature. In a meta-analysis of empirical studies on formal wage premiums, wages in the formal sector were found to be 19 percent above informal wages on average (box 4.1).

Patterns over time in informality, poverty, and inequality

Although informality is typically accompanied by poverty, the evidence that informality reduction is associated with lower poverty or income inequality is less conclusive. In some cases, the informal sector provides a critical source of income for the poorest and helps ward off poverty during adverse events (Rogan and Cichello 2020). Although policies to reduce informality in EMDEs have often been complemented by poverty-alleviation initiatives such as income support or unemployment protection programs, these initiatives can fail to reach the very poorest groups and can create their own disincentives for formal employment (Bloeck, Galiani, and Weinschelbaum 2019; Gasparini, Haimovich, and Olivieri

BOX 4.3 Informality, poverty, and income inequality (*continued*)

2009). Declines in informality and poverty often coincide with rapid economic growth, which can raise income inequality when structural factors that widen income disparities (such as urbanization and demographic change) are not offset by other policies (for example, tax and expenditure reforms; Jain-Chandra et al. 2018).

Methodology. A similar methodology to that used by Dollar and Kraay (2002) and Dollar, Kleineberg, and Kraay (2013) is applied here to investigate the link between within-country changes in informality over time and changes in poverty and inequality reduction (annex 4B). Income inequality is proxied by the Gini coefficient or the share of income of the poorest 40 percent of the population ("bottom 40 percent") within each country. The sample of country-year observations is assembled by starting with the first available observation for each country and selecting all available consecutive observations that are at least five years apart. This approach yields about 428 economy-year pairs over the period 1990-2018 for 32 advanced economies and up to 119 EMDEs. A median distance between observations is 5.5 years for EMDEs and 5.0 years for advanced economies. A cross-country fixed-effects regression estimates the changes in poverty and inequality associated with changes in informality.

Evolution of informality. Output and employment informality have declined steadily over the past three decades, but with considerable heterogeneity across and within EMDE regions (figure B4.3.1). In the median EMDE, output informality contracted by 4 percentage points of GDP between 1990-99 and 2010-18. It declined most in SAR (by about 10 percent of official GDP) and East Asia and the Pacific (EAP, by about 6 percent of official GDP). In Europe and Central Asia (ECA) and Latin America and the Caribbean (LAC), output informality fell by about 4 and 2 percentage points of official GDP, respectively.

Evolution of poverty and income inequality. Most EMDEs saw a substantial reduction in the share of population living below the $1.90 a day poverty line, although the pace of poverty reduction was slow in SSA (World Bank 2020b). Progress in improving shared prosperity was more heterogeneous across regions. Although the share of income captured by the bottom 40 percent increased by about 2 percentage points from 1990-99 to 2010-18 in a median EMDE, it did not change much in EAP and SAR despite a notable reduction in poverty.

Decline in informality and poverty reduction. The regression results suggest that a 1-percentage-point reduction in output informality in EMDEs has been associated with a 0.6-percentage-point decrease in the share of population living in extreme poverty (on less than $1.90 a day in 2011 U.S. dollars) and a significant decrease in the share of the population living on less than $3.20 a day (figure B4.3.1; table 4D.7).

BOX 4.3 Informality, poverty, and income inequality (*continued*)

Decline in informality and improvements in income inequality. Consistent with the literature on income inequality and economic development, no strong or statistically significant relationship was found here between declines in informality and changes in inequality indicators (Adams 2003; Banerjee and Duflo 2003). A reduction in informality may play only a small role in inequality reduction partly because workers who transition from informal to formal jobs are already in the upper tail of the wage distribution, such as informal workers in formal firms (Messina and Silva 2021). Unlike in poverty regressions, where GDP growth and reductions in informality are strongly associated with poverty reduction, neither economic growth nor declines in informality appear to be statistically significantly correlated with changes in shared prosperity indicators (table 4D.8).

Conclusion

Economies with higher informality also tend to have higher poverty and greater income inequality. Several forces contribute to this pattern. More constrained public spending envelopes in EMDEs with widespread informality limit governments' ability to provide public services, resulting in more limited coverage and adequacy of social security programs. Workers in the formal economy earn, on average, about a fifth more than workers in the informal economy; this earnings gap contributes to the higher levels of poverty and income inequality in EMDEs with more pervasive informality. Without establishing the causal relationship between changes in informality and changes in poverty or income inequality, the box finds that reductions in informality were typically accompanied by poverty reduction, but not by reductions in income inequality. The confirmation of a causal relationship between informality and poverty (and income inequality) presents an area for future research.

examine each correlate of informality individually. There is no presumption of causality going either from development to informality or vice versa.

To identify the most robust correlates of informality among this large menu, this chapter conducts a BMA estimation. The large number of (often intercorrelated) correlates of informality gives rise to concerns about model uncertainty (annex 4C). The BMA approach addresses model uncertainty formally—by recognizing that the identity of the true model is unknown and by combining various sets of potential correlates of informality, ranging from economic development to infrastructure quality. This approach also addresses concerns about omitted variables in the bilateral correlations depicted in the stylized facts.

FIGURE 4.5 **Informality and economic correlates**

Lower GDP per capita, lower labor productivity, and greater poverty, but also better-shared prosperity, tend to be found in countries with higher informality.

A. Economic correlates and informality

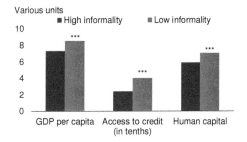

B. Labor productivity and informality

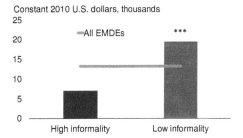

C. Informality and extreme poverty

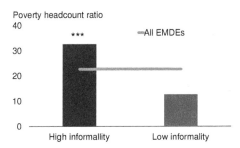

D. Informality and shared prosperity

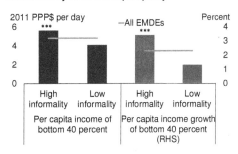

Sources: Barro and Lee (2013); Dieppe (2020); World Bank (World Development Indicators).
Note: DGE = dynamic general equilibrium; EMDEs = emerging market and developing economies; PPP = purchasing power parity; RHS = right-hand side. High informality (Low informality) = EMDEs with above-median (below-median) DGE-based estimates of informal output (in percent of official GDP). *** indicates group differences are not zero at 10 percent significance level.
A. "GDP per capita" is in thousands of 2010 U.S. dollars, "Access to credit" is domestic credit to the private sector in percent of GDP, and "Human capital" is measured as average years of schooling. Data are for EMDEs over the period 1990-2018
B-D. Simple group averages over the period 1990-2018 for countries with higher informality (above median) and those with lower informality (below median) are shown in bars. EMDE averages over the period 1990-2018 are shown in orange lines.
B. Labor productivity is proxied by output per employment in thousands of 2010 U.S. dollars.
C-D. "Per capita income of bottom 40 percent" measures the annualized average growth of per capita real survey mean consumption or income for the bottom 40 percent of the population.

Lack of development. Higher informality is associated with lower levels of per capita income and other measures of economic development.[13] For both output and employment informality, GDP per capita in EMDEs with below-median ("low") informality is about four times that in EMDEs with above-median ("high") informality (figure 4.5).[14] Because informal activity is concentrated in services and agriculture, more

---

[13] For empirical evidences on the link between informality and lack of development, please see La Porta and Shleifer (2014) and Loayza, Servén, and Sugawara (2010). However, there is also empirical evidence that the relationship between the extent of informality and the level of development has a U shape, with the informal economy tending to expand again (or at least to not shrink further) when economic development surpasses a certain threshold (Wu and Schneider 2019).

[14] Median informality amounts to about 36 percent of GDP for DGE-based informal output and 43 percent of total employment for self-employment.

manufacturing-based and more urban economies feature less informality. On average, about three-fifths of the population in EMDEs with below-median informality, but only two-fifths of the population in EMDEs with above-median informality, resides in urban areas. Past studies also show that more widespread informality has been associated with slower growth of output and investment and—in some studies—labor productivity (Perry et al. 2007; World Bank 2019).[15]

Poverty. Greater prevalence of informality is associated with greater prevalence of extreme poverty (figure 4.5; World Bank 2019). In 2000, the share of the population living on less than $1.90 a day was 44 percent in EMDEs with above-median informality—more than twice the share in EMDEs with below-median informality. In 2018, 1 in 4 people remained in extreme poverty in EMDEs with above-median informality, whereas fewer than 1 in 10 was in extreme poverty in EMDEs with below-median informality.

Financial development. Financial development, which reduces external financing costs, can incentivize entrepreneurs to join the formal sector and comply with tax obligations.[16] EMDEs with above-median informality significantly lag in financial development behind EMDEs with below-median informality (figure 4.3; chapter 6). People in EMDEs with below-median informality have access to significantly more commercial bank branches, automated teller machines (ATMs), and credit facilities than those in EMDEs with above-median informality. About half of the population in EMDEs with below-median informality holds an account at a financial institution or uses a mobile money service, which is significantly higher than the share in EMDEs with above-median informality, by about 18 percentage points. In financially less developed EMDEs, a higher share of entrepreneurs relies more on internal funding for starting, operating, or expanding their firms (figure 4.3; Epstein and Shapiro 2017; Farazi 2014).

International trade and financial openness. Although greater financial openness has been associated with lesser informality, the link between trade openness and informality is unclear. Higher capital account openness was associated with less output and employment informality (World Bank 2019). That said, the impact of major trade liberalizations on informality has varied across countries, differed between the short and the long term, and differed between workers and firms (Dix-Carneiro and Kovak 2017; Fugazza and Fiess 2010; Goldberg and Pavcnik 2003). Several studies show informality declining after trade liberalization.[17] In the presence of labor market rigidities, however, informal employment may rise in the short term after trade liberalization but not

---

[15] Other studies showing the association between informality and output growth, capital accumulation, and labor productivity include D'Erasmo and Moscoso Boedo (2012), Docquier, Müller, and Naval (2017), and Medina and Schneider (2019).

[16] Past studies on the link between informality and financial development include Blackburn, Bose, and Capasso (2012), Capasso and Jappelli (2013), and D'Erasmo and Moscoso Boedo (2012). See also chapter 6.

[17] Past studies, such as Boly (2018), Goldberg and Pavcnik (2004, 2007), and McCaig and Pavcnik (2018), find a decline in informality after trade liberalization.

necessarily in the long term.[18] In Brazil and Peru, trade liberalization and increased import competition were associated with increases in informality as informal firms exited and formal firms increasingly hired informal workers (Cisneros-Acevedo, forthcoming) or workers increasingly worked informally (Dix-Carneiro and Kovak 2019).

Informality and institutions

More informality is also associated with lower government revenues and expenditures, less effective public institutions, more burdensome tax and regulatory regimes, and weaker governance (for instance, Dabla-Norris, Gradstein, and Inchauste 2008; Enste and Schneider 1998; World Bank 2019).[19]

Government revenues and expenditures. On the basis of the various measures of informality, government revenues in EMDEs with above-median informality were, on average, 5-12 percentage points of GDP below those with below-median informality during 2000-18 (figure 4.6). The composition of tax revenues is also tilted toward trade taxes in economies with more pronounced informality, making the tax system less progressive but facilitating tax collection when income underreporting is widespread. Similarly, in EMDEs with more pervasive informality, government expenditures were 5-10 percentage points of GDP lower than in those with less informality.

Such constrained government spending is reflected in more limited provision of government services, contributing to poorer human development outcomes (Gaspar et al. 2019). During 2000-18, EMDEs with above-median informality spent about 2 percent of GDP on health, which was 1 percentage point of GDP lower than in EMDEs with below-median informality (figure 4.6). The average number of pupils per teacher in primary schools was about 35 in EMDEs with above-median informality—significantly higher, by 8 students per teacher, than in EMDEs with below-median informality. Access to medical resources, such as physicians and nurses, was also significantly more limited in EMDEs with a more pervasive informal sector (World Bank 2020a).

Regulatory burdens. Both empirical and theoretical studies suggest that heavier regulatory (or administrative) burdens are associated with greater informality (figure 4.6).[20] Over the period 2010-18, the average ease of doing business score for EMDEs with below-median informality (by DGE estimates) was higher by 7 points—two-thirds

---

[18] The changes of informal employment following trade liberalization, conditioning labor market rigidities, are studied in Attanasio, Goldberg, and Pavcnik (2004), Bosch, Goñi-Pacchioni, and Maloney (2012), Goldberg and Pavcnik (2003), Ponczek and Ulyssea (2018), and World Bank (2019).

[19] Access to the court system can also encourage formal production (Mendicino and Prado 2014; Schneider, Buehn, and Montenegro 2010).

[20] For studies that examine the link between informality and regulatory (or administrative) burdens, see Bruhn (2011), de Mel, McKenzie, and Woodruff (2013), Perry et al. (2007), Rocha, Ulyssea, and Rachter (2018), and Ulyssea (2010).

FIGURE 4.6 Informality, fiscal indicators, and institutional quality

Informality is associated with lower government revenues and expenditure capacity, hindering economies' abilities to provide health and education services. EMDEs with above-median informality tend to have more burdensome regulations and weaker governance.

A. Differential in government revenues between EMDEs with above- and below-median informality

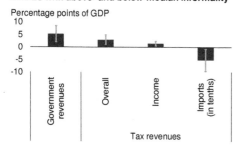

B. Government spending and informality

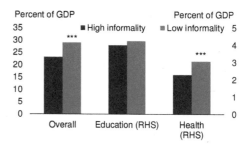

C. Access to education resources

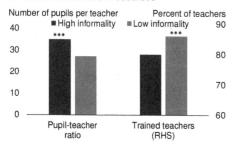

D. Access to medical resources

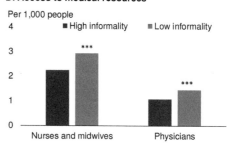

E. Regulatory burdens

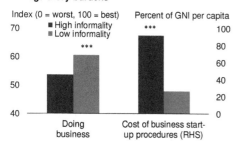

F. Governance

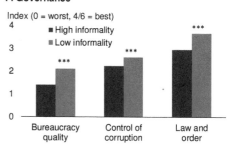

Sources: International Country Risk Guide (ICRG); International Monetary Fund (Government Finance Statistics, World Revenue Longitudinal Data); World Bank (*Doing Business,* World Development Indicators).

Note: Informality is proxied by DGE-based estimates of informal output in percent of GDP. Data for emerging market and developing economies (EMDEs). "High-informality" ("Low-informality") are EMDEs with above-median (below-median) DGE-based informal output measures. DGE = dynamic general equilibrium model; GNI = gross national income; RHS = right-hand side. *** indicates group differences are not zero at 10 percent significance level.

A. Differences in percentage points of GDP between the average fiscal indicators among EMDEs with above-median and below-median informality are in bars, with corresponding 90 percent confidence intervals shown by whiskers. All fiscal indicators and informality measures are 2000-18 averages for EMDEs with populations above 3.5 million (several oil-exporting outliers are dropped).

B. Simple group averages of public expenditure over the period 2000-18. Overall expenditures are for EMDEs with population above 3.5 million.

C. Simple group averages are in bars over the period 1990-2018. "Pupil-teacher ratio" measures the average number of pupils per teacher in primary school. "Trained teachers" captures the percentage of primary school teachers who have received the minimum organized teacher training (pre-service or in-service) required for teaching in a given country.

D. Simple group averages over the period 2010-18. Two outlier countries, Belarus and Belize, are excluded from the sample.

E.F. Simple group averages are in bars over the period 1990-2018. *Doing Business* score ranges from 0 (lowest performance) to 100 (best performance). Data for business registration costs are for 2003-18 (2010-18 for doing business scores). "Bureaucracy quality," "Control of corruption," and "Law and order" are from ICRG, with higher values corresponding to better outcomes.

of a standard deviation—than for EMDEs with above-median output informality.[21] Similarly, the average cost of business start-up procedures amounted to 92 percent of gross national income (GNI) per capita in EMDEs with above-median output informality, significantly higher than in EMDEs with below-median output informality, by about 65 percentage points.

Governance. A large literature has documented the coincidence of poor governance with pervasive informality in many EMDEs, especially in Latin America and the Caribbean (LAC) and Europe and Central Asia (ECA).[22] On average, EMDEs with above-median informality have had significantly poorer-quality bureaucracies, by about 1 standard deviation in terms of the rating by the *International Country Risk Guide* (ICRG), than EMDEs with below-median informality.[23] Similar differences pertain to the control of corruption and law and order. There are also country cases suggesting that informality declined faster in the presence of greater improvements in governance and better initial governance (World Bank 2019). For example, in Georgia, during 1996-2016, the transition to a market economy brought significant improvements in government effectiveness, control of corruption, and rule of law. With output growth averaging about 6 percent per year, the share of informal output fell from 66 percent to 57 percent of GDP, and the share of informal employment in total employment fell by a similar magnitude (World Bank 2019).

Informality and SDGs related to human development

Greater informality is associated with weaker human development outcomes. People living in EMDEs with more widespread informality suffer from a greater prevalence of hunger, poorer health and education, greater gender inequality, and lower human capital (figure 4.7; Docquier, Müller, and Naval 2017; Maloney 2004).

Hunger. EMDEs with more pervasive informality fared far worse during 1990-2018 in terms of the hunger-related SDGs than those with less pervasive informality. The share of the population suffering from stunting and wasting was significantly higher in EMDEs with above-median informality: more than a quarter of children under five years of age in EMDEs with above-median informality suffered from stunting, with more than 15 percent of the population being undernourished (Sachs et al. 2020). Both shares are significantly higher than in EMDEs with below-median informality, by about

---

[21] Similarly, the Heritage Foundation's Business Freedom Index was about three-quarters of a standard deviation higher in countries with below-median output informality than in countries with above-median informality.

[22] Sarte (2000) suggests that firms operate in the informal sector to avoid rent-seeking bureaucrats. Choi and Thum (2005) and Dreher and Schneider (2010) report an association between higher informality and weaker law and order and control of corruption. Dabla-Norris, Gradstein, and Inchauste (2008) show that the quality of the legal framework is important in determining the size of the informal sector.

[23] The measures of institutional quality used here are taken from the *International Country Risk Guide* (ICRG 2014). A higher value indicates better institutional quality. In the case of bureaucracy quality, high points are given to countries where the bureaucracy has the strength and expertise to govern without drastic changes in policy or interruptions in government services.

FIGURE 4.7 Informality and SDGs related to human development

EMDEs with more pervasive informality face more severe challenges in progressing toward SDGs related to human development. People in EMDEs with more informality tend to suffer more from hunger, poor health and education, and gender inequality.

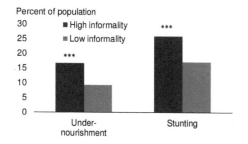

A. Hunger and informality

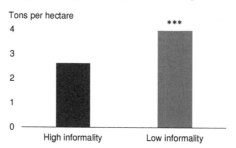

B. Agricultural productivity and informality

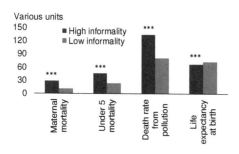

C. Health outcome indicators and informality

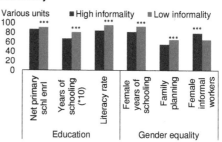

D. Educational attainment, gender equality, and informality

Sources: Sachs et al. (2018); Sachs et al. (2020); World Bank (World Development Indicators).
Note: "High informality" ("Low informality") are emerging market and developing economies (EMDEs) with above-median (below-median) DGE model-based informal output measure over the period 1990-2018. Figures show the latest available data. DGE = dynamic general equilibrium model; SDGs = Sustainable Development Goals. *** indicates that group differences are significant at 10 percent level.
A. Average shares of population (children under 5 years of age) that suffer from undernourishment (stunting) for corresponding country groups. Based on 144 EMDEs.
B. Agricultural productivity is measured as cereal yield (tons per hectare of harvested land). Based on 141 EMDEs.
C. Bars for group averages for the latest year available. "Maternal mortality" is measured per 10,000 live births. "Under 5 mortality" is measured per 1,000 live births. "Death rate from pollution" is age-standardized death rate (per 100,000 persons) due to household and ambient (outdoor) pollution. "Life expectancy" at birth is measured in years. Based on up to 153 EMDEs.
D. Bars for group averages for the latest year available. "Net primary school enrollment" rate ("net primate schl enrl") is measured in percentage points. Mean years of schooling are measured in years (in multiplier of 10; taken from Sachs et al. 2018). "Literacy rate" of 15-24 years old is measured in percent of population. "Female years of schooling" is measured in percent of male schooling years. "Family planning" measures the percentage of women reporting having their family planning needs attended. "Female informal workers" captures the percent of female workers informally employed among all female workers.

10 percentage points. The higher prevalence of hunger in EMDEs with above-median informality is partly explained by lower agricultural productivity. On average, the cereal yield in EMDEs with above-median informality is less than two-thirds of the yield in EMDEs with below-median informality (figure 4.7).

Health. People in EMDEs with more widespread informality face poorer health outcomes. According to the latest available data, in 2016, the average life expectancy at birth in EMDEs with above-median informality was about 67 years, which is about 6 years shorter than in EMDEs with below-median informality. Both the maternal mortality rate and the mortality rate of children under 5 years old in EMDEs with above-median informality were nearly twice the rates in EMDEs with below-median informality. In EMDEs with above-median informality, on average, about 133 deaths per 100,000 persons were caused by household air pollution and ambient pollution, which is significantly higher than in EMDEs with below-median informality by more than 50 deaths per 100,000 persons.

Education. Access to education is less available in EMDEs with more pervasive informality (Docquier, Müller, and Naval 2017). On average in EMDEs with above-median informality, people spent less than seven years in schooling, compared with eight to nine years in EMDEs with below-median informality. Less than 85 percent of the population aged 15-24 years in EMDEs with above-median informality is literate—more than 10 percentage points less than the population in EMDEs with below-median informality.

Gender equality. Female workers make up a disproportionate share of workers in the informal sector (Bonnet, Vanek, and Chen 2019; ILO 2018b). In EMDEs with above-median employment informality, 87 percent of employed women work in the informal sector, which is about three-quarters higher than in EMDEs with below-median employment informality (table 4D.12). In South Asia (SAR) and Sub-Saharan Africa (SSA), the regions where informality is most pervasive, about 80 percent of female workers in the nonagricultural sector are informally employed (UN Women 2016). In low-income countries, up to 92 percent of all employed women work in the informal sector (ILO 2018b; OECD/ILO 2019). Working in the informal sector exposes female workers to low remuneration, poor working conditions, and lack of or limited access to social protection and rights at work (ILO 2019; Otobe 2017).

EMDEs with more widespread informality are also associated with greater gender inequality in broader terms. The average years of schooling received by women in EMDEs with above-median informality are, on average, 20 percent less than the average years received by men, in stark contrast to EMDEs with below-median informality where no significant gender gap in schooling prevails. Only 55 percent of women in EMDEs with above-median informality have their family planning needs attended to, which is 10 percentage points lower than in EMDEs with below-median informality. In addition to factors such as traditional gender roles, lack of access to education and insufficient coverage of family planning needs constrain women's ability to participate in the formal sector (Malta et al. 2019).

Informality and SDGs related to infrastructure

More widespread informality is associated with poorer access to, and lower overall quality of, infrastructure, with causality running in both directions. Thus widespread informality tends to limit government revenue and hence public expenditure on infrastructure; conversely, poor access to infrastructure can discourage firms or workers from joining the formal sector and engaging with the government (Perry et al. 2007).

FIGURE 4.8 **Informality and SDGs related to infrastructure**

Higher infrastructure costs and lower quality of overall infrastructure are associated with more pervasive informality. People in EMDEs with above-median informality tend to have significantly less access to various types of infrastructure than people in those with below-median informality.

A. Quality of overall infrastructure

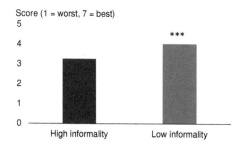

B. Access to clean water and sanitation

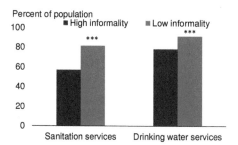

C. Access to energy

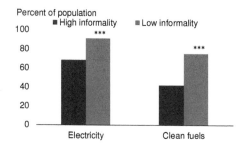

D. Access to ICT-related infrastructure

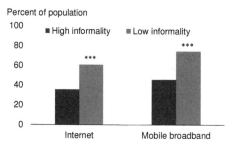

E. Access to roads

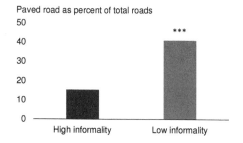

F. Road project costs

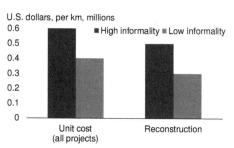

Sources: Sachs et al. (2018); Sachs et al. (2020); World Bank (Road Costs Knowledge System [ROCKS] database; World Development Indicators).

Note: "High informality" ("Low informality") are emerging market and developing economies (EMDEs) with above-median (below-median) DGE-based informal output, measured over the period 1990-2018. DGE = dynamic general equilibrium model; ICT = information and communication technology. *** indicates group differences are significant at 10 percent level.

A. Bars show the average overall infrastructure quality for the latest year available. The index is taken from Sachs et al. (2018) and ranges from 1 to 7, with higher values representing better overall infrastructure quality. Based on 115 EMDEs.

B.-E. Bars show the group means for the latest year available. Based on up to 153 EMDEs.

F. Bars show group averages for the latest year available. Data are for 51 EMDEs (outliers, Guinea, Malawi, and Peru, are dropped). "Unit cost (all projects)" excludes new 4-lane and 6-lane expressway projects because they cost much more than other projects and do not exist in EMDEs with above-median informality. Reconstruction is the most common road project by project number. Data are from the latest year available. Based on 77 EMDEs.

Infrastructure weaknesses create an additional obstacle to human capital accumulation and job creation, entrenching informality (Vorisek and Yu 2020). Lack of energy and communications infrastructure limits access to more and better job opportunities and slows productivity gains from digital technologies (Zaballos, Iglesias, and Adamowicz 2019). Poor transportation networks restrict factor mobility and market access, thus slowing productivity growth.[24] Weak within-city transportation networks prevent workers from accessing formal employment opportunities (Zarate 2019).

Sanitation and clean water. Greater informality is associated with more limited access to sanitation facilities and clean water (figure 4.8). In EMDEs with above-median informality, only about 55 percent of the population has access to basic sanitation services—about 30 percentage points less than in EMDEs with below-median informality. Whereas almost all people in EMDEs with below-median informality have access to clean drinking water, this essential infrastructure service is available to less than 80 percent of the population in EMDEs with above-median informality.

Access to energy and information and communication technology infrastructure. Access to infrastructure services such as electricity, clean fuels, the internet, and mobile broadband is more limited in EMDEs with above-median informality. As shown by the latest available data, about one-third of people living in EMDEs with above-median informality lacked access to electricity, whereas almost all in EMDEs with below-median informality had such access. The share of the population with access to clean fuels in EMDEs with above-median informality is about half of the share in EMDEs with below-median informality. Access to the internet and mobile broadband was available to 30-40 percent of the population in EMDEs with above-median informality—less than three-fifths of the share in EMDEs with below-median informality.

Road access. Despite progress made in recent years, road access remains more limited in EMDEs with above-median informality. The latest data show that only about 15 percent of roads were paved in EMDEs with above-median informality—one-third of the share in EMDEs with below-median informality. This could in part reflect higher costs of road construction in EMDEs with more pervasive informal sectors: on average, road construction costs amounted to $0.6 million per kilometer in EMDEs with above-median informality—significantly higher than the cost in EMDEs with below-median informality, by $0.2 million per kilometer.

Finding the needle in the haystack: The most robust correlates

The analysis so far has considered individual correlates of informality in isolation. This section aims to identify the most robust correlates of informality via a BMA approach.

---

[24] Banerjee, Duflo, and Qian (2020) find that proximity to transportation networks have a moderately sized positive causal effect on per capita GDP levels across sectors. De Soyres, Mulabdic, and Ruta (2020) and Francois and Manchin (2013) confirm the trade impact of transportation infrastrucutere.

FIGURE 4.9 **Results from Bayesian model averaging approach**

Widely ranging economic and institutional conditions, such as better governance, a more developed and diversified economy, and better human capital, are associated with less pervasive informality in EMDEs.

A. Effect of group correlates on the evolution of output informality

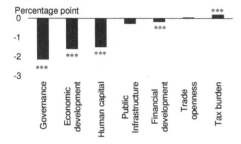

B. Probability of inclusion

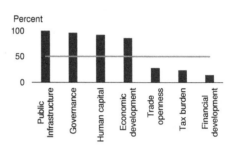

Source: World Bank.

Note: Based on the panel regression result using Bayesian model averaging technique. In A, *** denotes that the signs of the estimated coefficients are the same for 90 percent of the model, conditional on inclusion of the variable. The dependent variable is the share of informal economy in GDP using dynamic-general-equilibrium-based estimates on informal output as a share of official GDP. From an unbalanced panel from 67 emerging market and developing economies (EMDEs) and 5-year periods over 1998-2018. See annex 4C for details.

A. Predicted differences in the share of output informality for countries whose correlates differ by 1 standard deviation.

B. Probability of including at least one variable from the group to the regression (posterior inclusion probability). The groups whose posterior inclusion probabilities exceed the prior of 50 percent could be regarded as relevant.

The approach utilizes a large number of possible correlates that have been identified in the literature and reviewed in the previous sections. It recognizes the unknown nature of the true relationship between informality and various conditions and combines evidence from different models.

Methodology. Following Dieppe et al. (2020) and Durlauf, Kourtellos, and Tan (2008), independent variables that represent common concepts are grouped together to estimate their group marginal effects. The correlates of informality are sorted into seven groups, covering economic development, human capital, financial development, and governance (table 4D.9). Analyses are carried out at the level of output informality, proxied by the share of informal output in GDP, while using the levels of correlates as independent variables (table 4D.10). The results from a similar analysis using employment informality are broadly consistent (annex 4C). The sample comprises an unbalanced panel of 68 EMDEs, observed from 1998 to 2018 in five-year windows.

Results. The results are broadly consistent with existing studies about individual correlates. First, the posterior inclusion probabilities (PIPs) for several variable groups under consideration exceed 0.50 (figure 4.9). This finding suggests that most of these factors are related to the level of output informality. The group PIPs are highest—near 1—for economic development, human capital, and governance, indicating these factors' particularly strong association with informality. The results indicate their stronger association with the level of output informality than other groups of variables.

Second, all the correlates are associated with the level of informality in the expected manner (figure 4.9). EMDEs with better governance, a more developed and less agriculture-oriented economy, and stronger human capital tend to have lower informality. In particular, informal output as a share of official GDP is significantly lower, by about 1-2 percentage points of GDP, if the EMDE has 1-standard-deviation better governance, greater economic development, or larger human capital. In addition, tax burdens, measured as the share of government consumption or tax revenue in GDP, are significantly and negatively correlated with the size of output informality.

Conclusion

Pervasive informality is associated with a wide range of development challenges, from extreme poverty to lack of access to basic sanitation services. This chapter documented and quantified the wider gaps, relative to the SDGs, among EMDEs with greater informality. These shortcomings also make EMDEs with widespread informality particularly vulnerable to adverse global shocks, including the COVID-19 pandemic.

The wide range of correlates of informality suggests that informality is a phenomenon that reflects broad-based underdevelopment rather than a challenge that can be considered in isolation. Consequently, policy measures to address informality need to be equally broad-based. They include measures to enhance human capital and lift productivity, streamline regulations, and improve governance and the provision of public services and social safety nets. Policy options are discussed in detail in chapter 6.

Several areas for further development are worth exploring. First, the chapter does not demonstrate a causal link between informality and the various development outcomes. The exploration of causal relationships between informality and these outcomes, in either direction, is left for future studies. Second, because of data limitations, some variables, such as access to paved roads and bank account ownership, that are relevant to informality are not included in the current BMA analysis. Future studies can improve upon the work reported here by incorporating those variables. Third, future research could explore asymmetries in the challenges posed by informality. There may be interactions between country circumstances and worker or firm characteristics that can mitigate some of the challenges posed by informality. For firms, some of these interactions were explored in box 4.2 but other important interactions may yet come to light in future research.

ANNEX 4A Meta-regression analysis

A random-effects model assumes that there is a distribution of true effects rather than a common fixed effect across studies (DerSimonian and Laird 1986). In particular, a study-specific estimate of the informal-formal wage gap has a sampling distribution $\hat{\theta}_i \sim N(\theta_i, \sigma^2)$, where σ^2 is the within study variance of the estimate due to a sampling error; and the true effect has the following distribution $\theta_i \sim N(\mu, \tau^2)$. Meta-analysis pools information across many studies to estimate μ and τ^2, where τ^2 measure the degree of across-study variations.[25] The proportion of total variation in study estimates is equal to $I^2 = \tau^2/(\tau^2 + \sigma^2)$ and reflects the impact of across-study heterogeneity (Higgins and Thompson 2002). The meta-regression analysis (MRA) can be performed to associate this variation with any characteristics of the study or sample.

The MRA of estimated wage differentials between formal and informal jobs uses estimates of the wage gap drawn from each study as the dependent variable. The set of regressors, or moderator variables, includes study characteristics that are deemed consequential for the reported results, for example, identification and estimation methods, study design, and data sources. This, in particular, helps clarify the diversity of research outcomes on the size of the informal-formal wage gap and identify the sensitivity of reported wage gaps to study-specific methods and data. A random-effects MRA is performed by estimating the following regression:

$$\hat{\theta}_i = \mu + \sum_{j}^{k} \alpha_j X_{ij} + \epsilon_i + \vartheta_i, \qquad (4A.1)$$

where $\hat{\theta}_i$ is a study-specific estimate of the informal-formal wage gap, ϵ_i is a sampling error with a standard deviation that may vary across studies, and ϑ_i is an error term reflecting across-study variation of true effects with a constant across-study variance τ^2; finally, the set of moderator variables, X, includes the following:

- A dummy variable accounts for differences in methodology: FE_i is 1 if fixed effects were used to correct for unobserved workers' characteristics and 0 otherwise.

- Two dummy variables reflect the gender composition of the sample: $FEMALE_i$ is 1 if estimates were obtained for female workers only and 0 otherwise, $-MALE_i$ 1 if estimates were obtained for male workers only and 0 otherwise. The reference categories for this set of dummy variables are estimates obtained with samples containing both female and male workers.

- Regional dummy variables are included to account for regional heterogeneity.

- $Self\text{-}employed_i$ is a dummy variable indicating that a study measured the wage gap between self-employed and formal employees.

---

[25] The random-effects meta-analysis estimate is a special case of a generalized method of moments estimator, where each estimate is weighted proportionally to its sampling error. Thus, it can only be applied to studies that reported standard errors of their inform-formal wage gap estimates.

ANNEX 4B **Regression analysis**

Correlation between informality, poverty, and income inequality. The following cross-country ordinary least squares regression model is estimated to show the association between informality and levels of extreme poverty and income inequality:

$$\overline{y}_i = \alpha_0 + \theta_1\overline{x}_i + \theta_2\overline{LnGDPpc}_i + \epsilon_i \qquad (4B.1)$$

The results are reported in table 4D.6.

The dependent variable ($\overline{y}_i$) includes a range of measures for levels of poverty and income inequality averaged over 1990-2018 in country i. The level of poverty is proxied by the poverty headcount ratio at $1.90 a day (2011 purchasing power parity [PPP]) in percent of the total population. Measures for income inequality include the Gini coefficient (range from 0 to 100, with 0 being perfect equality and 100 being extreme inequality), survey mean consumption or income per capita of the lowest-income 40 percent of population, and the difference in consumption or income per capita levels between the bottom 40 percent of population and the total population (World Bank 2018). Last, the progress in shared prosperity, measured as the difference in the average annual growth in income or consumption of the poorest 40 percent of population and that of total population, is used as the dependent variable in column (6).

The variable of interest, $\overline{x}_i$, is the average level of informality in country i over the period 1990-2018, including the share of estimates based on DGE and multiple indicators multiple causes (MIMIC) models of informal output in official GDP and the share of self-employed in employed. All regressions control for income per capita, measured as the logged real GDP per capita in 2010 U.S. dollars averaged between 1990 and 2018 ($\overline{LnGDPpc}_i$). The proxies for poverty, income inequality, and shared prosperity are taken from World Development Indicators (WDI).

Declines in informality, poverty reduction, and income equalization. The association between within-country changes in informality and poverty and inequality reduction is explored using a similar sample setup and methodology as in Dollar and Kraay (2002) and Dollar, Kleineberg, and Kraay (2013). In particular, the sample of country-year observations is assembled by starting with the first available observation for each country and selecting all available consecutive observations with at least a five-year distance between them (sampling window). This approach yields 428 country-year pairs for 32 advanced economies 119 EMDEs with at least two observations per country and a median of four observations per country. A median distance between observations is 5.5 years for EMDEs and 5.0 years for advanced economies. The sample excludes fragile and conflict-affected states.

In table 4D.7, the dependent variables are changes in poverty rates at $1.90 and $3.20 per day (in PPP terms) poverty lines at the end of the sampling window. In table 4D.8, the dependent variables are changes in the Gini coefficient and shared prosperity at the end of the sampling window, where shared prosperity refers to the income share of the bottom 40 percent of the population.

The main variable of interest is the cumulative change of output (or employment) informality during the sampling windows. Employment informality is proxied by self-employment in percent of total employment, whereas output informality is measured by DGE-based estimates on informal output in percent of official GDP.

Additional control variables include initial poverty/inequality levels, which are measured at the start of the sampling windows, to capture persistence in poverty/inequality outcomes; initial levels of informality; cumulative GDP per capita growth during the sampling window; a constant; country and time fixed effects; and squared initial informality to control for the possible nonlinear relationship between informality and poverty.

ANNEX 4C Bayesian model averaging approach

Model uncertainty is a common issue in regressions that investigate the correlates of informality. Past theoretical models and empirical studies have identified many potential drivers and implications of informality, ranging from social and economic factors underlying underdevelopment to institutional conditions (Schneider, Buehn, and Montenegro 2010; World Bank 2019). The BMA approach can address model uncertainty formally—by recognizing that the identity of the true model is unknown and that it may be preferable to combine evidence from many different models. Here the BMA model is used to show the potential correlates of output informality in EMDEs. A hyper-g prior is used for each coefficient, following Feldkircher and Zeugner (2012), which may achieve greater robustness than the priors used in the earlier literature. Priors on the inclusion probabilities are discussed below.

Grouping variables. Multiple variables can represent the same broad concepts. For example, both the share of population with primary schooling and above and the share of population with secondary schooling and above can proxy for the quality of human capital in that country. BMA approaches should be designed to take this into account (Durlauf, Kourtellos, and Tan 2008; Ghosh and Ghattas 2015). In the analysis underlying this chapter, variables that represent common concepts are grouped together following Dieppe (2020) and Durlauf, Kourtellos, and Tan (2008). As in their work, a group is deemed relevant if the posterior probability of including at least one variable from the group exceeds the prior inclusion probability. To account for the dependency within groups, the prior inclusion probability of each variable is defined as follows:

$$m_j^i = 1 - (1 - p_j)^{\frac{1}{k_j}}$$

where m_j^i, p_j, and k_j are the prior inclusion probability of variable i in the group j, the probability of including at least one variable from the group j, and the number of variables in group j, respectively. m_j^i is set so that the prior probability of including at least one variable out of the k_j variables in the group is equal to p_j. The quantity p_j is set to 0.5 for all j, so there is no specific prior knowledge on the probability of a group's inclusion. Posterior distributions of the coefficients of the variables obtained from BMA are aggregated to the group level. The marginal impact of a group is defined as follows:

$$\beta_j^G = \sum_{\{i \in Group_j\}} \beta_i PIP_i \delta_{j,i}$$

where β_j^G is the marginal impact of the group j, β_i is a posterior mean of variable given inclusion of the variable, PIP_i is a posterior inclusion probability of a variable, and $\delta_{j,i}$ is the factor loading of variable i in group j. A factor of group j is defined as the variable within a group whose coefficient posterior mean multiplied by the posterior inclusion probability is the highest. $\delta_{j,i}$ is the coefficient from the linear regression of a variable on the factor. β_j^G can be interpreted as the marginal impact of the factor, accounting for the correlations of the variables within groups. It can also be interpreted as the hypothetical posterior mean when including only one variable per group. In a linear regression, the factor-loading weighted sum of the coefficients is identical to the coefficient obtained by another regression (one that includes one variable per group).

Empirical specification. Following Loayza, Servén, and Sugawara (2010), analyses are carried out at the country level as the dependent variable. The explanatory variables ($X_{j,t}$) are those identified as potential drivers or implications of informality by former theoretical or empirical studies.

Former studies show that the relationships between informality and its correlates in EMDEs may differ from those in advanced economies (Wu and Schneider 2019). To mitigate this issue, the analysis here includes only EMDEs. Based on data availability, the final sample covers an unbalanced panel for about 55 EMDEs over the period 1989-2018. Details about the list of group variables under investigation and their expected signs are summarized in table 4D.9.

The level of output informality in country j in the beginning of a five-year period is modeled as follows:

$$y_{j,t} = X_{j,t} \beta + \theta_t + \varepsilon_{j,t}$$

where $y_{j,t}$ captures levels of informality at time period t in country j. Two measures of informality are used: informality as DGE-based informal output in percent of official GDP and share of self-employment. $X_{j,t}$ is a vector of variables of interest, taking from the beginning year of period t and country j. θ_t controls for time fixed effects and $\varepsilon_{j,t}$ is a time-varying unobserved idiosyncratic factor. To understand the cross-sectional variation of informality, as well as the time-series variation, country fixed effects are not included. The results are summarized in tables 4D.10 (output informality) and 4D.11 (employment informality).

Limitations. The empirical strategy shown above tries to reduce country heterogeneity issues by restricting the sample to a relatively homogenous set. At the same time, it uses the BMA approach to overcome ad hoc variable selection and the arbitrary omission of variables. However, the approach taken here cannot be used to draw any conclusions about causal effects. Because many explanatory variables (for instance, tax rates, government effectiveness, and financial development) could be viewed as equilibrium outcomes, which are jointly determined with informality, it is hard to draw conclusions about causal effects. Meanwhile, strong and valid instrumental variables that deal with this issue are hard to find. The analysis summarized here should be interpreted as correlates of informality levels. Another limitation of the model here is the omission of cyclical determinants, such as unemployment and macroeconomic shocks. Due to the medium (to long)-run focus of the analysis here, cyclical factors that could be associated with short-run fluctuations in informality are not considered.

ANNEX 4D Tables

TABLE 4D.1 Data: Meta-regression analysis

Study	Countries/ estimates	Sample period	Methodology	Mean wage gap*
Aydin, Hisarciklilar, and Ikkaran (2010)	1/4	1998-2007	OLS, ML logit	57.75
Bargain and Kwenda (2014)	3/6	2001, 2005	OLS, FE	19.19
Baskaya and Hulagu (2011)	1/2	2005-09	OLS, PSM	15.45
Botelho and Ponczek (2011)	1/2	1995-2001	OLS, FE	11.76
Earle and Sakova (2000)	6/6	1993, 1994	ML Logit	-13.33
El Badaoui, Strobl, and Walsh (2008)	1/17	2001-03	OLS, DID, PSM	28.48
El Badaoui, Strobl, and Walsh (2010)	1/6	1994	OLS, PSM	25.65
Funkhouser (1997)	1/4	1991-92	OLS	23.82
Gindling (1991)	1/1	1982	OLS	28.50
Huber and Rahimov (2014)	1/2	2007	OLS	-34.98
Lehmann and Pignatti (2007)	1/2	2004	OLS	-6.80
Lehmann and Zaiceva (2013)	1/5	2003-11	OLS, QR, FE	6.90
Magnac (1991)	1/1	1980	OLS	30.30
Marcouiller, de Castilla, and Woodruff (1997)	3/6	1990	OLS	16.50
Nguyen, Nordman, Roubaud (2013)	1/4	2002-06	OLS, FE	4.83
Nordman, Rakotomana, and Roubaud (2016)	1/6	2000-04	OLS, FE	15.33
Pratap and Quintin (2006)	1/3	1993-95	OLS, FE	28.49
Tansel and Kan (2012)	1/6	2006-09	OLS, FE	11.56

Source: World Bank.
Note: The sample covers these emerging market and developing economies: Argentina, Brazil, Colombia, Costa Rica, Czech Republic, Ecuador, El Salvador, Hungary, Madagascar, Mexico, Peru, Poland, Russian Federation, Slovak Republic, South Africa, Tajikistan, Turkey, Ukraine, and Vietnam. DID = difference-in-difference estimators; FE = fixed-effects regression; ML logit = multinomial logit regression; OLS = pooled ordinary least squares; PSM = propensity score matching; QR = quantile regression.
*Average formal sector premium across all estimates, in percent; a negative number indicates a wage penalty for formal sector workers.

TABLE 4D.2 Regression: Meta-regression analysis

	(1)	(2)	(3)	(4)	(5)	(6)	(7)	(8)
μ	0.195***	0.11**	0.23***	0.21***	0.14***	0.24***	0.17***	0.18***
	(0.03)	(0.04)	(0.03)	(0.03)	(0.04)	(0.04)	(0.05)	(0.06)
Female		0.16*			0.15*		0.12	0.12
		(0.08)			(0.08)		(0.08)	(0.08)
Male		0.14**			0.13**		0.11*	0.10
		(0.06)			(0.06)		(0.06)	(0.06)
Fixed effects			-0.15**		-0.13**	-0.14**	-0.13**	-0.13**
			(0.07)		(0.06)	(0.06)	(0.06)	(0.07)
Self-employed				-0.34*		-0.32**	-0.25*	-0.26*
				(0.14)		(0.13)	(0.14)	(0.14)
Latin America and the Caribbean								0.00
								(0.07)
Europe and Central Asia								-0.03
								(0.07)
Adjusted R²		7.8	5.8	6.4	12.0	11.4	14.8	12.4
Number of obs.	83	83	83	83	83	83	83	83
τ²		0.06	0.05	0.05	0.05	0.05	0.05	0.05
I ²		99.6	99.5	99.4	99.5	99.4	99.4	99.4	99.1

Source: World Bank.
Note: Within study standard errors of the estimates are used as weights to correct for the heteroscedasticity. The dependent variable is the informal-formal wage gap estimates by former studies (listed in annex table 4D.1). τ ² = estimates of across-study variance; *I* ² = residual variance due to study heterogeneity. *** p<0.01, ** p<0.05, * p<0.1; standard errors are in parenthesis.

TABLE 4D.3 Labor productivity differential between types of firms (percent)

	Informal firms						Informal versus formal firms
	Manager has higher education	Main owner is male	Services sector	Firm has bank loan	Single-employee firm	Young firm (<=5 years)	
Angola	45.8	70.0	44.9	-60.0	225.0	20.0	-75.5***
Argentina	25.0	200***	0.0	0.0	11.1	-16.7	-92.5***
Burkina Faso	-6.2	-6.2	28.6	6.7	66.7	-10.0	-79.8***
Botswana	89.4*	72.7**	-29.1	100.0	-35.0	-18.2	-89.8***
Cabo Verde	133.3	-25.0	185.7	1585**	566.7*	100.0	0.89
Cameroon	-41.7*	36.4	77.8**	-24.0	140.0***	56.2**	-55.8***
Congo, Dem. Rep.	33.3	0.0	36.0**	50.0	50.0***	0.0	10.7
Côte d'Ivoire	0.0	25.0	66.7**	-40.0	50.0	40.0	-47.5*
Ghana	0.0	12.5	0.0	25.0	66.7***	0.0	-51.8***
Guatemala	25.0	46.7***	33.3**	50.0	57.1***	-20.0	-86.0***
Kenya	50.0***	6.7	-40***	44.0**	12.0	-20.0**	-81.6***
Madagascar	40.0	-33.3	100***	33.3	60.0*	8.3	-88.1***
Mali	13.2	14.3	-19.4	31.4	57.1	-46.2**	-71.3***
Mauritius	66.7*	6.7	114.3***	25.0	6.7	25.0	-82.9***
Myanmar	80.0*	-11.1	63.6***	11.3	31.2	0.0	-89.1***
Nepal	11.1	0.0	0.0	33.3	150.0***	-16.7	-56.5***
Peru	28.6*	12.5	-50***	-11.1	2.9	-7.4	-74.2***
Rwanda	50.0***	28.6**	25.0*	-25.9	50.0***	-11.1	-91.4***
All countries	48.1***	10.2	8.2	20.0**	41.2***	-6.7	-79.4***

Source: World Bank.

Note: Productivity differential between the median informal and the median formal firm (last column) or between median informal firms among different groups of firms (all other columns). For example, "Manager has higher education" shows the difference in the median productivity among informal firms with managers with higher education and those without higher education. Other firm characteristics are not controlled for, hence results are similar but not identical to column (1) in table 4D.4. Productivity is defined as annual sales (in 2009 U.S. dollars) relative to the number of workers. "All countries" is the unweighted average across each column. Significance is denoted by *** (1 percent), ** (5 percent), * (10 percent).

TABLE 4D.4 **Regression: Labor productivity of formal and informal firms**

	(1)	(2)	(3)	(4)	(5)
Informal firm: Yes 1 No 0	-1.400***	-0.648***	-1.131***	-1.200***	-1.008***
	(0.091)	(0.184)	(0.131)	(0.121)	(0.160)
Firm age (logs)	0.120***	0.285***	0.118***	0.116**	0.137***
	(0.045)	(0.053)	(0.045)	(0.045)	(0.045)
Firm size (logs, workers)	-0.102***	-0.119***	-0.056*	-0.104***	-0.108***
	(0.027)	(0.027)	(0.032)	(0.028)	(0.028)
Manufacturing: Yes 1 No 0	-0.402***	-0.407***	-0.401***	-0.401***	-0.399***
	(0.056)	(0.056)	(0.056)	(0.056)	(0.056)
Capital city: Yes 1 No 0	0.201***	0.190***	0.187***	0.394***	0.201***
	(0.061)	(0.061)	(0.061)	(0.087)	(0.061)
Manager experience (logs, years)	0.094**	0.141***	0.107***	0.091**	0.190***
	(0.040)	(0.041)	(0.040)	(0.040)	(0.055)
Informal firm * Firm age (logs)		-0.353***			
		(0.069)			
Informal firm * Firm size (logs, workers)			-0.208***		
			(0.066)		
Informal firm * Capital city: Yes 1 No 0				-0.360***	
				(0.114)	
Informal firm * Manager experience (logs, years)					-0.176***
					(0.060)
Country fixed effects	Yes	Yes	Yes	Yes	Yes
Constant	9.013***	8.552***	8.859***	8.909***	8.748***
	(0.131)	(0.164)	(0.149)	(0.139)	(0.162)
Number of observations	10,527	10,527	10,527	10,527	10,527
R-squared	0.291	0.296	0.293	0.293	0.292

Source: World Bank.

Note: Ordinary least squares regression with labor productivity as dependent variable, as proxied by annual sales (in 2009 U.S. dollars) per worker, based on a sample using World Bank's Enterprise Surveys data collected during 2007-14 for 4,036 informal firms and 7,558 formal firms in 18 countries. "Informal firm" is a dummy variable taking the value of 1 if a firm is unregistered and 0 otherwise. "Manufacturing" is a dummy variable taking the value of 1 if a firm operates in the manufacturing sector and 0 otherwise. "Capital city" is a dummy variable taking the value of 1 if a firm is located in the capital city and 0 otherwise. Standard errors in parenthesis. Significance is denoted by *** (1 percent), ** (5 percent), * (10 percent).

TABLE 4D.5 Regression: Labor productivity of formal firms facing informal competition

	(1)	(2)	(3)	(4)	(5)
Informal competition	-0.268***	-1.642***	-1.919***	-0.574***	-1.657***
(Proportion of firms in the cell that report competing with informal firms)	(0.067)	(0.602)	(0.618)	(0.059)	(0.307)
Number of workers (logs)	-0.197***	-0.150***	-0.175***	-0.166***	-0.179***
	(0.016)	(0.017)	(0.019)	(0.019)	(0.020)
Firm age (logs)	0.208***	0.215***	0.296***	0.286***	0.356***
	(0.023)	(0.026)	(0.032)	(0.029)	(0.032)
Firm belongs to manufacturing sector: Yes 1 No 0	0.137***	0.077*	0.164***	0.157***	0.139***
	(0.044)	(0.046)	(0.052)	(0.048)	(0.053)
Firm belongs to retail sector: Yes 1 No 0	0.695***	0.747***	0.896***	0.862***	0.879***
	(0.045)	(0.047)	(0.053)	(0.049)	(0.054)
Top manager is female: Yes 1 No 0	-0.051	-0.125**	-0.128*	-0.086	-0.063
	(0.048)	(0.058)	(0.073)	(0.067)	(0.070)
Exports (proportion of sales)	0.268**	0.403***	0.431***	0.385***	0.397***
	(0.114)	(0.117)	(0.145)	(0.133)	(0.148)
Firm has foreign owners: Yes 1 No 0	0.638***	0.836***	0.821***	0.658***	0.781***
	(0.063)	(0.062)	(0.070)	(0.066)	(0.074)
Log GDP per capita (PPP, 2009 Int'l Dollars)		0.631***			
		(0.043)			
Informal competition * Log GDP per capita		0.138**			
		(0.067)			
Distance to Frontier (Doing Business)			0.031***		
(Higher values imply better regulatory practices)			(0.006)		
Informal competition * DTF			0.022**		
			(0.010)		
Corruption (Governance Indicators)				0.574***	
(Higher values imply less corruption)				(0.048)	
Informal competition * corruption				0.177**	
				(0.085)	
Business Freedom Index (Economic Freedom of the World)					0.015***
(Higher values imply less regulation and more freedom for businesses)					(0.003)
Informal competition * Business Freedom Index					0.016***
					(0.005)
Constant	8.771***	3.818***	7.469***	9.410***	8.163***
	(0.178)	(0.390)	(0.381)	(0.088)	(0.224)
Country fixed effects	YES	NO	NO	NO	NO
Number of observations	45,996	45,996	44,770	45,996	43,760
R-squared	0.404	0.259	0.184	0.191	0.154

Source: World Bank.
Note: Ordinary least squares regression with labor productivity as dependent variable, as proxied by annual sales (in 2009 U.S. dollars) per worker, based on a sample of formal firms only using World Bank's Enterprise Surveys data collected during 2007-14 for 4,036 informal firms and 7,558 formal firms in 18 countries. "Informal competition" is the share of firms in a cell (a group of firms of similar size in the same region and sector) that report competition from informal firms. It is worth mentioning that one could use a firm-level dummy rather than the proportion of formal firms in a cell to proxy informal competition. However, endogeneity concerns may arise because the informal competition faced by a specific firm may also be driven by its productivity. Therefore, the proportion of formal firms facing informal competition in a cell, which would be uncorrelated with the productivity of a specific firm, should be more robust to endogeneity concerns. "Manufacturing" is a dummy variable taking the value of 1 if a firm operates in the manufacturing sector and 0 otherwise. "Capital city" is a dummy variable taking the value of 1 if a firm is located in the capital city and 0 otherwise. DTF = Distance to Frontier; PPP = purchasing power parity. Standard errors in parenthesis. Significance is denoted by *** (1 percent), ** (5 percent), * (10 percent).

TABLE 4D.6 Regression: Informality, poverty, and income inequality

	Extreme poverty headcount ratio	Gini coefficient	Income per capita for bottom 40 percent	Income per capita growth for bottom 40 percent	Difference in income per capita between bottom 40 percent and total population	Difference in income per capita growth between bottom 40 percent and total population
Output informality	0.08	0.16**	-0.01	-0.07**	-0.02	0.01
(DGE estimates)	(0.13)	(0.07)	(0.02)	(0.03)	(0.04)	(0.02)
GDP per capita	-16.12***	1.25*	2.38***	0.70**	-3.72***	0.50***
	(1.45)	(0.67)	(0.25)	(0.32)	(0.37)	(0.18)
Observations	110	110	58	58	58	58
R-squared	0.59	0.05	0.60	0.16	0.68	0.09
Output informality	0.02	0.13**	-0.01	-0.07**	-0.02	0.00
(MIMIC estimates)	(0.13)	(0.06)	(0.02)	(0.03)	(0.03)	(0.02)
GDP per capita	-16.42***	1.09	2.39***	0.71**	-3.71***	0.48***
	(1.44)	(0.69)	(0.25)	(0.32)	(0.37)	(0.18)
Observations	112	112	58	58	58	58
R-squared	0.59	0.04	0.60	0.17	0.68	0.09
Employment informality	0.30***	0.09**	-0.04**	-0.04	-0.02	-0.03**
(Self-employment)	(0.08)	(0.04)	(0.02)	(0.03)	(0.02)	(0.02)
GDP per capita	-10.44***	2.54**	1.62***	0.28	-3.90***	-0.03
	(2.10)	(0.99)	(0.37)	(0.53)	(0.46)	(0.25)
Observations	118	118	60	60	60	60
R-squared	0.64	0.05	0.65	0.14	0.69	0.19

Source: World Bank.
Note: DGE = dynamic general equilibrium model; MIMIC = multiple indicators multiple causes model. Robust standard errors in parentheses. *** $p<0.01$, ** $p<0.05$, * $p<0.1$. Self-employment is in percent of total employment. Output informality measures are in percent of official GDP.

TABLE 4D.7 Regression: Changes in informality and poverty reduction

	Poverty at $1.90 per day							
	Output informality				Employment informality			
	World (1)	World (2)	EMDEs (1)	EMDEs (2)	World (1)	World (2)	EMDEs (1)	EMDEs (2)
Lagged poverty	-0.73*	-0.73*	-0.76*	-0.75*	-0.42*	-0.42*	-0.44*	-0.44*
	(0.07)	(0.07)	(0.07)	(0.07)	(0.09)	(0.09)	(0.11)	(0.11)
Change in informality	0.72**	0.69*	0.63	0.60**	0.10	0.08	0.112	0.004
	(0.38)	(0.33)	(0.40)	(0.36)	(0.06)	(0.08)	(0.08)	(0.07)
x lagged poverty		0.001		0.001		0.001		0.01
		(0.02)		(0.01)		(0.03)		(0.008)
Lagged informality	2.53*	2.53*	2.61*	2.62*	-0.09	-0.11	-0.34	-0.47
	(0.82)	(0.84)	(0.88)	(0.91)	(0.23)	(0.25)	(0.40)	(0.38)
Squared lagged informality	-0.016**	-0.016**	-0.017*	-0.017*	0.001	0.001	0.004	0.005
	(0.008)	(0.008)	(0.008)	(0.009)	(0.003)	(0.003)	(0.005)	(0.005)
GDP growth	-0.08*	-0.08*	-0.07	-0.07	-0.04	-0.04	-0.02	-0.02
	(0.04)	(0.04)	(0.05)	(0.05)	(0.03)	(0.03)	(0.04)	(0.04)
R-squared	0.66	0.66	0.69	0.69	0.65	0.65	0.74	0.75
Observations	366	366	262	262	266	266	164	164
Number of countries	117	117	85	85	92	92	60	60

	Poverty at $3.20 per day							
	Output informality				Employment informality			
	World (1)	World (2)	EMDEs (1)	EMDEs (2)	World (1)	World (2)	EMDEs (1)	EMDEs (2)
Lagged poverty	-0.59*	-0.59*	-0.65*	-0.65*	-0.42*	-0.41*	-0.46*	-0.49*
	(0.07)	(0.07)	(0.08)	(0.08)	(0.1)	(0.1)	(0.13)	(0.135
Change in informality	1.87*	1.87*	1.74**	1.74**	-0.23	0.20**	-0.57*	0.18
	(0.58)	(0.58)	(0.60)	(0.60)	(0.19)	(0.10)	(0.26)	(0.13)
x lagged poverty	-0.02**		-0.02*		0.014*		0.03*	
	(0.01)		(0.01)		(0.006)		(0.009)	
Lagged informality	2.88*	2.88*	2.88*	2.88*	-0.88**	-0.49	-1.53*	-0.98
	(0.98)	(0.98)	(1.04)	(1.04)	(0.45)	(0.42)	(0.65)	(0.67)
Squared lagged informality	-0.026*	-0.026*	-0.03*	-0.03*	0.01*	0.005	0.017*	0.011
	(0.01)	(0.01)	(0.01)	(0.01)	(0.005)	(0.005)	(0.008)	(0.007)
GDP growth	-0.15*	-0.15*	-0.12*	-0.12*	-0.14*	-0.14*	-0.15*	-0.17*
	(0.04)	(0.04)	(0.05)	(0.05)	(0.05)	(0.05)	(0.06)	(0.07)
R-squared	0.59	0.59	0.64	0.64	0.64	0.61	0.72	0.68
Observations	366	366	262	262	266	266	164	164
Number of countries	117	117	85	85	92	92	60	60

Source: World Bank.

Note: The sample of country-year observations starts with the first available observation for each country and all consecutive observations with at least five-year minimum window between them. Sample excludes fragile and conflict states. "Employment informality" is self-employment in percent of total employment. "Output informality" is proxied by DGE-based estimates on informal output in percent of official GDP. Dependent variables are changes in poverty rates at $1.90 and $3.20 per day. "GDP growth" denotes cumulative change in GDP per capita during the time window between observations. "Change in informality" denotes change in output (employment) informality during the time window between observations in percent of official GDP (in percent of official employment). "Lagged informality" denotes informality levels at t-1. Control variables include a constant, country and time fixed effects, and squared lagged informality to control for a possible nonlinear relationship between informality and poverty. A positive coefficient on change in informality indicates that formalization reduces poverty. DGE = dynamic general equilibrium model; EMDEs = emerging market and developing economies. Robust standard errors in parentheses; *p<0.05, ** p<0.1.

TABLE 4D.8 Regression: Changes in informality and improvement in income inequality

	Gini coefficient				Shared prosperity			
	Output informality		Employment informality		Output informality		Employment informality	
	World	EMDEs	World	EMDEs	World	EMDEs	World	EMDEs
Lagged inequality	-0.90*	-0.84*	-0.86*	-0.80*	-0.90*	-0.85*	-0.84*	-0.77*
	(0.06)	(0.07)	(0.09)	(0.12)	(0.06)	(0.07)	(0.09)	(0.12)
Change in informality	**-0.18**	**-0.22**	**0.02**	**0.006**	**0.10**	**0.12**	**-0.006**	**-0.01**
	(0.17)	(0.18)	(0.07)	(0.08)	(0.07)	(0.07)	(0.03)	(0.04)
Lagged informality	-0.28	-0.36	0.29	0.28	0.16	0.21	-0.12	-0.14
	(0.41)	(0.46)	(0.18)	(0.29)	(0.20)	(0.22)	(0.08)	(0.13)
Squared lagged informality	0.006	0.007	-0.004*	-0.004	-0.003	-0.003	0.002*	0.002
	(0.004)	(0.005)	(0.002)	(003)	(0.002)	(0.002)	(0.001)	(0.001)
GDP growth	0.01	0.02	0.012	0.04	-0.007	-0.009	-0.003	-0.02
	(0.02)	(0.03)	(0.030)	(0.05)	(0.014)	(0.014)	(0.014)	(0.023)
R^2	0.70	0.72	0.65	0.70	0.68	0.70	0.65	0.71
Observations	366	262	266	164	366	262	366	164
Number of countries	117	85	92	60	117	85	117	60

Source: World Bank.

Note: "Shared prosperity" refers to the income share of the bottom 40 percent of population. The sample of country-year observations starts with the first available observation for each country and all consecutive observations with at least five-year minimum window between them. Sample excludes fragile and conflict-affected states. "Employment informality" is self-employment in percent of total employment and "output informality" is proxied by DGE-based estimates on informal output in percent of official GDP. Dependent variables are two measures of inequality: the change in Gini coefficient and shared prosperity. "GDP growth" denotes cumulative change in GDP per capita during the time window between observations. "Change in informality" denotes change in output (employment) informality during the time window between observations in percent of official GDP (in percent of official employment). "Lagged informality" denotes informality levels at t-1. Control variables include a constant, country and time fixed effects, and squared lagged informality to control for a possible non-linear relationship between informality and inequality. A positive coefficient on change in informality indicates that formalization reduces shared prosperity (the income share of the bottom 40 percent of population). DGE = dynamic general equilibrium model; EMDEs = emerging market and developing economies. Robust standard errors in parentheses; *p<0.05, ** p<0.1.

TABLE 4D.9 Data: Bayesian model averaging approach

Group	Expected sign (group)	Variable	Source
Economic development	(-)	Share of population in urban area	WDI
		Labor productivity (in logs)	WDI
		Share of manufacturing (in percent of value added)	WDI
		Share of manufacturing (in percent of employment)	WDI
Human capital	(-)	Human capital	UNDP
		Share of population with primary schooling and above	Wittgenstein Center for Demography and Global Human Capital
		Share of population with secondary schooling and above	
Financial development	(-)	Domestic credit to private sector (in percent of GDP)	WDI
Trade openness	(-/+)	GVC position index	UNCTAD
		GVC participation index	UNCTAD
Governance	(-)	Political rights index	Freedom house
		Civil rights index	Freedom house
		Accountability	WGI
		Regulatory Quality	WGI
		Control of corruption	WGI
		Political stability	WGI
Tax burdens	(+)	Government expenditure (in percent of GDP)	WDI
		Tax revenues (in percent of GDP)	IMF GFS
Access to public infrastructure	(-)	Electricity consumption per capita	WDI
		Access to basic water, rural/urban	WDI
		Air goods transported	WDI
		Road length per capita	World Road Statistics

Source: World Bank.

Note: The expected signs are for each group of variables. They summarize the relationship between each group of variables and the level of informality suggested by past studies. "(-)" ("+") suggests that an increase in the corresponding group variable would be associated with a lower (higher) level of output informality. Among all groups, only the group of variables on tax burdens are expected to be positively associated with output informality, suggesting that higher tax burdens are associated with a higher level of informal output. In the case of trade openness, its relationship with informality could be either positive or negative, as suggested by former studies (chapter 6). GVC = global value chain; IMF GFS = International Monetary Fund Government Finance Statistics database; UNCTAD = United Nations Conference on Trade and Development; UNDP = United Nations Development Programme; WDI = World Development Indicators; WGI = Worldwide Governance Indicators.

TABLE 4D.10 PIP and posterior means (output informality)

Variable	PIP	Posterior Mean	Group	Group PIP	Group coef	Group coef positive prob.
Share of manufacturing (percent of value added)	0.22	-0.30				
Labor productivity (log)	0.05	0.00				
Share of population in urban area	0.06	-0.03	Economic development	0.88	-1.66	0.00
Share of manufacturing (percent of employment)	0.67	-1.08				
Agriculture export share	0.30	-0.25				
Share of population with primary schooling and above	0.34	0.15				
Share of population with secondary schooling and above	0.08	0.00	Human capital	0.92	-1.49	0.01
Human capital	0.88	-1.65				
Domestic credit to private sector (percent of GDP)	0.13	-0.14	Financial development	0.13	-0.14	0.01
Civil rights index	0.18	-0.01				
Political rights index	0.20	-0.31				
Accountability	0.21	-0.03	Governance	0.96	-2.18	0.00
Control of corruption	0.70	-3.31				
Regulatory quality	0.58	2.18				
Political stability	0.42	-0.70				
Electricity consumption per capita	0.28	0.15				
Access to basic water, rural	0.29	0.32	Access to public infrastructure	1.00	-0.36	0.26
Access to basic water, urban	0.81	1.40				
Road length per area (log)	0.28	0.03				
Air goods transported (log)	0.97	-2.26				
Government expenditure (percent of GDP)	0.12	0.09	Tax burdens	0.25	0.21	0.99
Tax revenues (percent of GDP)	0.14	0.12				
GVC participation index	0.16	0.12	Trade openness	0.25	0.08	0.64
GVC position index	0.10	-0.05				

Source: World Bank.

Note: Based on the panel regression result using Bayesian model averaging technique. The dependent variable is the share of informal economy in GDP using dynamic general equilibrium-based measures. From unbalanced panel from 67 emerging market and developing economies, using five-year panel from 1998-2018. GVC = global value chain; PIP = posterior inclusion probability.

TABLE 4D.11 **PIP and posterior means (employment informality)**

Variable	PIP	Posterior mean	Group	Group PIP	Group coef	Group coef positive prob.
Share of manufacturing (percent of value added)	0.29	-1.04				
Labor productivity (log)	0.22	-0.01	Economic development	0.99	-7.39	0.00
Share of population in urban area	0.03	-0.04				
Share of manufacturing (percent of employment)	0.48	-1.71				
Agriculture export (percent exports)	0.98	-4.59				
Share of population with primary schooling and above	0.24	0.25	Human capital	1.00	-8.02	0.00
Share of population with secondary schooling and above	0.12	0.34				
Human capital	1.00	-8.60				
Domestic credit to private sector (percent of GDP)	0.09	0.23	Financial development	0.09	0.23	0.95
Civil rights index	0.32	1.36				
Political rights index	0.07	0.18				
Accountability	0.37	2.07	Governance	1.00	-7.74	0.00
Control of corruption	0.74	-5.76				
Regulatory quality	0.04	0.03				
Political stability	0.94	-5.62				
Electricity consumption per capita	0.59	-6.62				
Access to basic water, rural	0.58	2.87	Access to public infrastructure	1.00	-6.59	0.16
Access to basic water, urban	0.55	2.38				
Road length per area (log)	0.96	-4.81				
Air goods transported (log)	0.16	-0.48				
Government expenditure (percent of GDP)	0.06	-0.10	Tax burdens	0.11	0.06	0.59
Tax revenues (percent of GDP)	0.07	0.16				
GVC participation index	0.06	0.05	Trade openness	0.17	0.28	0.93
GVC position index	0.11	0.23				

Source: World Bank.
Note: Based on the panel regression result using Bayesian model averaging technique. The dependent variable is the share self employment. From unbalanced panel from 64 emerging market and developing economies, using five-year panel from 1998-2018. GVC = global value chain; PIP = posterior inclusion probability.

TABLE 4D.12 **Correlates of employment informality in EMDEs**

	High informality	Low informality	P-value for t-test
SDG global index rank	113.6	77.0	0.00
Extreme poverty headcount (2000, percent of population)	39.7	11.6	0.01
Extreme poverty headcount (latest, percent of population)	24.0	5.4	0.00
Agriculture sector (value added, percent of GDP)	19.6	5.4	0.00
Agriculture sector (employment, percent of employment)	45.5	10.8	0.00
Finance constraint (percent of firms)	32.3	28.9	0.24
Bank finance (percent of firms)	20.7	30.9	0.00
Internal finance (percent of investment)	73.6	66.3	0.00
Basic training	1.9	2.0	0.31
Business infrastructure	2.8	3.0	0.09
Physical infrastructure	3.6	3.4	0.03
Adequacy of social insurance programs (percent of household income)	27.4	34.1	0.04
Coverage of unemployment benefits (percent of population)	5.0	5.2	0.91
GDP per capita (in thousands of 2010 U.S. dollars)	2.0	9.6	0.00
Access to credit (percent of GDP)	24.3	43.1	0.00
Human capital (years of schooling)	5.2	8.1	0.00
Trade openness (percent of GDP)	71.9	92.9	0.00
Labor productivity (in thousands of 2010 U.S. dollars)	5.5	21.3	0.00
Per capita income of bottom 40 percent (2011 PPP$ per day)	3.2	6.6	0.00
Per capita income growth of bottom 40 percent (2011 PPP$ per day)	1.5	3.1	0.02
Government revenues (percent of GDP)	20.4	31.9	0.00
Tax revenues (overall, percent of GDP)	13.4	19.0	0.00
Tax revenues (income, percent of GDP)	4.4	6.0	0.00
Tax revenues (imports, percent of GDP)	1.3	0.3	0.00
Government expenditures (overall, percent of GDP)	23.2	32.8	0.00
Government expenditures (education, percent of GDP)	4.0	4.6	0.00
Government expenditures (health, percent of GDP)	2.2	3.6	0.00
Undernourishment (percent of population)	17.7	6.6	0.00
Stunting (percent of population)	28.1	12.1	0.00
Agricultural productivity (tons per hectare)	2.3	4.3	0.00
Maternal mortality (per 10,000 births)	267.4	65.1	0.00
Under 5 mortality (per 1,000 births)	43.8	17.4	0.00

TABLE 4D.12 **Correlates of employment informality in EMDEs (*continued*)**

	High informality	Low informality	P-value for t-test
Death rate from pollution (per 100,000 persons)	136.7	67.2	0.00
Life expectancy at birth (years)	67.4	73.4	0.00
Net primary school enrollment	88.6	90.6	0.24
Literacy rate (percent of people aged 15-24)	84.6	97.9	0.00
Female years of schooling (percent of male schooling)	77.8	97.8	0.00
Family planning	55.4	65.3	0.00
Female informal workers	86.6	50.3	0.00
Doing Business score	53.8	61.8	0.00
Cost of business start-up procedures (percent of GNI per capita)	79.9	22.8	0.00
Bureaucracy quality	1.49	2.03	0.00
Control of corruption	2.27	2.57	0.01
Law and order	3.02	3.59	0.00
Quality of overall infrastructure	4.0	3.3	0.00
Access to sanitation services (percent of population)	55.6	88.8	0.00
Access to drinking water services (percent of population)	78.3	95.1	0.00
Access to electricity (percent of population)	69.4	96.3	0.00
Access to clean fuels (percent of population)	36.7	83.2	0.00
Access to internet (percent of population)	35.2	65.3	0.00
Access to mobile broadband (percent of population)	46.2	73.4	0.00
Paved road (percent of total roads)	14.0	47.8	0.00
Road project unit costs (all, U.S. dollars per km, millions)	0.5	0.4	0.22
Road project unit costs (reconstruction, U.S. dollars per km, millions)	0.5	0.3	0.22

Source: World Bank.
Note: See the notes to figures 4.1-4.8 for detailed definitions and data sources. The columns "High" ("Low") informality show simple averages for emerging market and developing economies (EMDEs) with above (below)-median employment informality (proxied by self-employment as a share of total employment). GNI = gross national income; PPP = purchasing power parity; SDG = Sustainable Development Goal.

TABLE 4D.13 Correlates of informality in EMDEs: MIMIC-based informal activity and WEF index

	MIMIC-based output informality			Perceived informality (WEF)		
	High	Low	P-val	High	Low	P-val
GDP per capita	7.3	8.4	0.00	7.4	8.4	0.00
Access to credit	23.0	39.1	0.00	22.7	42.3	0.00
Human capital	5.8	7.1	0.01	5.7	7.5	0.00
Trade openness	73.7	82.3	0.15	7.0	8.7	0.00
Doing Business score	53.3	59.8	0.00	53.3	62.1	0.00
Cost of business start-up procedures	96.2	26.8	0.00	86.7	22.5	0.00
Bureaucracy quality	1.4	2.1	0.04	1.5	2.0	0.00
Control of corruption	2.2	2.6	0.00	2.3	2.6	0.00
Law and order	2.9	3.6	0.00	2.9	3.8	0.00

Sources: Barro and Lee (2013); *International Country Risk Guide* (ICRG); World Bank (*Doing Business*, World Development Indicators).

Note: Data are from emerging market and development economies (EMDEs) and the period 1990-2018. "High" are EMDEs with above median MIMIC-based informal output measures (perceived informality measured by the World Economic Forum's index, reversed order), while "Low" are EMDEs with below median MIMIC-based informal output measures (perceived informality). "P-val" shows the p-values of the t-tests conducted for the group comparisons. The correlates include GDP per capita (in logs; 2010 U.S. dollars); access to credit (domestic credit to private sector in percent of GDP); human capital (average years of schooling); trade openness (the sum of imports and exports in percent of GDP); the ease of doing business score (the score is reflected on a scale from 0 to 100, where 0 represents the lowest and 100 represents the best performance); bureaucracy quality; control of corruption; and law and order (ICRG). Higher values corresponding to better outcomes. MIMIC = multiple indicators multiple causes model; WEF = World Economic Forum.

TABLE 4D.14 Regression: Developmental challenges and DGE-based output informality in EMDEs

Dependent variable =	Lowest quartile (Q1)	2nd quartile (Q2) -Q1	3rd quartile (Q3) -Q1	Highest quartile (Q4) -Q1	Obs	R-sq
	(1)	(2)	(3)	(4)	(5)	(6)
SDG global index rank	84.500***	3.638	28.017***	20.362**	117	0.088
	(6.380)	(9.165)	(9.973)	(9.837)		
Extreme poverty headcount (2000, percent of population)	13.140**	13.760	29.560**	40.310**	17	0.298
	(5.439)	(17.815)	(13.628)	(18.508)		
Extreme poverty headcount (latest, percent of population)	7.336***	1.418	23.579***	12.435**	111	0.199
	(1.908)	(3.204)	(5.318)	(4.925)		
Agriculture sector (value added, percent of GDP)	4.846***	3.589**	14.358***	15.348***	157	0.298
	(1.074)	(1.705)	(2.281)	(2.288)		
Agriculture sector (employment, percent of employment)	10.366***	10.350***	32.082***	34.126***	157	0.360
	(2.372)	(3.907)	(4.433)	(3.939)		
Finance constraint (percent of firms)	24.295***	5.775*	14.365***	8.257*	109	0.108
	(2.325)	(3.371)	(3.958)	(4.201)		
Bank finance (percent of firms)	28.650***	-0.276	-8.426**	-10.278***	109	0.126
	(2.406)	(3.482)	(3.324)	(3.367)		
Internal finance (percent of investment)	68.843***	-1.446	6.834**	5.311*	109	0.086
	(2.015)	(3.152)	(2.775)	(3.165)		
Basic training	1.937***	0.128	-0.076	-0.028	68	0.041
	(0.102)	(0.127)	(0.149)	(0.123)		
Business infrastructure	2.941***	-0.001	-0.053	-0.081	68	0.019
	(0.075)	(0.085)	(0.104)	(0.094)		
Physical infrastructure	3.675***	-0.201	-0.296**	-0.230	68	0.070
	(0.088)	(0.129)	(0.121)	(0.157)		
Adeq. of social insurance program (percent household income)	36.281***	-6.164	-10.095*	-6.798	93	0.050
	(3.530)	(4.372)	(5.335)	(4.811)		
Coverage of unemployment benefits (percent of population)	6.519***	0.326	-2.290	-3.653*	59	0.092
	(1.823)	(2.399)	(2.069)	(2.025)		
GDP per capita (logs)	8.769***	-0.697**	-1.645***	-1.317***	121	0.263
	(0.220)	(0.293)	(0.296)	(0.274)		
Access to credit (percent of GDP)	44.818***	-9.466	-23.791***	-18.603***	122	0.139
	(4.988)	(6.533)	(5.731)	(6.649)		
Human capital (years of schooling)	7.253***	-0.524	-1.432*	-1.270**	99	0.055
	(0.363)	(0.573)	(0.747)	(0.594)		
Trade openness (percent of GDP)	83.269***	-8.021	-7.312	-9.606	119	0.013
	(6.215)	(8.878)	(8.266)	(8.375)		
Labor productivity (in thousands of 2010 U.S. dollars)	27.342***	-15.96***	-20.522***	-20.254***	116	0.235
	(5.092)	(5.338)	(5.270)	(5.328)		
Per capita income of bottom 40 percent (2011 PPP$ per day)	6.344***	-1.911*	-2.426**	-2.044*	58	0.095
	(0.790)	(1.054)	(1.206)	(1.107)		
Per capita income growth of bottom 40 percent (2011 PPP$ per day)	3.215***	0.307	-1.581*	-2.270**	58	0.132
	(0.702)	(1.178)	(0.841)	(1.071)		

TABLE 4D.14 Regression: Developmental challenges and DGE-based output informality in EMDEs (*continued*)

Dependent variable =	Lowest quartile (Q1)	2nd quartile (Q2) -Q1	3rd quartile (Q3) -Q1	Highest quartile (Q4) -Q1	Obs	R-sq
	(1)	(2)	(3)	(4)	(5)	(6)
Government revenues	26.745***	-1.311	-4.068	-4.735*	83	0.050
(percent of GDP)	(1.678)	(2.704)	(2.459)	(2.578)		
Tax revenues	15.655***	-0.020	-0.730	-1.706	83	0.016
(overall, percent of GDP)	(1.297)	(1.705)	(1.892)	(1.605)		
Tax revenues	5.517***	-0.929	-1.075	-1.212	83	0.035
(income, percent of GDP)	(0.677)	(0.825)	(0.906)	(0.815)		
Tax revenues	0.968*	0.152	0.317	0.023	69	0.008
(imports, percent of GDP)	(0.492)	(0.593)	(0.546)	(0.549)		
Government expenditures	28.156***	0.071	-3.477	-5.270**	83	0.075
(overall, percent of GDP)	(1.755)	(2.685)	(2.357)	(2.520)		
Government expenditures (education,	4.332***	-0.233	-0.085	-0.610*	118	0.025
percent of GDP)	(0.247)	(0.391)	(0.373)	(0.365)		
Government expenditures	3.240***	-0.372	-1.090***	-0.838**	122	0.076
(health, percent of GDP)	(0.287)	(0.417)	(0.345)	(0.407)		
Pupil - teacher ratio	21.369***	4.821*	14.413***	12.430***	120	0.162
(primary education)	(1.489)	(2.561)	(3.008)	(3.584)		
Trained teachers in primary edu	86.299***	0.438	-12.399**	-0.440	103	0.100
(percent of teachers)	(3.034)	(3.891)	(4.954)	(4.589)		
Undernourishment	8.738***	0.830	6.340**	10.087***	113	0.119
(percent of population)	(1.667)	(2.137)	(2.797)	(3.440)		
Stunting	15.486***	3.293	11.487***	9.455***	118	0.121
(percent of population)	(2.390)	(3.288)	(3.493)	(3.197)		
Agricultural productivity	4.778***	-1.697*	-2.550***	-1.726	119	0.074
(tons per hectare)	(0.812)	(0.876)	(0.841)	(1.175)		
Maternal mortality	82.677***	50.356	206.452***	198.189***	122	0.146
(per 10,000 births)	(20.641)	(38.247)	(50.318)	(58.552)		
Under 5 mortality	19.368***	7.919	28.871***	23.192***	122	0.156
(per 1,000 births)	(3.040)	(5.157)	(6.358)	(7.116)		
Death rate from pollution	75.419***	11.181	70.000***	46.281***	122	0.155
(per 100,000 persons)	(9.292)	(14.843)	(15.546)	(17.098)		
Life expectancy at birth	72.871***	-0.784	-6.739***	-5.198***	122	0.169
(years)	(1.098)	(1.491)	(1.593)	(1.767)		
Net primary school enrollment	91.268***	-1.443	-6.683**	-3.401	117	0.053
	(1.448)	(2.238)	(3.163)	(2.312)		
Literacy rate	96.585***	-3.306	-14.395***	-10.544***	118	0.142
(percent of people aged 15-24)	(0.942)	(2.093)	(3.562)	(3.538)		
Female years of schooling	8.497***	-0.930	-2.210***	-1.313**	122	0.083
(percent of male schooling)	(0.400)	(0.587)	(0.735)	(0.624)		
Family planning	69.000***	-8.123*	-16.607***	-11.750**	121	0.094
(percent of women with needs)	(2.709)	(4.642)	(4.304)	(4.902)		

TABLE 4D.14 Regression: Developmental challenges and DGE-based output informality in EMDEs (*continued*)

Dependent variable =	Lowest quartile (Q1)	2nd quartile (Q2) -Q1	3rd quartile (Q3) -Q1	Highest quartile (Q4) -Q1	Obs	R-sq
	(1)	(2)	(3)	(4)	(5)	(6)
Female informal workers (percent of female workers)	60.138*** (4.865)	11.028 (7.157)	19.612** (8.026)	17.188** (6.939)	67	0.112
Doing Business score	62.683*** (1.253)	-4.368* (2.258)	-9.435*** (2.099)	-8.453*** (2.481)	122	0.133
Cost of business start-up procedures (percent of GNI per capita)	17.574*** (4.245)	18.013** (8.728)	70.237*** (17.750)	78.590*** (22.164)	122	0.153
Bureaucracy quality	2.271*** (0.105)	-0.340* (0.184)	-0.927*** (0.173)	-0.824*** (0.148)	95	0.279
Control of corruption	2.808*** (0.108)	-0.394** (0.151)	-0.550*** (0.142)	-0.640*** (0.166)	95	0.183
Law and order	4.029*** (0.171)	-0.746*** (0.255)	-1.147*** (0.220)	-1.050*** (0.255)	95	0.230
Quality of overall infrastructure	4.295*** (0.152)	-0.576** (0.227)	-1.158*** (0.201)	-0.936*** (0.211)	108	0.246
Access to sanitation services (percent of population)	83.694*** (3.702)	-4.642 (5.880)	-27.935*** (6.741)	-25.588*** (6.561)	122	0.179
Access to drinking water services (percent of population)	93.046*** (1.952)	-4.307 (3.300)	-15.721*** (3.660)	-14.017*** (3.886)	122	0.157
Access to electricity (percent of population)	92.750*** (2.817)	-3.920 (4.544)	-28.945*** (6.764)	-19.955*** (6.152)	122	0.176
Access to clean fuels (percent of population)	82.268*** (4.393)	-14.314* (7.399)	-43.833*** (8.216)	-37.288*** (8.000)	120	0.225
Access to internet (percent of population)	65.353*** (4.137)	-9.966* (5.811)	-32.517*** (6.151)	-26.623*** (5.780)	122	0.245
Access to mobile broadband (percent of population)	83.712*** (8.220)	-18.885* (9.981)	-42.583*** (9.599)	-33.104*** (10.050)	122	0.182
Paved road (percent of total roads)	40.100*** (8.154)	-1.265 (12.626)	-19.772** (9.118)	-29.360*** (8.416)	45	0.247
Road project unit costs (all, U.S. dollars per km, millions)	0.389*** (0.108)	-0.085 (0.124)	0.156 (0.254)	0.209 (0.186)	67	0.037
Road project unit costs (reconstruction, U.S. dollars per km, millions)	0.441*** (0.157)	-0.149 (0.188)	0.184 (0.412)	-0.094 (0.223)	31	0.044

Source: World Bank.

Note: See the notes to figures 4.1-4.8 for detailed definitions and data sources for various dependent variables. Development outcomes are regressed against a set of dummies that categorize emerging market and developing economies (EMDEs) into quantiles of shares of informality using DGE-based estimates on informal output in percent of official GDP. The constant from the regression results show the development outcomes for the lowest quartile; coefficients show the difference between the corresponding quartile and the lowest quartile. All regressions are cross-sectional, with variables averaged during (up to) 1990-2018 (or otherwise specified period or latest year available). DGE = dynamic general equilibrium model; PPP = purchasing power parity; SDG = Sustainable Development Goal. Robust standard errors in parentheses. *** p<0.01, ** p<0.05, * p<0.1

TABLE 4D.15 Regression: Developmental challenges and self-employment in EMDEs

Dependent variable =	Lowest quartile (Q1) (1)	2nd quartile (Q2) -Q1 (2)	3rd quartile (Q3) -Q1 (3)	Highest quartile (Q4) -Q1 (4)	Obs (5)	R-sq (6)
SDG global index rank	67.033***	22.467***	26.733***	65.863***	119	0.382
	(5.576)	(8.264)	(8.004)	(7.356)		
Extreme poverty headcount	9.283*	5.577	12.457	53.497***	21	0.752
(2000, percent of population)	(5.126)	(7.034)	(9.287)	(7.376)		
Extreme poverty headcount	4.163***	2.420	7.777**	32.323***	119	0.439
(latest, percent of population)	(1.210)	(2.432)	(3.392)	(3.835)		
Agriculture sector	3.241***	4.387***	9.684***	23.135***	170	0.580
(value added, percent of GDP)	(0.612)	(1.109)	(1.243)	(1.808)		
Agriculture sector	6.184***	9.979***	25.441***	53.426***	161	0.765
(employment, percent of emp.)	(1.148)	(1.977)	(2.190)	(2.602)		
Finance constraint	26.429***	5.117	-3.481	15.571***	114	0.220
(percent of firms)	(2.172)	(3.743)	(2.945)	(3.699)		
Bank finance	34.543***	-7.428**	-11.221***	-16.531***	114	0.196
(percent of firms)	(2.214)	(3.669)	(3.004)	(3.009)		
Internal finance	65.445***	1.701	3.691	12.792***	114	0.147
(percent of investment)	(2.072)	(3.161)	(3.419)	(2.680)		
Basic training	2.000***	0.013	-0.084	-0.079	72	0.015
	(0.084)	(0.114)	(0.129)	(0.125)		
Business infrastructure	2.966***	-0.021	-0.140*	-0.095	72	0.044
	(0.056)	(0.077)	(0.081)	(0.100)		
Physical infrastructure	3.643***	-0.093	-0.159	-0.395***	72	0.111
	(0.079)	(0.121)	(0.126)	(0.148)		
Adequacy of social insurance programs	36.782***	-5.376	-8.182*	-10.646**	100	0.058
(percent of household income)	(3.319)	(4.421)	(4.350)	(5.074)		
Coverage of unemployment benefits	6.644***	-3.069	-1.378	-1.909	61	0.044
(percent of population)	(1.705)	(1.851)	(2.385)	(2.021)		
GDP per capita	9.131***	-0.862***	-1.471***	-2.461***	133	0.580
(in logs)	(0.153)	(0.190)	(0.221)	(0.185)		
Access to credit	50.592***	-15.457***	-19.843***	-32.891***	131	0.245
(percent of GDP)	(4.629)	(5.709)	(5.964)	(5.228)		
Human capital	8.626***	-1.131**	-2.201***	-4.686***	99	0.500
(years of schooling)	(0.258)	(0.499)	(0.463)	(0.406)		
Trade openness	98.526***	-11.076	-24.556***	-29.558***	129	0.095
(percent of GDP)	(5.327)	(10.325)	(7.770)	(7.393)		
Labor productivity	30.441***	-18.349***	-22.537***	-28.026***	119	0.383
(in thousands of 2010 dollars)	(4.531)	(4.654)	(4.812)	(4.543)		
Per capita income of bottom 40 percent	8.200***	-3.622***	-3.746***	-6.341***	61	0.583
(2011 PPP$ per day)	(0.766)	(0.839)	(0.899)	(0.812)		
Per capita income growth of bottom 40 percent	3.393***	-0.506	-1.152	-2.762**	61	0.130
(2011 PPP$ per day)	(0.812)	(1.155)	(0.891)	(1.100)		

TABLE 4D.15 Regression: Developmental challenges and self-employment in EMDEs (*continued*)

Dependent variable =	Lowest quartile (Q1)	2nd quartile (Q2) -Q1	3rd quartile (Q3) -Q1	Highest quartile (Q4) -Q1	Obs	R-sq
	(1)	(2)	(3)	(4)	(5)	(6)
Road project unit costs	0.536***	-0.247	0.088	-0.112	69	0.041
(all, U.S. dollars per km, millions)	(0.152)	(0.171)	(0.254)	(0.203)		
Road project unit costs	0.447***	-0.241*	-0.170	0.282	34	0.112
(reconstruction, U.S. dollars per km, millions)	(0.114)	(0.138)	(0.144)	(0.407)		
Government revenues	33.473***	-9.163***	-11.665***	-13.253***	83	0.327
(percent of GDP)	(1.829)	(2.608)	(2.409)	(2.227)		
Tax revenues	19.586***	-6.703***	-4.357**	-6.630***	83	0.242
(overall, percent of GDP)	(1.255)	(1.651)	(1.812)	(1.334)		
Tax revenues	5.867***	-1.504*	-1.093	-1.853**	83	0.076
(income, percent of GDP)	(0.683)	(0.809)	(0.913)	(0.790)		
Tax revenues	0.669	1.016	0.484	0.755	70	0.033
(imports, percent of GDP)	(0.435)	(0.935)	(0.539)	(0.489)		
Government expenditures	33.438***	-5.909**	-10.147***	-10.691***	83	0.247
(overall, percent of GDP)	(2.074)	(2.862)	(2.468)	(2.344)		
Government expenditures	4.674***	-0.371	-0.873**	-0.475	123	0.042
(education, percent of GDP)	(0.376)	(0.449)	(0.432)	(0.440)		
Government expenditures	4.089***	-0.812*	-1.374***	-2.542***	126	0.277
(health, percent of GDP)	(0.371)	(0.471)	(0.435)	(0.392)		
Pupil - teacher ratio	17.443***	5.350***	11.154***	24.265***	125	0.501
(primary education)	(1.066)	(1.499)	(2.544)	(2.106)		
Trained teachers in primary edu.	85.695***	0.894	-0.401	-9.355*	107	0.060
(percent of teachers)	(2.789)	(3.856)	(4.362)	(4.779)		
Undernourishment	4.607***	3.935**	8.496***	18.253***	123	0.346
(percent of population)	(0.871)	(1.541)	(2.049)	(2.606)		
Stunting	8.969***	6.473***	14.698***	23.889***	125	0.450
(percent of population)	(1.351)	(2.329)	(2.631)	(2.109)		
Agricultural productivity	5.715***	-2.830***	-2.921***	-3.896***	124	0.188
(tons per hectare)	(1.014)	(1.058)	(1.038)	(1.035)		
Maternal mortality	37.242***	55.851*	98.539***	368.820***	129	0.434
(per 10,000 births)	(6.469)	(29.142)	(24.735)	(45.042)		
Under 5 mortality	12.850***	9.253**	14.768***	47.802***	133	0.470
(per 1,000 births)	(1.794)	(4.052)	(3.712)	(4.704)		
Death rate from pollution	58.061***	19.158*	36.939***	122.033***	129	0.466
(per 100,000 persons)	(4.963)	(11.268)	(10.401)	(11.641)		
Life expectancy at birth	74.394***	-1.991*	-3.122***	-11.022***	129	0.423
(years)	(0.617)	(1.125)	(1.156)	(1.117)		
Net primary school enrollment	91.533***	-1.935	0.751	-6.626***	128	0.092
	(1.111)	(2.087)	(1.613)	(2.443)		
Literacy rate	98.876***	-2.581**	-5.672***	-22.994***	123	0.424
(percent aged 15-24)	(0.228)	(1.106)	(1.587)	(3.375)		

TABLE 4D.15 Regression: Developmental challenges and self-employment in EMDEs (*continued*)

Dependent variable =	Lowest quartile (Q1) (1)	2nd quartile (Q2) -Q1 (2)	3rd quartile (Q3) -Q1 (3)	Highest quartile (Q4) -Q1 (4)	Obs (5)	R-sq (6)
Female years of schooling	9.788***	-1.300***	-2.239***	-5.222***	131	0.500
(percent of male schooling)	(0.234)	(0.442)	(0.475)	(0.384)		
Family planning	63.142***	3.554	-1.058	-13.977***	129	0.125
(percent of women with needs)	(3.244)	(4.293)	(4.844)	(4.278)		
Female informal workers	37.304***	26.815***	42.878***	56.091***	70	0.724
(percent of female workers)	(3.654)	(5.184)	(5.013)	(3.835)		
Doing Business score	64.187***	-4.942***	-6.484***	-14.312***	134	0.293
	(1.194)	(1.849)	(1.977)	(1.828)		
Cost of business start-up procedures	14.904***	16.091**	25.022***	106.249***	134	0.353
(percent of GNI per capita)	(3.551)	(7.362)	(7.597)	(17.265)		
Bureaucracy quality	2.275***	-0.485***	-0.547***	-1.020***	96	0.253
(ICRG)	(0.132)	(0.178)	(0.161)	(0.210)		
Control of corruption	2.803***	-0.463***	-0.552***	-0.517***	96	0.161
(ICRG)	(0.108)	(0.164)	(0.143)	(0.145)		
Law and order	4.055***	-0.921***	-0.944***	-1.134***	96	0.229
(ICRG)	(0.152)	(0.255)	(0.218)	(0.217)		
Quality of overall infrastructure	4.352***	-0.788***	-0.826***	-1.227***	111	0.270
	(0.131)	(0.183)	(0.194)	(0.209)		
Access to sanitation services	92.238***	-6.793**	-18.251***	-56.234***	133	0.599
(percent of population)	(1.760)	(3.213)	(4.457)	(3.942)		
Access to drinking water services	96.573***	-3.219**	-8.487***	-28.303***	133	0.522
(percent of population)	(0.879)	(1.495)	(2.380)	(2.739)		
Access to electricity	98.099***	-3.622	-10.983***	-47.426***	133	0.517
(percent of population)	(1.175)	(2.521)	(3.811)	(4.852)		
Access to clean fuels	88.398***	-10.309*	-30.273***	-73.766***	131	0.586
(percent of population)	(3.502)	(5.779)	(6.279)	(4.645)		
Access to internet	71.024***	-12.388***	-24.094***	-47.731***	133	0.498
(percent of population)	(3.444)	(4.340)	(4.984)	(4.337)		
Access to mobile broadband	82.942***	-18.727*	-28.295***	-46.673***	133	0.209
(percent of population)	(8.002)	(9.703)	(9.093)	(9.114)		
Paved road	57.567***	-23.393*	-41.977***	-45.587***	41	0.446
(percent of total roads)	(10.160)	(12.608)	(10.394)	(10.399)		

Source: World Bank.
Note: See the notes to figures 4.1-4.8 for detailed definitions and data sources for various dependent variables. Development outcomes are regressed against a set of dummies that categorize emerging market and developing economies (EMDEs) into quantiles of shares of informality using self-employment in percent of total employment. The constant from the regression results show the development outcomes for the lowest quartile and coefficients show the difference between the corresponding quartile and the lowest quartile. All regressions are cross-sectional regressions with variables averaged during (up to)1990-2018 (or otherwise specified period or latest year available). Robust standard errors in parentheses. *** p<0.01, ** p<0.05, * p<0.1. ICRG = *International Country Risk Guide*; PPP = purchasing power parity; SDG = Sustainable Development Goal.

References

Abraham, R. 2019. "Informal Employment and the Structure of Wages in India: A Review of the Trends." *Review of Income and Wealth* 65 (S1): S102-22.

Adams, R. 2003. "Economic Growth, Inequality, and Poverty: Findings from a New Data Set." Policy Research Working Paper 2972, World Bank, Washington, DC.

Al Masri, D., V. Flamini, and F. G. Toscani. 2021. "The Short-Term Impact of COVID-19 on Labor Markets, Poverty and Inequality in Brazil." IMF Working Paper 2166, International Monetary Fund, Washington, DC.

Ali, N., and B. Najman. 2017. "Informal competition, firms' productivity and policy reforms in Egypt." In *The Informal Economy: Exploring Drivers and Practices*, edited by I. A. Horodnic, P. Rodgers, C. C. Williams, and L. Momtazian. Abingdon, U.K.: Routledge (in press).

Allen, J., and T. Schipper. 2016. "Understanding the Informal Sector: Do Formal and Informal Firms Compete?" Unpublished manuscript.

Amaral, P. S., and E. Quintin. 2006. "A Competitive Model of the Informal Sector." *Journal of Monetary Economics* 53 (7): 1541-53.

Amarante V., R. Arim, and M. Yapor, 2016. "Decomposing Inequality Changes in Uruguay: The Role of Formalization in the Labor Market." *IZA Journal of Labor & Development* 5 (1): 1-20.

Amin, M., and X. Huang. 2014. "Does Firm-Size Matter in the Informal Sector?" Enterprise Note 28, World Bank, Washington, DC.

Amin, M., and A. Islam. 2015. "Are Large Informal Firms More Productive than the Small Informal Firms? Evidence from Firm-Level Surveys in Africa." *World Development* 74 (C): 374-85.

Amin, M., F. Ohnsorge, and C. Okou. 2019. "Casting a Shadow: Productivity of Formal Firms and Informality." Policy Research Working Paper 8945, World Bank, Washington, DC.

Amin, M., and C. Okou. 2020. "Casting a Shadow: Productivity of Formal Firms and Informality." *Review of Development Economics* 24 (4): 1610-30.

Amuedo-Dorantes, C. 2004. "Determinants and Poverty Implications of Informal Sector Work in Chile." *Economic Development and Cultural Change* 52 (2): 347-68.

Arias, O., and M. Khamis. 2008. "Comparative Advantage, Segmentation and Informal Earnings: A Marginal Treatment Effects Approach." IZA Discussion Paper 3916, Institute for the Study of Labor, Bonn, Germany.

Ariza, J., and G. Montes-Rojas. 2017. "Labour Income Inequality and the Informal Sector in Colombian Cities." *Cuadernos de Economía* 36 (72): 77-98.

Attanasio, O., P. Goldberg, and N. Pavcnik. 2004. "Trade Reforms and Wage Inequality in Colombia." *Journal of Development Economics* 74 (2): 331-66.

Auriol, E., and M. Walters. 2005. "Taxation Base in Developing Countries." *Journal of Public Economics* 89 (4): 625-46.

Autor, D. and Reynolds, E., 2020. "The Nature of Work after the COVID Crisis: Too Few Low-Wage Jobs." The Hamilton Project, Brookings Institution, Washington, DC.

Aydin, E., M. Hisarciklilar, and I. Ikkaracan. 2010. "Formal versus Informal Labor Market Segmentation in Turkey in the Course of Market Liberalization." Topics *in Middle Eastern and North African Economies* 12 (September).

Banerjee, A., and E. Duflo. 2003. "Inequality and Growth: What Can the Data Say?" *Journal of Economic Growth* 8: 267-99.

Banerjee, A., E. Duflo, and N. Qian. 2020. "On the Road: Access to Transportation Infrastructure and Economic Growth in China." *Journal of Development Economics* 145 (June): 102442.

Bargain, O., and P. Kwenda. 2014. "The Informal Sector Wage Gap: New Evidence Using Quantile Estimations on Panel Data." *Economic Development and Cultural Change* 63 (1): 117-53.

Barro, R. J., and L. W. Lee. 2013. "A New Data Set of Educational Attainment in the World, 1950–2010." *Journal of Development Economics* 104 (September): 184-98.

Baskaya, Y. S., and T. Hulagu. 2011. "Informal-Formal Worker Wage Gap in Turkey: Evidence from A Semi-Parametric Approach." Working Paper 11/15, Central Bank of the Republic of Turkey, Ankara.

Benjamin, N., and A. Mbaye. 2012. "The Informal Sector, Productivity, and Enforcement in West Africa: A Firm-Level Analysis." *Review of Development Economics* 16 (4): 664-80.

Berdiev, A., J. Saunoris, and F. Schneider. 2020. "Poverty and the Shadow Economy: The Role of Governmental Institutions." *The World Economy* 43 (4): 921-47.

Besley, T., and T. Persson. 2014. "Why Do Developing Countries Tax So Little?" *Journal of Economic Perspectives* 28 (4): 99-120.

Blackburn, K., N. Bose, and S. Capasso. 2012. "Tax Evasion, the Underground Economy and Financial Development." *Journal of Economic Behavior & Organization* 83 (2): 243-53.

Blanchflower, D.G., A. Oswald, and A. Stutzer. 2001. "Latent Entrepreneurship across Nations." *European Economic Review* 45 (4-6): 680-91.

Bloeck, M., S. Galiani, and F. Weinschelbaum. 2019. "Poverty Alleviation Strategies under Informality: Evidence for Latin America." *Latin American Economic Review* 28 (1): 14.

Boly, A. 2018. "On the Short- and Medium-Term Effects of Formalisation: Panel Evidence from Vietnam." *The Journal of Development Studies* 54 (4): 641-56.

Bonnet, F., J. Vanek, and M. Chen. 2019. *Women and Men in the Informal Economy—A Statistical Brief.* Manchester, U.K.: Women in Informal Employment: Globalizing and Organizing.

Bosch, M., E. Goñi-Pacchioni, and W. Maloney. 2012. "Trade Liberalization, Labor Reforms and Formal-Informal Employment Dynamics." *Labour Economics* 19 (5): 653-67.

Bose, N., S. Capasso, and M. Wurm, 2012. "The Impact of Banking Development on the Size of Shadow Economies." *Journal of Economic Studies* 39 (6): 620-38.

Botelho, F., and V. Ponczek. 2011. "Segmentation in the Brazilian Labor Market." *Economic Development and Cultural Change* 59 (2): 437-63.

Brandt, L., J. Van Biesenbroeck, and Y. Zhang. 2012. "Creative Accounting or Creative Destruction? Firm-Level Productivity Growth in Chinese Manufacturing." *Journal of Development Economics* 97 (2): 339-51.

Bruhn, M. 2011. "License to Sell: The Effect of Business Registration Reform on Entrepreneurial Activity in Mexico." *The Review of Economics and Statistics* 93 (1): 382-86.

Canelas, C. 2019. "Informality and Poverty in Ecuador." *Small Business Economics* 53: 1097-115.

Capasso, S., and T. Jappelli. 2013. "Financial Development and the Underground Economy." *Journal of Development Economics* 101 (March): 167-78.

Capp, J., H. Elstrodt, and W. Jones Jr. 2005. "Reining in Brazil's Informal Economy." *McKinsey Quarterly*. http://www.mckinseyquarterly.com.

Chen, M., J. Vanek, and J. Heintz. 2006. "Informality, Gender, and Poverty: A Global Picture." *Economic and Political Weekly* 41 (21): 2131-39.

Cho, J., and D. Cho. 2011. "Gender Difference of the Informal Sector Wage Gap: A Longitudinal Analysis for the Korean Labor Market." *Journal of the Asia Pacific Economy* 16 (4): 612-29.

Choi, J., and M. Thum. 2005. "Corruption and the Shadow Economy." *International Economic Review* 46 (3): 817-36.

Chong, A., and M. Gradstein. 2007. "Inequality and Informality." *Journal of Public Economics* 91 (1-2): 159-79.

Cisneros-Acevedo, C. Forthcoming. "Unfolding Trade Effect in Two Margins of Informality: The Peruvian Case." *The World Bank Economic Review.*

Cunningham, W. V., and W. F. Maloney. 2001. "Heterogeneity among Mexico's Microenterprises: An Application of Factor and Cluster Analysis." *Economic Development and Cultural Change* 50 (1): 131-56.

Cusolito, A. P., and W. F. Maloney. 2018. *Productivity Revisited: Shifting Paradigms in Analysis and Policy.* Washington, DC: World Bank.

D'Erasmo, P. N., and H. J. Moscoso Boedo. 2012. "Financial Structure, Informality and Development." *Journal of Monetary Economics* 59 (3): 286-302.

Dabla-Norris, E., M. Gradstein, and G. Inchauste. 2008. "What Causes Firms to Hide Output?" *Journal of Development Economics* 85 (1-2): 1-27.

Dabla-Norris, E., L. J. Mayor, F. Lima, and A. Sollaci. 2018. "Size Dependent Policies, Informality, and Misallocation." IMF Working Paper 18/179, International Monetary Fund, Washington DC.

de Mel, S., D. McKenzie, and C. Woodruff. 2011. "What is the Cost of Formality? Experimentally Estimating the Demand for Formalization." Working Paper, University of Warwick, Coventry, U.K.

de Mel, S., D. McKenzie, and C. Woodruff. 2013. "The Demand for, and Consequences of, Formalization among Informal Firms in Sri Lanka." *American Economic Journal: Applied Economics* 5 (2): 122-50.

de Soto, Hernando. 1989. *The Other Path: The Invisible Revolution in the Third World.* New York: Harper & Row.

de Soyres, F., A. Mulabdic, and M. Ruta. 2020. "Common Transport Infrastructure: A Quantitative Model and Estimates from the Belt and Road Initiative." *Journal of Development Economics* 143 (March): 102415.

Deininger, K., S. Jin, and M. Sur. 2007. "Sri Lanka's Rural Non-Farm Economy: Removing Constraints to Pro-Poor Growth," *World Development* 35 (12): 2056-78.

Dell'Anno, R. 2016. "Inequality and Informality in Transition and Emerging Countries." *IZA World of Labor.* 325. doi:10.15185/izawol.325.

DerSimonian, R., and N. Laird. 1986. "Meta-Analysis in Clinical Trials." *Controlled Clinical Trials* 7 (3): 177-88.

Devicienti F., F. Groisman, and A. Poggi. 2009. "Informality and Poverty: Are These Processes Dynamically Interrelated? Evidence from Argentina," Working Papers 146, Society for the Study of Economic Inequality, Palma, Spain.

Dieppe, A., ed. 2020. *Global Productivity: Trends, Drivers, and Policies.* Washington, DC: World Bank.

Dieppe, A., A. Kawamoto, Y. Okawa, C. Okou, and J. Temple. 2020. "What Explains Productivity Growth." In *Global Productivity: Trends, Drivers, and Policies,* edited by A. Dieppe, 39-94. Washington, DC: World Bank.

Distinguin, I., C. Rugemintwari, and R. Tacneng. 2016. "Can Informal Firms Hurt Registered SMEs' Access to Credit?" *World Development* 84 (August): 18-40.

Dix-Carneiro, R., and B. Kovak. 2017. "Trade Liberalization and Regional Dynamics." *American Economic Review* 107 (10): 2908-46.

Dix-Carneiro, R., and B. Kovak. 2019. "Margins of Labor Market Adjustment to Trade." *Journal of International Economics* 117 (C): 125-42.

Docquier, F., and Z. Iftikhar. 2019. "Brain Drain, Informality and Inequality: A Search-and-Matching Model for Sub-Saharan Africa." *Journal of International Economics* 120 (September): 109-25.

Docquier, F., T. Müller, and J. Naval. 2017. "Informality and Long-Run Growth." *The Scandinavian Journal of Economics* 119 (4): 1040-85.

Dollar, D., T. Kleineberg, and A. Kraay. 2013. "Growth Still Is Good for the Poor." Policy Research Working Paper 6568, World Bank, Washington DC.

Dollar, D., and A. Kraay. 2002. "Growth Is Good for the Poor." *Journal of Economic Growth* 7: 195-225.

Dreher, A., and F. Schneider. 2010. "Corruption and the Shadow Economy: An Empirical Analysis." *Public Choice* 144 (1-2): 215-38.

Duranton, G., and D. Puga. 2004. "Chapter 48—Micro-Foundations of Urban Agglomeration Economies." *Handbook of Regional and Urban Economics* 4: 2063-117.

Durlauf, S. N., A. Kourtellos, and C. M. Tan. 2008. "Are Any Growth Theories Robust?" *The Economic Journal* 118 (527): 329-46.

Earle, J. S., and Z. Sakova. 2000. "Business Start-Ups or Disguised Unemployment? Evidence on the Character of Self-Employment from Transition Economies." *Labour Economics* 7 (5): 575-601.

El Badaoui, E., E. Strobl, and F. Walsh. 2008. "Is There an Informal Employment Wage Penalty? Evidence from South Africa." *Economic Development and Cultural Change* 56 (3): 683-710.

El Badaoui, E., E. Strobl, and F. Walsh. 2010. "The Formal Sector Wage Premium and Firm Size." *Journal of Development Economics* 91 (1): 37-47.

Elgin, C., and A. Elveren. 2019. "Informality, Inequality, and Feminization of Labor." Working Paper 483, Political Economy Research Institute, University of Massachusetts Amherst.

Enste, D., and F. Schneider. 1998. "Increasing Shadow Economies all over the World—Fiction or Reality." IZA Discussion Paper 26, IZA Institute of Labor Economics, Bonn, Germany.

Epstein, B., and A. F. Shapiro. 2017. "Employment and Firm Heterogeneity, Capital Allocation, and Countercyclical Labor Market Policies." *Journal of Development Economics* 127 (July): 25-41.

Fajnzylber, P., W. Maloney, and G. Montes-Rojas 2011. "Does Formality Improve Micro-Firm Performance? Evidence from the Brazilian SIMPLES Program." *Journal of Development Economics* 94 (2): 262-76.

Falco, P., A. Kerr, N. Rankin, J. Sandefur, and F. Teal. 2011. "The Returns to Formality and Informality in Urban Africa." *Labour Economics* 18: S23-S31.

Farazi, S. 2014. "Informal Firms and Financial Inclusion: Status and Determinants." *Journal of International Commerce, Economics and Policy* 5 (3): 1440011.

Farrell, D. 2004. "The Hidden Dangers of Informal Economy." *McKinsey Quarterly* 3: 27-37.

Feldkircher, M., and S. Zeugner. 2012. "The Impact of Data Revisions on the Robustness of Growth Determinants—A Note on 'Determinants of Economic Growth: Will Data Tell?'" *Journal of Applied Econometrics* 27(4): 686-94.

Fernandes, A. M. 2008. "Firm Productivity in Bangladesh Manufacturing Industries." *World Development* 36 (10): 1725-44.

Fernandez, C., E. Ley, and M. Steel. 2001. "Model Uncertainty in Cross-Country Growth Regressions." *Journal of Applied Econometrics* 16 (5): 563-76.

Fields, G. S. 1975. "Rural-Urban Migration, Urban Unemployment and Underemployment, and Job-Search Activity in LDCs." *Journal of Development Economics* 2 (2): 165-87.

Fields, G. S. 1990. "Labour Market Modelling and the Urban Informal Sector: Theory and Evidence". In *The Informal Sector Revisited*, edited by D. Turnham, B. Salomé, and A. Schwarz. Paris: Organisation for Economic Co-operation and Development.

Fields, G. S. 2005. "A Guide to Multisector Labor Market Models." Employment Policy Primer, World Bank, Washington, DC.

Fields, G. S., and J. Pieters. 2018. *Employment and Development: How Work Can Lead from and into Poverty.* Oxford, U.K.: Oxford University Press.

Francois, J., and M. Manchin. 2013. "Institutions, Infrastructure, and Trade." *World Development* 46 (June): 165-75.

Friedman, E., S. Johnson, D. Kaufmann, and P. Zoido-Lobatón. 2000. "Dodging the Grabbing Hand: The Determinants of Unofficial Activity in 69 Countries." *Journal of Public Economics* 76 (3): 459-93.

Friesen, J., and K. Wacker. 2013. "Do Financially Constrained Firms Suffer from More Intense Competition by the Informal Sector? Firm-Level Evidence from the World Bank Enterprise Surveys." Discussion Paper 139, Courant Research Centre, Göttingen, Germany.

Fugazza, M., and N. Fiess. 2010. "Trade Liberalization and Informality: New Stylized Facts." Policy Issues in International Trade and Commodities Study Series No. 43, United Nations, New York and Geneva.

Funkhouser, E. 1997. "Mobility and Labor Market Segmentation: The Urban Labor Market in El Salvador." *Economic Development and Cultural Change* 46 (1): 123-53.

Galiani, S., F. Weinschelbaum. 2012. "Modeling Informality Formally: Households and Firms." *Economic Inquiry* 50 (3): 821-38.

Gandelman, N., and A. Rasteletti. 2017. "Credit Constraints, Sector Informality and Firm Investments: Evidence from a Panel of Uruguayan Firms." *Journal of Applied Economics* 20 (2): 351-72.

García, G. A., and E. R. Badillo. 2018. "Rationing of Formal Sector Jobs and Informality: The Colombian Case." *Journal of International Development* 30 (5): 760-89.

Gaspar, V., D. Amaglobeli, M. Garcia-Escriabno, D. Prady, and M. Soto. 2019. "Fiscal Policy and Development: Human, Social, and Physical Investments for the SDGs." Staff Discussion Note 19/03, International Monetary Fund, Washington, DC.

Gasparini, L., F. Haimovich, and S. Olivieri. 2009. "Labor Informality Bias of a Poverty-Alleviation Program in Argentina." *Journal of Applied Economics* 12 (2): 181-205.

Gasparini, L., and L. Tornarolli. 2007. "Labor Informality in Latin America and the Caribbean: Patterns and Trends from Household Survey Microdata." CEDLAS Working Paper, Centro de Estudios Distributivos, Laborales y Sociales, Universidad Nacional de La Plata, Argentina.

Ghosh, J. and A. E. Ghattas. 2015. "Bayesian Variable Selection Under Collinearity." *The American Statistician* (69): 165-73.

Gindling, T. 1991. "Labor Market Segmentation and the Determination of Wages in the Public, Private- Formal, and Informal Sectors in San José, Costa Rica." *Economic Development and Cultural Change* 39 (3): 585-605.

Gindling, T., N. Mossaad, and D. Newhouse. 2016. "Earnings Premiums and Penalties for Self-Employment and Informal Employees around the World." Policy Research Working Paper 7530, World Bank, Washington, DC.

Gindling, T., N. Mossaad, and D. Newhouse. 2020. "Self-Employment Earnings Premiums/Penalties and Regulations: Evidence from Developing Economies." *Small Business Economics* 55 (1): 507-27.

Goldberg, P. K., and N. Pavcnik. 2003. "The Response of the Informal Sector to Trade Liberalization." *Journal of Development Economics* 72 (2): 463-96.

Goldberg, P. K., and N. Pavcnik. 2004. "Trade, Inequality, and Poverty: What Do We Know? Evidence from Recent Trade Liberalization Episodes in Developing Countries." NBER Working Paper 10593, National Bureau of Economic Research, Cambridge, MA.

Goldberg, P. K., and N. Pavcnik. 2007. "Distributional Effects of Globalization in Developing Countries." *Journal of Economic Literature* 45 (1): 39-82.

Gong, X., A. van Soest, and E. Villagomez. 2004. "Mobility in the Urban Labor Market: A Panel Data Analysis for Mexico." *Economic Development and Cultural Change* 53 (1): 1-36.

Gonzalez, A., and F. Lamanna. 2007. "Who Fears Competition from Informal Firms?" Policy Research Working Paper 4316, World Bank, Washington, DC.

Grimm, M., P. Knorringa, and J. Lay. 2012. "Constrained Gazelles: High Potentials in West Africa's Informal Economy." *World Development* 40 (7): 1352-68.

Günther, I., and A. Launov. 2006. "Competitive and Segmented Informal Labor Markets." IZO Discussion Paper 2349, Institute for the Study of Labor, Bonn, Germany.

Haltiwanger, J. C., J. I. Lane, and J. R. Spletzer. 1999. "Productivity Differences across Employers: The Roles of Employer Size, Age, and Human Capital." *American Economic Review* 89 (2): 94-8.

Harris, J. R., and M. P. Todaro. 1970. "Migration, Unemployment, and Development: A Two Sector Analysis." *American Economic Review* 60 (1): 126-42.

Hazans, M. 2011. "Informal Workers across Europe: Evidence from 30 Countries." IZO Discussion Paper 5871, Institute for the Study of Labor, Bonn, Germany.

Heckman, J. J., and X. Li. 2003. "Selection Bias, Comparative Advantage and Heterogeneous Returns to Education: Evidence from China in 2000." NBER Working Paper 9877, National Bureau of Economic Research, Cambridge, MA.

Heredia, J., A. Flores, C. Geldes, and W. Heredia. 2017. "Effects of Informal Competition on Innovation Performance: The Case of Pacific Alliance." *Journal of Technology Management and Innovation* 12 (4): 22-8.

Higgins, J. P. T., and S. G. Thompson. 2002. "Quantifying Heterogeneity in a Meta-Analysis." *Statistics in Medicine* 21 (11): 1539-58.

Huber, P., and U. Rahimov. 2014. "Formal and Informal Sector Wage Differences in Transition Economies: Evidence from Tajikistan." Working Papers in Business and Economics 48/2014, Mendel University in Brno, Czech Republic.

Hussmanns, R. 2004. "Measuring the Informal Economy: From Employment in the Informal Sector to Informal Employment." ILO Working Paper 42, International Labour Office, Geneva.

ICRG (*International Country Risk Guide*). 2014. "ICRG Methodology." PRS Group, Syracuse, NY. https://www.prsgroup.com/wp-content/uploads/2014/08/icrgmethodology.pdf.

Ihrig, J., and K. S. Moe. 2004. "Lurking in the Shadows: The Informal Sector and Government Policy." *Journal of Development Economics* 73 (2): 541-57.

ILO (International Labour Organization). 2013. *Measuring Informality: A Statistical Manual on The Informal Sector and Informal Employment.* Geneva: International Labour Office.

ILO (International Labour Organization). 2018a. *World Employment and Social Outlook—Trends 2018.* Geneva: International Labour Office.

ILO (International Labour Organization). 2018b. *Women and Men in the Informal Economy: A Statistical Picture.* Geneva: International Labour Office.

ILO (International Labour Organization). 2019. *Global Wage Report 2018/19: What Lies behind Gender Pay Gaps.* Geneva: International Labour Office.

Iriyama, A., R. Kishore, and D. Talukda. 2016. "Playing Dirty or Building Capability? Corruption and HR Training as Competitive Actions to Threats from Informal and Foreign Firm Rivals." *Strategic Management Journal* 51 (2): 315-34.

Islam, A. 2018. "The Burden of Water Shortages on Informal Firms." Policy Research Working Paper 8457, World Bank, Washington, DC.

Jain-Chandra, S., N. Khor, R. Mano, J. Schauer, J. Wingender, and J. Zhuang. 2018. "Inequality in China—Trends, Drivers and Policy Remedies." IMF Working Paper 2018/127, International Monetary Fund, Washington, DC.

Jones, I. C., and W. Nordhaus. 2008. "Comment on A. Shleifer and R. La Porta's 'The Unofficial Economy and Economic Development.'" *Brookings Papers on Economic Activity* 2008 (2): 353-63.

Joshi, A., W. Prichard, and C. Heady. 2014. "Taxing the Informal Economy: The Current State of Knowledge and Agendas for Future Research." *Journal of Development Studies* 50 (10): 1325-47.

Jovanovic, B. 1982. "Selection and Evolution of Industry." *Econometrica* 50 (3): 649-70.

Kahyalar, N., S. Fethi, S. Katircioglu, and B. Ouattara. 2018. "Formal and Informal Sectors: Is There Any Wage Differential?" *The Service Industries Journal* 38 (11-12): 789-823.

Kanbur, R. 2017. "Informality: Causes, Consequences and Policy Responses." *Review of Development Economics* 21 (4): 939-61.

Kim, B. 2005. "Poverty and Informal Economy Participation: Evidence from Romania." *Economics of Transition* 13 (1): 163-85.

La Porta, R., and A. Shleifer. 2008. "The Unofficial Economy and Economic Development." *Brookings Papers on Economic Activity* 2008 (2): 275-352.

La Porta, R., and A. Shleifer. 2014. "Informality and development." *Journal of Economic Perspectives* 28 (3): 109-26.

Lehmann, H., and N. Pignatti. 2007. "Informal Employment Relationships and Labor Market Segmentation in Transition Economies: Evidence from Ukraine." IZO Discussion Paper 3269, Institute for the Study of Labor, Bonn, Germany.

Lehmann, H., and A. Zaiceva. 2013. "Informal Employment in Russia: Incidence, Determinants and Labor Market Segmentation." DSE Working Paper 903, Department of Economics, University of Bologna, Italy.

Loayza, N. V. 1996. "The Economics of the Informal Sector: A Simple Model and Some Empirical Evidence from Latin America." *Carnegie-Rochester Conference Series on Public Policy* 45: 129-62.

Loayza, N. V. 2016. "Informality in the Process of Development and Growth." *The World Economy* 39 (12): 1856-916.

Loayza, N. V. 2018. "Informality: Why Is It So Widespread and How Can It Be Reduced?" Research & Policy Brief, World Bank, Kuala Lumpur, Malaysia.

Loayza, N., and J. Rigolini. 2006. "Informality Trends and Cycles." Policy Research Working Paper 4078, World Bank, Washington, DC.

Loayza, N., L. Servén, and N. Sugawara. 2010. "Informality in Latin America and the Caribbean." In *Business Regulation and Economic Performance*, edited by N. Loayza and L. Servén. Washington, DC: World Bank.

Luttmer, E. G. J. 2007. "Selection, Growth, and the Size Distribution of Firms." *The Quarterly Journal of Economics* 122 (3): 1103-44.

Magnac, T. 1991. "Segmented or Competitive Labor Markets." *Econometrica* 59 (1): 165-87.

Maloney, W. 1999. "Does Informality Imply Segmentation in Urban Labor Markets? Evidence from Sectoral Transitions in Mexico." *The World Bank Economic Review* 13 (2): 275-302.

Maloney, W. F. 2004. "Informality Revisited." *World Development* 32 (7): 1159-78.

Malta, V., L. Kolovich, A. Marinez, and M. Tavares. 2019. "Informality and Gender Gaps Going Hand in Hand?" IMF Working Paper 19/112, International Monetary Fund, Washington, DC.

Marcouiller, D., V. R. de Castilla, and C. Woodruff. 1997. "Formal Measures of the Informal-Sector Wage Gap in Mexico, El Salvador, and Peru." *Economic Development and Cultural Change* 45 (2): 367-92.

Marjit S., V. Mukherjee, and M. Kolmar. 2006. "Poverty, Taxation, and Governance." The *Journal of International Trade & Economic Development* 15 (3): 325-33.

Matano, A., M. Obaco, and V. Royuela. 2020. "What Drives the Spatial Wage Premium for Formal and Informal Workers? The Case of Ecuador." *Journal of Regional Science* 60 (4): 823-47.

McCaig, B., and N. Pavcnik. 2018. "Export Markets and Labor Allocation in a Low-Income Country." *American Economic Review* 108 (7): 1899-1941.

McKenzie, D., and Y. Sakho. 2010. "Does It Pay Firms to Register for Taxes? The Impact of Formality on Firm Productivity." *Journal of Development Economics* 91 (1): 15-24.

Medina, M., and F. Schneider. 2018. "Shadow Economies around the World: What Did We Learn over the Last 20 Years?" IMF Working Paper 18/17, International Monetary Fund, Washington, DC.

Medina, M., and F. Schneider. 2019. "Shedding Light on the Shadow Economy: A Global Database and the Interaction with the Official One." CESifo Working Paper 7981. CESifo Group Munich.

Meghir, C., R. Narita, and J. M. Robin. 2015. "Wages and Informality in Developing Countries." *American Economic Review* 105 (4): 1509-46.

Melitz, M. J. 2003. "The Impact of Trade on Intra-Industry Reallocations and Aggregate Industry Productivity." *Econometrica* 71 (6): 1695-725.

Mendi, P., and Costamagna, R. 2017. "Managing Innovation under Competitive Pressure from Informal Producers." *Technological Forecasting and Social Change* 114: 192-202.

Mendicino, C., and M. Prado. 2014. "Heterogeneous Firms and the Impact of Government Policy on Welfare and Informality." *Economics Letters* 124 (1): 151-6.

Messina, J., and J. Silva. 2021. "Twenty Years of Wage Inequality in Latin America." *The World Bank Economic Review* 35 (1): 117-47.

Mishra, A., and R. Ray. 2010. "Informality, Corruption, and Inequality," Department of Economics Working Papers 13/10, University of Bath, Department of Economics.

Nazier, H., & Ramadan, R. 2015. "Informality and Poverty: A Causality Dilemma with Application to Egypt." *Advances in Management and Applied Economics* 5 (4): 1-4.

Nguyen, H. C., C. J. Nordman, and F. Roubaud. 2013. "Who Suffers the Penalty? A Panel Data Analysis of Earnings Gaps in Vietnam." *Journal of Development Studies* 49 (12): 1694-710.

Nordman C. J., F. Rakotomana, and F. Roubaud. 2016. "Informal versus Formal: A Panel Data Analysis of Earnings Gaps in Madagascar." IZO Discussion Paper 9970, Institute for the Study of Labor, Bonn, Germany.

OECD/ILO (Organisation for Economic Co-operation and Development/International Labour Organization). 2019. "Addressing the Gender Dimension of Informality." In *Tackling Vulnerability in the Informal Economy*. Paris: OECD Publishing.

Ordóñez, J. 2014. "Tax Collection, the Informal Sector, and Productivity." *Review of Economic Dynamics* 17 (2): 262-86.

Otobe, N. 2017. "Gender and the Informal Economy: Key Challenges and Policy Response." ILO Employment Working Paper 236, International Labour Office, Geneva.

Oviedo, A. M. 2009. *Economic Informality: Causes, Costs, and Policies: A Literature Survey of International Experience*. Washington, DC: World Bank.

Oviedo, A., M. Thomas, and K. Karakurum-Özdemir. 2009. "Economic Informality: Causes, Costs, and Policies—A Literature Survey." Working Paper 167, World Bank, Washington, DC.

Perry, G. E., W. F. Maloney, O. S. Arias, P. Fajnzylber, A. D. Mason, and J. Saavedra-Chanduvi. 2007. *Informality: Exit and Exclusion*. Washington, DC: World Bank.

Ponczek, V., and G. Ulyssea. 2018. "Enforcement of Labor Regulation and the Labor Market Effects of Trade: Evidence from Brazil," IZA Discussion Papers 11783, IZA Institute of Labor Economics, Bonn, Germany.

Prado, M. 2011. "Government Policy in the Formal and Informal Sectors." *European Economic Review* 55 (8): 1120-36.

Pratap, S., and E. Quintin. 2006. "Are Labor Markets Segmented in Developing Countries? A Semiparametric Approach." *European Economic Review* 50 (7): 1817-41.

Quintin, E. 2008. "Contract Enforcement and the Size of the Informal Economy." *Economic Theory* 37 (3): 395-416.

Rauch, J. E. 1991. "Modelling the Informal Sector Formally." *Journal of Development Economics* 35 (1): 33-47.

Rocha, R., G. Ulyssea, and R. Rachter. 2018. "Do Lower Taxes Reduce Informality? Evidence from Brazil." *Journal of Development Economics* 134 (September): 28-49.

Rogan, M., and P. Cichello. 2020. "(Re)conceptualising Poverty and Informal Employment." In *The Informal Economy Revisited: Examining the Past, Envisioning the Future*, edited by M. Chen and F. Carré. Routledge: New York.

Rosenthal, S. S., and W. C. Strange. 2004. "Chapter 49—Evidence on the Nature and Source of Agglomeration Economies." *Handbook of Regional and Urban Economics* 4: 2119-71.

Rosser B., M. Rosser, and E. Ahmed. 2000. "Income Inequality and the Informal Economy in Transition Economies." *Journal of Comparative Economics* 28 (1): 156-71.

Rozenberg, J., and M. Fay. 2019. *Beyond the Gap: How Countries Can Afford the Infrastructure They Need while Protecting the Planet*. Washington, DC: World Bank.

Sachs, J. D., G. Schmidt-Traub, C. Kroll, G. Lafortune, and G. Fuller. 2018. *SDG Index and Dashboards Report 2018*. New York: Bertelsmann Stiftung and Sustainable Development Solutions Network.

Sachs, J. D., G. Schmidt-Traub, C. Kroll, G. Lafortune, G. Fuller, and F. Woelm. 2020. *Sustainable Development Report 2020: The Sustainable Development Goals and COVID-19*. Cambridge, U.K.: Cambridge University Press.

Sanfey, P., and U. Teksoz. 2007. "Does Transition Make You Happy?" *Economics of Transition* 15 (4): 707-31.

Saracoğlu, D. S. 2008. "The Informal Sector and Tax on Employment: A Dynamic General Equilibrium Investigation." *Journal of Economic Dynamics and Control* 32 (2): 529-49.

Sarte, P.-D. G. 2000. "Informality and Rent-Seeking Bureaucracies in a Model of Long-Run Growth." *Journal of Monetary Economics* 46 (1): 173-97.

Schipper, T. 2020. "Informality, Innovation, and Aggregate Productivity Growth." *Review of Development Economics* 24 (1): 125-43.

Schneider, F., A. Buehn, and C. E. Montenegro. 2010. "Shadow Economies All over the World: New Estimates for 162 Countries from 1999 to 2007." Policy Research Working Paper 5356, World Bank, Washington, DC.

Shleifer, A., and R. W. Vishny. 1993. "Corruption." *The Quarterly Journal of Economics* 108 (3): 599-617.

Stanley, T. D., H. Doucouliagos, M. Giles, H. Heckemeyer, R. J. Johnston, P. Laroche, J. P. Nelson. 2013. "Meta-Analysis of Economics Research Reporting Guidelines: Reporting Guidelines for Meta-Regression Analysis in Economics." *Journal of Economic Surveys* 27 (2): 390-94.

Tansel, A., and E. Kan. 2012. "The Formal/Informal Employment Earnings Gap: Evidence from Turkey." ERC Working Paper 1204, Economic Research Center, Middle East Technical University, Ankara, Turkey.

Tansel, A., H. Keskin, and Z. Ozdemir. 2020. "Is There an Informal Employment Wage Penalty in Egypt? Evidence from Quantile Regression on Panel Data." *Empirical Economics* 58 (6): 2949-79.

Ulyssea, G. 2010. "Regulation of Entry, Labor Market Institutions and the Informal Sector." *Journal of Development Economics* 91 (1): 87-99.

Ulyssea, G. 2018. "Firms, Informality, and Development: Theory and Evidence from Brazil." *American Economic Review* 108 (8): 2015-47.

Ulyssea, G. 2020. "Informality: Causes and Consequences for Development." *The Annual Review of Economics* 12 (1): 525-46.

UN SDSN (Sustainable Development Solutions Network). 2019. *SDG Costing & Financing for Low-income Developing Countries*. SDSN: New York.

UN Women. 2016. *Progress of the World's Women 2015/2016: Transforming Economies, Realizing Rights*. UN Women: New York.

van der Sluis, J., M. van Praag, and W. Vijverberg. 2005. "Entrepreneurship Selection and Performance: A Meta-Analysis of the Impact of Education in Developing Economies." *World Bank Economic Review* 19 (2): 225-61.

Vargas, J. P. M. 2015. "Informality in Paraguay: Macro-Micro Evidence and Policy Implications." Working Paper 15/245, International Monetary Fund, Washington, DC.

Vorisek, D., and S. Yu. 2020. "Understanding the Cost of Achieving the Sustainable Development Goals." Policy Research Working Paper 9164, World Bank, Washington, DC.

WHO (World Health Organization). 2017. *Tracking Universal Health Coverage: 2017 Global Monitoring Report.* Geneva: World Health Organization.

WIEGO (Women in Informal Employment: Globalizing and Organizing). 2019. "Extending Social Protection to Informal Workers." Briefing Note March 2019. Cambridge, MA: WIEGO.

World Bank. 2018. *Poverty and Shared Prosperity 2018: Piecing Together the Poverty Puzzle.* Washington, DC: World Bank.

World Bank. 2019. *Global Economic Prospects: Darkening Skies.* January. Washington, DC: World Bank.

World Bank. 2020a. *Global Economic Prospects.* June. Washington, DC: World Bank.

World Bank. 2020b. *Poverty and Shared Prosperity 2020: Reversals of Fortune.* Washington, DC: World Bank.

World Bank. 2021. *Global Economic Prospects.* January. Washington, DC: World Bank.

Wu, D., and F. Schneider. 2019. "Nonlinearity between the Shadow Economy and Level of Development." IMF Working Paper 19/48, International Monetary Fund, Washington, DC.

Yoshida, N., A. Narayan, and H. Wu. 2020. "How COVID-19 Affects Households in Poorest Countries—Insights from Phone Surveys." *Voices: Perspectives on Development* (blog), December 10, 2020. https://blogs.worldbank.org/voices/how-covid-19-affects-households-poorest-countries-insights-phone-surveys.

Zaballos, A., E. Iglesias, and A. Adamowicz. 2019. *The Impact of Digital Infrastructure on the Sustainable Development Goals: A Study for Selected Latin American and Caribbean Countries.* Washington, DC: Inter-American Development Bank.

Zarate, R. 2019. "Does Transit Infrastructure Reduce Informality in Developing Countries? Guest Post by Román David Zárate." *Development Impact* (blog), December 6, 2019. https://blogs.worldbank.org/impactevaluations/does-transit-infrastructure-reduce-informality-developing-countries-guest-post.

Zenker, S., and F. Kock. 2020. "The Coronavirus Pandemic—A Critical Discussion of a Tourism Research Agenda." *Tourism Management* 81 (December): 104-64.

CHAPTER 5

Informality in Emerging Market and Developing Economies: Regional Dimensions

Emerging market and developing economies experienced a decline in informality over the two decades before the COVID-19 (coronavirus) pandemic. Output informality declined most in East Asia and Pacific and South Asia, while employment informality fell most in the Middle East and North Africa, South Asia, and Sub-Saharan Africa. Yet the incidence of informality remains high in all regions. In South Asia and Sub-Saharan Africa, pervasive informality has been associated with low human capital and large agricultural sectors. In Europe and Central Asia, Latin America and the Caribbean, and the Middle East and North Africa, heavy regulatory and tax burdens and weak institutions have been important factors. Also important have been legacies of the transition from central planning to market economies in Europe and Central Asia and disruptions related to conflict in the Middle East and North Africa and Sub-Saharan Africa. In East Asia and Pacific, employment informality is associated with lagging social protection in cities following large-scale rural-to-urban migration. A balanced policy mix tailored to economy-specific circumstances can help mitigate the adverse effects of informality.

Introduction

Informal economic activity is pervasive in emerging market and developing economies (EMDEs), accounting for one-third of gross domestic product (GDP), on average. Self-employment, a commonly used proxy for informal employment, averages about two-fifths of total employment. For various reasons, including flexibility, some firms and workers choose to remain informal. In some cases, informal work may be the only option. High levels of informality are associated with low labor productivity and low tax revenues, and can further entrench poverty and inequality.

On average, informality fell in EMDEs in the two decades before the COVID-19 (coronavirus) pandemic, although the pace of decline varied across regions and countries. The correlates of informality also vary across regions, shaped by distinctive regional cultures and histories, as well as economic, social, and policy structures.

This chapter addresses the following questions:

- How has informality evolved over the past two decades in each EMDE region?

Note: This chapter was prepared by Dana Vorisek, Gene Kindberg-Hanlon, Wee Chian Koh, Yoki Okawa, Temel Taskin, Ekaterine T. Vashakmadze, and Lei Sandy Ye. Research assistance was provided by Hrisyana Doytchinova and Arika Kayastha.

- What are the correlates of informality in each region?

- What policy options are available to address the challenges associated with informality in each region?

Several techniques have been developed to measure informality (chapter 2).[1] For the analysis here, output informality is proxied by estimates based on the dynamic general equilibrium (DGE) model, in percent of official GDP, and employment informality refers to the share of self-employment in total employment, unless otherwise indicated. These measures are chosen because of their extensive economy and time-series coverage.

Contributions. The chapter makes several contributions to the literature. First, the chapter brings a regional perspective to the existing literature on informality in EMDEs. Past studies either grouped all economies together or focused on one or a few economies or a specific region. The chapter distills commonalities among EMDEs within each region and differences across regions. Second, the chapter brings together multiple strands of literature by investigating two key types of informality—output and employment informality—thus helping policy makers better understand the nature of informality in their respective regions (chapter 4). Previous studies typically examined either output informality or employment informality. Last, the chapter provides policy recommendations that are tailored to region-specific needs and conditions. Former studies tend to have a broad overview of all relevant policies without applying them to the regional context.

Main findings. First, the chapter documents large differences in the evolution of informality across regions. Output informality is highest in Europe and Central Asia (ECA), Latin America and the Caribbean (LAC), and Sub-Saharan Africa (SSA), while employment informality is highest in East Asia and Pacific (EAP), South Asia (SAR), and SSA. Output informality declined most in EAP and SAR between 1990-99 and 2010-18, while employment informality fell most in the Middle East and North Africa (MNA), SAR, and SSA. Despite declines in output informality, and consistent with slower productivity growth in the informal than the formal sector, employment informality remained broadly unchanged in EAP, ECA, and LAC between 1990-99 and 2010-18.

Second, a combination of cross-regional, intraregional, and economy-specific factors is associated with informality in EMDEs. Key correlates of high informality include low human capital, large agricultural sectors, and poor business climates. But there are also

---

[1] Three methods of estimating informal output are used in this book. The DGE method refers to the dynamic general equilibrium (DGE) model of Elgin and Oztunali (2014). It estimates the allocation of labor between the formal and informal sectors based on the assumption of utility maximization by an infinitely lived representative household endowed with certain units of productive capital and time. An alternative, multiple indicators multiple causes (MIMIC) method is based on a model comprising structural equations that use observable causes and indicators to capture the latent level of informal output. A third method uses survey data on perceptions of informal activity obtained by the World Economic Forum, World Values Survey, and World Bank Enterprise Surveys. Chapter 2 contains a detailed discussion of these and other measures of informality and their limitations.

important region-specific factors, such as insufficient social protection coverage, trade liberalization, and economic disruptions due to armed conflict. Reflecting regional as well as national differences in informality, balanced policy mixes tailored to economy circumstances are required to set the right conditions for informality to fall.

The remainder of the chapter is structured as follows. The next section provides an overview of informality in EMDEs. The subsequent sections discuss the evolution of informality in each of the six EMDE regions. Each of these sections examines the correlates of informality and presents region-specific policy options to address the challenges associated with informality. The last section concludes with a discussion of emerging opportunities and policy challenges.

Informality in EMDEs

Informality is far more widespread in EMDEs than in advanced economies (figure 5.1). Informal output in EMDEs was, on average, 33 percent of official GDP between 2010 and 2018, whereas self-employment accounted for 42 percent of total employment. These shares were 18 and 14 percent, respectively, in advanced economies. Of the six EMDE regions, output informality is highest in ECA, LAC, and SSA. Employment informality is highest in EAP, SAR, and SSA.

Informality has declined in both advanced economies and EMDEs over the past two decades, but by more in EMDEs (figure 5.1; chapter 2). In EMDEs, output informality decreased by 8 percentage points between 1990 and 2018, whereas employment informality fell by about 9 percentage points, with increases in the mid-1990s and early 2000s subsequently reversed.

EMDEs account for half of the world's informal output and more than 90 percent of its informal employment (figure 5.2). Three EMDE regions—EAP, LAC, and ECA— account for more than one-third of the world's informal output. These are also the largest EMDE regions in terms of official GDP. EAP and SAR account for the largest shares, by far, of informal employment at the global level. These two regions' shares of global informal employment are three times and eight times as large, respectively, as their shares of global informal output, implying that productivity is particularly low among informal workers in EAP and SAR.

EAP and SAR also experienced the largest declines in output informality between 1990-99 and 2010-18, in large part reflecting rapid economic development in China and India. The sharpest decline in employment informality occurred in SAR, followed by MNA and SSA. Despite declines in output informality, employment informality increased slightly in EAP and LAC. This may reflect, in part, rigid labor markets and burdensome regulations (LAC) and mismatch between rapidly expanding jobs during urbanization and lagging social protection coverage as demographic conditions changed (EAP). Informality—especially employment informality—is most prevalent in EMDEs with low income per capita, reflecting the role of informality as both a driver and a consequence of poverty (figure 5.2; La Porta and Shleifer 2014).

FIGURE 5.1 **Evolution of informality in advanced economies and EMDEs**

Informality is far more widespread in EMDEs than in advanced economies. Output and employment informality have declined in both groups, but by more in EMDEs.

A. Output informality

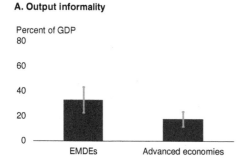

B. Employment informality

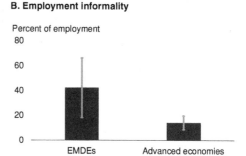

C. Output informality, 1990-2018

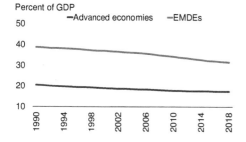

D. Employment informality, 1990-2018

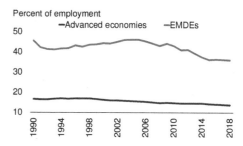

Sources: International Labour Organization; World Bank.
Note: Informal output is proxied by DGE-based estimates, in percent of official GDP. Informal employment is the share of self-employment in total employment. DGE = dynamic general equilibrium model; EMDEs = emerging market and developing economies.
A.B. Bars show unweighted group averages for 2010-18 and vertical lines show +/-1 standard deviation.
C.D. Lines show unweighted group averages for each year.

Informality in EMDEs is associated with numerous factors, well documented in the literature. EMDEs with the highest incidence of informality tend to have weak human capital (less educated and less skilled workers), large agricultural sectors, and poor institutional environments (for instance, high corruption or restrictive regulations; figure 5.3; chapter 4). In SAR, and SSA, for instance, agricultural production still makes up a large share of employment in many economies.

Other key correlates of informality differ among regions. In EAP, large-scale rural-to-urban migration in recent decades supported rapid growth and industrialization. Although this migration has been accompanied by falling output informality, employment informality increased, because of lagging social protection. In ECA, the high shares of informal output in some economies are partly a legacy of the transition from centrally planned to market economies. In LAC, trade liberalization reforms of the 1990s contributed to growing informality in some economies, as formal firms that were unable to compete in a liberalized formal economy retreated into informality. In MNA

FIGURE 5.2 **Informality in EMDE regions**

Employment informality tends to be higher than output informality in EMDE regions. Low per capita income is associated with high informality, especially employment informality.

A. Output and employment informality

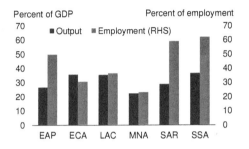

B. EMDE regions' shares of world output and employment

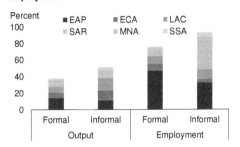

C. Output informality

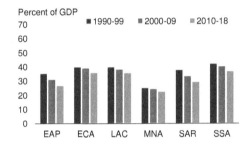

D. Employment informality

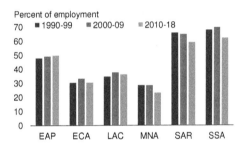

E. GDP per capita and output informality

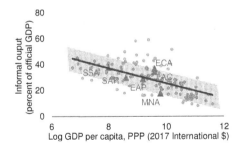

F. GDP per capita and employment informality

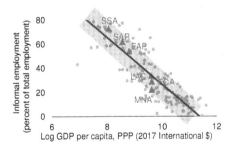

Sources: International Labour Organization; World Bank.

Note: Informal output is proxied by DGE-based estimates, in percent of official GDP. Informal employment is the share of self-employment in total employment. DGE = dynamic general equilibrium model; EAP = East Asia and Pacific; ECA = Europe and Central Asia; EMDE = emerging market and developing economy; LAC = Latin America and the Caribbean; MNA = Middle East and North Africa; PPP = purchasing power parity; RHS = right-hand side; SAR = South Asia; SSA = Sub-Saharan Africa.

A.C.D. Bars show unweighted group averages for 2010-18.

B. Estimates are based on economies' shares of output and employment averaged over 2010-18.

E.F. Gray markers show unweighted average log GDP (PPP, constant 2017 international $) relative to informal output and employment in individual EMDEs, with the fitted line shown in blue and the corresponding +/-1 standard errors shown in shaded grey areas. Red markers show median GDP per capita and median informal output and employment in EMDE regions. Data are for 2010-18. Sample includes 154 economies for output informality and 147 economies for employment informality.

FIGURE 5.3 Correlates of informality in EMDE regions

EMDE regions with higher employment informality tend to have larger agricultural sectors, lower educational attainment, heavier tax burdens, and poorer governance than regions with smaller informal sectors.

A. Share of agricultural output in output

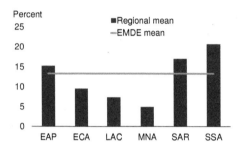

B. Years of schooling

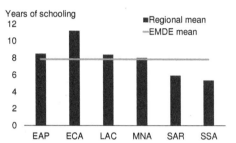

C. Corporate tax rates

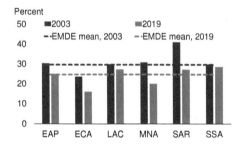

D. Control of corruption

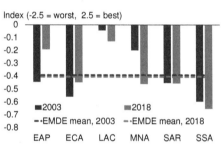

Sources: Barro and Lee (2013); Végh and Vuletin (2015), World Bank (World Development Indicators, World Governance Indicators).
Note: EAP = East Asia and Pacific; ECA = Europe and Central Asia; EMDE = emerging market and developing economy; LAC = Latin America and the Caribbean; MNA = Middle East and North Africa; SAR = South Asia; SSA = Sub-Saharan Africa.
A. Data for 2010-18.
B. Average years of schooling for those aged 15 and older. Data for 2010.
C.D. Bars show unweighted group averages.
D. The dashed lines are unweighted averages for EMDEs in 2003 and 2018, respectively.

and SSA, economic disruptions during armed conflicts have forced people to earn their livelihoods in the informal economy.

The COVID-19 pandemic has hit the informal sector hard. An estimated three-quarters of the world's informal workers were significantly affected by lockdowns in early 2020 (ILO 2020). In many economies, informal firms are concentrated in the services sector, which has been subject to more disruption from government-imposed mobility restrictions than the industrial or agricultural sectors because it relies on face-to-face interactions. However, because informal workers are often not registered in government systems, many have been out of reach of social assistance programs. If unreachable through benefits programs, informal workers are likely to feel compelled to continue working, despite the health risks (Maloney and Taskin 2020). Encouragingly, the policy response to COVID-19 in some EMDEs has included the provision of benefits to informal workers, including through digital platforms, although the adequacy and coverage of benefits to informal workers were far from complete (Dabla-Norris and Rhee 2020; Díez et al. 2020; Frost, Gambacorta, and Shin 2021).

East Asia and Pacific

The EAP region experienced a sharp decline in output informality over the past two decades. This decline was broad-based within the region. However, there remain pockets of high informality, in particular in several lower-middle-income economies characterized by large rural sectors, poor governance, weak institutions, and low human capital (Cambodia, Lao People's Democratic Republic, and Myanmar).

Although many economies in the region have made considerable progress in integrating rural migrants into urban labor markets, they still face challenges related to urban informality. EAP has large slum populations. Many urban dwellers are informal workers with inadequate social protection and without access to basic services like clean water and public transportation. Although cities across East Asia have propelled the region's rapid economic growth, there remain challenges in expanding opportunities, including to unregistered migrants living in urban peripheries. Reforms to urban planning can help expand access to opportunities.

The COVID-19 pandemic is taking a severe toll on micro, small, and medium enterprises (SMEs), which are the sources of livelihood for most informal workers. The pandemic and resulting lockdowns, given the limited access in the informal sector to social support and digital technologies, are likely to have increased inequality. Policies that focus on skills upgrading and improving access to resources, such as business development services, can help reverse this.

Evolution of informality in EAP

Informal output in EAP was equivalent to 27 percent of official GDP, on average, in 2010-18, below the EMDE average and down from 35 percent of GDP in 1990-99 (figure 5.4). Survey-based measures of informality in EAP, such as perceptions of informal activity, also indicate a decline. However, informal employment (as measured by self-employment), at 50 percent of total employment, was higher than the EMDE average in 2010-18 and has increased slightly over the past two decades. In an alternative measure of employment informality, the share of labor without basic pension coverage, approximately 75 percent of EAP employment can be categorized as informal in recent years.

Declining output informality in EAP has been accompanied by sustained economic growth, rapid industrialization and urbanization, and improvements in institutional quality (Loayza 2016; World Bank 2015). Between 1990-99 and 2010-18, the share of informal output declined rapidly in the fastest-growing economies, in part reflecting the effects of comprehensive reforms. For example, the share of informal output in GDP in Myanmar fell by 33 percentage points, to below 30 percent in 2010-18, following broad-based liberalization measures (figure 5.4).

FIGURE 5.4 **Informality in East Asia and Pacific**

Compared with other EMDE regions, EAP's share of informal output is moderate, whereas its share of informal employment is above average. Informality is particularly high in lower-income economies, which are also characterized by more stringent labor regulations and lack of enforcement.

A. Output informality

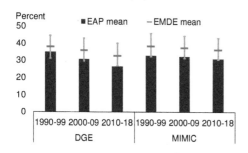

B. Employment informality and perceptions of informality

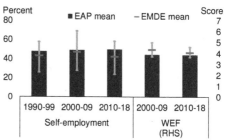

C. Output informality in selected economies

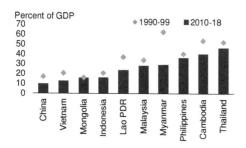

D. Range between employment and output informality

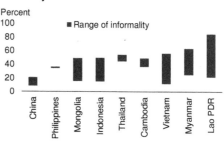

Sources: International Labour Organization; World Bank; World Economic Forum (2018).
Note: DGE = dynamic general equilibrium model; EAP = East Asia and Pacific; EMDE = emerging market and developing economy; MIMIC = multiple indicators multiple causes model; RHS = right-hand side; WEF = World Economic Forum.
A.B. Blue bars show unweighted averages of the informal economy of the region. Red markers show unweighted averages of all EMDEs and the vertical lines denote the interquartile range of all EMDEs.
A. DGE and MIMIC models estimate the size of the informal sector as a percent of official GDP. DGE sample includes 12 EAP economies and 122 EMDEs; MIMIC sample includes 14 EAP economies and 124 EMDEs.
B. Self-employment is measured as percent of total employment. The WEF asks the following question: "In your country, how much economic activity do you estimate to be undeclared or unregistered? (1 = Most economic activity is undeclared or unregistered; 7 = Most economic activity is declared or registered)." The average responses are used to capture the extent of perceived informality. The index is reversed here so that a lower WEF index indicates a larger informal economy. Self-employment sample includes 19 EAP economies and 134 EMDEs; WEF sample includes 19 EAP economies and 134 EMDEs.
C. Output informality is based on DGE estimates, in percent of official GDP.
D. The upper bound of each bar indicates the latest available share of self-employment in total employment. The lower bound indicates the latest available share of informal output in official GDP, based on DGE estimates. For Malaysia, not shown, the level of informal output is slightly higher than the level of informal employment. Data for last available year.

Employment informality in upper-middle-income economies is about two-fifths lower than in lower-middle-income economies. In a pattern consistent with per capita incomes, output informality is also lower, by about one-tenth.[2]

---

[2] Although the commonly observed link between per capita income and informality generally holds in the EAP region, there are outliers. Thus, informality is relatively high in Thailand despite its higher-middle-income status.

In lower-middle-income economies, the share of informal employment far exceeds the share of informal output, reflecting low labor productivity in the informal sector. The differentials are particularly pronounced in Indonesia, Lao PDR, Mongolia, and Vietnam (figure 5.4).

Correlates of informality in EAP

The extent of informality in EAP is associated with several economic and institutional factors, particularly the size of the agricultural sector and human capital development, as well as firm structure, regulatory burdens and the quality of governance. Informality is also correlated with such socioeconomic variables as poverty and inequality, which may exacerbate the vulnerability to shocks of households in the informal sector (chapter 4).

Urbanization. EAP is the world's most rapidly urbanizing region: the urban population grew by an average of 3 percent annually during 1978-2015 (Judy and Gadgil 2017). Rapid industrialization in EAP has supported large-scale rural-to-urban migration and stimulated growth of output, labor productivity, and employment (Ghani and Kanbur 2013). Urbanization has coincided with a shift from agriculture to manufacturing and services in China and other fast-growing East Asian economies (McMillan, Rodrik, and Sepúlveda 2017; Rodrik 2015). In general, larger nonagricultural sectors are associated with lower informal output, and informality in manufacturing is significantly lower than in services (figure 5.5; Atesagaoglu, Bayram, and Elgin 2017). In economies such as Indonesia, Lao PDR, and Myanmar, informal employment accounts for about 80 percent of total nonagricultural employment (World Bank 2020a).

However, rapid growth of cities in EAP has been accompanied by rising urban informality and policy challenges, such as lack of affordable housing, growing slums, poor provision of basic services, and widening income inequality among urban dwellers. In China, for example, there is unequal access to public services between citizens with urban household registration under the *hukou* system and those without, with many unregistered urban households still lacking essential social protection (Park, Wu, and Du 2012; World Bank 2014). Despite having the lowest employment and output informality in EAP, China is estimated to have approximately 120 million to 150 million rural-to-urban migrants who are not registered to work in cities (Gagnon, Xenogiani, and Xing 2011; Huang 2009; Jutting and Xenogiani 2007). Much of the urban slum population is informally employed, with significantly lower wages than in the formal sector (Judy and Gadgil 2017). The cities with the largest numbers of urban poor are in China, Indonesia, and the Philippines, while the highest urban poverty rates are in the Pacific Island countries of Papua New Guinea, Timor-Leste, Vanuatu, as well as in Indonesia and Lao PDR.

Firm structure. Economic reforms in China and Vietnam that began in the 1970s have allowed the emergence of private sector activity in the form of unregulated micro-enterprises, family enterprises, and individual entrepreneurs (Park, Wu, and Du 2012). The informal economy in these and other economies mostly comprises such enterprises. For example, in Indonesia, most informal firms have fewer than five employees. These

FIGURE 5.5 Correlates of informality in East Asia and Pacific

Better institutions and business environments, industrialization, and urbanization are associated with relatively low informality in higher-income economies. Economies with higher shares of informality have lower levels of educational attainment.

A. Employment informality and agricultural employment

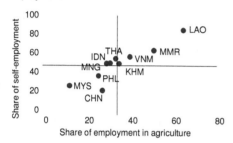

B. Share of urban population in total population

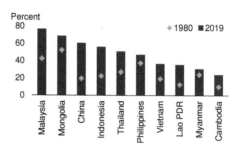

C. Employment informality and human capital

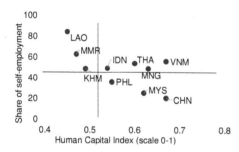

D. Years of schooling

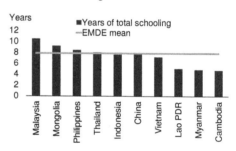

E. Institutional factors in economies with high and low informal employment

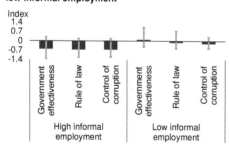

F. Institutions and income per capita

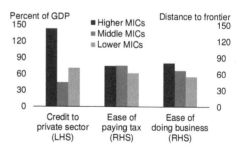

Sources: Barro and Lee (2013); International Labour Organization; World Bank (*Doing Business*, World Development Indicators, Worldwide Governance Indicators).

Note: CHN = China; EAP = East Asia and Pacific; EMDE = emerging market and developing economy; IDN = Indonesia; KHM = Cambodia; LAO = Lao PDR; LHS = left-hand side; MICs = middle-income countries; MMR = Myanmar; MNG = Mongolia; MYS = Malaysia; PHL = the Philippines; RHS = right-hand side; THA = Thailand; VNM = Vietnam.

A. Agricultural employment and self-employment are share of employment in agriculture and share of self-employed in total employment, respectively. Data for 2018.

C. The Human Capital Index calculates the contributions of health and education to worker productivity. The final index ranges from zero to one and measures the productivity as a future worker of a child born today relative to the benchmark of full health and complete education. The vertical and horizonal lines denote EMDE averages. Data for the latest year available.

D. Total years of schooling is the average years of education completed by people over age 15. Data for the latest year available.

E. A higher value indicates better institutional quality. Error bars reflect values from all EMDEs in EAP. "High informal employment" includes EAP EMDEs with above-median informality over the period 2010-18; "low informal employment" includes those with below-median informality over the same period. Data for the latest year available.

F. "Higher MICs" include China, Malaysia, and Thailand. "Middle MICs" include Indonesia, Mongolia, and the Philippines. "Lower MICs" include Cambodia, Lao PDR, Myanmar, and Vietnam. These groupings are based on GDP per capita.

firms also tend to be less productive than larger firms, and they pay lower wages. Their operations predominantly supply local markets, and they have little ambition for expansion (Rothenberg et al. 2016).

Policy options to address informality challenges in EAP

A distinctive feature of EAP is its large number of slum dwellers. Informality tends to be high among these populations. Targeted policies to improve urban planning can improve living conditions and provide more equal opportunities to informal workers in these settlements. In lower-middle-income economies, underinvestment in human capital and persistently low labor productivity warrant attention. In addition, complementary broad-based measures, such as improving governance and removing disincentives to formal employment, could be pursued.

The COVID-19 pandemic has exposed the challenges in protecting informal workers and vulnerable households in Asia. But it has also provided an opportunity to address long-standing inequalities—in access to health and basic services, finance, and the digital economy—and to enhance social protection for informal workers (Dabla-Norris and Rhee 2020).

Urban planning reforms. Agglomeration benefits can lower the unit costs of public service provision in cities, enabling governments to extend access to basic services to more people (Ghani and Kanbur 2013). To leverage these benefits, urban plans must be well-designed to help improve access to jobs, affordable housing, commercial services, public transportation, and health and education services, thus providing more equal opportunities to disadvantaged communities (Judy and Gadgil 2017; World Bank 2015). Examples of effective metropolitan governance include Beijing, Jakarta, Kuala Lumpur, Metro Manila, and Shanghai (World Bank 2015; World Bank and DRCSC 2014).

Increasing labor productivity. A shift into the formal sector does not necessarily increase labor productivity in firms (Demenet, Razafindrakoto, and Roubaud 2016). Supporting policies need to be in place, including to improve access to business development services, decrease red tape and corruption, facilitate access to financial services, and offer better education and training (OECD 2009; World Bank 2019a). These policies are especially important for small agricultural enterprises, which engage a large share of EAP's workforce.

Reducing regulatory burdens. Removing disincentives to formal employment could encourage a shift of informal firms into the formal sector. Policies can include less burdensome registration procedures and costs and simpler tax assessment and payment regimes. Such broad-based reforms to improve the business climate are also important for formal firms, incentivizing them to invest, grow, and create more jobs. These measures could be complemented with strengthening enforcement to increase the benefits of regulatory compliance.

Widening social protection coverage. Investment in social support systems can be scaled up; systems can be more effectively targeted and, where possible, linked with existing education, health, and employment support mechanisms. The tax base can be widened, the progressivity in taxation increased, and financing of social insurance schemes can be expanded (OECD 2019). The pandemic provides an important opportunity for policy makers to take measures to strengthen social protection systems, including ability to adapt to future shocks (World Bank 2020a).

Europe and Central Asia

The incidence of informality in ECA differs markedly between the eastern and western portions of the region. The east, with weaker institutions and less conducive business climates, has significantly higher informality than the western part (figure 5.6). Higher informality in the east can also be attributed partly to larger agricultural sectors and to sizable remittance inflows, which have provided capital to establish small, informal businesses.

Some ECA economies have had success with policies to promote lower informality, including reductions in tax compliance burdens and tax rates. Policies to promote more flexible labor markets have also been associated with reductions in informal employment. For economies in the east, building stronger institutions, strengthening enforcement, and controlling corruption can encourage businesses to operate in the formal economy.

Evolution of informality in ECA

With the collapse of central planning in ECA in the late 1980s, the informal sector expanded dramatically. Many firms chose to operate informally to avoid regulations, taxation, or corruption, but also because informal activities were profitable due to rationing of consumer goods and high inflation (Johnson, Kaufmann, and Shleifer 1997). During 1989-95, the size of the informal economy more than doubled. Since then, informality in ECA has fallen slightly, from an average of 39 percent of official GDP in 1990-99 to 36 percent in 2010-18; it is still slightly higher than the EMDE average (figure 5.6). Survey-based measures of informality in ECA, such as perceptions of informal activity, also indicate a downward trend. Employment informality (measured by self-employment), however, was unchanged between 1990-99 and 2010-18, at 30 percent of total employment.

Since the 1990s, the western portion of ECA has experienced a faster decline in informality than the east, reflecting more progress with market liberalization and other reforms and less corruption than in the east (Kaufmann and Kaliberda 1996). Notwithstanding the larger decline in informality in the west of the region, 1 in 10 formal employees in Central Europe still received "envelope wages" as recently as 2006.[3]

---

[3] "Envelope wages" refers to the practice of paying a portion of wages in undeclared cash to avoid tax and social security contributions (Williams and Padmore 2013).

FIGURE 5.6 **Informality in Europe and Central Asia**

Output informality in ECA has been higher than the EMDE median since the 1990s and has declined at roughly the same pace as in other regions. But employment informality in ECA has been lower than the EMDE average. Within ECA, informality has been higher and has declined more gradually in the east.

A. Output informality

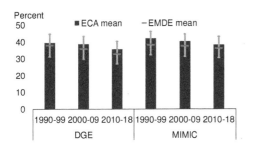

B. Employment informality and perception of informality

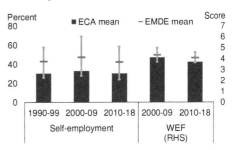

C. Output informality in the eastern and western parts of the region

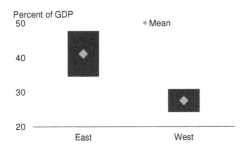

D. Output informality

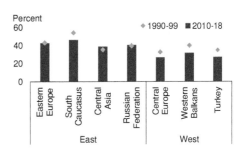

Sources: International Labour Organization; World Bank; World Economic Forum (2018).
Note: DGE = dynamic general equilibrium model; ECA = Europe and Central Asia; EMDE = emerging market and developing economy; MIMIC = multiple indicators multiple causes model; RHS = right-hand side.
A.B. Blue bars show unweighted averages of the informal economy of the region. Red markers show unweighted averages of all EMDEs and the vertical lines denote the interquartile range of all EMDEs.
A. DGE and MIMIC models estimate the size of the informal sector as a percent of official GDP.
B. Self-employment is measured as percent of total employment. The World Economic Forum (WEF) asks the following question: "In your country, how much economic activity do you estimate to be undeclared or unregistered? (1 = Most economic activity is undeclared or unregistered; 7 = Most economic activity is declared or registered)." The average responses are used to capture the extent of perceived informality. The index is reversed here so that a lower WEF index indicates a larger informal economy.
C.D. Output informality is based on DGE estimates, in percent of official GDP. "East" includes Eastern Europe (Belarus, Moldova, and Ukraine), South Caucasus (Armenia, Azerbaijan, and Georgia), Central Asia (Kazakhstan, Kyrgyz Republic, Tajikistan, and Uzbekistan) and Russian Federation. "West" includes Central Europe (Bulgaria, Croatia, Hungary, Poland, and Romania), the Western Balkans (Albania, Bosnia and Herzegovina, Kosovo, North Macedonia, Montenegro, and Serbia), and Turkey.
C. Data are for the latest year available, in most cases, for 2018. Orange diamonds indicate subsample averages and blue bars indicate the 1-standard-deviation range. Output informality is based on DGE estimates, in percent of official GDP.

Correlates of informality in ECA

Informality in ECA has been associated with several economic and institutional factors, including the size of the agriculture sector, remittances, and institutional quality. Informality has also had socioeconomic consequences, such as greater income inequality arising from lower wages in the informal sector and lower fiscal revenues and capacity, because informal firms do not pay taxes.

Remittances. Several economies in ECA (in particular, the Kyrgyz Republic and Tajikistan) are among the most remittance-reliant in the world in terms of inflows as a share of GDP (World Bank 2020b). At the household level, high levels of remittances inflows are associated with a higher likelihood of working informally in ECA (Ivlevs 2016). Remittances can provide capital to help establish small businesses, which tend to be informal, and income support that can make it easier to engage in less secure but often more lucrative informal work (Chatterjee and Turnovsky 2018; Shapiro and Mandelman 2016).

Institutions. Institutional quality is better in ECA, on average, than the EMDE average, but it varies widely, with much weaker indicators in the eastern part of the region (figure 5.7). The west has seen marked improvements in its institutional environment, including more effective government, better regulatory quality, strengthened enforcement, and less corruption, in part owing to reforms implemented in the context of the European Union (EU) accession process (Kaufmann and Kaliberda 1996). These gains have contributed to substantial improvements in the business environment, encouraging firms to operate in the formal sector.[4]

Wage gaps. Traditionally, workers are thought to seek informal work when formal employment opportunities are scarce and when they are less productive (box 4.1). But the informal sector can also provide opportunities to develop human capital helpful for eventual formal employment or self-employment, as has been found for the Russian Federation and Turkey (Guariglia and Kim 2006; Taymaz 2009). In some ECA economies (Romania, Russia, Tajikistan, and Ukraine), informal workers have been found to earn a wage *premium* over formal workers, which may compensate for the lack of social security and lower job security (see, for instance, Lehmann and Norberto 2018; Shehu and Nilsson 2014; Staneva and Arabsheibani 2014; Zahariev 2003). Relatively high wages in the informal sector may encourage skilled professionals to forgo emigration opportunities in highly regulated economies experiencing high rates of emigration, such as Tajikistan (Abdulloev, Gang, and Landon-Lane 2011).

Fiscal revenues. Within ECA, large informal sectors are associated with lower tax revenues and lower provision of public goods (figure 5.7). However, the magnitude of revenues lost because of informality is a matter of debate. One estimate is that tax revenue losses from informality could have been as high as 7 percent of GDP in Armenia in 2004 (Grigorian and Davoodi 2007). Survey data, however, point to only modest potential revenue gains (0.03-0.07 percent of GDP) from turning informal workers into formal workers in Ukraine in 2009, because the newly formal sector workers would typically be low-skilled and subject to low tax rates (World Bank 2011).

---

[4] However, the transition from economies dominated by large state-owned enterprises to economies more friendly to private business can sometimes create more informal employment and a larger informal sector (Earle and Sakova 2000).

FIGURE 5.7 **Correlates of informality in Europe and Central Asia**

As in other regions, employment informality in ECA tends to be higher in countries with larger agricultural sectors. Output informality is higher in the eastern part than in the western part of the region, in part reflecting differences in institutional quality.

A. Employment informality and agricultural employment

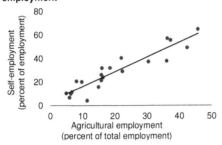

B. Regulatory quality and rule of law

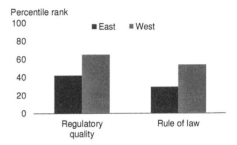

C. Government effectiveness and control of corruption

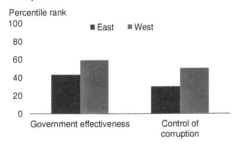

D. Public finance

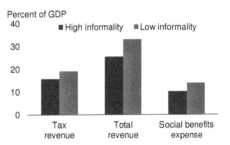

Sources: European Bank for Reconstruction and Development; International Labour Organization; International Monetary Fund (Government Finance Statistics); World Bank (Worldwide Governance Indicators).

Note: ECA = Europe and Central Asia.

A. Agricultural employment and self-employment are share of employment in agriculture and share of self-employed in total employment, respectively. Data for 2018. Sample includes 21 ECA countries.

B.C. Data for 2016 in most cases. "East" includes Armenia, Azerbaijan, Belarus, Georgia, Kazakhstan, Kyrgyz Republic, Moldova, Russia Federation, Tajikistan, Ukraine, and Uzbekistan. "West" includes Albania, Bosnia and Herzegovina, Bulgaria, Croatia, Hungary, Kosovo, Montenegro, North Macedonia, Poland, Romania, Serbia, and Turkey.

D. Values are latest available five-year averages for tax revenue, total revenue, and social benefit expenditure from the general government including social security system. High/low informality are median of top/bottom 50 percent of output informality in ECA sample of economies, as measured by average dynamic general equilibrium (DGE) estimates during 2010-18.

Policy options to address informality challenges in ECA

Policies that are effective in other EMDE regions or even in a particular economy within ECA could be counterproductive for another economy in the region. This underscores the importance of tailoring reforms to economy-specific circumstances. In ECA, policies to tackle informality have centered around fiscal policies, reforms of institutional environments, and labor market policies.

Fiscal reforms. Within ECA, large informal sectors are associated with lower tax revenues and lower provision of public goods, which is a general pattern in EMDEs (figure 5.7; chapter 4). However, the magnitude of revenues lost because of informality depends on economy circumstances. Typically, reducing the tax compliance burden and tax rates, as well as subsidizing the transition to formality, has been accompanied by declines in informality.[5]

- *Preferential tax schemes.* One form of tax simplification that has been used in ECA is the introduction of presumptive taxation for the self-employed and small firms (IFC 2007). This can encourage entrepreneurship, increase revenue collection from hard-to-tax sectors, and ease the transition from informal to formal work. However, these schemes may also inadvertently encourage formal workers to avoid taxes by shifting into presumptive tax status, and encourage firms to remain small (Packard, Koettl, and Montenegro 2012).

- *Other taxes.* Shifting from labor income taxes, which constitute a wedge between informal and formal employment, to less distorting and more easily enforced taxes, such as value added taxes and progressive real estate or land taxes, can shrink the informal economy (Packard, Koettl, and Montenegro 2012). Such shifts occurred in several ECA economies, such as Azerbaijan and Georgia, after 2000 (Végh and Vuletin 2015).

- *Subsidies.* A formal employment subsidy introduced in Turkey in 2004 and 2005 led to an increase in the number of registered jobs by encouraging informal workers to transition to formal employment, including through better social protection (Betcherman, Daysal, and Pagés 2010).

Building institutions. Better governance and more effective tax collection authorities can reduce the size of the informal economy and increase tax revenue. Corruption has been associated with greater informal activity in Poland and Romania (Johnson et al. 2000). Conversely, better control of corruption has reduced the extent of informal activities, particularly in countries that joined the EU in the mid-2000s (Fialová and Schneider 2011). The eastern part of the region, which has much weaker institutions, could focus on improving governance, strengthening enforcement, and fighting corruption, to mimic the favorable outcomes observed in the west.

Labor market regulations. More restrictive employment protection legislation has been associated with higher informal output and employment in ECA, supporting the case for increasing labor market flexibility (Fialová and Schneider 2011; Lehmann and Muravyev 2009). This can take the form of less restrictive regulations with respect to hiring and dismissal, working arrangements, and wage levels.

COVID-19. With informal and formal workers both having lost wages during the COVID-19 pandemic, new wage support programs have targeted both types of workers.

---

[5] On one hand, higher labor tax rates encourage a movement into untaxed informal employment, especially for low-wage earners (Koettl and Weber 2012). On the other hand, higher labor tax rates have in some cases been associated with a lower share of informal employment, because higher revenue allows governments to provide better public goods that can be accessed only in formal employment (Fialová and Schneider 2011; Friedman et al. 2000).

Success in reaching the informal sector has been uneven across economies, however. Support programs in ECA, including cash transfers, have also covered informal workers and firms, albeit to a smaller degree than formal workers (World Bank 2020c). Meanwhile, in Central Asia, large informal sectors and low digitalization may have slowed the transition to online sales that has helped other countries weather the pandemic (EBRD 2020).

Latin America and the Caribbean

A confluence of factors—labor market inefficiencies, burdensome regulations and taxation, corruption, and vast economic and social inequalities—create an environment that has allowed informality to flourish in LAC. Although output informality in LAC has steadily declined over the past two decades, it remains slightly higher than the EMDE median. The trend in employment informality has been less clear. The COVID-19 pandemic has brought new challenges: providing income support to informal workers, many of whom were already living hand-to-mouth before the pandemic and have faced severe income losses during it, became an urgent priority.

Although the quality of institutions in LAC is on average stronger than in EMDEs as a whole, countries in the region with low institutional quality indicators have higher informality. Informality has increased in countries with rampant corruption. High tax rates or burdensome tax regulations may also have encouraged firms to stay in the informal sector. Informality in LAC has been associated with weak growth of output and labor productivity, as well as worse poverty and inequality outcomes. Redesigning tax policy, increasing enforcement of labor laws, and improving the business climate have had some success in reducing informality in the region.

Evolution of informality in LAC

Output informality in LAC has fallen over the past two decades. On average, informal output was equivalent to 35 percent of official GDP in 2010-18, marginally higher than the EMDE average, down from 40 percent in 1990-99 (figure 5.8). A survey-based measure of perceptions of informal activity has also fallen. However, informal employment (measured by self-employment) as a share of total employment increased by about 2 percentage points from 1990-99 to 2010-18, to 36 percent, which was still below the EMDE average. The COVID-19 pandemic is likely to have sharply increased the informal share of employment, at least temporarily, and at the same time, informal workers have suffered disproportionately large income losses.

The decline in output informality over the past two decades has been broad-based across the region (figure 5.8). Several of the countries with the highest incidence of output informality, such as Bolivia, Panama, and Peru, experienced some of the largest declines over the past two decades, in part due to rapid formal job creation in the context of strong output growth. In most countries, employment informality is higher than output informality, reflecting lower productivity in the informal than the formal sector.

FIGURE 5.8 **Informality in Latin America and the Caribbean**

Output-based informality in LAC has fallen since the 1990s, on average, but remains above the EMDE median. Employment-based informality has been stable in the region as a whole; it has increased in several countries.

A. Output informality

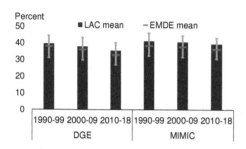

B. Employment informality and perceptions of informality

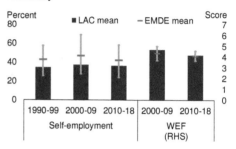

C. Output informality in selected economies

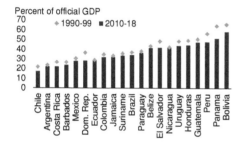

D. Employment informality in selected economies

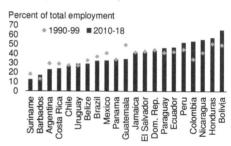

Sources: International Labour Organization; World Bank; World Economic Forum (2018).
Note: DGE = dynamic general equilibrium model; Dom. Rep. = Dominican Republic; EMDE = emerging market and developing economy; LAC = Latin America and the Caribbean; MIMIC = multiple indicators multiple causes model; RHS = right-hand side.
A.B. Blue bars show unweighted averages of the informal economy of the region. Red markers show unweighted averages of all EMDEs and the vertical lines denote the interquartile range of all EMDEs.
A. DGE and MIMIC models estimate the size of the informal sector as a percent of official GDP. DGE sample includes 26 LAC economies and 122 EMDEs; MIMIC sample includes 25 LAC economies and 124 EMDEs.
B. Self-employment is measured as percent of total employment. The World Economic Forum (WEF) asks the following question: "In your country, how much economic activity do you estimate to be undeclared or unregistered? (1 = Most economic activity is undeclared or unregistered; 7 = Most economic activity is declared or registered)." The average responses are used to capture the extent of perceived informality. The index is reversed here so that a lower WEF index indicates a larger informal economy. Self-employment sample includes 32 LAC economies and 134 EMDEs; WEF sample includes 25 LAC economies and 114 EMDEs.
C. Output informality is based on DGE estimates, in percent of official GDP.
D. Employment informality is based on self-employment as a share of total employment.

The broad-based decline in output informality in recent decades did not occur for employment informality, in part reflecting the effects of trade liberalizations in the 1990s in contexts of heavily regulated labor markets (figure 5.8; chapter 4). In fact, informal employment in countries such as Bolivia, Colombia, Honduras, and Peru increased. Even where employment informality fell overall, the decline was not always widespread. In Argentina and Brazil, two of the largest economies in LAC, middle-aged men, the highly skilled, and full-time workers were the most likely to shift from informal to formal employment during the 2000s (Maurizio 2015).

Correlates of informality in LAC

Informality in LAC is associated with economic and institutional factors such as trade liberalization, worker characteristics, tax policy, and governance.

Trade liberalization. The reduction of trade barriers in LAC in the 1980s and 1990s led to fears that domestic firms in the formal sector would become uncompetitive and shift to the informal sector to reduce costs. The effects of trade liberalization on informality have actually been mixed across countries and different in the short run from the long run (Bosch, Goñi-Pacchioni, and Maloney 2012; Menezes-Filho and Muendler 2011). It has been found that, in the presence of labor market rigidities, informal employment may rise in the short term after trade liberalization but not necessarily in the long term (Ponczek and Ulyssea 2018; World Bank 2019b). In Brazil and Peru, trade liberalization was associated with increases in informality as formal firms exited to the informal sector or increasingly hired informal workers, or workers increasingly worked informally (Cisneros-Acevedo, forthcoming; Dix-Carneiro and Kovak 2019). In Colombia, trade liberalization was associated with a slight increase in informality, but only before a subsequent reform that increased labor market flexibility (Goldberg and Pavcnik 2003).

Voluntary movement between formal and informal employment. Switching between the formal and informal sectors is common in the largest economies in the region (Bosch and Maloney 2010; Fiess, Fugazza, and Maloney 2008; Perry et al. 2007). This may reflect responses to swings in employment and income opportunities in the formal sector. Other structural factors, such as poor education and skills, could also account for employment informality (Fernández and Villar 2016).

Tax burdens. High tax rates or burdensome tax regulations have encouraged informality in the region (Loayza 1997; Ordóñez 2014; Vuletin 2008). During 2010-18, average corporate and personal incomes tax rates were significantly higher in EMDEs with above-median output informality than in those with below-median output informality (chapter 6). Both corporate and personal income tax rates tend to be higher in LAC than in EMDEs on average—indeed, LAC is the only EMDE region where the average personal income tax rate has risen since the early 2000s (figure 5.9).

Institutional quality. In LAC, most of the institutional measures associated with informality are at, or slightly better than, the EMDE average. But there is heterogeneity within the region. LAC economies with weak institutional quality have also tended to be those with high informality (figure 5.9). For instance, higher employment informality in Peru than in Chile has been attributed to poorer governance in Peru (Loayza and Wada 2010). Informality in LAC countries has also been attributed to restrictive business and labor regulations, which discourage firms from entering the formal sector (see, for instance, Dougherty and Escobar 2013; Estevão and de Carvalho Filho 2012; Loayza 1997; Loayza, Servén, and Sugawara 2010; Vuletin 2008).

Policy options to address informality challenges in LAC

Designing policies to address informality requires an understanding of its causes and characteristics. These vary considerably in LAC, even within individual countries

FIGURE 5.9 Correlates of informality in Latin America and the Caribbean

In LAC economies where government effectiveness is poor, output-based informality tends to be high. Self-employment tends to be high where labor market efficiency is low. As of 2019, both corporate and personal income tax rates were higher in LAC than the average in all EMDEs.

A. Corporate income tax rates

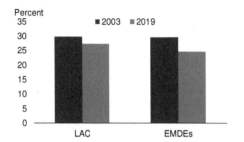

B. Personal income tax rates

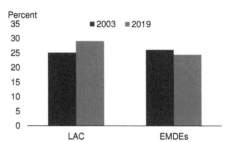

C. Output informality and government effectiveness

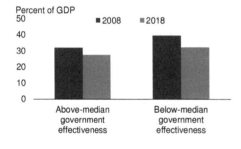

D. Employment informality and labor market efficiency

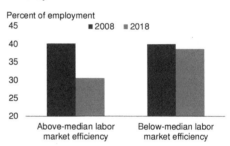

Sources: International Labour Organization; Végh and Vuletin (2015); World Bank (Worldwide Governance Indicators); World Economic Forum (2018).
Note: EMDEs = emerging market and developing economies; LAC = Latin America and the Caribbean.
A.B. Unweighted sample averages.
A Sample includes 17 LAC economies and 49 EMDEs.
B. Sample includes 17 LAC economies and 47 EMDEs.
C. Output informality is based on dynamic general equilibrium (DGE) model estimates, in percent of official GDP. "Above (Below) median" are EMDEs in the LAC region with above- and below-median government effectiveness within the corresponding year (2008 or 2018). Sample includes 32 LAC economies.
D. Employment informality is self-employment as a share of total formal employment. Bars show medians. "Above (Below) median" are EMDEs in the LAC region with above- and below-median labor market efficiency within the corresponding year (2008 or 2018). Labor market efficiency measures flexibility and efficient use of talent. Sample includes 16 LAC economies.

(Fernández and Villar 2016; Perry et al. 2007). Policies that have been successful in addressing informality in LAC have taken account of these factors, focusing variously on reducing tax burdens, strengthening enforcement of labor regulations, and removing disincentives to formal employment.

Tax policy reforms. Making tax policy less burdensome, by simplifying tax systems or lowering tax rates, could incentivize firms to become formal and increase demand for formal workers. Indeed, a large reduction in payroll tax rates in Colombia in 2012 reduced employment informality in the main metropolitan areas by about 7 percentage points (Fernández and Villar 2016). A reduction and simplification of business taxes in Brazil in 1996 was associated with a significant increase in the incidence of formal firms, and the newly formal firms achieved higher revenue and profits than those operating informally (Fajnzylber, Maloney, and Montes-Rojas 2011). The impact of Brazil's reform on informality varied across economic sectors, however, because of differences in incentives to become formal (Monteiro and Assuncáo 2012).

Labor market regulations. Tighter enforcement of labor regulations has been effective in reducing informality in the region, through various mechanisms. In Brazil, tighter enforcement of regulations raised wages and output by improving the allocation of workers between the formal and informal sectors (Meghir, Narita, and Robin 2015). More frequent inspections in Brazil also induced some informal workers to become formal (Almeida and Carneiro 2012). Moreover, inspections have been found to be more effective than incentives in convincing firms in Brazil to operate in the formal sector (de Andrade, Bruhn, and McKenzie 2013).

Other regulations. Policy reforms to ease barriers to entering the formal sector have had mixed results. A reform that simplified the process of opening a business in Mexico was successful in increasing the number of registered businesses, but had no impact on informality: the owners of the new businesses were former employees of formal firms, not informal workers (Bruhn 2011; Kaplan, Piedra, and Seira 2011). Financial deepening contributed to a reduction in informality in Uruguay, particularly for women and older workers (Gandelman and Rasteletti 2016).

COVID-19 response. The provision of income support to informal workers during the COVID-19 pandemic has been challenging. In some cases, existing programs have been successfully scaled up, particularly for the lowest-income informal workers. But even where informal workers have been reached, there have been challenges related to coverage (Busso et al. 2020). One lesson is that the provision of social safety nets needs to be more agile, with low barriers to enrollment and provisions for rapid rollout (Arnold, Garda, and Gonzalez-Pandiella 2020).

Middle East and North Africa

On average, MNA has the lowest output and employment informality among all EMDE regions. There is particularly wide divergence within the region, however, consistent with the wide range of per capita incomes across MNA economies (figure 5.10). Output informality in oil importers and in oil exporters that are not members of the Gulf Cooperation Council (GCC) is well above that in GCC countries, reflecting a sizable presence of agriculture sectors in some countries, as well as histories in some cases of prolonged armed conflict with associated migration, and high reliance on public sector employment. Informal activity in these economies absorbs a large proportion of the region's high numbers of unemployed youth. By contrast, employment informality in GCC countries is very low, averaging 3 percent of total employment in 2010-18. This is broadly in line with the high per capita incomes of GCC countries.

FIGURE 5.10 **Informality in the Middle East and North Africa**

Informal sector output in MNA accounts for about one-quarter of official GDP, lower than in other EMDE regions. However, perceptions of informality in MNA have risen somewhat, while they have declined in the median EMDE. Informal activity is relatively low in GCC economies.

A. Output informality

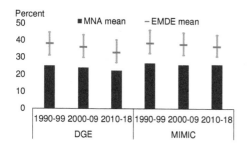

B. Employment informality and perceptions of informality

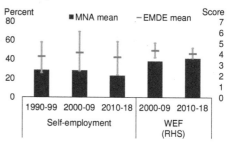

C. Informality by economy groups

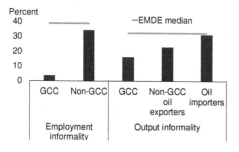

D. Output informality in selected economies

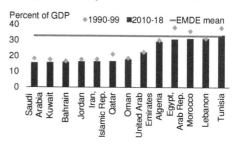

Sources: International Labour Organization; World Bank; World Economic Forum (2018).
Note: DGE = dynamic general equilibrium model; GCC = Gulf Cooperation Council; EMDE = emerging market and developing economy; MIMIC = multiple indicators multiple causes model; MNA = Middle East and North Africa; RHS = right-hand side.
A.B. Blue bars show unweighted averages of the informal economy of the region. Red markers show unweighted averages of all EMDEs and the vertical lines denote the interquartile range of all EMDEs.
A. DGE and MIMIC models estimate the size of the informal sector as a percent of official GDP. DGE sample includes 15 MNA economies and 122 EMDEs; MIMIC sample includes 16 MNA economies and 124 EMDEs.
B. Self-employment is measured as percent of total employment. The World Economic Forum (WEF) asks the following question: "In your country, how much economic activity do you estimate to be undeclared or unregistered? (1 = Most economic activity is undeclared or unregistered; 7 = Most economic activity is declared or registered)." The average responses are used to capture the extent of perceived informality. The index is reversed here so that a lower WEF index indicates a larger informal economy. Self-employment sample includes 16 MNA economies and 134 EMDEs; WEF sample includes 16 MNA economies and 114 EMDEs.
C. Output informality is based on DGE estimates, in percent of official GDP. Employment informality is self-employment as a share of total employment. Bars and lines show medians of economy averages during 2010-18 in corresponding economy groups. Sample includes 6 GCC economies and 10 non-GCC economies (employment informality) and 6 GCC economies, 2 oil exporters, and 5 oil importers (output informality).
D. Output informality is based on DGE estimates, in percent of official GDP. Bars and diamonds show unweighted period averages. The line shows the unweighted average for EMDEs over the period 2010-18.

Several non-GCC economies have reduced informality over the past two decades. Policies that could be effective in further addressing informality in MNA include building better institutions to spur private sector activity, fiscal reforms to reduce tax burdens and improve revenue collection, increased access to finance, and better education and training for vulnerable groups.

Evolution of informality in MNA

On average in 2010-18, informal output in MNA was equivalent to 22 percent of GDP and informal employment stood at 23 percent of total employment (figure 5.10), substantially below the EMDE average. Output informality in MNA declined slightly over the past three decades, by 3 percentage points of GDP between 1990-99 and 2010-18, while employment informality fell by 6 percentage points of total employment. Perceptions of informal activity, however, have risen.[6]

In most of the region, declines in informality in recent decades have been very limited (figure 5.10). Some non-GCC economies, such as the Arab Republic of Egypt, Morocco, and Tunisia, have made progress in reducing output informality. Among GCC countries, informality in Qatar has declined the most.

Correlates of informality in MNA

Informality in MNA reflects economic and development challenges ranging from limited private sector activity to armed conflict. Large informal sectors have been associated with weak human capital, low labor productivity and wages, and less inclusive growth. Although informality can provide helpful employment opportunities where the formal sector suffers from severe distortions and governance is poor, the structural, policy, and institutional causes of informality pose challenges for efforts to diversify economies and reduce reliance on commodity production and the public sector.

Economic structure. Low informality in GCC countries in part reflects high reliance on expatriate workers and, in some countries, high public employment of nationals (World Bank 2018a). Urban workers in MNA are less likely to be informally employed than rural workers (Angel-Urdinola and Tanabe 2012).

Conflict. The MNA region has experienced numerous armed conflicts, some prolonged, in recent decades. In Iraq and the Syrian Arab Republic, violent conflicts have severely limited the number of public sector jobs, and many workers have moved into the informal sector for lack of alternatives (Ianchovichina and Ivanic 2014; World Bank 2017). In Jordan and Lebanon, the massive influx of refugees—many of whom are unregistered—has enlarged the informal sector, where jobs tend to be labor-intensive and low skilled (Verme et al. 2016).

Governance and business climate. Informality in MNA economies is closely and negatively correlated with the quality of governance (Elbadawi and Loayza 2008). In non-GCC economies, government effectiveness and regulatory quality are substantially

---

[6] Before 2012, perceptions of informal activity in MNA were broadly constant. The recent increase could be due to the Arab Spring in 2011 and associated disruptions of activity and policing and enforcement (for instance, for Egypt and Tunisia; Brown, Kafafy, and Hayder 2017). Informal employment and employment outside the formal sector have also increased in Egypt (Elsayed and Wahba 2019; ILO 2018), whereas self-employment has remained stable.

worse than EMDE averages, after deteriorating markedly between 2010 and 2018 (figure 5.11). These issues are further compounded by poor public services and burdensome taxation, both of which raise the costs of operating in the formal sector (World Bank 2016).[7] Such hindrances incentivize firms and workers to remain in the informal sector, where labor productivity is lower.[8]

Policy options to address informality challenges in MNA

Widespread informality in non-GCC MNA economies reflects deep-rooted structural challenges, such as high youth unemployment and bloated public sectors that can no longer absorb additional public servants (IMF 2018).[9] Public sector employment constitutes more than a quarter of total employment in these economies, on average— well above the EMDE average (figure 5.11). The focus has therefore been on multi-pronged policies that aim to create a more vibrant private sector, especially to encourage small firms to grow and boost the human capital of workers so that they can be productively employed in a reinvigorated private sector. Policies targeting specific vulnerable groups can lessen the negative externalities associated with informality.

Fiscal reforms. Burdensome taxation has been a major constraint on formal sector firms in MNA (Gatti et al. 2014). In non-GCC MNA economies, reforms to align tax systems with international best practices and strengthen enforcement could encourage formalization while also raising revenues. Such reforms could include reducing excessive corporate tax burdens and enhancing revenue collection through harmonized electronic filing systems (for example, Morocco) or the introduction of a value added tax (for example, Egypt). In Egypt, reduction of the corporate tax burden has been associated with higher revenues through a broader tax base (Gatti et al. 2014).

Building institutions. Public sector effectiveness and regulatory quality in non-GCC MNA economies have deteriorated in the last decade (figure 5.11). Corruption is cited among the biggest hindrances to MNA firm operations, incentivizing firms and workers to operate informally (World Bank 2016). Policies that reduce regulatory costs help increase the movement of informal firms to the formal sector, and reforms that strengthen property rights may assist rural and agricultural sector populations to access financing (for example, enabling collateralized loans). Policies to promote entrepreneurial activities, such as easing of business licensing requirements, can also facilitate entry of informal workers into more productive jobs in the formal sector.

Increasing access to finance. Access to finance is a more binding constraint on doing business in MNA than in most other EMDE regions (figure 5.11; Farazi 2014).

---

[7] Although informal business operations are likely to make lower contributions to government revenues, they may add to utilization of public services, such as provision of infrastructure (Galal 2005).

[8] Based on Enterprise Survey data, a sizable proportion of firms in oil-importing economies, such as Morocco and Tunisia, consider competitors' practices in the informal sector as hindering their own business operations (World Bank 2004).

[9] These two issues may be linked. Informality is high among the young, in part reflecting the entrance of workers into public sector jobs at a later age (Angel-Urdinola and Tanabe 2012; Elbadawi and Loayza 2008).

FIGURE 5.11 **Correlates of informality in the Middle East and North Africa**

High informality in non-GCC MNA economies reflects deep-rooted structural challenges, such as high youth unemployment and bloated public sectors that can no longer absorb additional public servants. Policies to improve access to finance and government effectiveness can help shift resources from the informal to the formal sector.

A. Youth not employed and not in education

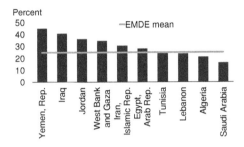

B. Public sector employment

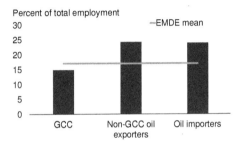

C. Firms citing access to finance as biggest obstacle

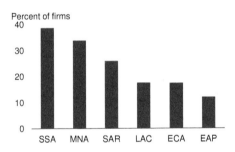

D. Government effectiveness and regulatory quality in non-GCC economies

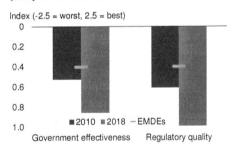

Sources: International Labour Organization; World Bank (Enterprise Surveys, Worldwide Governance Indicators).
Note: EAP = East Asia and Pacific; ECA = Europe and Central Asia; EMDEs = emerging market and developing economies; GCC = Gulf Cooperation Council; LAC = Latin America and the Caribbean; MNA = Middle East and North Africa; SAR = South Asia; SSA = Sub-Saharan Africa.
A. Bars show data for latest available year from 2010 onward. Line shows unweighted average of 121 EMDEs using data for latest available year from 2010-20.
B. Bars show unweighted averages of 6 GCC economies, 3 non-GCC oil exporters, 7 oil importers, and 131 EMDEs. Public sector employment includes employment in the government and publicly owned companies. Based on the latest available data from 2010-20.
C. Percent of firms citing access to finance as their biggest obstacle, based on World Bank Enterprise Surveys (surveys in the MNA region exclude GCC economies). Bars show unweighted averages.
D. EMDEs denotes unweighted average during 2010-18. Sample includes 13 non-GCC economies.

Improving such access, including through stronger legal frameworks and improved credit protection regimes, can promote formal private sector activity by increasing the transparency of firms to investors and facilitating investment (Straub 2005). Several MNA economies have recently implemented policies in this area, such as new insolvency resolution laws in Egypt, Saudi Arabia, and the United Arab Emirates. The adoption of financial technologies (fintech), such as innovations that automate financial transactions, can also facilitate access to financial services by informal unbanked individuals and SMEs (Lukonga 2018; World Bank 2018b).

Investing in human capital. Policies that expand job training are especially relevant for the young, who are commonly informally employed in MNA, to facilitate their entry into more productive, formal jobs (figure 5.11; Angel-Urdinola and Tanabe 2012). Training programs may be particularly effective if they are coupled with mechanisms to increase women's mobility, which is constrained in the region, and offer a combination of soft and hard skills (figure 5.11). The extension of training to rural areas, where education levels are low, could also be especially beneficial; the region's training programs currently tend to serve higher-income and more educated individuals (Angel-Urdinola, Semlali, and Brodmann 2010). A holistic approach that combines job training with job creation, such as through public-private sector programs, could boost informal workers' earnings (Steel and Snodgrass 2008). In MNA, unemployment rates are higher among university graduates than among low-skilled workers. Thus, education system reforms that are coupled with private sector development (the demand side of the labor market) may be more effective at generating high-quality employment.

South Asia

Employment informality in SAR is pervasive. SAR is home to the highest number of informal workers among the six EMDE regions, accounting for close to two-fifths of the world total. Output informality has declined in recent decades, however. Low labor productivity is a long-standing feature of the region's informal sector.

The pervasiveness of employment informality reflects large artisanal and agricultural sectors and the dominance of micro and small business units, often family businesses. High unemployment among the low-skilled, rural, female, and young populations pushes workers into the informal sector. High informality in the region is also associated with weak institutions and poor business climates. Policies that focus on improving the business environment and addressing skills gaps in vulnerable groups can help promote movement to the formal sector.

Evolution of informality in SAR

Informal employment in SAR (measured by self-employment) was 59 percent of total employment in 2010-18, the second highest among all EMDE regions, and well above the EMDE average of 42 percent. However, employment informality has also declined the most of any region since the 1990s (figure 5.12). Using an alternative measure, lack of basic pension coverage, about 90 percent of the labor force in SAR works informally.

Although there is evidence that the COVID-19 pandemic has been accompanied by a movement of formal workers into the informal sector, informal workers were more vulnerable to loss of employment in the early stage of the pandemic, when lockdown measures were most stringent (World Bank 2020d). In India, lockdown measures are estimated to have tripled the urban unemployment rate in the early stages of the pandemic. The income losses associated with these lost jobs were exacerbated by the fact that some 60-85 percent of urban workers had no access to social protection benefits,

FIGURE 5.12 **Informality in South Asia**

SAR's share of informal employment is the largest among EMDE regions, despite a below-average share of informal output. Employment informality in the region has remained broadly unchanged over the past two decades, but output informality has declined rapidly. Persistent low productivity has therefore been a long-standing feature of the region's informal sector.

A. Output informality

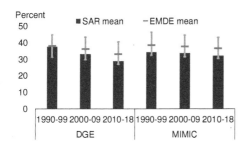

B. Employment informality and perceptions of informality

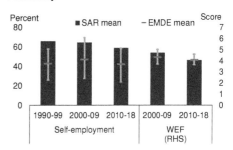

C. Output informality in selected economies

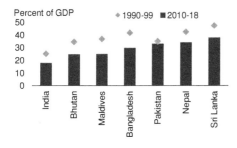

D. Ratio of informal to total labor productivity

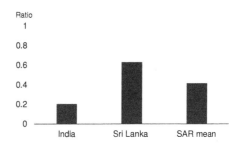

Sources: International Labour Organization; World Bank; World Economic Forum (2018).
Note: DGE = dynamic general equilibrium model; EMDEs = emerging market and developing economies; MIMIC = multiple indicators multiple causes model; RHS = right-hand side; SAR = South Asia.
A.B. Blue bars show unweighted averages of the informal economy of the region. Red markers show unweighted averages of all EMDEs and the vertical lines denote the interquartile range of all EMDEs.
A. DGE and MIMIC models estimate the size of the informal sector as a percent of official GDP. DGE sample includes 7 SAR economies and 122 EMDEs; MIMIC sample includes 7 SAR economies and 124 EMDEs.
B. Self-employment is measured as percent of total employment. The World Economic Forum (WEF) asks the following question: "In your country, how much economic activity do you estimate to be undeclared or unregistered? (1 = Most economic activity is undeclared or unregistered; 7 = Most economic activity is declared or registered)." The average responses are used to capture the extent of perceived informality. The index is reversed here so that a lower WEF index indicates a larger informal economy. Self-employment sample includes 7 SAR economies and 134 EMDEs; WEF sample includes 6 SAR economies and 114 EMDEs.
C. Output informality is based on DGE estimates, in percent of official GDP.
D. SAR sample includes 7 economies.

making reaching them through relief programs more challenging (Bussolo, Kotia, and Sharma 2021; Dhingra 2020).

Output informality in SAR has also fallen, to 29 percent of official GDP in 2010-18 from 38 percent in 1990-99—the largest decline of the six EMDE regions. Survey-based measures of perceptions of informal activity also indicate a decline.

Sri Lanka has the highest output informality in the region, at 38 percent of GDP in 2010-18, whereas India has the lowest, at 18 percent (figure 5.12). India has the highest employment informality, however, at 77 percent of total employment in 2010-18, reflecting large disparities in labor productivity between the formal and informal sectors.

Correlates of informality in SAR

High employment informality in SAR is associated with weak human capital development, poor business conditions, and limited access to financial resources. Informality has adverse implications for poverty and inequality reduction, especially where fiscal revenues available to fund development objectives are limited.

Human capital. SAR has the second-lowest average years of schooling among EMDE regions, behind only SSA (Barro and Lee 2013).[10] Low levels of education limit opportunities for employment in the formal economy. Conditions in slums, home to 130 million South Asians, entrench large education gaps (Ellis and Roberts 2016). In Bangladesh, for example, the net school enrollment rate of children living in informal communities is 15 percentage points below the national average (Kabir and Parajuli 2016).

COVID-19 impact. The negative effects of the COVID-19 pandemic on human capital accumulation may have implications for future informality in SAR. A decline in the duration of schooling during the pandemic may ultimately push more of the labor force into the informal sector, where they will face lower earnings. It is estimated that average lifetime earnings in South Asia will decline by 5 percent because of the pandemic (Azevedo et al. 2020; World Bank 2020d).

Worker characteristics. South Asia's informal labor force consists predominantly of low-skilled, rural, female, or young workers (Goldar and Aggarwal 2012; Gunatilaka 2008; Parajuli 2014). Such worker characteristics contributed to a wider labor productivity gap between formal and informal sectors in SAR than in other EMDE regions (Loayza 2018). For many, the informal sector is the only option for earning a livelihood. In Pakistan, the characteristics of individuals, such as being older and having higher levels of education, have been found to be more predictive of formal employment than the institutional environment (Williams, Shahid, and Martinez 2016).

Business climate. Over the past decade, SAR has suffered greater corruption and weaker government effectiveness than EMDEs on average (figure 5.13). The business environment in SAR—such as the burden of tax rates and compliance, labor regulations, and the ease of starting a business—is also less favorable than in the average EMDE and has been associated with high informality (Goldar and Aggarwal 2012; Vij, Khanna, and Srivastava 2017; Waseem 2018).

---

[10] Average years of schooling in Afghanistan, Nepal, and Pakistan were lower than the SAR average in 2010, the most recent year of available data.

FIGURE 5.13 **Correlates of informality in South Asia**

Weak control of corruption, low government effectiveness, and heavy tax burdens have likely contributed to high employment informality in SAR. Unemployment is higher among women, who represent a larger share of informal workers than men.

A. Institutional indicators

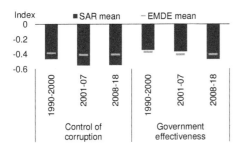

B. *Doing Business* indicators

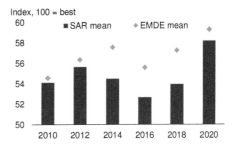

C. Burden of paying taxes

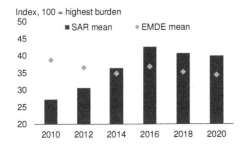

D. Unemployment rates

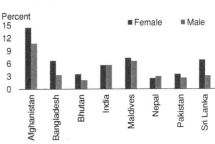

Sources: International Labour Organization; World Bank (*Doing Business*, Worldwide Governance Indicators).
Note: EMDEs = emerging market and developing economies; SAR = South Asia.
A. The score ranges from -2.5 to 2.5. A higher score represents better performance.
B. The index represents the distance to the frontier in the World Bank's *Doing Business* data set. An economy's ease of doing business score is calculated` on a scale from 0 to 100.
C. The index represents the distance to the frontier of the ease of paying taxes indicator in the World Bank's *Doing Business* data set. The value is subtracted from 100 to reflect tax burden.
D. Bars show unemployment rates for the labor force ages 15 and above during 2010-20.

Policy options to address informality challenges in SAR

Policies to address the challenges related to informality in SAR could prioritize addressing weak human capital in vulnerable groups and improving access to finance and public services. Also important, including for the creation of a more conducive climate for private sector development, would be strengthening governance and reducing regulatory burdens.

The COVID-19 pandemic has highlighted structural problems in the informal sector in SAR (Kesar et al. 2021; World Bank 2020d). In the short run, policy makers can provide relief to the informal sector and, in the long run, increase the inclusivity of universal social protection systems.

Investing in human capital. Unemployment is particularly high among young, low-skilled, female, and rural workers (figure 5.13). These groups often seek employment in the informal sector. Policies targeting training and education of these groups, especially in rural areas, could help their transition to formal employment (Khera 2016).

Increasing access to resources. Greater access to credit for informal workers could encourage formalization in SAR (Beck and Hoseini 2014; Ghani, Kerr, and O'Connell 2013). Expanding access to microfinance has led to increasing investment and productivity in the informal sector (Donou-Adonsou and Sylwester 2017; Imai and Azam 2012). High-quality public services can also provide an incentive for informal firms to become formal in order to access them.

Building institutions. There is significant room for improvement in SAR's business environment, including improving government effectiveness and controlling corruption. Measures to reduce regulatory burdens would also improve the business climate and foster growth (Vij, Khanna, and Srivastava 2017). This could reduce informality by reducing the costs of entry to, and operating in, the formal sector. Enhanced monitoring and enforcement, including of tax regulations, could help discourage informality (Ilzetzki and Lagakos 2017). In India, the recent introduction of a Goods and Services Tax is expected to encourage formalization of activity.

Sub-Saharan Africa

Informality in SSA is very high by multiple measures. In some countries, informal employment exceeds 80 percent of total employment. In others, informal output is equivalent to more than half of official GDP. SSA had the highest employment informality of the six EMDE regions in 2010-18 and, along with ECA and LAC, also had the highest output informality.

Numerous factors related to underdevelopment are associated with informality in SSA, including weak institutions, large rural and agricultural sectors, armed conflicts, and low human capital. The high incidence of poverty and inequality is also closely linked to the prevalence of large informal sectors.

Governments in SSA have struggled with how to address high levels of informality. There is a growing recognition of the key role of the informal economy in the region's development, and of the potential of the resources it employs if policies were more attuned to their mobilization.

Evolution of informality in SSA

Informal output in SSA was 36 percent of official GDP, on average, in 2010-18, the highest among EMDE regions and slightly above the shares in ECA and LAC (figure 5.14). Informal employment (measured by self-employment), at 62 percent of total employment, was also the highest among the EMDE regions. Alternative measures of informality, such as the share of labor without pension coverage (above 90 percent) and perceptions of informal activity, are also among the highest of EMDE regions.

Over the past two decades, both output and employment informality in SSA have fallen somewhat, by 5 and 6 percentage points, respectively. Relative to other EMDE regions, the decline in employment informality was large, whereas the fall in output informality was broadly in line with the EMDE average. That said, several SSA countries have made more significant progress in lowering output informality (figure 5.14).

Informality is higher in low-income countries (LICs), fragile states, and commodity exporters. Informal employment exceeded 85 percent of total employment, on average, in countries such as Benin, Burundi, and Madagascar during 2010-18, whereas it was less than 20 percent in countries such as Mauritius and South Africa. Among sub-regions, central and western Africa had the highest average shares of informal employment during 2010-18, at 80 percent and 74 percent, respectively, compared to 50 percent in southern Africa.

Correlates of informality in SSA

High informality in SSA reflects wide-ranging economic and development challenges, including poor institutions, labor and product market rigidities, armed conflict, limited access to resources, and a dearth of skilled labor (Lince 2011; Xaba, Horn and Motala 2002).

Fragility and conflict. As of 2021, SSA hosts all but six of the world's 29 LICs and more than half of the world's 39 fragile states. In general, informality is higher in low-income SSA countries—especially in fragile states with weak state capacity—than elsewhere in the region. Economic disruptions related to conflict and violence have been an important factor forcing people to earn their livelihoods in the informal economy (Heintz and Valodia 2008).

Economic structure. In commodity-exporting countries, the capital-intensive mining sector creates few formal employment opportunities (and artisanal mining creates informal employment opportunities). Moreover, most economies in SSA have large agricultural sectors that have high rates of self-employment. In nonagricultural sectors, there is also considerable self-employment in labor-intensive services, such as street vendors, craftspeople, and home-based activities (Fox and Sohnesen 2012). Rural-to-urban migration and increased labor force participation, especially among women, have been mostly absorbed by the informal sector (Kessides 2005). In countries where social norms restrict the mobility of women, their only employment options are in the informal sector (ILO 2009).

Regulatory burden and governance. SSA has considerably heavier regulatory burdens than other EMDE regions (figure 5.15). Burdensome regulations such as lengthy business registration processes, cumbersome procedures for filing taxes, costly documentary compliance for exports and imports, rigid labor regulations, and high taxes

FIGURE 5.14 Informality in Sub-Saharan Africa

SSA has the highest output and employment informality of the six EMDE regions, although both measures have fallen somewhat in recent decades. Informality is highest in western and central Africa, low-income countries, fragile states, and commodity exporters.

A. Output informality

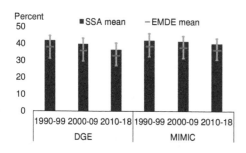

B. Employment informality and perceptions of informality

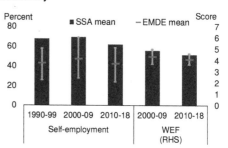

C. Output informality in selected economies

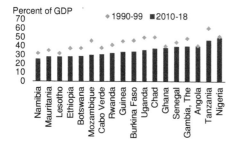

D. Employment informality by economy groups

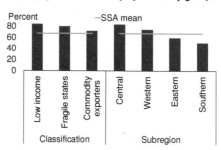

Sources: International Labour Organization; World Bank; World Economic Forum (2018).
Note: DGE = dynamic general equilibrium model; EMDEs = emerging market and developing economies; MIMIC = multiple indicators multiple causes model; RHS = right-hand side; SSA = Sub-Saharan Africa.
A.B. Blue bars show unweighted averages of the informal economy of the region. Red markers show unweighted averages of all EMDEs and the vertical lines denote the interquartile range of all EMDEs.
A. DGE and MIMIC models estimate the size of the informal sector as a percent of official GDP.
B. Self-employment is measured as percent of total employment. The World Economic Forum (WEF) asks the following question: "In your country, how much economic activity do you estimate to be undeclared or unregistered? (1 = Most economic activity is undeclared or unregistered; 7 = Most economic activity is declared or registered)." The average responses are used to capture the extent of perceived informality. The index is reversed here so that a lower WEF index indicates a larger informal economy.
C. Output informality is based on DGE estimates, as percent of official GDP.
D. World Bank classifications. Bars show unweighted group averages over the period 1990-2018. Lines show unweighted averages for SSA over the same period.

can make it prohibitively expensive to operate in the formal economy (Mbaye and Benjamin 2015). SSA also has considerably weaker governance and institutions than other EMDE regions, which can result in failures in enforcing regulations and containing corruption and an environment in which informal enterprises can easily conceal their activities and evade taxes.

Labor productivity. Differences in labor productivity between formal and informal sectors are large: value added per worker in informal firms is only 14 percent that in formal firms in the median SSA country, lower than the corresponding ratio in other

FIGURE 5.15 **Correlates of informality in Sub-Saharan Africa**

Low human capital, limited access to resources, heavy regulatory burdens, and weak governance are potentially important drivers of informality in SSA.

A. Economic and social characteristics

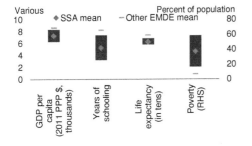

B. Economic factors

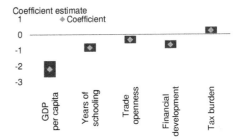

C. *Doing Business* indicators

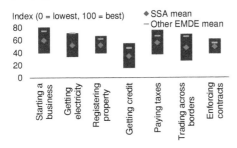

D. Governance indicators

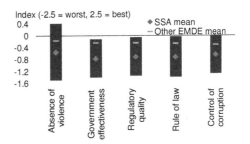

E. Regulation and governance

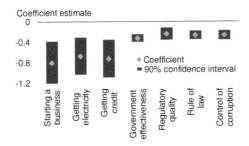

F. Macroeconomic and social outcomes

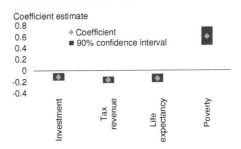

Sources: Barro and Lee (2013); International Labour Organization; World Bank (*Doing Business*, World Development Indicators, Worldwide Governance Indicators).

Note: EMDE = emerging market and developing economies; Other EMDE = EMDEs excluding those in Sub-Saharan Africa; PPP = purchasing power parity; RHS = right-hand side; SSA = Sub-Saharan Africa. Data are for 1990-2018 unless otherwise specified.

A.C.D. Blue bars are +/- 1 standard deviation of SSA mean.

A.B.F. GDP per capita is measured as thousands of 2011 PPP dollars (in logarithm). Life expectancy at birth is in years (in tens). Poverty is the headcount at $1.90 per day (2011 PPP) as percent of population. Trade openness is the sum of exports and imports as a share of GDP. Financial development is proxied by private credit as a share of GDP. Tax burden is the total tax rate. Investment is gross fixed capital formation as a percentage of GDP. Tax revenue is expressed as a share of GDP.

B.E.F. The orange diamonds show the coefficient estimates and the blue bars denote the 90 percent confidence intervals. Ordinary least squares (OLS) estimators are applied, with country means over the sample period used for both the dependent and independent variables. The share of self-employment in total employment is the dependent variable in panels B and E and the independent variable in panel F. The coefficient estimate measures the effect on the dependent variable of a unit change in the independent variable. Sample includes 37 SSA countries.

C. The index represents the distance to the frontier in the World Bank's *Doing Business* data set. An economy's ease of doing business score is calculated on a scale of 0 (lowest performance) to 100 (best performance). Data are for 2004-18.

D. Data are for 1996-2018.

E. The correlates are the distance to frontier in *Doing Business* (for 2004-16) and scores from the Worldwide Governance Indicators (for 1996-2018). The coefficients for the governance and regulatory indicators are in 100ths.

EMDEs (La Porta and Shleifer 2014). Although Enterprise Surveys conducted in SSA indicate that practices of competitors in the informal sector are only the third-largest obstacle to the activities of formal firms (after access to electricity and finance), these obstacles are more problematic in SSA than in other EMDE regions (figure 5.16; Dinh, Mavridis, and Nguyen 2010; La Porta and Shleifer 2016; Nguimkeu 2014).

COVID-19 impact. The large pool of informal workers in SSA, already highly vulnerable to economic shocks, was poorly positioned to withstand the unprecedented supply and demand shocks caused by the COVID-19 pandemic. Further, evidence suggests that the presence of large informal sectors in the region, where workers gather in close proximity to one another, exacerbated the spread of COVID-19 (Nguimkeu and Okou 2020, 2021).

Policy options to address informality challenges in SSA

Although informality is more pervasive in SSA than in other EMDE regions, the environment is conducive to a policy push to shift informal to formal activity. More SSA formal firms started out as informal and the duration of their informality was shorter than in other EMDEs (figure 5.16). Population surveys in SSA also tend to show a more positive attitude toward starting a business than surveys in other EMDE regions, despite a higher proportion of entrepreneurs who became such out of necessity. Thus in one survey 65 percent of respondents believed that they had the required skills and knowledge to start a business, 59 percent indicated that they saw good opportunities to start a firm, and 43 percent intended to start a business within three years. This entrepreneurial spirit, despite high regulatory burdens, may make the informal sector a reservoir of untapped economic potential if allowed to flourish (de Soto 1989; Grimm, Knorringa, and Lay 2012).

Policy makers are focusing their efforts on a combination of strategies aimed at making work more skilled and more productive. Investing in human capital, including increasing the duration of schooling and improving learning outcomes, is a critical pillar in the region's development strategy.[11] Other policies that have been successful in addressing informality have focused on increasing access to resources, such as leveraging technology to make banking accessible to the general public and bridging small informal firms to formal markets (Benhassine et al. 2018; Nguimkeu and Okou 2019). Building better institutions would also help to foster a more conducive business environment, encouraging informal firms to operate in the formal sector and incentivizing formal firms to invest and create more job opportunities.

Investing in human capital. Policies to improve human capital can be prioritized. Fewer than 20 percent of primary school students in SSA pass a minimum proficiency threshold in learning assessment, the lowest among EMDE regions (World Bank

---

[11] In Kenya, for example, improved managerial skills and new marketing channels induced by competition helped metalwork enterprises in the Kariobangi Light Industries grow and transition to the formal economy (Sonobe, Akoten, and Otsuka 2011). The local government provided little support other than designating an area for these artisans to operate, but that proved sufficient.

FIGURE 5.16 Informality indicators and entrepreneurial conditions in Sub-Saharan Africa

In SSA, on average, more than 80 percent of surveyed firms lack formal registration, while about three-quarters of formal firms face competition from firms in the informal sector. There are indications of widespread entrepreneurial ambition in SSA, but potential entrepreneurs are deterred from entering the formal sector by low human capital, limited access to resources, heavy regulatory burdens, and weak governance.

A. Informal competition

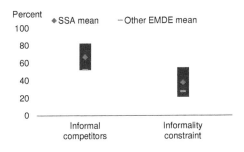

B. Formal registration of firms

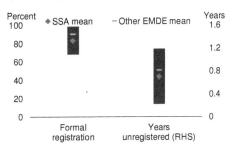

C. Entrepreneurship attitudes

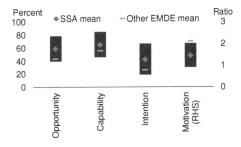

D. Entrepreneurial framework conditions

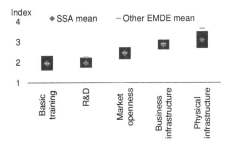

Sources: Global Entrepreneurship Monitor; World Bank (Enterprise Surveys).

Note: EMDEs = emerging market and developing economies; Other EMDE = EMDEs excluding those in Sub-Saharan Africa; RHS = right-hand side; SSA = Sub-Saharan Africa. Blue bars are +/- 1 standard deviation of SSA mean.

A.B. "Informal competitors" shows the percent of firms competing against unregistered or informal firms. "Informality constraint" shows the percent of firms identifying practices of competitors in the informal sector as a major constraint. "Formal registration" shows the percent of firms formally registered when they started operations in the country. "Years unregistered" shows the number of years firms operated without formal registration. Data for 2006-18.

C. "Opportunity" is the percent of population ages 18-64 who see good opportunities to start a firm in the area where they live. "Capability" is the percent of population ages 18-64 who believe they have the required skills and knowledge to start a business. "Intention" is the percent of population ages 18-64 (individuals involved in any stage of entrepreneurial activity excluded) who are latent entrepreneurs and who intend to start a business within three years. "Motivation" is the percent of those who are either a nascent entrepreneur or an owner-manager of a new business that is improvement-driven and opportunity-motivated, divided by the percentage that is necessity-motivated (a lower ratio indicates a higher proportion that is necessity-driven). Data for 2000-19.

D. Scores range from 1 to 9. A higher score represents better perceived condition. "Basic training" is the extent to which training in creating or managing small and medium enterprises (SMEs) is incorporated within the education and training system at primary and secondary levels. "R&D" is the extent to which national research and development will lead to new commercial opportunities and is available to SMEs. "Market openness" is the extent to which new firms are free to enter existing markets. "Business infrastructure" is the presence of property rights, commercial, accounting and other legal and assessment services and institutions that support or promote SMEs. "Physical infrastructure" is the ease of access to physical resources, communications, utilities, transportation, land, or space at a price that does not discriminate against SMEs. Data for 2000-19.

2019a). Teachers are often absent from classrooms. The ensuing learning deficiencies compound over time and eventually appear as a weakly skilled labor force. Although technically and politically difficult, efforts to improve learning outcomes are essential. There is also a need to address issues related to health care. COVID-19 is likely to set back human capital further, by disrupting schooling and livelihoods. To cushion the negative effects of the pandemic, concessional financing and enhanced domestic resource mobilization will be critical to ensure sufficient investment in human capital, as well as green energy and digital infrastructure, amid elevated public debt (World Bank 2021).

Improving labor productivity. Small informal firms, lacking in human capital, cannot be expected to raise the productivity of their labor forces just by registering (La Porta and Shleifer 2016). Large informal firms are likely to resemble formal firms much more than their small informal counterparts: labor productivity differentials between large informal firms and formal ones tend to be minor (Benjamin and Mbaye 2012). In west Africa, the largest and fastest-growing sectors are dominated by large, informal firms. This argues for policies to encourage small firms to grow into larger, more productive ones, through skills upgrading and better access to inputs and resources such as business development services, transport and communications connectivity, financial services, health services, land and property rights, infrastructure, digital technology, and product markets (Nguimkeu and Okou 2019; Oosthuizen et al. 2016; World Bank 2021).[12] As these firms become more productive, with higher-quality products, they may be able to participate in formal-sector supply chains (La Porta and Shleifer 2016). For large firms or those that voluntarily remain informal to evade taxes or avoid labor codes, incentives to encourage formal registration can be combined with tighter enforcement (Mbaye and Benjamin 2015).

Building institutions. Regulatory and institutional reforms to build public trust can strengthen incentives for firms to operate formally (Mbaye and Benjamin 2015). This includes improving the business environment by removing unnecessary regulatory barriers, strengthening monitoring and enforcement capabilities, combatting corruption, and upholding legal and judicial systems. These policies apply equally to formal firms because an enabling environment is critical for investment and employment generation. Improving macroeconomic stability with sound fiscal and monetary policy frameworks is also essential.

Stakeholder engagement. Governments can actively engage with the informal community to put in place the conditions for informality to end. This can involve educating informal firms on the benefits of formal registration, providing information on formalization and the procedures involved, participating in social dialogues to understand pressing issues for informal firms, customizing household surveys to better capture important aspects of informality, and collaborating with informal actors to design and implement effective development policies.

---

[12] For example, training programs in Côte d'Ivoire have had significant positive economic results for informal workers in the agricultural and electronics sectors (Verner and Verner 2005).

Conclusion

The varied nature of informality in EMDEs indicates the need for policy mixes that are appropriate to each economy's circumstances. Cross-economy experiences also highlight the importance of the right policy mix. Policies that have been successful in addressing informality fall broadly into four categories: investing in human capital, improving access to resources, easing regulatory and tax burdens, and strengthening governance.

- *Investing in human capital.* In Côte d'Ivoire and Pakistan, for example, training programs boosted worker income and firm revenue in the informal sector (Burki and Abbas 1991; Verner and Verner 2005).

- *Improving access to resources.* In Bangladesh and Kenya, providing informal firms with better access to markets or finance helped increase firm profitability and investment, easing transition to the formal sector (see, for instance, Donou-Adonsou and Sylwester 2017; Imai and Azam 2012; Sonobe, Akoten, and Otsuka 2011).

- *Ease regulatory and tax burdens.* Policies to reduce tax rates and simplify tax systems have incentivized firms to transition to the formal sector in countries such as Colombia, Egypt, Mexico, and Russia (see, for instance, Bruhn 2011; Fernandez and Villar 2016; Gatti et al. 2014; Slonimczyk 2012).

- *Strengthen governance.* In Georgia, during 1996-2016, the transition to a market economy brought significant improvements in government effectiveness, control of corruption, and law and order (World Bank 2019b). This was accompanied by a steep decline in informality.

The COVID-19 pandemic has taken an especially heavy toll on informal workers, who have not only faced severe income losses but also been difficult for social safety nets to reach to offset some of the income losses. Restrictions on physical interaction and mobility, to impede the spread of the virus, have been difficult to enforce for informal workers because many already live on the cusp of poverty, in turn blunting the public health benefits of lockdowns (Alon et al. 2020).

With good policies, effective enforcement of sensible regulations can help reduce the presence of the informal sector (Loayza 2018). In Brazil, labor inspections helped induce informal workers and firms to formalize (Almeida and Carneiro 2012; de Andrade, Bruhn, and McKenzie 2013). In ECA, better control of corruption reduced the extent of informal activities in the countries that joined the EU in the mid-2000s (Fialová and Schneider 2011). In SSA, policies have focused on unlocking the latent economic potential of the informal sector through investing in human capital and improving access to resources to increase labor productivity. Such policies offer a pathway for informal firms to improve product quality and participate in formal-economy supply chains. In contrast, in ECA, LAC, and non-GCC MNA economies, successful policies have centered around easing regulatory and tax burdens and building more effective and accountable institutions—in particular, strengthening enforcement and reducing corruption. Supportive macroeconomic, structural, and social policies—such as reducing labor market rigidities and enhancing public service delivery and social protection—can ease the implementation of these reforms and facilitate smoother transitions to the formal sector.

The importance of comprehensive strategies, based on thorough economy-specific diagnoses, merits emphasis. In some instances, well-intentioned policies have turned out to aggravate the problems associated with informality. Often these policies were implemented in isolation without complementary measures. For example, trade liberalization reforms were followed by greater informality in some LAC countries; however, when the reforms were accompanied by supporting policies, such as more flexible labor market regulations and well-designed social safety nets, the outcomes were more favorable.

Digital platforms offer governments opportunities to reduce regulatory burdens, strengthen tax administration, and improve the coverage of social protection programs (see, for instance, Awasthi and Engelschalk 2018; Gupta et al. 2017; Junquera-Valera et al. 2017; World Bank 2020d). In Georgia, for example, successful tax reforms were accompanied by the introduction of an electronic tax filing system, which led to improved efficiency, a doubling of the tax-revenue-to-GDP ratio, and a reduction in employment informality by 8 percentage points between 2004 and 2011 (Akitoby 2018). In response to the COVID-19 pandemic, new online platforms (Brazil and Thailand) and new mobile payment devices (Morocco) have been utilized to help governments expand the coverage of existing social protection programs to reach informal workers (World Bank 2020e).

References

Abdulloev, I., I. N. Gang, and J. Landon-Lane. 2011. "Migration as a Substitute for Informal Activities: Evidence from Tajikistan." *Research in Labor Economics* 34 (6236): 205-27.

Akitoby, B. 2018. "Raising Revenue: Five Country Cases Illustrate How Best to Improve Tax Collection." *Finance & Development* 55 (1): 18-21.

Almeida, R., and P. Carneiro. 2012. "Enforcement of Labor Regulation and Informality." *American Economic Journal: Applied Economics* 4 (3): 64-89.

Alon, T., M. Kim, D. Lagakos, and M. VanVuren. 2020. "How Should Policy Responses to the COVID-19 Pandemic Differ in the Developing World?" Working Paper 27273, National Bureau of Economic Research, Cambridge, MA.

Angel-Urdinola, D. F., A. Semlali, and S. Brodmann. 2010. "Non-Public Provision of Active Labor Market Programs in Arab-Mediterranean Countries: An Inventory of Youth Programs." Social Protection Discussion Paper 55673, World Bank, Washington, DC.

Angel-Urdinola, D. F., and K. Tanabe. 2012. "Micro-Determinants of Informal Employment in the Middle East and North Africa Region." Social Protection Discussion Paper 1201, World Bank, Washington, DC.

Arnold, J., P. Garda, and A. Gonzalez-Pandiella. 2020. "Reaching Out to Informal Workers in Latin America: Lessons from COVID-19." *Ecoscope* (blog), June 20, 2020. https://oecdecoscope .blog/2020/06/29/reaching-out-to-informal-workers-in-latin-america-lessons-from-covid-19/.

Atesagaoglu, O., D. Bayram, and C. Elgin. 2017. "Informality and Structural Transformation." *Central Bank [of Turkey] Review* 17 (4): 117-26.

Awasthi, R., and M. Engelschalk. 2018. "Taxation and the Shadow Economy: How the Tax System Can Stimulate and Enforce the Formalization of Business Activities." Policy Research Working Paper 8391, World Bank, Washington, DC.

Azevedo, J. P., A. Hasan, D. Goldemberg, S. A. Iqbal, and K. Geven. 2020. "Simulating the Potential Impacts of COVID-19 School Closures on Schooling and Learning Outcomes: A Set of Global Estimates." Policy Research Working Paper 9284, World Bank, Washington, DC.

Barro, R., and J-W. Lee. 2013. "A New Data Set of Educational Attainment in the World, 1950-2010." *Journal of Development Economics* 104 (September): 184-98.

Beck, T., and M. Hoseini. 2014. "Informality and Access to Finance: Evidence from India." CentER Discussion Paper Series 2014-052. Tilburg University - Center for Economic Research, Tilburg.

Benhassine, N., D. McKenzie, V. Pouliquen, and M. Santini. 2018. "Does Inducing Informal Firms to Formalize Make Sense? Experimental Evidence from Benin." *Journal of Public Economics* 157 (1): 1-14.

Benjamin, N., and A. A. Mbaye. 2012. *The Informal Sector in Francophone Africa: Firm Size, Productivity and Institutions.* Washington, DC: World Bank.

Betcherman, G., N. M. Daysal, and C. Pagés. 2010. "Do Employment Subsidies Work? Evidence from Regionally Targeted Subsidies in Turkey." *Labour Economics* 17 (4): 710-22.

Bosch, M., E. Goñi-Pacchioni, and W. Maloney. 2012. "Trade Liberalization, Labor Reforms, and Formal-Informal Employment Dynamics." *Labour Economics* 19 (5): 653-67.

Bosch, M., and W. Maloney. 2010. "Labor Dynamics in Developing Countries: Comparative Analysis Using Markov Processes: An Application to Informality." *Labour Economics* 17 (4): 621-31.

Brown, A., N. Kafafy, and A. Hayder. 2017. "Street Trading in the Shadows of the Arab Spring." *Environment and Urbanization* 29 (1): 283-98.

Bruhn, M. 2011. "License to Sell: The Effect of Business Registration Reform on Entrepreneurial Activity in Mexico." *Review of Economics and Statistics* 93 (1): 382-86.

Burki, A. A., and Q. Abbas. 1991. "Earnings Functions in Pakistan's Urban Informal Sector: A Case Study." *The Pakistan Development Review* 30 (4): 695-706.

Busso, M., J. Camacho, J. Messina, and G. Montenegro. 2020. "Social Protection and Informality in Latin America during the COVID-19 Pandemic." Working Paper 10849, Inter-American Development Bank, Washington, DC.

Bussolo, M., A. Kotia, and S. Sharma. 2021. "Workers at Risk: Panel Data Evidence on the COVID-19 Labor Market Crisis in India." Policy Research Working Paper 9584, World Bank, Washington, DC.

Chatterjee, S., and S. J. Turnovsky. 2018. "Remittances and the Informal Economy." *Journal of Development Economics* 133 (July): 66-83.

Cisneros-Acevedo, C. Forthcoming. "Unfolding Trade Effect in Two Margins of Informality: The Peruvian Case." *The World Bank Economic Review*.

Dabla-Norris, E., and C. Rhee. 2020. "A New Deal for Informal Workers in Asia." *IMF Blog*, April 30, 2020. https://blogs.imf.org/2020/04/30/a-new-deal-for-informal-workers-inasia.

de Andrade, G. H., M. Bruhn, and D. McKenzie. 2013. "A Helping Hand or the Long Arm of the Law? Experimental Evidence on What Governments Can Do to Formalize Firms." Policy Research Working Paper 6435, World Bank, Washington, DC.

de Soto, H. 1989. *The Other Path: The Invisible Revolution in the Third World*. New York: Harper and Row.

Demenet, A., M. Razafindrakoto, and F. Roubaud. 2016. "Do Informal Businesses Gain from Registration and How? Panel Data Evidence from Vietnam." *World Development* 84 (August): 326-41.

Dhingra, S. 2020. "Protecting Informal Workers in Urban India: The Need for a Universal Job Guarantee." *VoxEU.Org* (blog), May 2, 2020. https://voxeu.org/article/protecting-informal-workers-urban-india.

Díez, F., R. Duval, C. Maggi, Y. Li, I. Shibata, and M. Mendes Tavares. 2020. "Options to Support the Incomes of Informal Workers during COVID-19." International Monetary Fund Special Series on COVID-19, Washington, DC.

Dinh, H. T., D. A. Mavridis, and H. B. Nguyen. 2010. "The Binding Constraint on the Growth of Firms in Developing Countries." Policy Research Working Paper 5485, World Bank, Washington, DC.

Dix-Carneiro, R., and B. Kovak. 2019. "Margins of Labor Market Adjustment to Trade." *Journal of International Economics* 117 (March): 125-42.

Donou-Adonsou, F., and K. Sylwester. 2017. "Growth Effect of Banks and Microfinance: Evidence from Developing Countries." *The Quarterly Review of Economics and Finance* 64 (May): 44-56.

Dougherty, S., and O. Escobar. 2013. "The Determinants of Informality in Mexico's States." OECD Economics Department Working Paper 1043, Organisation for Economic Co-operation and Development, Paris.

Earle, J. S., and Z. Sakova. 2000. "Business Start-Ups or Disguised Unemployment? Evidence on the Character of Self-Employment from Transition Economies." *Labour Economics* 7 (5): 575-601.

EBRD (European Bank for Reconstruction and Development). 2020. "Regional Economic Prospects in the EBRD Regions. Covid-19: Early Estimates of the Damage, Uncertain Prospects." European Bank for Reconstruction and Development, London.

Elbadawi, I., and N. Loayza. 2008. "Informality, Employment and Economic Development in the Arab World." *Journal of Development and Economic Policies* 10 (2): 27-75.

Elgin, C., and O. Oztunali. 2014. "Institutions, Informal Economy, and Economic Development." *Emerging Markets Finance and Trade* 50 (4): 117-34.

Ellis, P., and M. Roberts. 2016. *Leveraging Urbanization in South Asia: Managing Spatial Transformation for Prosperity and Livability*. South Asian Development Matters. Washington, DC: World Bank.

Elsayed, A., and J. Wahba. 2019. "Political Change and Informality." *Economics of Transition and Institutional Change* 27 (1): 31-66.

Estevão, M., and I. de Carvalho Filho. 2012. "Institutions, Informality, and Wage Flexibility: Evidence from Brazil." IMF Working Paper 12/84, International Monetary Fund, Washington, DC.

Fajnzylber, P., W. Maloney, and G. Montes-Rojas. 2011. "Does Formality Improve Micro-Firm Performance? Evidence from the Brazilian SIMPLES Program." *Journal of Development Economics* 94 (2): 262-76.

Farazi, S. 2014. "Informal Firms and Financial Inclusion: Status and Determinants." Policy Research Working Paper 6778, World Bank, Washington, DC.

Fernández, C., and L. Villar. 2016. "Informality and Inclusive Growth in Latin America: The Case of Colombia." IDS Working Paper 469, Institute of Development Studies, Brighton, U.K.

Fialová, K., and O. Schneider. 2011. "Labor Institutions and Their Impact on Shadow Economies in Europe." Policy Research Working Paper 5913, World Bank, Washington, DC.

Fiess, N., M. Fugazza, and W. Maloney. 2008. "Informality and Macroeconomic Fluctuations." IZA Discussion Paper 3519, Institute for the Study of Labor, Bonn.

Fox, L., and T. P. Sohnesen. 2012. "Household Enterprises in Sub-Saharan Africa: Why They Matter for Growth, Jobs, and Livelihoods." Policy Research Working Paper 6184, World Bank, Washington, DC.

Friedman, E., S. Johnson, D. Kaufmann, and P. Zoido-Lobatón. 2000. "Dodging the Grabbing Hand: The Determinants of Unofficial Activity in 69 Countries." *Journal of Public Economics* 76 (3): 459-93.

Frost, J., L. Gambacorta, and H. S. Shin. 2021. "From Financial Innovation to Inclusion." *Finance & Development* (March).

Gagnon, J., T. Xenogiani, and C. Xing, 2011. "Are All Migrants Really Worse Off in Urban Labour Markets? New Empirical Evidence from China." IZA Discussion Paper 6268, Institute for the Study of Labor, Bonn.

Galal, A. 2005. "The Economic of Formalization: Potential Winners and Losers from Formalization in Egypt." In *Investment Climate, Growth, and Poverty,* edited by G. Kochendorfer-Lucius and B. Pleskovic. Washington, DC: World Bank.

Gandelman, N., and A. Rasteletti. 2016. "The Impact of Bank Credit on Employment Formality: Evidence from Uruguay." *Emerging Markets Finance and Trade* 52 (7): 1661-78.

Gatti, R., D. F. Angel-Urdinola, J. Silva, and A. Bodor. 2014. *Striving for Better Jobs: The Challenge of Informality in the Middle East and North Africa.* Washington, DC: World Bank.

Ghani, E., and R. Kanbur. 2013. "Urbanization and (In)Formalization." Policy Research Working Paper 6374, World Bank, Washington, DC.

Ghani, E., W. Kerr, and S. O'Connell. 2013. "The Exceptional Persistence of India's Unorganized Sector." Policy Research Paper 6454, World Bank, Washington, DC.

Goldar, B., and S. C. Aggarwal. 2012. "Informalization of Industrial Labor in India: Effects of Labor Market Rigidities and Import Competition." *The Developing Economies* 50 (2): 141-69.

Goldberg, P., and N. Pavcnik. 2003. "The Response of the Formal Sector to Trade Liberalization." *Journal of Development Economics* 72 (2): 463-96.

Grigorian, D. A., and H. R. Davoodi. 2007. "Tax Potential vs. Tax Effort: A Cross-Country Analysis of Armenia's Stubbornly Low Tax Collection." IMF Working Paper 07/106, International Monetary Fund, Washington, DC.

Grimm, M., P. Knorringa, and J. Lay. 2012. "Constrained Gazelles: High Potential in West Africa's Informal Economy." *World Development* 40 (7): 1352-68.

Guariglia, A., and B.-Y. Kim. 2006. "The Dynamics of Moonlighting in Russia: What Is Happening in the Russian Informal Economy?" *Economics of Transition* 14 (1): 1-45.

Gunatilaka, R. 2008. "Informal Employment in Sri Lanka: Nature, Probability of Employment, and Determinants of Wages." ILO Asia-Pacific Working Paper Series, International Labour Organization, New Delhi.

Gupta, S., M. Keen, A. Shah, and G. Verdier. 2017. *Digital Revolutions in Public Finance.* Washington, DC: International Monetary Fund.

Heintz, J., and I. Valodia. 2008. "Informality in Africa: A Review." WIEGO Working Paper 3, Women in Informal Employment: Globalizing and Organizing, Cambridge, MA.

Huang. P. 2009. "China's Neglected Informal Economy. Reality and Theory." *Modern China* 35 (4): 405-38.

Ianchovichina, E., and M. Ivanic. 2014. "Economic Effects of the Syrian War and the Spread of the Islamic State on the Levant." Policy Research Working Paper 7135, World Bank, Washington, DC.

IFC (International Finance Corporation). 2007. *Designing a Tax System for Micro and Small Businesses: Guide for Practitioners.* Washington, DC: World Bank.

ILO (International Labour Organization). 2009. *The Informal Economy in Africa: Promoting Transition to Formality: Challenges and Strategies.* Geneva: International Labour Office.

ILO (International Labour Organization). 2018. *Women and Men in the Informal Economy: A Statistical Picture.* Geneva: International Labour Office.

ILO (International Labour Organization). 2020. *ILO Monitor: COVID-19 and the World of Work.* Third edition. Geneva: International Labour Organization.

Ilzetzki, E., and D. Lagakos. 2017. "The Macroeconomic Benefits of Tax Enforcement in Pakistan." International Growth Centre, London School of Economics.

Imai, S., and S. Azam. 2012. "Does Microfinance Reduce Poverty in Bangladesh? New Evidence from Household Panel Data." *The Journal of Development Studies* 48 (5): 633-53.

IMF (International Monetary Fund). 2018. "Public Wage Bill in the Middle East and Central Asia Region." IMF Departmental Paper, International Monetary Fund, Washington, DC.

Ivlevs, A. 2016. "Remittances and Informal Work." *International Journal of Manpower* 37 (7): 1172-90.

Johnson, S., D. Kaufmann, J. McMillan, and C. Woodruff. 2000. "Why Do Firms Hide? Bribes and Unofficial Activity After Communism." *Journal of Public Economics* 76 (3): 495-520.

Johnson, S., D. Kaufmann, and A. Shleifer. 1997. "The Unofficial Economy in Transition." *Brookings Papers on Economic Activity* 1997 (2): 159-239.

Judy, L., and B. G. U. Gadgil. 2017. *East Asia and Pacific Cities: Expanding Opportunities for the Urban Poor*. Washington, DC: World Bank.

Junquera-Varela R. F., M. Verhoeven, G. P. Shukla, B. Haven, R. Awasthi, and B. Moreno-Dodson. 2017. *Strengthening Domestic Resource Mobilization: Moving from Theory to Practice in Low- and Middle-Income Countries*. Washington, DC: World Bank.

Jutting, J., and T. Xenogiani. 2007. "Informal Employment and Internal Migration: The Case of China." OECD Publishing, Paris.

Kabir, M., and D. Parajuli. 2016. "When Urbanization Is Messy, Students Fall Through the Cracks." *End Poverty in South Asia* (blog), February 10, 2016. https://blogs.worldbank.org/endpoverty insouthasia/when-urbanization-messy-students-fall-through-cracks.

Kaplan, D. S., E. Piedra, and E. Seira. 2011. "Entry Regulation and Business Start-Ups: Evidence from Mexico." *Journal of Public Economics* 95 (11-12): 1501-15.

Kaufmann, D., and A. Kaliberda. 1996. "Integrating the Unofficial Economy into the Dynamics of Post-Socialist Economies: A Framework of Analysis and Evidence." Policy Research Working Paper 1691, World Bank, Washington, DC.

Kesar, S., R. Abraham, R. Lahoti, P. Nath, and A. Basole. 2021. "Pandemic, Informality, and Vulnerability: Impact of COVID-19 on Livelihoods in India." *Canadian Journal of Development Studies/Revue Canadienne D'Etudes du Développement*: 1-20. https://doi.org/10.1080/02255189 .2021.1890003.

Kessides, C. 2005. "The Urban Transition in Sub-Saharan Africa: Implications for Economic Growth and Poverty Reduction." Africa Region Working Paper 97, World Bank, Washington, DC.

Khera, P. 2016. "Macroeconomic Impacts of Gender Inequality and Informality in India." IMF Working Paper 16/16, International Monetary Fund, Washington, DC.

Koettl, J., and M. Weber. 2012. "Does Formal Work Pay? The Role of Labor Taxation and Social Benefit Design in the New EU Member States." *Research in Labor Economics* 34 (April): 167-204.

La Porta, R., and A. Shleifer. 2014. "Informality and Development." *Journal of Economic Perspectives* 28 (3): 109-26.

La Porta, R., and A. Shleifer. 2016. "The Unofficial Economy in Africa." In *African Successes, Volume 1: Government and Institutions*, edited by S. Edwards, S. Johnson, and D. N. Weil. Chicago: University of Chicago Press.

Lehmann, H., and A. Muravyev. 2009. "How Important Are Labor Market Institutions for Labor Market Performance in Transition Countries?" IZA Discussion Paper 4673, Institute for the Study of Labor, Bonn, Germany.

Lehmann, H., and P. Norberto. 2018. "Informal Employment Relationships and the Labor Market: Is There Segmentation in Ukraine?" *Journal of Comparative Economics* 46 (3): 838-57.

Lince, S. 2011. "The Informal Sector in Jinja, Uganda: Implications of Formalization and Regulation." *African Studies Review* 54 (2): 73-93.

Loayza, N. 1997. "The Economics of the Informal Sector: A Simple Model and Some Empirical Evidence from Latin America." Policy Research Working Paper 1727, World Bank, Washington, DC.

Loayza, N. 2016. "Informality in the Process of Development and Growth." *The World Economy* 39 (12): 1856-916.

Loayza, N. 2018. "Informality: Why Is It So Widespread and How Can It Be Reduced?" *Research & Policy Brief*, World Bank, Kuala Lumpur.

Loayza, N., L. Servén, and N. Sugawara. 2010. "Informality in Latin America and the Caribbean." In *Business Regulation and Economic Performance*, edited by N. Loayza and L. Servén, 157-96. Washington, DC: World Bank.

Loayza, N., and T. Wada. 2010. "Informal Labor: Basic Measures and Determinants." Unpublished manuscript.

Lukonga, L. 2018. "Fintech, Inclusive Growth and Cyber Risks: Focus on the MNAP and CCA Regions." IMF Working Paper 18/201, International Monetary Fund, Washington, DC.

Maloney, W., and T. Taskin. 2020. "Determinants of Social Distancing and Economic Activity during COVID-19: A Global View." Working Paper 9242, World Bank, Washington, DC.

Maurizio, R. 2015. "Transitions to Formality and Declining Inequality." *Development and Change* 46 (5): 1047-79.

Mbaye, A. A., and N. Benjamin. 2015. "Informality, Growth, and Development in Africa." In *The Oxford Handbook of Africa and Economics*, edited by C. Monga and J. Y. Lin. New York: Oxford University Press.

McMillan, M., D. Rodrik, and C. Sepúlveda. 2017. *Structural Change, Fundamentals, and Growth: A Framework and Case Studies*. Washington, DC: International Food Policy Research Institute.

Meghir, C., R. Narita, and J.-M. Robin. 2015. "Wages and Informality in Developing Countries." *American Economic Review* 105 (4): 1509-46.

Menezes-Filho, N. A., and M.-A. Muendler. 2011. "Labor Reallocation in Response to Trade Reform." NBER Working Paper 17372, National Bureau of Economic Research, Cambridge, MA.

Monteiro, J. C. M., and J. J. Assuncão. 2012. "Coming Out of the Shadows? Estimating the Impact of Bureaucracy Simplification and Tax Cut on Formality in Brazilian Microenterprises." *Journal of Development Economics* 99 (1): 100-15.

Nguimkeu, P. 2014. "A Structural Econometric Analysis of the Informal Sector Heterogeneity." *Journal of Development Economics* 107 (March): 175-91.

Nguimkeu, P., and C. Okou. 2019. "Informality." In *The Future of Work in Africa: Harnessing the Potential of Digital Technologies for All*, edited by J. Choi, M. A. Dutz, and Z. Usman, 107-139. Washington, DC: World Bank.

Nguimkeu, P., and C. Okou. 2020. "A Tale of Africa Today: Balancing Lives and Livelihoods of Informal Workers during the COVID-19 Pandemic." Africa Knowledge in Time Policy Brief, World Bank, Washington, DC.

Nguimkeu, P., and C. Okou. 2021. "Does Informality Increase the Spread of COVID-19 in Africa? A Cross-Country Examination." *Applied Economics Letters* (online): 1-5.

OECD (Organisation for Economic Co-operation and Development). 2009. *Is Informal Normal? Towards More and Better Jobs in Developing Countries*. Paris: OECD Publishing.

OECD (Organisation for Economic Co-operation and Development). 2019. *Society at a Glance: Asia/ Pacific 2019*. Paris: OECD .

Oosthuizen, M., K. Lilenstein, F. Steenkamp, and A. Cassim. 2016. "Informality and Inclusive Growth in Sub-Saharan Africa." ELLA Regional Evidence Paper, ELLA Network, Lima.

Ordóñez, J. C. L. 2014. "Tax Collection, the Informal Sector, and Productivity." *Review of Economic Dynamics* 17 (2): 262-86.

Packard, T., J. Koettl, and C. E. Montenegro. 2012. *In from the Shadow: Integrating Europe's Informal Labor*. Washington, DC: World Bank.

Parajuli, R. 2014. "Determinants of Informal Employment and Wage Differential in Nepal." *Journal of Development and Administrative Studies* 22 (1-2): 37-50.

Park, A., Y. Wu, and Y. Du. 2012. "Informal Employment in Urban China: Measurement and Implications." World Bank, Washington, DC.

Perry, G., W. Maloney, O. Arias, P. Fajnzylber, A. Mason, and J. Saavedra-Chanduvi. 2007. *Informality: Exit and Exclusion*. Washington, DC: World Bank.

Ponczek, V., and G. Ulyssea. 2018. "Enforcement of Labor Regulation and the Labor Market Effects of Trade: Evidence from Brazil." Discussion Paper DP15960, Centre for Economic Policy Research, London.

Rodrik, D. 2015. "Premature Deindustrialisation." NBER Working Paper 20935, National Bureau of Economic Research, Cambridge, MA.

Rothenberg, A. D., A. Gaduh, N. E. Burger, C. Chazali, I. Tjandraningsih, R. Radikun, C. Sutera, and S. Weilant. 2016. "Rethinking Indonesia's Informal Sector." *World Development* 80 (April): 96-113.

Shapiro, A. F., and F. S. Mandelman. 2016. "Remittances, Entrepreneurship, and Employment Dynamics over the Business Cycle." *Journal of International Economics* 103 (November): 184-99.

Shehu, E., and B. Nilsson. 2014. *Informal Employment among Youth: Evidence from 20 School-to-Work Transition Surveys*. Geneva: International Labour Organization.

Slonimczyk, F. 2012. "The Effect of Taxation on Informal Employment: Evidence from the Russian Flat Tax Reform." In *Informal Employment in Emerging and Transition Economies*, edited by H. Lehmann and K. Tatsiramos. Bingley, U.K.: Emerald Group Publishing Limited.

Sonobe, T., J. E. Akoten, and K. Otsuka. 2011. "The Growth Process of Informal Enterprises in Sub-Saharan Africa: A Case Study of a Metalworking Cluster in Nairobi." *Small Business Economics* 36 (3): 323-35.

Staneva, A. V., and G. R. Arabsheibani. 2014. "Is There an Informal Employment Wage Premium? Evidence from Tajikistan." *IZA Journal of Labor and Development* 3 (1): 1-24.

Steel, W., and D. Snodgrass. 2008. "Raising Productivity and Reducing Risks of Household Enterprises." Diagnostic Methodology Framework, World Bank, Washington, DC.

Straub, S. 2005. "Informal Sector: The Credit Market Channel." *Journal of Development Economics* 78 (2): 299-321.

Taymaz, E. 2009. "Informality and Productivity: Productivity Differentials between Formal and Informal Firms in Turkey." ERC Working Paper 0901, Economic Research Centre, Middle East Technical University, Ankara, Turkey.

Végh, C., and G. Vuletin. 2015. "How Is Tax Policy Conducted over the Business Cycle?" *American Economic Journal* 7 (3): 327-70.

Verme, P., C. Gigliarano, C. Wieser, K. Hedlund, M. Petzoldt, and M. Santacroce. 2016. *The Welfare of Syrian Refugees: Evidence from Jordan and Lebanon.* Washington, DC: World Bank.

Verner, D., and M. Verner. 2005. "Economic Impacts of Professional Training in the Informal Sector of Côte d'Ivoire: Evaluation of the PAFPA." Policy Research Working Paper 3668, World Bank, Washington, DC.

Vij, J., A. Khanna, and P. Srivastava, eds. 2017. Informal Economy in India: Setting the Framework for Formalisation. New Delhi: Federation of Indian Chambers of Commerce and Industry (FICCI) and Konrad-Adenauer-Stiftung.

Vuletin, G. 2008. "Measuring the Informal Economy in Latin America and the Caribbean." IMF Working Paper 08/102, International Monetary Fund, Washington, DC.

Waseem, M. 2018. "Taxes, Informality and Income Shifting: Evidence from a Recent Pakistani Tax Reform." *Journal of Public Economics* 157 (January): 41-77.

Williams, C., and J. Padmore. 2013. "Envelope Wages in the European Union." *International Labour Review* 152 (3-4): 411-30.

Williams, C., M. Shahid, and A. Martinez. 2016. "Determinants of the Level of Informality in Informal Micro-Enterprises: Some Evidence from the City of Lahore, Pakistan." *World Development* 84 (August): 312-25.

World Bank. 2004. *Unlocking the Employment Potential in the Middle East and North Africa.* MNA Development Report. Washington, DC: The World Bank.

World Bank. 2011. "The Scope and Main Characteristics of Informal Employment in Ukraine." Technical Note for the Government of Ukraine, World Bank, Washington, DC.

World Bank. 2014. *East Asia Pacific at Work: Employment, Enterprise, and Well-Being.* Washington, DC: World Bank.

World Bank. 2015. *East Asia's Changing Urban Landscape: Measuring a Decade of Spatial Growth.* Washington, DC: World Bank.

World Bank. 2016. *What's Holding Back the Private Sector in MNA? Lessons from the Enterprise Survey.* Washington, DC: World Bank.

World Bank. 2017. "The Economics of Post-Conflict Reconstruction in MNA." *Middle East and North Africa Economic Monitor.* Washington, DC: World Bank.

World Bank. 2018a. *Gulf Economic Monitor: Deepening Reforms; In Focus: Pension Systems in the Gulf.* February. Washington, DC: World Bank.

World Bank. 2018b. *Middle East and North Africa Economic Monitor: A New Economy for Middle East and North Africa.* October. Washington, DC: World Bank.

World Bank. 2019a. *World Development Report 2019: The Changing Nature of Work.* Washington, DC: World Bank.

World Bank. 2019b. *Global Economic Prospects: Darkening Skies.* January. Washington, DC: World Bank.

World Bank. 2020a. *Europe and Central Asia Economic Update: East Asia and Pacific in the Time of COVID-19*. Fall. Washington, DC: World Bank.

World Bank. 2020b. "Phase II: COVID-19 Crisis through a Migration Lens." Migration and Development Brief 33, World Bank, Washington, DC.

World Bank. 2020c. *Europe and Central Asia Economic Update: COVID-19 and Human Capital*. Fall. Washington, DC: World Bank.

World Bank. 2020d. *South Asia Economic Focus: Beaten or Broken? Informality and COVID-19*. Washington, DC: World Bank.

World Bank. 2020e. "Social Protection and Jobs Responses to COVID-19: A Real-Time Review of Country Measures." Living paper version 14 (December 11, 2020), World Bank, Washington DC.

World Bank. 2021. *Africa's Pulse: COVID-19 and the Future of Work in Africa*. April. Washington, DC: World Bank.

World Bank and DRCSC (Development Research Center of the State Council, the People's Republic of China). 2014. *Urban China: Toward Efficient, Inclusive, and Sustainable Urbanization*. Washington, DC: World Bank.

World Economic Forum. 2018. *The Global Competitiveness Report 2018*. Geneva: World Economic Forum.

Xaba, J., P. Horn, and S. Motala. 2002. "The Informal Sector in Sub-Saharan Africa." ILO Working Paper on the Informal Economy 2002/10, International Labour Organization, Geneva.

Zahariev, A. 2003. "Tax Avoidance in Bulgaria: The Human Capital Approach." *SSRN Electronic Journal* (5).

The high incidence of informality is a major challenge for the realization of decent work for all and sustainable and inclusive development.

Rafael Diez de Medina (2018)
Director
Department of Statistics, International Labour Organization

PART III

Policies

CHAPTER 6

Tackling Informality: Policy Options

Overcoming the challenges of informal economic activity requires a combination of policies tailored to economy-specific circumstances. In countries where informality is predominantly a reflection of poor governance, an appropriate policy package could streamline regulatory and tax frameworks while improving the efficiency of public revenue collection and regulatory enforcement as well as strengthening public service delivery to bolster tax morale. In countries where informality is predominantly a reflection of underdevelopment, an appropriate policy package could include measures to expand access to finance, markets, and inputs to foster firm productivity and growth; better education to facilitate formal sector employment; and enhanced safety nets to cushion household risks. Several such policy improvements have been associated with sustained declines in informality.

Introduction

Widespread informality is a common policy challenge in emerging market and developing economies (EMDEs). Theoretical models present two major reasons for the emergence of informal economic activity: lack of development (Harris and Todaro 1970; Loayza 2016) and poor governance (de Soto 1989). These two reasons suggest different policy approaches to address informality. The former refers to factors such as an inability of an urban, modern, formal sector to absorb rural migrants; limited financial development to provide finance for formal sectors; and insufficient human capital that prevents workers from finding jobs in the formal sector.[1] The latter refers to factors such as excessively burdensome tax and regulatory frameworks that encourage firms to remain informal, excessive labor regulations that increase the cost of formal employment, and poor governance and regulatory quality that discourage formal participation (chapter 2). The former reason emphasizes the inability to benefit from participating in the formal sector, whereas the latter emphasizes the costs associated with formal-sector participation.[2]

Many EMDE governments have implemented a wide range of policy reforms in the past few decades that may have helped to reduce informality (figure 6.1; Jessen and Kluve 2021).[3] These reforms have often been implemented to either increase the benefits of

---

Note: This chapter was prepared by Franziska Ohnsorge and Shu Yu. Research assistance was provided by Hrisyana Doytchinova and Lorez Qehaja.

[1] See, for example, Amaral and Quintin (2006); Fields (1975); Harris and Todaro (1970); and Loayza (2016).

[2] See Loayza (2018); Oviedo, Thomas, and Karakurum-Özdemir (2009); and chapter 2 for a review of costs and benefits associated with formal (informal) sector participation and how optimizing participants may choose formality (or informality).

[3] Some of these reforms had their roots in the "Washington Consensus" (Birdsall, de La Torre, and Caicedo 2010; Naim 1999; Williamson 2000).

FIGURE 6.1 Policies to address challenges of informality in EMDEs

Governments have implemented a wide range of reforms that could affect informality.

A. Reforms in advanced economies and EMDEs

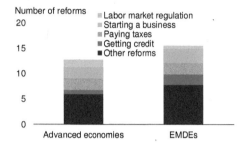

B. Reforms across EMDE regions

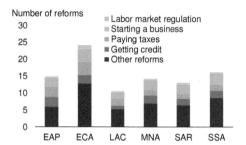

C. Reforms by EMDE region, 2008-18

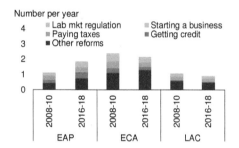

D. Reforms by EMDE region, 2008-18 (continued)

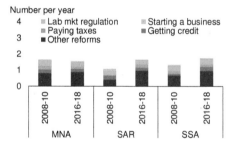

E. Economies with improvement in control of corruption

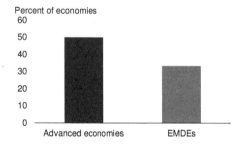

F. Economies with improvement in the ease of doing business

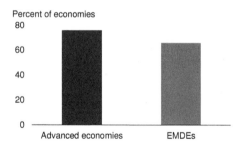

Sources: International Country Risk Guide (ICRG); World Bank (*Doing Business*).

Note: See World Bank *Doing Business* database for reform details. EAP = East Asia and Pacific; ECA = Europe and Central Asia; EMDEs = emerging market and developing economies; LAC = Latin America and the Caribbean; MNA = Middle East and North Africa; SAR = South Asia; SSA = Sub-Saharan Africa.

A.B. For an average economy, the number of policy reforms that have been implemented after year 2008 and are regarded as "improvement" in the ease of doing business or "neutral" (which applies only to "labor market regulation") by *Doing Business* 2008-18.

C.D. For an average economy, the average number of policy reforms per year that have been implemented during 2008-10 in comparison to the annual average number of reforms conducted during 2016-18 (shown in bars).

E.F. Bars show the shares of economies with improved control of corruption (in E; the ease of doing business in F) between 2010 and 2018.

formal-sector participation or reduce the costs of formal activity. For instance, both corporate and personal income tax rates in EMDEs have been reduced, from 37-39 percent on average in the early 1990s to about 24 percent in 2019 (Végh and Vuletin 2015). Time spent on paying taxes was cut by about one-third in EMDEs between 2006 and 2020. Value added taxes, which can lower tax burdens through a refund on input taxes, had been adopted in 71 EMDEs by 2020 (World Bank 2020a). Access to financial services has broadened, with access to automatic teller machines (ATMs) per 100,000 adults and the share of the population with an account at a financial institution both increasing by more than 50 percent between 2010 and 2018. Over the same period, one-third to two-thirds of EMDEs improved their governance and institutional quality.

A review of past policy reforms indicates that some reforms had unintended consequences for informality. Policy reforms often had more benign effects on informality when they were implemented in a supportive institutional and macroeconomic environment. For instance, trade liberalization programs were often associated with greater informality in the short term—unless they were accompanied by greater labor market flexibility and an upgrading of skills in the labor force (Goldberg and Pavcnik 2003; McCaig and Pavcnik 2015; World Bank 2019b).

The current pandemic has provided a reminder of the developmental challenges posed by the informal sector. Informal participants have suffered more adverse economic and health consequences from COVID-19 (coronavirus) than their formal counterparts (box 2.1). The untapped potential of informal sectors, if harnessed to boost income growth and resilience, can help EMDEs build back better from the severe global recession of 2020. This is especially important against the backdrop of a steady decline in potential growth, the growth an economy can sustain at full employment and capacity, over the past decade as all fundamental drivers of growth weakened (World Bank 2018a, 2020b). Specifically, this chapter addresses the following questions:

- Which fiscal measures can help reduce informality?

- Which other policies can help reduce informality?

- What should be the elements of a comprehensive policy package to tackle informality?

Contributions. The chapter makes the following contributions to the literature. First, it offers a systematic review of policies that could affect informality, ranging from fiscal policies to labor market regulations and policies to encourage financial development. It covers both policies that are intentionally designed to encourage formalization and ones that could incidentally affect the informal sector.

Second, the chapter describes novel empirical estimates of the cumulative changes in informality following various policy changes, obtained using a local projection model. Policy-related variables examined include tax rates, access to credit by the private sector,

BOX 6.1 Financial development and the informal economy

Financial development reduces the costs of accessing external financing and thus incentivizes firms and households to invest, including in higher-productivity projects. It also incentivizes participants of the informal sector to join the formal sector. In emerging market and developing economies (EMDEs) with above-median informality, a significantly larger share of firms relies on internal finance and identifies access to finance as a major business obstacle than in EMDEs with below-median informality. Also, in EMDEs with more prevalent informality, a significantly smaller share of households has access to commercial bank branches, automated teller machines (ATMs), and credit. Over the past three decades, growing access to financial services and credit has coincided with a falling share of the informal economy.

Introduction

In recent decades, much research has been devoted to understanding the determinants of informal economic activity, including the role of financial development (Loayza 2018; Ulyssea 2020). Financial development can influence firms' and individuals' choices to engage in informal activity and may also, conversely, be affected by the level of informality (for instance, Capasso and Jappelli 2013; Elgin and Uras 2013; Straub 2005). Easier access to non-cash-based payments—whether via mobile phones, cards, or online—can improve the government's ability to reach and support informal participants during a recession like COVID-19 (World Bank 2019c).[a]

Firms in the informal sector are typically characterized by small scale, low capital-to-labor ratios, lack of investment, a low propensity to implement new and even high-return technologies, and unskilled managers (Capasso and Jappelli 2013; Dabla-Norris, Gradstein, and Inchauste 2008; Quintin 2008). By influencing firms' behavior, financial development can encourage capital accumulation and productivity improvements, and thus enhance long-run economic growth, particularly in the presence of informality (Antunes and Cavalcanti 2007).

Against this background, this box addresses the following questions:

- What links between informality and financial development have been identified by the literature?

- How does financial development differ between EMDEs with high and low informality?

- How has financial development in EMDEs evolved?

Note: This box was prepared by Salvatore Capasso, Franziska Ohnsorge, and Shu Yu.
a. Also see Fang, Kennedy, and Resnick (2020) for detailed examples.

BOX 6.1 **Financial development and the informal economy** **(continued)**

The box examines the nexus between financial development and informality both theoretically and empirically. It first provides a short literature review on the channels through which limited financial development can encourage informality, followed by a summary of existing empirical evidence. It then uses both descriptive statistics and regression analysis to show that greater informality is associated with less financial development, and that better access to finance is associated with lower informality. The conclusion offers policy recommendations.

Lessons from the literature

Theoretical models suggest that financial development reduces informality, whereas the existence of informality could also hinder financial development. Such theoretical findings are supported by empirical studies.

Theoretical models. As informal participants hide all or part of their income and wealth from the authorities, they face high costs of providing collateral or signaling their profitability to lenders and are often credit-rationed (Blackburn, Bose, and Capasso 2012; Capasso and Jappelli 2013). The choice of operating formally or informally thus involves a trade-off between higher financial costs, as well as restricted access to public goods, and the benefits of lower tax and regulatory burdens (Franjo, Pouokam, and Turino 2020; Straub 2005). This trade-off can be faced at the level of the firm or household (extensive margin) or at the level of individual transactions within a firm (intensive margin).

Theory predicts that, as financial markets develop, the size of the informal sector will decrease. Financial development, which involves innovations ranging from the emergence of new and more efficient monitoring and screening technologies to more intermediated funds, typically reduces the average costs of accessing financial resources and incentivizes firms and entrepreneurs to operate formally. Several mechanisms have been explored.

- *Lower collateral requirements.* By improving screening and monitoring technologies, financial development will tend to reduce the minimum collateral required for borrowing, which will tend to attract entrepreneurs into the formal sector (Straub 2005).

- *Stronger legal enforcement.* By strengthening financial contract enforceability, financial development can lower credit costs, which will also tend to attract entrepreneurs into the formal sector (Amaral and Quintin 2006; Antunes and Cavalcanti 2007; Quintin 2008).

BOX 6.1 Financial development and the informal economy (continued)

- *Expanding pool of formal finance.* By expanding the pool of formal-sector funding, financial development can lower the relative cost of formal finance and attract entrepreneurs into the formal sector (Blackburn, Bose, and Capasso 2012; Capasso and Jappelli 2013).

- *More efficient tax auditing.* Financial development can facilitate the enforcement of tax compliance, which is likely to discourage informal activity (Guo and Hung 2020).

Conversely, some studies point to informality as holding back financial development, through several channels.

- *Tax evasion.* Tax evasion, which is often at the core of informality, erodes government revenue bases. Countries with pervasive tax evasion have often used financial transaction taxes to boost revenues. These taxes increase financial intermediation costs and may slow financial development (Elgin and Uras 2013; Roubini and Sala-i-Martin 1992, 1995).

- *Higher bank monitoring costs.* Where informality is prevalent, the lack of formal, declared incomes and assets may force banks to incur higher screening and monitoring expenses. This raises borrowing costs (Capasso, Monferrà, and Sampagnaro 2015).

Empirical evidence. Several measures of financial development have been found to be statistically significantly associated with smaller informal activity (Bittencourt, Gupta, and Stander 2014; Bose, Capasso, and Wurm 2012; Gatti and Honorati 2008). The empirical association has been robust to different model specifications and estimation methodologies (See table 6B.1 for a detailed summary).

- *Firm-level evidence.* Firms that rate financing as a major obstacle to their businesses have, on average, a 16 percent probability of hiding at least 50 percent of their sales, whereas this probability drops below 6 percent for firms that consider financing to be a minor obstacle (Dabla-Norris, Gradstain, and Inchauste 2008). More tax-compliant firms have reported significantly easier access to credit, and this relationship was stronger in more formalized economies (Gatti and Honorati 2008).

- *Household-level evidence.* Italian households reported greater informal activity, especially in the construction sector, in regions with weaker financial development (Capasso and Jappelli 2013).

- *Cross-economy evidence.* Among 137 economies during 1995-2007, both greater efficiency and depth of the banking sector were associated with

BOX 6.1 Financial development and the informal economy (continued)

significantly lower informality (Bose, Capasso, and Wurm 2012). Among 150 economies during 1980-2009, faster broad money growth and a smaller differential between lending and deposit interest rates were associated with statistically significantly smaller informal economies, even when controlling for institutional quality and central bank independence (Bittencourt, Gupta, and Stander 2014).[b]

Stylized facts

Firms and workers in the informal sector have less access to credit and financial services in EMDEs with above-median informality than in EMDEs with below-median informality.

Methodology and data. A sample of 122 EMDEs for 1990-2018 (or the latest available year) is split into those with above-median and below-median shares of informality by output (as proxied by the dynamic general equilibrium model-based share of informal output in official gross domestic product [GDP]) and employment (proxied by the share of self-employment in total employment).[c] Financial development is proxied, first, by firms' reported access to bank credit and capital markets, their difficulty in accessing credit, and the share of internal finance used in investment. Second, at the household level, financial development is proxied by the number of commercial bank branches, ATMs, and bank credit as well as account ownership and reported use of mobile payment services. Data are available from World Bank Enterprise Surveys, the World Bank's Global Financial Development Database, and the World Development Indicators. In addition, the International Monetary Fund's Financial Development Index and its subcomponents are used as proxies for overall financial development and for development in "financial institutions" and "financial markets."[d] Simple averages of the financial development indicators for EMDEs with above-median informality and those with below-median

---

b. Several studies have found nonlinear relationships between informality and financial development. The impact of financial development on informality is greater in more financially developed economies or when GDP exceeds a certain level (Canh and Thanh 2020; Gharleghi and Jahanshahi 2020) or may even be inverse-U-shaped (Elgin and Uras 2013).

c. The results from output informality and employment informality are largely consistent. This box mainly relies on results from output informality.

d. The "financial markets" development index captures access to, and depth and efficiency of, an economy's stock and debt markets, which is less relevant for informal participants in EMDEs. The "financial institutions" development index measures how developed financial institutions are in terms of their depth (size and liquidity), access (ability of individuals and companies to access financial services), and efficiency (ability of institutions to provide financial services at low cost and with sustainable revenues).

**BOX 6.1 Financial development and the informal economy
(continued)**

informality (grouped above) are tested for statistically significant differences. There is no presumption of causality going either from financial development to informality or vice versa.

Firms. Firms in the informal sector have reported more restricted access to credit from the banking sector and capital markets, which limits their ability to invest, including in productivity-enhancing new technologies (Capasso and Jappelli 2013; D'Erasmo 2016; Ferreira-Tiryaki 2008). In EMDEs with above-median output informality, on average, 36 percent of firms identified access to finance as a major constraint—about 9 percentage points more than in other EMDEs (figure B6.1.1). Firms also rely more on internal finance for operating, starting, or expanding firms in EMDEs with more pervasive informality (Farazi 2014). On average in EMDEs with above-median informality, 75 percent of firms depend on internal finance to invest and 19 percent of firms can use bank funds to fulfill their investment needs, compared with 68 percent and 29 percent of firms, respectively, on average in EMDEs with below-median informality.

Households. Households in EMDEs with below-median informality have access to significantly more commercial bank branches, ATMs, and credit than those in EMDEs with above-median informality (figure B6.1.1). About 50 percent of the population in EMDEs with below-median informality owns an account at a financial institution or recently used a mobile money service—about 17 percentage points more than in EMDEs with above-median informality.

Evolution of financial development and its implications

EMDE financial systems have deepened and financial access has broadened over the past three decades. This has coincided with a steady decline in the shares of informal output and employment.

Methodology. A local projection model is used to estimate the cumulative changes in the share of informal output or informal employment over one to five years following a shift in financial development (annex 6A). Two dimensions of financial development that are particularly relevant for informal participants are examined. The first is the ability of individuals and companies to access financial services, which is proxied by the number of commercial bank branches per 100,000 adults. The second dimension, financial system depth, is proxied by domestic credit to the private sector in percent of GDP (Svirydzenka 2016; World Bank 2020c). The estimation controls for per capita GDP. The sample covers 125 EMDEs over 1990-2018.

Financial development in EMDEs. Measures to improve access to credit have been a common policy reform in East Asia and the Pacific, the Middle East and

BOX 6.1 Financial development and the informal economy (continued)

FIGURE B6.1.1 Financial development and informality in EMDEs

Firms and workers in EMDEs with more pervasive informality are more likely to be financially constrained, less likely to obtain bank finance, and more likely to have limited access to other financial services than those in EMDEs with less pervasive informality. As a result, firms in EMDEs with more pervasive informality rely more on internal financing.

A. Financial constraint facing firms and informality

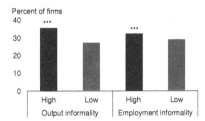

B. Financing options facing firms

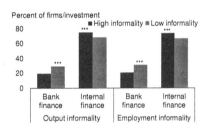

C. Access to finance and output informality (households)

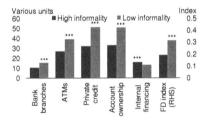

D. Access to finance and employment informality (households)

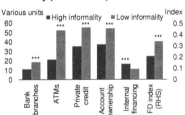

Sources: International Monetary Fund (Financial Development Index Database); World Bank (Enterprise Surveys, Global Financial Development Database, World Development Indicators).

Note: Data are from EMDEs and the period 1990-2018. Output informality is measured by DGE-based estimates on informal output (in percent of official GDP). Employment informality is proxied by self-employment in percent of total employment. In A-D, *** denotes that the group differences are not zero at 10 percent significance level. "High informality" ("Low informality") are EMDEs with above-median (below-median) DGE-based informal output measure (or employment informality proxied by self-employment shares) over the period 2000-18 (2010-2018 in C-D). ATM = automated teller machine; DGE = dynamic general equilibrium model; EMDEs = emerging market and developing economies; IMF = International Monetary Fund; RHS = right-hand side.

A.B. Bars are simple group means using data from latest year available for EMDEs with "high informality" and those with "low informality." "Finance constraint" measures the percent of firms identifying access to finance as a major constraint in an economy. "Bank finance" measures the percent of firms using banks to finance investment in an economy. "Internal finance" measures the average share of investment financed internally using personal savings.

C.D. Bars are unweighted averages of various financial development indicators for EMDEs with "high informality" and those with "low informality" over the period 2010-18. Output informality is used in C and employment informality is used in D. "Bank branches" measures the number of commercial bank branches per 100,000 adults. "ATMs" measures the number of ATMs per 100,000 adults. "Private credit" measures domestic credit to private sector in percent of GDP. "FD index" is the financial development index from the International Monetary Fund, which measures the overall level of financial development. "Account ownership" is the percentage of survey respondents (aged 15 or above) who report having an account (by themselves or together with someone else) at a bank or another type of financial institution or report personally using a mobile money service in the past 12 months. "Internal financing" is captured by the percentage of respondents (aged 15 or above) who report saving or setting aside any money in the past 12 months to start, operate, or expand a farm or business.

BOX 6.1 Financial development and the informal economy (continued)

North Africa, South Asia, and, more recently, Sub-Saharan Africa (chapter 5). Measures to expand access to finance have included better personal property registration to facilitate borrowing by informal firms (for example, Czech Republic; World Bank 2012) and digital payment systems to encourage a shift away from informal finance (World Bank 2017).

Overall, access to finance and and the size of financial institutions increased in more than three-fifths of EMDEs over 2010-18 (figure B6.1.2). The number of ATMs per 100,000 adults rose from 26 to 40, and the share of population with an account at a financial institution increased from 33 to 51 percent (Svirydzenka 2016). Domestic credit to the private sector in EMDEs increased by more than 4 percentage points of GDP, on average, over the same period.

Changes in informality following financial development. Financial development was associated with significant contractions in both output and employment informality (figure B6.1.3; annex 6A). First, 10 more bank branches per 10,000 adults—about the difference between the averages for EMDEs with above-median and below-median informality—were associated with a 0.1- to 0.3-percentage-point decline in the share of informal output in the following one to five years. The share of informal employment also declined statistically significantly. Second, a 10-percentage-point-of-GDP increase in domestic credit to the private sector was associated with a significant contraction in the shares of output and employment informality in subsequent years.[e]

Conclusion

Both theory and empirical evidence indicate that more advanced financial development is associated with a smaller informal economy, although the direction of causality remains a matter of debate and may run both ways. Financial development is considerably weaker in countries with more pervasive informality. Financial systems have deepened, and access to financial services has broadened, in EMDEs over the past three decades.

Policy measures to reduce informality, however, need to go beyond improving the financial system and facilitating access to credit. Evidence suggests that the impact of financial development on informality depends on the quality of the legal and regulatory systems, the level of economic development, and financial

---

e. The results remain broadly unchanged when levels of informal output and employment are used as robustness checks (see figure 6A.1 for results using levels of informal output). The robust results suggest that any movement in the informal share of output or employment is determined by changes in informal activity (the numerator), not by only changes in formal activity (the denominator).

BOX 6.1 Financial development and the informal economy (*continued*)

FIGURE B6.1.2 Evolution of financial development in EMDEs

In EMDEs, access to financial institutions and the depth of their activities improved between 1990 and 2018.

A. Financial development, 1990-2018

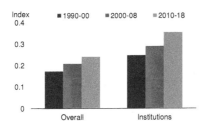

B. EMDEs with improved financial development

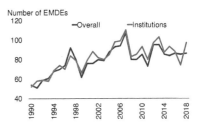

C. Access to finance

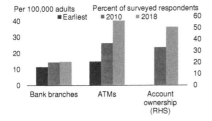

D. Domestic credit to private sector

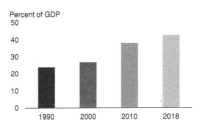

Sources: International Monetary Fund (Financial Development Index Database); World Bank (Global Financial Development Database, World Development Indicators).

Note: Data are from EMDEs and the period 1990-2018. Output informality is measured by DGE-based estimates on informal output (in percent of official GDP). Employment informality is proxied by self-employment in percent of total employment. ATMs = automated teller machines; DGE = dynamic general equilibrium model; EMDEs = emerging market and developing economies; IMF = International Monetary Fund; RHS = right-hand side.

A.B. Bars (A) and lines (B) show simple EMDE averages for corresponding time periods. "Overall" is the aggregate financial development index obtained from the IMF. It measures the overall level of financial development and captures development in both "financial institutions" and "financial markets." The latter is about the access, depth, and efficiency of a economy's stock and debt market, which was less relevant for informal participants in EMDEs. The "Institutions" index measures how developed financial institutions are in terms of their depth (size and liquidity), access (ability of individuals and companies to access financial services), and efficiency (ability of institutions to provide financial services at low cost and with sustainable revenues). Some of the subindicators for "Institutions" are used in C-D to show the access (C) and depth (D) of financial institutions.

C. Bars show simple EMDE averages in earliest possible year (2004), 2010, and 2018. "Bank branches" measures the number of commercial bank branches per 100,000 adults. "ATMs" measures the number of ATMs per 100,000 adults. "Private credit" measures domestic credit to private sector in percent of GDP. "Account ownership" is the percentage of survey respondents (aged 15 or above) who report having an account (by themselves or together with someone else) at a bank or another type of financial institution or report personally using a mobile money service in the past 12 months. In the case of "account ownership," data from closest years are used.

D. Bars show simple EMDE averages in corresponding years. The indicators captures domestic credit to private sector as a share of GDP.

BOX 6.1 Financial development and the informal economy (continued)

FIGURE B6.1.3 Evolution of output informality following financial development in EMDEs

Financial development is found to have been associated with significant subsequent contractions in output informality. Financial development, especially better access to financial institutions and increased depth of financial institutions, helps reduce output informality.

A. Cumulative changes in output informality following a 10-unit increase in the number of bank branches per 100,000 adults

B. Cumulative changes in output informality following a 10-percentage-point-of-GDP increase in domestic credit to the private sector

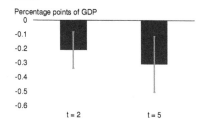

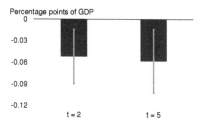

Source: World Bank.
Note: Data are from EMDEs and the period 1990-2018. Output informality is measured by DGE-based estimates on informal output in percent of official GDP. The results are obtained via a local projection method where informality measures are detrended using Hodrick-Prescott (HP) filter. See annex 6A for detailed model specifications. DGE = dynamic general equilibrium model; EMDEs = emerging market and developing economies.
A.B. Bars show the cumulative changes in DGE-based output informality in percent of GDP following a 10-unit increase in the number of bank branches per 100,000 people (in A) and 10-percentage-point-of-GDP increase in the share of domestic credit to the private sector in percent of GDP (in B). Whiskers show the upper and lower bounds of the corresponding 90 percent confidence intervals. "t = n" shows cummulative changes over the n years after the policy change.

development itself. In addition, the effect of measures to promote financial development may be temporary and differ depending on the structure of financial markets.

In particular, improvements in the legal system may be a precondition for achieving broader access to credit that can draw informal firms into the formal sector. Measures to improve contract enforcement and investor protection may be particularly effective in EMDEs, which often fall well behind best practices.

Greater competition and access to markets may foster the productivity gains that are needed for firms to be able to service debt, one aspect of financial development. The possibility of reverse causality suggests that, in some instances, measures to reduce informality by streamlining regulations and improving their enforcement may create a virtuous circle of lowering informality and spurring financial development.

labor market efficiency, governance, and regulatory quality. This is the first study to conduct such empirical analysis for a wide range of policies. It is also the first to examine the share of informality in both economic output and employment: earlier studies have tended to focus on either informal output, or informal employment, or informal firms.[4]

Third, the chapter is the first published attempt to comprehensively examine the link between financial development and informality both theoretically and empirically (box 6.1). It reviews the literature identifying the channels through which limited financial development can discourage formalization. It uses both descriptive statistics and regression approaches to show that informality is associated with lack of financial development, and that improvements in access to finance are associated with declining informality.

Main findings. First, macroeconomic policies, governance, and business climates have become more conducive to lowering informality over the past three decades. Over that period, EMDEs have reduced tax burdens, improved governance and regulatory quality, and expanded access to finance, education, and public services.

Second, policies that seek to streamline tax regulation, strengthen tax administration, and improve public service delivery have been associated with declines in informality. Separately, policies aimed at invigorating private sector activity broadly, such as measures to increase labor market flexibility, streamline regulatory frameworks for firm start-up, expand access to finance, and improve governance have also been associated with declines in informality.

Third, policy measures can have unintended consequences. For instance, trade liberalization that raised competition in the tradable sector was sometimes associated with greater informality in the short run, unless accompanied by measures that increase labor market flexibility. Also, reductions in informality have tended to be greater for reforms accompanied by business development and training programs, public awareness campaigns, and stronger enforcement.

Fourth, financial development has been associated with declining informality (box 6.1). It reduces the average costs of access to external financing and incentivizes firms to invest in higher-productivity projects and to join the formal sector. Over the past three decades, increased access to financial services and increased credit availability have been followed by declining informality.

Fifth, a comprehensive policy package tailored to country circumstances offers the greatest chance of success in reducing informality. A combination of measures to strengthen economic development, boost productivity in both formal and informal sectors, streamline regulations, and ensure effective enforcement can address multiple

---

[4] See Bosch, Goñi-Pacchioni, and Maloney (2012); Fajnzylber, Maloney, Montes-Rojas (2011); Ihrig and Moe (2004); and Rocha, Ulyssea, and Rachter (2018).

sources of informality. The relative priorities will depend on the economy-specific features of informality.

The rest of the chapter is organized as follows. It first presents a range of fiscal policy options that may be used to help remove barriers to joining the formal sector. It then discusses a wide range of policies that can ease the transition from the informal to the formal sector. The chapter also illustrates the importance of having a comprehensive and complementary policy package to tackle the challenges posed by informality and how to implement it successfully. In addition, the chapter describes the implications of digital technologies for coping with informality. The final section summarizes the conclusions.

Data and methodology

This chapter relies on the database detailed in chapter 2 for measures of output and employment informality. It applies several statistical tests to quantify the links between a wide range of policies and informality, without establishing or assuming causality. It then estimates a series of local projection models to help quantify the cumulative response of informality to various policy actions over the short and medium terms.

Data. Both output and employment informality are considered here. Output informality is proxied by estimates based on the dynamic general equilibrium (DGE) model in percent of official gross domestic product (GDP), and employment informality is proxied by self-employment in percent of total employment. Both measures are available for up to 121 EMDEs over the period 1990-2018.[5] For the local projection estimation, all data series on informality are detrended using the Hodrick-Prescott filter to mitigate concerns that the results are driven by the declining trend in informality (chapter 2). A wide range of policy measures is considered here, ranging from changes in corporate tax rates to actions to improve the ease of doing business (table 6B.2). Detailed data descriptions are provided in annex 6A.

Empirical strategy. The chapter applies two empirical approaches to assess the links between informality and policies.

First, differences between average policies in EMDEs with above-median and below-median informality are tested for statistical significance. The sample of EMDEs is grouped into those with an above-median share of informal output and those with a below-median share of informal output, on average during (up to) 1990-2018.[6] For each subsample, simple averages of policy indicators are generated and the difference between these two group averages is tested for statistical significance. EMDEs with high

---

[5] In the case of financial development, absolute levels of informal output and informal employment, rather than their relative share of official GDP or total employment, are used as robustness checks when a local projection model is estimated (figure 6A.1). Using absolute levels of informal output and informal employment avoids the possibility that the results are driven by movements in total official GDP or total employment (the denominator) rather than movements in output or employment in the informal sector (the numerator).

[6] The results are the same when EMDEs are grouped according to employment informality (table 6B.3).

informality refer to EMDEs with above-median informality, and EMDEs with low informality refer to EMDEs with below-median informality.

Second, a local projection model as in Jordà (2005), Teulings and Zubanov (2014), and World Bank (2018a) is estimated to identify the effects of policy changes on informality over time for a sample of up to 125 EMDEs during 1990-2018. The model estimates the cumulative changes in informality after policy changes over different time horizons while controlling for country fixed effects and per capita income levels (table 6B.4).[7] Policy changes are defined as a unit change in the corresponding policy indicator. For instance, a 1-percentage-point increase in the personal income tax rate is considered a tax policy change. Annex 6A details the model specification.

Fiscal measures

High tax rates or payments, complicated tax codes, and administrative burdens have been commonly cited as reasons for informal activity (Auriol and Warlters 2005; Perry et al. 2007; Waseem 2018). Lax tax enforcement facilitates poor tax compliance (Slemrod 2019). Poor government services—often underfunded and inefficiently delivered—will tend to erode tax morale (Awasthi and Engelschalk 2018). In a sweeping survey of the literature, measures to address such issues have been identified as having been particularly effective at encouraging a shift into formal activity (Jessen and Kluve 2021; World Bank 2019b).

Tax rates

Higher tax rates in more informal EMDEs. On average during 2010-2018, average corporate and personal incomes tax rates were significantly higher, by 3 (corporate) to 4 (personal) percentage points in EMDEs with above-median output informality than in those with below-median output informality. Value added tax (VAT) rates were also statistically significantly higher in EMDEs with above-median output informality than in those with below-median output informality.[8]

Over time, shift away from income taxes. Since 1990, both corporate and personal income tax rates have been lowered in EMDEs whereas the use of VAT has expanded. Average corporate and personal income tax rates in EMDEs have fallen by 13 and 15 percentage points, respectively, from close to 40 percent in the beginning of the 1990s to about 24 percent in 2020 (figure 6.2). About two-thirds of EMDEs lowered their statutory personal income tax rates and more than three-quarters lowered their statutory

---

[7] The results are robust to using self-employment as a measure of employment informality (table 6B.5). As further robustness checks, both ordinary least squares and quantile regressions are performed using the same set of policy for both output and employment informality measures. The regression results are largely in line with the findings from the group comparison approach (tables 6B.6-6B.7).

[8] In contrast, EMDEs with high or low informality often do not differ significantly in their average statutory rates for social security contributions nor their revenue collections from such taxes, but they do differ significantly in the amount of social security they provide (see below).

FIGURE 6.2 Tax rates and informality in EMDEs

Income tax rates remain higher in EMDEs with more pervasive informality—even where governments have cut rates and shifted toward value added taxation. Informality declined after income tax rate reductions but not after VAT rate reductions.

A. Tax rates and output informality

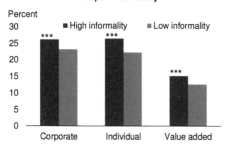

B. Tax rates, 1990-2020

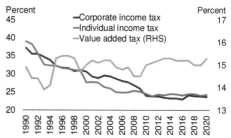

C. Cumulative changes in output informality following a 10-percentage-point increase in corporate income tax rate

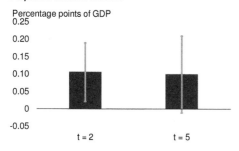

D. Cumulative changes in output informality following a 10-percentage-point increase in individual income tax rate

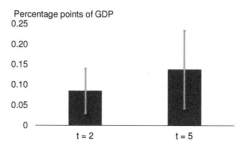

E. Number of economies with VAT

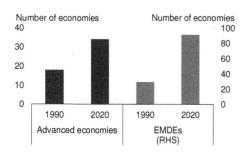

F. Cumulative changes in output informality following a 10-percentage-point increase in VAT rate

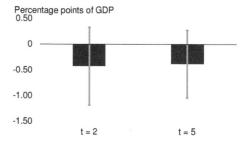

Sources: Cnossen (1998); KPMG; University of Michigan; Organisation for Economic Co-operation and Development; Végh and Vuletin (2015); World Bank (*Doing Business*).

Note: DGE = dynamic general equilibrium model; EMDEs = emerging market and developing economies; RHS = right-hand side; VAT = value added tax.

A. Bars are group means for EMDEs with above-median DGE-based estimates on informal output ("high informality") or those with below-median DGE-bases estimates on informal output ("low informality") over the period 2010-2018. Data are from about 100 EMDEs (in the case of individual tax rate, China is dropped as an outlier). Bolivia, Georgia, Panama, and Zimbabwe are dropped as outliers. *** denotes that the group differences are not zero at 10 percent significance.

B. Lines are simple group averages for EMDEs.

C.D., F. Bars show the cumulative changes in DGE-based output informality in percent of GDP following 10-percentage-point increase in corporate income tax rate (C), individual income tax rate (D), and VAT rate (F). Whiskers show the upper and lower bounds of the corresponding 90 percent confidence intervals. "t = n" indicates the cumulative changes in output informality over the n years after a policy change. Data are for EMDEs over the period 2010-18. See annex 6A for detailed model specifications.

E. Bars show the number of EMDEs and advanced economies that adopted VAT.

corporate income tax rates over the sample period.[9] These efforts often coincided with a streamlining of tax regulations and a broadening of the tax base (Kopczuk 2005).

Although income tax rates were lowered, often to reduce distortions that discourage employment, VAT was introduced, which could be less distortionary than income tax but may lead to a more regressive tax system (Cnossen 1998).[10] Many economies in Latin America introduced VAT regimes in the 1970s and 1980s, and their ranks were joined by a large number of economies in Europe and Central Asia (ECA) during the 1990s. Between 1990 and 2020, the number of EMDEs with VAT systems increased from 29 to 91 (Végh and Vuletin 2015; World Bank 2020a).

Lower informality after tax rate cuts. Lower corporate or personal income tax rates can reduce the incentives of firms and households to operate in the informal economy to lower their costs. In one EMDE, for example, a tax hike in 2010 reduced the number of formal firms and their sales revenues to such an extent that tax revenues three years after the hike were lower than they would have been without the tax hike (Waseem 2018). A sweeping review of past government interventions suggests that tax cuts were particularly effective in reducing informality (Jessen and Kluve 2021). Similarly, a review of policies showed that tax simplification and tax cuts were associated with lower informality (World Bank 2019b).

Meanwhile, the introduction of VAT may strengthen incentives to register in order to qualify for VAT refunds—or, conversely, may strengthen incentives to operate informally to offer lower prices excluding VAT. A VAT regime imposes an input tax on informal firms that do not qualify for refunds but source from formal firms, which in the right circumstance can motivate them to register, thus raising government revenue collection (de Paula and Scheinkman 2010; Loayza 2018; World Bank 2018c).[11] A requirement to digitalize sales receipts for accelerated VAT refunds could further strengthen incentives to register and correctly report sales (Fan et al. 2020). In one case, electronic invoicing for VAT purposes was rolled out in waves between 2014 and 2018 and resulted in more than 5 percent higher reported firm sales, purchases, and value added in the first year after adoption (Bellon et al. 2019).

Indeed, since 1990, a 10-percentage-point decrease in the corporate income tax rate has been associated with a cumulative decline in output informality of about 0.1 percentage point of GDP, relative to trend, over the following two years (figure 6.2). A similarly sized reduction in the personal income tax rate has been associated with a slightly stronger, and deepening, fall in output informality in the following five years. Despite finding significant falls in informality following tax cuts, these falls are generally small in

---

[9] The sample contains up to 53 EMDEs for which data are available in 2020 and 1990.

[10] That said, the presence of an informal economy could lead to incomplete coverage and inefficiencies in the VAT system (Keen 2008; Piggott and Whalley 2001; Emran and Stigliz 2005). In some case, labor informality was found to be associated with lower overall VAT collection (Caro and Sacchi 2021).

[11] Poorer households tend to spend a larger share of their budgets in the informal sector than richer households. As a result, households in the richest quintile can face an effective consumption tax rate that is twice that of the poorest quintile (Bachas, Gadenne, and Jensen 2020).

size, suggesting that cutting tax rates alone is not enough to move all participants from the formal sector to the informal sector. Other policy measures are needed (Loayza 2018). Meanwhile, increases in VAT have not been associated with any significant change in output informality. This suggests that some informal firms source their inputs from informal markets that operate outside the VAT system. The results are robust to using employment informality, instead of output informality.

Tax compliance

More burdensome tax compliance in more informal EMDEs. Beyond tax rates, tax compliance can be costly and time-consuming and, thus, discourage formal registration by firms, especially those with poor profitability (Morales and Medina 2016; Rocha, Ulyssea, and Rachter 2018; Ulyssea 2018). On average, in EMDEs with above-median informality during 2010-18, it took the average firm 33 hours longer and required statistically significantly more payments, estimated at 11 per year, to comply with tax regulations than in EMDEs with below-median informality (figure 6.3). As a result, despite higher corporate and personal income tax rates in EMDEs with above-median informality, revenue collections were lower: on average in EMDE with above-median output informality, personal and corporate income tax revenues were statistically significantly lower, by 0.6 and 0.8 percentage point of GDP, than in EMDEs with below-median informality.

Similar administrative challenges have troubled the administration of VAT regimes in countries with high informality. During 2016-18, firms spent 29 hours a year, on average, complying with VAT refund requirements in EMDEs with above-median informality—7 hours more than in EMDEs with below-median informality, though the difference is not statistically significant.[12] It took about 40 weeks for firms in EMDEs with above-median informality to receive VAT refunds—significantly longer than the 31 weeks in EMDEs with below-median informality.

Over time, less burdensome tax compliance. Firms' tax compliance costs have declined in EMDEs in the past few decades. Since 2006, the time spent by firms on paying taxes has fallen by 68 hours a year, on average, in EMDEs and the average number of tax payments per year has declined by one-third, to 26 payments per year in 2020 (figure 6.3). In ECA, the introduction of electronic tax filing and payment systems has reduced the average tax filing time from 473 hours in 2006 to 225 hours in 2020 (World Bank and PwC 2019).

Efforts to lower tax burdens have been among the most common policy reforms in EMDEs, especially in East Asia and Pacific (EAP) and Latin America and the Caribbean (LAC). Measures to make tax compliance less burdensome have ranged widely (Awasthi

---

[12] In the case of employment informality, the average annual number of hours spent on complying with VAT refund requirements amounted to 37 in EMDEs with above-median informality—20 hours per year significantly more than in EMDEs with below-median informality (table 6B.3).

FIGURE 6.3 **Firms' tax compliance burdens and informality in EMDEs**

Tax compliance burdens on firms remain higher in EMDEs with more pervasive informality than in those with less pervasive informality, despite recent declines. Past efforts to lower compliance costs were not followed by immediate declines in informality.

A. Ease of paying taxes and output informality

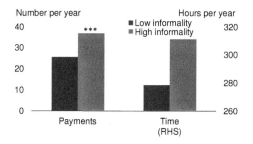

B. Ease of paying taxes over time

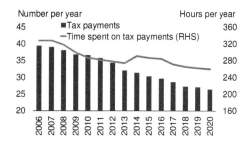

C. Time to comply with and obtain VAT refund and output informality

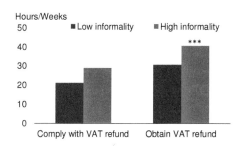

D. Cumulative changes in output informality following a 1-point increase in the score for ease of paying taxes

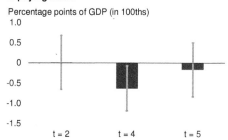

Source: World Bank (*Doing Business*).
Note: DGE = dynamic general equilibrium model; EMDEs = emerging market and developing economies; RHS = right-hand side; VAT = value added tax.
A.C. Bars are group means using data from latest year available for EMDEs with "high informality" and those with "low informality." "High informality" ("low informality") are EMDEs with above-median (below-median) DGE model-based informal output measure over the period 2010-18. Data are from about 100 EMDEs. *** denotes that the group differences are not zero at 10 percent significance.
B. Bars show the average number of tax payments per year by a medium-size company. The line shows the average time spent on paying taxes per year by a medium-size company. Data are for EMDEs.
D. Bars show the cumulative changes in DGE-based output informality in percent of GDP following a 1-point increase in the score for ease of paying taxes. Whiskers show the upper and lower bounds of the corresponding 90 percent confidence intervals. "t = n" indicates the cumulative changes in output informality over the n years after a policy change. Data are for EMDEs over the period 1990-2018. See annex 6A for detailed model specifications.

and Engelschalk 2018; Slemrod 2019). Tax bases have been simplified in industries with a high percentage of undeclared workers (for example, domestic work), and tax regulations have been harmonized across different types of firms (Oviedo, Thomas, and Karakurum-Özdemir 2009). At the same time, tax enforcement has been stepped up by expanding the use of information technology and communication tools, encouraging a switch from cash-based transactions to bank-based ones, and strengthening the capacity of tax administrations (for example, Nguimkeu and Okou 2019; Prichard et al. 2019).[13]

---

[13] See Chodorow-Reich et al. (2018); Crouzet, Gupta, and Mezzanotti (2020); and Lahiri (2020) for the impact of demonetization.

Lower informality after measures to facilitate tax compliance. Measures to reduce the burden of tax compliance or firm registration can lower the cost for informal firms of moving into the formal sector (Rocha, Ulyssea, and Rachter 2018). Coordination of minimum tax thresholds across different types of tax, such as personal income tax, VAT, and social security contributions, could increase tax compliance and improve welfare (Kanbur and Keen 2014). Measures to harmonize tax provisions or other regulations across different types of firms can reduce incentives for firms to evade taxation and remain small and informal (Dabla-Norris, Gradstein, and Inchauste 2018; Harju, Matikka and Rouhanen 2019). Measures to strengthen tax administration can increase the likelihood of detection of informal firms that do not comply with taxes (Carrillo, Pomeranz, and Singhal 2017; Naritomi 2019).

Measures to facilitate tax compliance have been accompanied by statistically significant declines in output informality (figure 6.3). The effects have not been immediate, being insignificant in the first year, but have strengthened over time. Thus four years after reforms that increased the score for the ease of paying taxes by 1 point, the share of output informality was 0.1 percentage point of GDP lower—a statistically significant difference.

Tax morale

Weaker tax morale in more informal economies. Tax morale is weaker in EMDEs with above-median informality. On average, in EMDEs with above-median output informality, the average household scores 2.5 points on a scale of 0 to 10, with 10 indicating that underreporting of income for tax purposes is always justifiable—that score is 0.4 index points, and statistically significantly, higher than in EMDEs with below-median informality (figure 6.4).

Among the many reasons for weaker tax morale is a lack of trust in the government or dissatisfaction with the quality of public service delivery.[14] Indeed, entrepreneurs in EMDEs with above-median output informality report significantly poorer access to government support and programs as well as poorer physical and services infrastructure than entrepreneurs in EMDEs with below-median output informality (figure 6.4; chapter 4). Similarly, significantly better access to commercial and professional infrastructure is reported by businesses in EMDEs with above-median tax morale than those in EMDEs with below-median tax morale. Coverage of unemployment benefits is significantly lower, by about 3 percentage points of the population, in EMDEs with above-median informality than in those with below-median informality. On average , in EMDEs with below-median informality, social insurance programs can cover about 34 percent of the annual income or consumption of the beneficiary household, which is significantly lower, by 6 percentage points, than in EMDEs with above-median informality.

---

[14] See Daude, Gutiérrez, and Mulguizo (2012) for a review of drivers of tax morale. OECD (2019) suggests that there is a positive association between tax morale and public service provision in Africa, whereas tax morale in Latin America is more linked with trust in the government.

FIGURE 6.4 **Tax morale and informality in EMDEs**

Tax morale is higher in EMDEs with lower informality. Higher tax morale has been associated with better government services such as social security, infrastructure, education, and health care systems.

A. Tax morale and informality

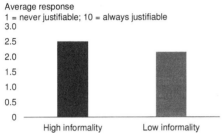

B. Government support and informality

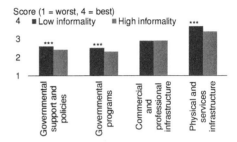

C. Tax morale and access to government services

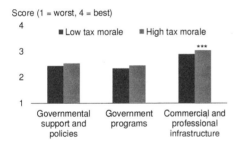

D. Adequacy of social security and informality

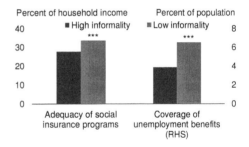

E. Access to infrastructure and informality

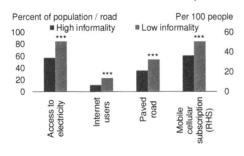

F. Health and education outcomes and informality

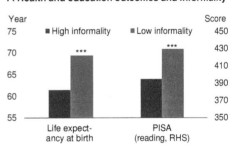

Sources: Global Entrepreneurship Monitor; Programme for International Student Assessment (PISA) database; World Bank (World Development Indicators); World Road Statistics (WRS).

Note: Data are from EMDEs and the period 1990-2018. "High (Low) informality" are EMDEs with above (below)-mediaDGE-based estimates on informal output in percent of GDP. All scores on government support and public infrastructure in B and C are for the period 2000-18 and range from 1 (worst) to 4 (best). DGE = dynamic general equilibrium model; EMDEs = emerging market and developing economies; RHS = right-hand side. *** denotes that the group differences are not zero at 10 percent significance.

A. Bars show simple group averages between 1990 and 2018. World Value Survey asks whether cheating on taxes is justifiable, with a higher level suggesting that the economy is more tolerant toward the informal sector.

B.C. Bars show simple group averages. "Governmental support and policies" measures the extent to which policies support entrepreneurship as a relevant economic issue. "Government programs" captures the presence and quality of programs directly assisting small and medium enterprises (SMEs) at all levels of government (national, regional, municipal). "Commercial and professional infrastructure" captures the presence of property rights, commercial, accounting, and other legal and assessment services and institutions that support or promote SMEs. "Physical and service infrastructure" measures the ease of access to physical resources at a price that does not discriminate against SMEs.

D. Adequacy of social insurance programs is measured as total transfer amount received by population participating in social insurance programs in percent of total income or expenditures of beneficiary households.

E. Bars show simple group averages.

F. PISA testing scores are for students aged 15.

Education and health outcomes are significantly poorer in EMDEs with above-median informality, with Programme for International Student Assessment (PISA) test scores for 15-year-old students in EMDEs with above-median informality being lower by about 10 percent than in those with below-median informality, and life expectancy eight years lower in EMDEs with above-median informality. The poorer outcomes are partly due to more limited government expenditures on education and health in EMDEs with more pervasive informality (chapter 4).

Over time, stable tax morale, despite better government services. In contrast to output and employment informality, tax morale has remained stable over the past three decades. In the early 1990s, households in EMDEs gave an average score of 2.5 to the justifiability of cheating on taxes (where a score of 1 means that cheating on taxes is never justifiable and 10 means that it is always justifiable)—virtually the same as in 2010.[15] As one of the social capital measures with deep roots in culture, tax morale is slow-moving by nature (Luttmer and Singhal 2014). In contrast, entrepreneurs in EMDEs have, on average, perceived statistically significant improvements in government support or programs for small and medium enterprises (SMEs) and in improving commercial and professional infrastructure available to SMEs (figure 6.5).

Meanwhile, actual government service delivery has improved by several measures. The adequacy of social insurance programs has risen in EMDEs from an average of 31 percent of household income in the 2000s to 34 percent a decade later. Infrastructure—for example, road kilometers, access to reliable power, and access to internet services—has improved considerably since 2000. Mobile cellular subscriptions rose from 28 to 95 per 100 people between the 2000s and the 2010s. EMDEs' test scores on PISA indicators of education outcomes have risen significantly, by 17 points, and life expectancy has risen by four years, on average, in EMDEs.

A range of measures has been introduced over the past three decades to cultivate better tax morale, including public appeals to declare activities, campaigns to encourage a culture of commitment to declaration, and efforts to change perceptions of the tax system's fairness (Williams and Schneider 2016). Other measures have included steps to shift the burden of payments of social security contributions from employers to employees (for example, in Latvia, Poland, and Slovenia), to reduce employers' social security contributions (for example, in Bulgaria), and to link social benefits to personal contributions (for example, in most of the economies in the European Union; Oviedo, Thomas, and Karakurum-Özdemir 2009).[16]

Lower informality after improvements in government services. Improvements in the perception that tax dollars are spent judiciously—that is, for appropriate objectives and in an efficient way—can encourage greater tax compliance and lessen informality (Sung,

---

[15] The indicator for tax morale is taken from World Values Surveys, conducted in various years. The current round of World Values Surveys will complete its data collection in December 2021.

[16] Transitions from an employment-based social security system to a well-designed model of risk sharing can further improve the safety net for informal workers and help protect both formal and informal workers during economic downturns (World Bank 2013, 2018c).

FIGURE 6.5 **Government services in EMDEs, 2000-18**

Although infrastructure, social security systems, and health care systems have improved in EMDEs over the past several decades, entrepreneurs' perceptions of the adequacy of government services have remained stable and poor.

A. Government support perceived by entrepreneurs

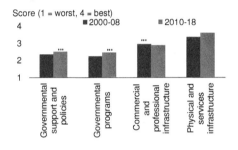

B. Social security

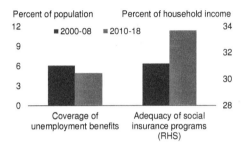

C. Public infrastructure

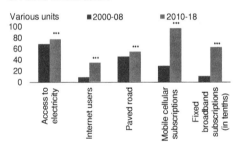

D. Health and education outcomes

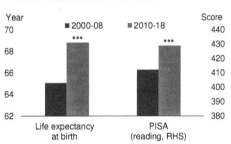

Sources: Global Entrepreneurship Monitor; Programme for International Student Assessment (PISA) database; World Bank (World Development Indicators); World Road Statistics (WRS).

Note: Data are from emerging market and development economies (EMDEs) and the period 2000-2018. All scores on government support and public infrastructure in A are taken from the National Expert Survey of the Global Entrepreneurship Monitor for the period 2000-18. The scores range from 1 to 4 with a lower score representing poorer entrepreneurial conditions. Bars show simple period averages for 2000-08 and 2010-2018, correspondingly, with *** indicating that the period differences are not zero at 10 percent significance level. RHS = right-hand side.

A. "Government support and policies" measures the extent to which policies support entrepreneurship as a relevant economic issue. "Government programs" captures the presence and quality of programs directly assisting small and medium enterprises (SMEs) at all levels of government (national, regional, municipal). "Commercial and professional infrastructure" captures the presence of property rights, commercial, accounting, and other legal and assessment services and institutions that support or promote SMEs. "Physical and service infrastructure" measures the ease of access to physical resources—communication, utilities, transportation, land, or space—at a price that does not discriminate against SMEs.

B. Adequacy of social insurance programs are measured in percent of total welfare of beneficiary households.

C-D. PISA scores are for students aged 15. "Paved road" is calculated as 100 minus the share of unpaved road in percent of total road. "Access to electricity" and "Internet users" are in percent of population. "Mobile cellular subscriptions" and "fixed broadband subscriptions" are measured as per 100 people.

Awasthi, and Lee 2017). Better education or infrastructure can help raise labor productivity in both formal and informal activities, thus facilitating a move of previously insufficiently productive, informal firms into the formal sector.[17]

---

[17] See, for instance, Benjamin and Mbaye (2012); Kim, Loayza, and Meza-Cuadra (2016); Oviedo, Thomas, and Karakurum-Özdemir (2009); and World Bank (2018c). Better access to education or infrastructure may boost productivity growth more in the formal sector than in the informal sector, resulting in a fall in the relative share of informal output in total economic output.

FIGURE 6.6 Informality after improvements in government services

After improvements in government services, informality has declined.

A. Cumulative changes in output informality following a 1-point increase in the presence and quality of government programs in EMDEs

B. Cumulative changes in output informality following a 1-point increase in commercial and professional infrastructure in EMDEs

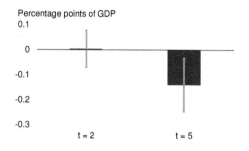

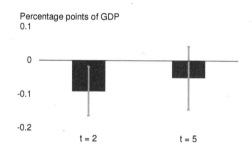

Source: World Bank.

Note: Data are from EMDEs and the period 2000-18. Both scores taken from National Expert Survey of the Global Entrepreneurship Monitor for the period 2000-18. The scores range from 1 (worst) to 4 (best). DGE = dynamic general equilibrium model; EMDEs = emerging market and developing economies.

A.B. Bars show the cumulative response of DGE-based output informality in percent of GDP to a 1-point increase in "government programs" index (A) and "commercial and professional infrastructure" (B). Whiskers show the upper and lower bounds of the corresponding 90 percent confidence intervals. The results are obtained via a local projection method. Output informality in percent of GDP is detrended using Hodrick-Prescott filter. "t = n" indicates the cumulative changes over the n years after a policy change. See annex 6A for detailed model specifications.

Empirically, declines in output informality followed improvements in government services, although the small country sample of data for tax morale blunts the significance of coefficient estimates (figure 6.6). Measures perceived to improve government support for SMEs by 1 standard deviation were followed by a 0.1-percentage-point decline in the share of output informality five years later. A similar, 1-standard-deviation improvement in SMEs' access to quality commercial and professional infrastructure was also followed by a 0.1-percentage-point decline in the informal output share after two years, although the effect subsequently dissipated.

Other policies

Many reforms designed to invigorate private sector growth can also help lower informality, such as reducing corruption, improving business climates and governance, strengthening enforcement of taxes and regulations, and liberalizing labor and product markets, including through trade liberalization.[18] Financial development, by lowering financing costs, can incentivize firms to operate formally, and has often been associated with a shrinking informal sector (box 6.1). Policy measures that narrow the earnings gap

---

[18] Kuddo (2018) shows that about 60 percent of the reforms implemented between 2007 and 2017 throughout the world aimed at improving labor market flexibility. Among measures to improve product market flexibility, trade liberalization has been associated with increased informality unless complementary reforms improved labor market flexibility (World Bank 2019b).

between informal and formal workers or reduce the labor productivity gap between informal and formal firms, such as measures that improve access to education or training programs, can also help reduce informal activity.

Labor market regulations

More restrictive regulations in more informal economies. Although higher minimum wages may attract informal workers into the formal sector, they are also likely to discourage firms from hiring workers, resulting in unclear effects on employment of minimum wages (especially in the presence of imperfect competition).[19] In a development context, in which agricultural sectors are large and urbanization is still under way, a higher minimum wage can slow capital accumulation and push workers into informal employment (Loayza 2016).

Empirically, labor market regulations in EMDEs with above-median informality are more restrictive than in EMDEs with below-median informality (figure 6.7). Minimum wages in EMDEs with above-median output informality average 5.5 percent of per capita income, which is 1.3 percentage points, and significantly, higher than in EMDEs with below-median output informality. Flexibility of working hours, often measured by the inverse of restrictions on night and overtime work, holiday work, and the length of the work week, is significantly less in EMDEs with above-median output informality than in EMDEs with below-median output informality.

Over time, increased labor market flexibility. Labor market flexibility and efficiency have increased in EMDEs over the past three decades (figure 6.7). EMDEs have lowered their minimum wage by 0.6 percentage points of GDP per capita from its level in the 1990s (Loayza 2016). Between 2010 and 2018 alone, about one-quarter of EMDEs increased their perceived labor market efficiency, which measures the extent to which the labor market matches workers with the most suitable jobs for their skillset (WEF 2020). About 40 percent of EMDEs changed regulations to make the hiring and dismissal of workers more flexibly determined by employers. During the same period, 4 out of 10 EMDEs reduced the costs of advance notice requirements, severance payments, and the penalties due when dismissing a worker with a 10-year tenure.

These changes reflect several decades of labor market reforms especially in ECA, Sub-Saharan Africa (SSA), and, more recently, LAC. Regulations with respect to hiring and dismissal, working hours, and wage rates have been eased in ECA (EBRD 2018). Incentives have been provided for worker registration—for example, legalization of undocumented workers—while enforcement of existing labor laws has been tightened (Anand and Khera 2016; Munkacsi and Saxegaard 2017). In EMDEs, the reduction of

---

[19] The employment effects of minimum wages have been unclear (Manning 2021). An increase in the real minimum wage has been associated with a lower probability of being hired in the formal sector, or employment in general (Gindling and Terrell 2007; Maloney and Nuñez Mendez 2004). However, employment effect was not found in studies like Hohberg and Lay (2015); Lemos (2009); and Urzua and Saltiel (forthcoming).

FIGURE 6.7 Labor market reforms and informality in EMDEs

Labor market regulations are more restrictive in EMDEs with high informality than in those with low informality. About one-third of EMDEs have improved their labor market efficiency and eased labor market regulations over the past several decades.

A. Labor market regulations and output informality

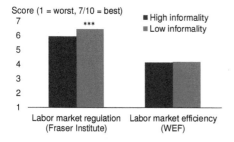

B. Minimum wage and output informality

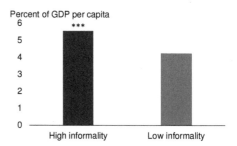

C. Specific labor market regulations and output informality

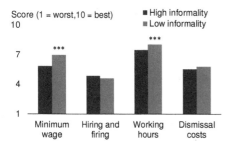

D. EMDEs with liberalized labor market regulations between 2010 and 2018

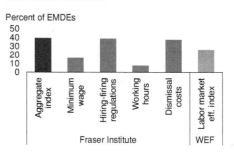

Sources: Fraser Institute; International Labour Organization (ILO); World Economic Forum (WEF).

Note: The labor market regulation index from the Fraser Institute covers issues such as minimum wage, hiring and firing regulations, centralized collective bargaining, mandated cost of hiring, mandated cost of worker dismissal, regulation of hours, and conscription. DGE = dynamic general equilibrium model; EMDEs = emerging market and developing economies.

A.-C. Bars are group means using data available between 1990 and 2018 for EMDEs with "high informality" and those with "low informality." "High informality" ("Low informality") are EMDEs with above-median (below-median) DGE-based informal output measure over the period 1990-2018. In B, data are between 1994 and 2018. Data on labor market regulations are obtained from the Fraser Institute (in A and C) and are between 1990 and 2018. The WEF index is available between 2007 and 2017.The labor market efficiency index from WEF measures the extent to which the labor market matches workers with the most suitable jobs for their skillset (1 = worst, 7 = best). The labor market regulation index from the Fraser Institute measures the extent to which these restraints (listed in C) upon economic freedom are present in the labor market (1 = worst, 10 = best). *** denotes that the group differences are not zero at 10 percent significance.

D. Bars show the share of EMDEs with improved labor market regulations between 2010 and 2018. "Labor market eff. index" is the labor market efficiency index obtained from WEF.

minimum wages encouraged formalization of employment (Betcherman, Meltem Daysal, and Pagés 2010; Kugler, Kugler, and Herrera-Prada 2017).

Lower informality after labor market reforms. Excessive labor market regulations, such as excessively high minimum wages, can distort the labor market and provide incentives for firms to hire workers informally (Kugler 2004; Loayza 2016; Ulyssea 2010). Increases in labor market flexibility and efficiency have been associated with significant falls in output informality (figure 6.8). A 1-standard-deviation increase in the Fraser Institute's index of hiring and firing regulation, which gauges the extent to which the

FIGURE 6.8 **Informality after labor market reforms in EMDEs**

Efforts to increase labor market flexibility and efficiency have been followed by declines in output informality.

A. Cumulative changes in output informality following a 1-point increase in Fraser Institute index of hiring and firing regulations in EMDEs

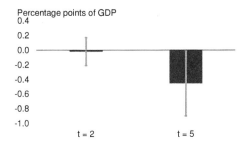

B. Cumulative response of output informality to a 1-point increase in WEF index of labor market efficiency in EMDEs

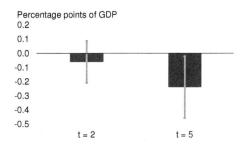

Source: World Bank.
Note: The labor market efficiency index from WEF measures the extent to which the labor market matches workers with the most suitable jobs for their skillset (1 = worst, 7 = best). The index on hiring and firing regulations is from the Fraser Institute, which measures the extent to which hiring and firing regulation are restricting economic freedom in the labor market (1 = worst, 10 = best). Data are for EMDEs over the period 1990-2018. DGE = dynamic general equilibrium model; EMDEs = emerging market and developing economies; WEF = World Economic Forum.
A.B. Bars show the cumulative changes in DGE-based output informality in percent of GDP to a 1-point increase in the Fraser Institute's index on hiring and firing regulations (1-point increase in WEF labor market efficiency index in B). Whiskers show the upper and lower bounds of the corresponding 90 percent confidence intervals. The results are obtained via a local projection method. Output informality in percent of GDP is detrended using Hodrick-Prescott filter. "t = n" indicates the cumulative changes in output informality over the n years after a policy change. See annex 6A for detailed model specifications.

hiring and dismissal of workers is at the employer's discretion, was associated with a significant drop in output informality, by 0.5 percentage point, over the following five years. A 1-point increase in the World Economic Forum's labor market efficiency index was associated with a cumulative drop in output informality by about 0.2 percentage point of GDP over the following five years.[20]

Firm start-up costs

More difficult firm start-up in more informal economies. Starting a new firm is more challenging in EMDEs with more pervasive informality (figure 6.9). On average, the costs of business start-up amount to about 90 percent of per capita gross national income (GNI) in EMDEs with above-median output informality—three times the level in other EMDEs. It takes 33 days to start a business in EMDEs with above-median informality— about 1 day longer than in other EMDEs, although the difference is not statistically significant.

Over time, easier firm start-up. Business start-up costs have fallen steadily in EMDEs over the past two decades. Between 2003 and 2018, the costs of business start-up fell

---

[20] A similarly sized increase in labor market efficiency was associated with a decline in employment informality by 2 percentage points of employment, cumulatively, over the following two to three years.

FIGURE 6.9 Firm start-up cost and informality in EMDEs

Firm start-ups are more challenging in EMDEs with above-median informality than in those with below-median informality. Over the past two decades, EMDEs have taken measures to facilitate firm start-up. Reduced start-up costs have been followed by significant contractions in informal output.

A. Firm start-up costs and output informality

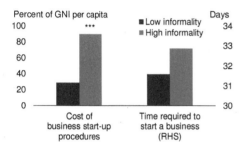

B. Firm start-up costs, 2003-18

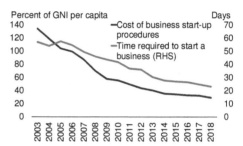

C. Cumulative changes in output informality after the cost of business start-up procedures falls by 10 percentage points of GNI per capita

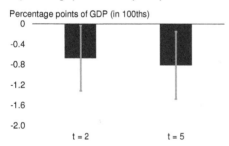

D. Cumulative changes in output informality following a 1-unit decrease in the number of days required to start a business

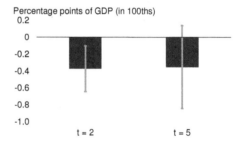

Source: World Bank (*Doing Business*).
Note: Data are from EMDEs and the period 1990-2018. DGE = dynamic general equilibrium model; EMDEs = emerging market and developing economies; GNI = gross national income; RHS = right-hand side.
A. The bars show unweighted group averages. "High-informality" ("Low-informality") are EMDEs with above-median (below-median) DGE-based informal output measures. The data are from 2003-18.*** denotes that the group differences between EMDEs with above median informality and those with below-median informality are significant at 10 percent level.
B. Lines show unweighted averages for EMDEs for the period 2003-18.
C.D. Bars show the cumulative changes in DGE-based output informality in percent of GDP following a decrease of 10 percentage points of GNI per capita in the cost of business start-up procedures (C; or following a 1-unit increase in the number of days required to start a business in D). Whiskers show the upper and lower bounds of the corresponding 90 percent confidence intervals. "t = n" indicates the cumulative changes in output informality over the n years after a policy change. See annex 6A for detailed model specifications.

from above 130 percent of per capita GNI to below 30 percent, and the number of days required to start a business declined by two-thirds, to 23 days. There has also been a reduction in the number of procedures needed to start a business (World Bank 2020a).

Various regulations have been used to encourage formal firm start-up. "One-stop-shop" registrations have been created (for example, in Ukraine) to simplify the firm start-up process. Similar reforms have been carried out in several other EMDEs (World Bank 2009, 2010, 2011). EMDEs in ECA and SSA have implemented an above-average number of reforms to reduce the costs of starting a business during the past decade.

Lower informality after regulatory easing. Easier and less costly firm registration reduces the costs for firms of entering the formal sector (Haltiwanger, Jarmin, and Miranda 2013; Loayza 2018; Nguimkeu 2015). Empirically, a reduction in the costs of business start-up by 10 percentage points of GNI per capita was associated with a significant reduction in output informality, by 0.1 percentage point of GDP over the following five years. Similarly, a one-day reduction in the number of days required to start a business was associated with a significant contraction in output informality, by 0.4 percent point of GDP over the following two years.

Governance

Weaker governance in more informal economies. More corruption, less effective government, and weaker law and order have been associated with larger informal sectors in EMDEs (figure 6.10; chapter 4). On average in the past three decades, EMDEs with above-median output informality scored significantly lower (by about half of a standard deviation) on government effectiveness, control of corruption, and rule of law than other EMDEs. Using the *International Country Risk Guide* (ICRG) indicators, bureaucracy quality, control of corruption, and law and order in EMDEs with above-median output informality are significantly lower, by 0.4-0.7 standard deviation, than in EMDEs with below-median informality.

Over time, improved governance. Governance has generally improved in EMDEs since 1990. Both bureaucracy quality and law and order improved by 0.2-0.6 standard deviation between 1990 and 2018. Control of corruption, law and order, and bureaucracy quality strengthened in the early 1990s but weakened again in the second half of the 1990s with the economic, social, and political disruptions in transition economies, before stabilizing in the early 2000s.

To improve governance and regulatory quality, countries have increased the frequency of inspections (for example, in most EU15 economies and Bangladesh), created a national-level firm or employee registry (Poland), and launched public awareness campaigns regarding tax compliance (for example, China, Republic of Korea).[21] Such measures have been most effective in reducing informality when implemented in conjunction with steps to improve labor market functioning and when applied even-handedly to both formal and informal firms (Loayza 2018). In Georgia, during 1996-2016, the transition to a market economy brought significant improvements in government effectiveness, control of corruption, and law and order (World Bank 2019b).[22] With output growth averaging about 6 percent per year, the share of informal output fell by 9 percentage points of GDP, and the share of informal employment in total employment fell by a similar magnitude.

---

[21] See, for instance, Awasthi and Engelschalk (2018); Bruhn and McKenzie (2014); De Giorgi, Ploenzke, and Rahman (2018); and Oviedo, Thomas, and Karakurum-Özdemir (2009). The EU15 were the members of the Euroean union before 2004.

[22] From 1996 to 2016, Georgia's global ranking on regulatory quality improved from 150th to 34th place, and its ranking on government effectiveness improved from 123th to 55th place.

FIGURE 6.10 **Governance and informality in EMDEs**

Governance and regulatory quality tend to be weaker in EMDEs with more pervasive informality but have improved over the past several decades. Such improvement has often been followed by declines in informality.

A. Governance and informality: ICRG indicators

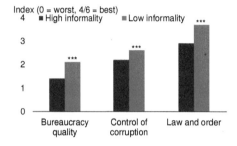

B. Governance in EMDEs, 1990-2018

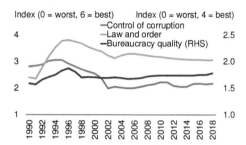

C. Perceived level of corruption in EMDEs, 2012-20

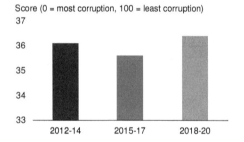

D. Cumulative change in output informality following a 1-point improvement in control of corruption (ICRG)

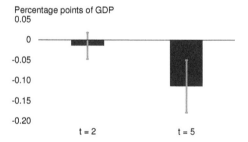

Sources: Transparency International - Corruption Perceptions Index (data set); *International Country Risk Guide* (ICRG) data set; World Bank.
Note: Data are from EMDEs and the period 1990-2018. DGE = dynamic general equilibrium model; EMDEs = emerging market and developing economies; RHS = right-hand side.
A. The bars show the unweighted group averages. "High (Low)-informality" are EMDEs with above-median (below-median) DGE-based informal output measures. *** denotes that the group differences are significant at 10 percent level.
B. Lines show simple averages for EMDEs using various indicators from ICRG. A higher value indicates better governance.
C. Bars show the unweighted averages of the perceived level of corruption in EMDEs. The measure ranges from 0 (the highest level of perceived corruption) and 100 (the least level of perceived corruption).
D. Bars show the cumulative changes in DGE-based estimates on output informality to a 1-point increase in control of corruption. Whiskers show the upper and lower bounds of the corresponding 90 percent confidence intervals. "t = n" indicates the cumulative changes in output informality over the n years after a policy change. The results are obtained via a local projection method. Output informality in percent of GDP is detrended using Hodrick-Prescott filter. See annex 6A for detailed model specifications.

Lower informality after governance reforms. Stricter enforcement of government regulations and a better legal framework can increase the costs of remaining in the informal economy (Dabla-Norris, Gradstein, and Inchauste 2008). Anti-corruption efforts and stronger law and order may allow fewer opportunities for informal firms to avoid the obligations of formal firms (Choi and Thum 2005; Dreher and Schneider 2010; Iriyama, Kishore, and Talukdar 2016). Better control of corruption can also reduce informality via the tax morale channel (DeBacker, Heim, and Tran 2015; Luttmer and Singhal 2014). Empirically, a 1-standard-deviation improvement in the control of corruption was associated with a cumulative decrease in output informality by about 0.1 percentage point of GDP in the following three to five years.

Education and training programs

Poorer education associated with greater informality. Informal workers tend to be less skilled, and therefore also less productive, than formal-economy workers (chapter 4; Loayza 2018; Perry et al. 2007). In fact, wage differentials between formal and informal workers have primarily reflected differences in educational backgrounds and experience (box 4.1). Workers in EMDEs with above-median output informality have, on average, one year less of schooling than those in other EMDEs (figure 6.11). Poorer access to schooling and qualified teachers has resulted in significantly poorer education outcomes, measured by PISA test scores, in EMDEs with above-median output informality. Entrepreneurship training, at all levels of education, including education programs aimed at equipping entrepreneurs to create and manage SMEs, is significantly less accessible in EMDEs with above-median output informality.

Over time, improved education and training. Since 1990, education outcomes and skill levels have improved: thus, on average in EMDEs, average years of schooling have increased by about two years (figure 6.11). Entrepreneurship training has also become more accessible in EMDEs, and the improvement has been statistically significantly more pronounced in EMDEs with above-median informality. In some EMDEs, training programs have boosted worker income and firm revenue in the informal sectors (Burki and Abbas 1991; Verner and Verner 2005). These training programs were also supported by general improvements in access to primary education and literacy rates (Aziz et al. 2014; Hathaway 2005).

Lower informality after improvements to training and education. To the extent that workers remain in the informal sector for lack of human capital or skills, better and more accessible public education may help workers (or their dependents) move into better paid formal employment (Andrews, Sánchez, and Johansson 2011; Maloney 2004; Perry et al. 2007).

Empirically, additional entrepreneurship training and improved education outcomes have been accompanied by significant declines in output informality. Five years after a 2-standard-deviation increase in access to entrepreneurship training and education at primary and secondary levels, output informality was statistically significantly lower, by 0.2 percentage point of GDP.[23] A 10-point increase in the PISA reading score was associated with a significant decline in output informality, by about 0.1 percentage point of GDP, over the following two years.

---

[23] Such an improvement was accompanied by a significant reduction in employment informality, by 1.3 percentage points of employment, over three to four years.

FIGURE 6.11 **Education and informality in EMDEs**

Workers in EMDEs with more pervasive informality are, on average, less educated and trained than those in EMDEs with less pervasive informality. Training focused on SMEs has improved over the past two decades, especially in EMDEs with above-median informality. Better education and training have coincided with declines in informality.

A. Education and informality

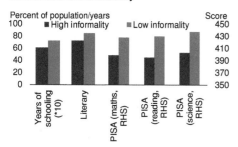

B. Education, 1990 vs. 2015

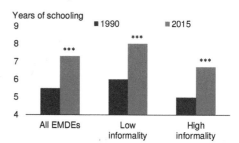

C. Entrepreneurship training and informality

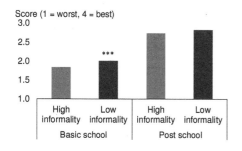

D. Entrepreneurship training, 2000-18

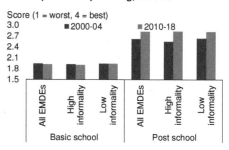

E. Cumulative changes in output informality following a 1-point improvement in basic school entrepreneurial education and training

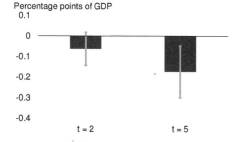

F. Cumulative changes in output informality following a 10-point increase in national average PISA score on reading

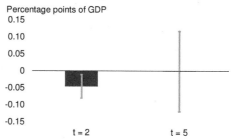

Sources: Barro and Lee (2013); Global Entrepreneurship Monitor; Program for International Student Assessment (PISA) database; World Bank (World Development Indicators).

Note: Data are from EMDEs and the period 1990-2018. "High (Low) informality" are EMDEs with above (below)-median output informality proxied by DGE-based estimates in percent of GDP. All scores regarding entrepreneurship training and education (in C-F) range from 1 (worst) to 4 (best). "Basic school" measures the extent to which training in creating or managing small SMEs is incorporated within the education and training system at primary and secondary levels. "Post school" measures the extent to which training in creating or managing SMEs is incorporated within the education and training system in higher education. DGE = dynamic general equilibrium model; EMDEs = emerging market and developing economies; RHS = right-hand side; SME = small and medium enterprise. *** denotes that the group differences are not zero at 10 percent significance.

A.C. Bars show simple group averages. PISA scores are for 15-year-old students.

B.D. Bars show simple group averages for corresponding time periods.

E.F. Bars show the cumulative changes in DGE-based output informality in percent of GDP to a 1-point increase in "Basic school" score from the Global Entrepreneurship Monitor (10-point increase in PISA reading scores). Whiskers show the upper and lower bounds of the corresponding 90 percent confidence intervals. "t = n" indicates the cumulative changes in output informality over the n years after a policy change. See annex 6A for detailed model specifications. PISA scores are for 15-year-old students.

Access to finance

Less access to finance in more informal economies. Firms in the informal sector have less access to credit from the banking sector and capital markets, which restricts their ability to invest, including in productivity-enhancing technologies (Capasso and Jappelli 2013; D'Erasmo 2016; Ferreira-Tiryaki 2008; box 6.1; figure 6.12). In EMDEs with above-median informality, about one-third of firms identified access to finance as a major constraint—8 percentage points higher than in EMDEs with below-median informality. Households in EMDEs with below-median informality have access to significantly more commercial bank branches, ATMs, and credit than those in other EMDEs. About half of the population in EMDEs with below-median informality owns an account at a financial institution or used a mobile money service recently—about 17 percentage points higher than in EMDEs with below-median informality.

Over time, expanded access to finance. EMDEs, especially in EAP, Middle East and North Africa (MNA), South Asia (SAR), and, more recently, SSA, have implemented a series of reforms to improve access to finance. Such reforms mainly aim to strengthen credit reporting systems and improve the effectiveness of collateral and bankruptcy laws (World Bank 2020a). Overall, financial development improved in about 90 out of 142 of EMDEs over the period 2010-18 (figure 6.12). The number of ATMs per 100,000 adults rose by 50 percent between 2010 and 2018, and the share of population with an account at a financial institution increased from 33 percent to 51 percent. Domestic credit to the private sector increased by about 4 percentage points of GDP over the same period. Access to credit has been facilitated for firms in the informal sector by introducing credit information bureaus and better use of information and communication technology (Capasso, Monferrà, and Sampagnaro 2018). Personal property registration has also made loans more accessible for firms operating in the informal economy (for example, in the Czech Republic; World Bank 2012). Digital payment systems have provided an entry point into the formal financial system and encouraged a shift away from informal finance (for example, in Kenya; World Bank 2017).

Lower informality after expanded access to finance. Lower financing costs and easier access to credit can entice informal firms with promising investment projects that require external finance to enter the formal economy (box 6.1). Empirically, adding 10 more bank branches per 100,000 adults was followed by a decline of 0.1 to 0.3 percentage point in the share of informal output in the following one to five years. A 10-percentage-point-of-GDP increase in domestic credit to the private sector was associated with a significant contraction in output informality, by 0.1 percentage point of GDP over the subsequent one to five years.

Conclusion

The COVID-19 (coronavirus) pandemic plunged the global economy into an unprecedented contraction in 2020, and it is likely to leave lasting scars on long-term

FIGURE 6.12 **Access to finance and informality in EMDEs**

Firms and workers in EMDEs with more pervasive informality are more likely to be financially constrained, less likely to obtain bank finance, and more likely to have limited access to other financial services. Access and depth of financial systems in EMDEs improved between 1990 and 2018. Financial development has been followed by significant declines in output informality.

A. Access to finance and output informality

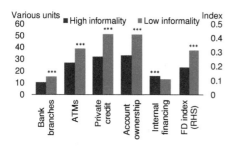

B. Financial constraints facing firms and output informality

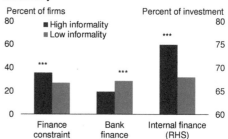

C. EMDEs with improved financial development, 1990-2018

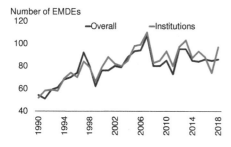

D. Domestic credit to private sector, 1990-2018

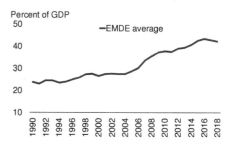

E. Cumulative changes in output informality following a 10-unit increase in the number of bank branches per 100,000 adults

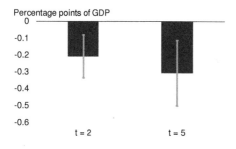

F. Cumulative changes in output informality following a 10-percentage-point-of-GDP increase in domestic credit to the private sector

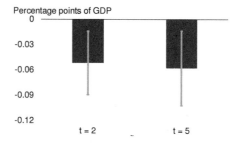

Sources: International Monetary Fund (IMF); World Bank.
Note: Data are from EMDEs and the period 1990-2018. Output informality is measured by DGE-based estimates on informal output (in percent of official GDP). See notes below figure B6.1.1 for detailed variable descriptions in A-D. ATM = automated teller machine; DGE = dynamic general equilibrium model; EMDEs = emerging market and developing economies; RHS = right-hand side. In A-B, *** denotes that the group differences are not zero at 10 percent significance level.
A.B. Bars are unweighted averages for EMDEs with above-median ("high") informality and those with below-median ("low") informality over the period 2010-18 (in A; and 2000-18 in B). In B, bars are group means using data from latest year available for EMDEs.
C.D. Lines show simple EMDEs averages for corresponding time periods. "Overall" is the aggregate financial development index obtained from the IMF. The "Institutions" index subcomponent measures how developed financial institutions are.
E.F. Bars show the cumulative changes in DGE-based output informality in percent of GDP to a 1-unit increase in the number of bank branches per 100,000 people (E) or 10-percentage-point-of-GDP increase in domestic credit to the private sector (F). Whiskers show upper and lower bounds of 90 percent confidence intervals. "t = n" indicates n years after the rise in bank branches of private credit. See annex 6A for detailed model specifications.

potential output (World Bank 2020b, 2021). Informal sector workers have been among the hardest hit because they are disproportionately employed in the services sector that has been particularly disrupted by the pandemic, work in crowded conditions where the virus can spread easily, and have limited access to savings or government support programs (box 2.1). The limited access to sanitation facilities and medical resources in EMDEs with more pervasive informality illustrates further the development challenges posed by informality. The pandemic has served as a reminder of the long-standing need for policies to address the challenges associated with, and caused by, informality. To achieve the Sustainable Development Goals, policy makers need to boost productivity growth in both formal and informal sectors and reduce the vulnerabilities of firms and workers in the informal economy.

Policies are more likely to succeed in addressing the challenges of informality if they are comprehensive and tailored to country circumstances. Past failures of reforms to lower informality and boost productivity have in part been attributed to reform design that was not tailored to country specifics and not sufficiently embedded in a supportive institutional and business environment, in addition to not being consistently implemented (Birdsall, de La Torre, and Caicedo 2010; Loayza 2018).

A comprehensive strategy: The right policy mix. Individual policy interventions in isolation may have only a limited impact on informality, and have unwelcome unintended consequences (annex 6A; Oviedo, Thomas, and Karakurum-Özdemir 2009; Ulyssea 2018). A coherent reform strategy is needed, with reforms that complement each other and address the complexity of informality (Loayza 2018). Success also depends on careful monitoring of potential unintended consequences and on a supportive macroeconomic, political, and institutional environment. The latter should ensure the political and fiscal viability of reform implementation and reduce the transition costs for workers moving from the informal sector to the formal sector.

A tailored strategy: Addressing economy-specific priorities. Because the causes and features of informality differ considerably across countries, policy makers need to identify economy-specific reform priorities. In countries where informality is predominantly associated with poor governance, a policy package could streamline regulatory and tax frameworks while improving the efficiency of public revenue collection and regulatory enforcement as well as strengthening public service delivery to bolster tax morale. In countries where informality is predominantly a reflection of underdevelopment, a policy package could include expanded access to finance, markets, and inputs to foster firm productivity and growth; better education to facilitate formal sector employment; and enhanced safety nets to cushion household risks. In SSA, SAR, and MNA economies that are not members of the Gulf Cooperation Council, for example, general education and training programs to raise human capital could be prioritized (World Bank 2019b; chapter 5). In LAC, reducing high tax and regulatory costs faced by businesses could incentivize firms to join the formal sector. In ECA, improving government effectiveness and reducing corruption could be policy priorities.

New policy challenges. The emerging "gig" economy poses opportunities and policy challenges with its higher accessibility, more fluid labor arrangements, and greater reliance on digital technology than more traditional forms of informality. Because "gig" workers do not fully participate in the social security system, they are, by some definitions, informal workers (Loayza, Servén, and Sugawara 2010). Regulatory changes, especially in the context of social security systems, can help ensure that "gig" workers' economic risks are manageable and that they do not permanently lose access to the formal economy (World Bank 2014, 2016, 2018c). These workers may take on many different assignments over the course of their careers, making the ability to learn and adapt essential. Policies can support this adaptability with more provision of education and (re)training programs (Card, Kluve, and Weber 2018; World Bank 2019a). Increased emphasis on the development of cognitive skills in primary and secondary education can also help (Almeida, Behrman, and Robalino 2012; World Bank 2018a, 2018c).

New policy opportunities. New technologies offer governments opportunities both to reduce the incentives for and increase the cost of operating informally while also providing boosts to productivity that can propel firms into the formal economy. New technologies can help strengthen tax administration and improve access to finance, including by making it easier to broaden the tax net and assess credit worthiness.[24] Digitalization can lower regulatory burdens. For example, Costa Rica reduced the time required to register a business by digitizing tax registration records and company books in 2009 (World Bank 2009). This was followed by a drop in informal employment by 4 percentage points of total employment and a fall in informal output by about 2 percentage points of official GDP during 2009-16 (World Bank 2019b). Similar reforms have been carried out in Guyana (2010) and Kenya (2011; World Bank 2010, 2011).

Safeguarding informal workers during severe shocks. COVID-19 has taken an especially heavy humanitarian and economic toll on EMDEs with large informal sectors (World Bank 2020b). The vulnerabilities of the informal sector, associated with low incomes and limited access to government benefits and public services, have amplified the economic shock from COVID-19 and the related threat to livelihoods (OECD 2020). In many countries, the pandemic has revealed severe shortcomings in social security systems and governments' ability to support vulnerable groups (Busso et al. 2020; Loayza and Pennings 2020).[25] Despite their high costs, untargeted programs may be warranted during such a crisis to maximize the reach to informal-economy participants; their long-term fiscal burden can be minimized by prioritizing temporary and reversable measures. To prevent hysteresis in formal-sector job losses, policies can aim to preserve formal-sector employment opportunities while protecting the poor and informal workers through food aid and cash transfers (Alfaro, Becerra, and Eslava 2020).

---

[24] See Awasthi and Engelschalk (2018); Capasso, Monferrà, and Sampagnaro (2018); Gupta et al. (2017); and Junquera-Varela et al. (2017).

[25] See Fang, Kennedy, and Resnick (2020) for a review of social protection policies implemented under COVID-19.

Future research. Some policy areas remain underexplored in the literature. First, digitalization is a recent development in EMDEs that holds great potential for informal-economy participants and policy makers. Yet little is known about the impact of digitalization of government services or private economic activity on the informal economy, including relative to the formal economy. The possibility that digitalization will disproportionately benefit formal firms, and thus shrink the relative size of the informal sector, deserves examination. Second, past studies have focused on the impact of policies on formalization without looking into their effects on the resilience of the informal economy. Future studies could examine policies that can improve the resilience of the informal economy and prevent informal participants from being tipped into poverty by negative shocks such as COVID-19. Last, the chapter has not touched upon some emerging ideas regarding how governments can better engage with informal businesses, such as providing a simplified, intermediate, and temporary legal status to informal businesses that could be aligned with both business needs and government goals (Marusic et al. 2020).

ANNEX 6A **Policies and informality**

The link between policies and informality is analyzed via the local projection model. It focuses on showing the cumulative change in informality following policy changes.

Definitions

Both output informality and employment are considered in the regression analyses here. Output informality is proxied by estimates based on the dynamic general equilibrium (DGE) model in percent of official GDP, and employment informality is proxied by self-employment in percent of total employment. Both measures cover up to 125 EMDEs over the period 1990-2018. For the estimation of the local projection model, all data series are detrended using the Hodrick-Prescott (HP) filter.

Policy indicators

The following policy measures were considered, covering up to 121 EMDEs for 1990-2018 (table 6B.2).[26]

Tax rates. Corporate, individual, and VAT rates from Végh and Vuletin (2015; updated to 2019) using data from the Organisation for Economic Co-operation and Development, University of Michigan, and KPMG.

---

[26] Although the data for some indicators are available for more than 121 EMDEs, the regressions cover up to 121 EMDEs.

Cost of tax compliance. Ease of paying taxes score from the World Bank's *Doing Business* database (World Bank 2020a; 0 = worst, and 100 = best);

Access to finance. Domestic credit to the private sector in percent of GDP, a common measure for depth of financial institutions, is provided by the World Development Indicators (WDI; World Bank 2020c); the number of commercial bank branches per 100,000 adults, a common measure for the access to financial institutions, is obtained from Global Financial Development Database (World Bank 2019c);

Labor market regulation. Labor market efficiency index from World Economic Forum's Global Competitiveness Report (ranging from 1 to 7 with a higher score indicating a more efficient labor market) and the index for hiring and firing regulation from Fraser Institute (Fraser Institute 2020; 1 = firing and hiring are most determined by regulations but not by the employer, and 10 = firing and hiring are mostly determined by the employer but not by regulations).

Governance. Bureaucracy quality, control of corruption, and law and order are from the *International Country Risk Guide* (ICRG; 1 = worst governance, and 4/6 = best governance).

Government services. Survey responses on the presence and quality of programs directly assisting SMEs at all levels of government (national, regional, municipal; "government programs") and on the presence of property rights, commercial, accounting, and other legal and assessment services and institutions that support or promote SMEs ("commercial and professional infrastructure"), taken from the National Expert Surveys of the Global Entrepreneurship Monitor for the period 2000-19 (ranging from 1 to 4 with a lower score representing poorer entrepreneurial conditions). Survey responses on the extent to which training in creating or managing SMEs is incorporated within the education and training system at primary and secondary levels ("basic school") are also taken from the National Expert Surveys of the Global Entrepreneurship Monitor. Mobile phone subscriptions per 100 people are taken from World Development Indicators.

Firm start-up costs. Cost of business start-up procedures in percent of GNI per capita and time required to start a business in days are from *Doing Business* (World Bank 2020a).

Education and health outcomes. Life expectancy at birth and PISA test scores for reading (students aged 15) are from WDI (World Bank 2020c).

Model specification: The local projection model

A local projection model as in Jordà (2005), Teulings and Zubanov (2014), and World Bank (2018c) is used to identify the effects of policy changes on informality over time. In impulse responses, the model estimates the effect of policy changes on cumulative changes in the cyclical component of (DGE-based) informal output in percent of official

FIGURE 6A.1 Robustness checks: Evolution of informal output levels following financial development in EMDEs

Similar to the results on ratios of informality, improved access and depth of financial institutions are linked with significant contractions in levels of informal output in the following years.

A. Cumulative changes in informal output levels following a 10-unit increase in the number of bank branches per 100,000 people

B. Cumulative changes in informal output levels following a 10-percentage-point-of-GDP increase in domestic credit to the private sector

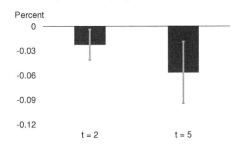
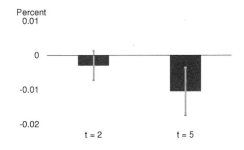

Source: World Bank.
Note: Data for the period 1990-2018 and EMDEs. Here informal output level is measured by DGE-based estimates on informal output (in constant 2011 U.S. Dollars). The results are obtained via a local projection method where informality measures are detrended using Hodrick-Prescott filter. See annex 6A for detailed model specifications. DGE = dynamic general equilibrium model; EMDEs = emerging market and developing economies.
A-B. Bars show the cumulative changes in DGE-based output informality in percent of GDP following a 10-unit increase in the number of bank branches per 100,000 people (A) and 10-percentage-point-of-GDP increase in the share of domestic credit to the private sector in percent of GDP (B). Whiskers show the upper and lower bounds of the corresponding 90 percent confidence intervals. "t = n" indicates the cumulative changes in output informality over the n years after a policy change.

GDP (or self-employment in percent of total employment) over a time horizon h while controlling for country fixed effects and per capita income levels:[27]

$$y_{i,t+h} - y_{i,t-1} = \alpha^h + \beta^h d.policy_{i,t-1} + \theta^h X_{i,t} + fixed\ effects + \epsilon_{i,t}^h$$

where $y_{i,t}$ is the cyclical component of informality in country i and year t. The variable $d.policy_{i,t-1}$ is the variable of interest, which measures the change in policy indicators in country i and year $t-1$. The policy change variable is lagged here to deal with potential endogeity issues. Real GDP per capita (constant 2010 U.S. dollars, obtained from the WDI) is included as the control variable ($X_{i,t}$).[28] Results are shown in tables 6B.4-6B.5.

---

[27] The results are robust to using levels of DGE-based informal output (figure 6A.1).

[28] In the case of corporate and individual tax rates, the levels of both tax rates at year t in country i are also included as control variables. The results do not change when these two control variables are dropped. Similarly, when labor tax and contributions is the variable of interest, the level of labor tax and contributions at year t in country i is included as one of the control variables.

ANNEX 6B Tables

TABLE 6B.1 A summary of empirical studies on financial development and informality

Paper	Measure of financial development (FD).	Measure of the informal economy (IE)	Estimators	Main database	Results
Gatti and Honorati (2008)	Access to credit, indicating whether the firm has a credit or overdraft line.	Percentage of firms' sales reported to tax authority.	OLS (ordinary least squares) and FE (fixed effects) estimation.	World Bank investment climate surveys.	Less informality is robustly and significantly related with more access to credit. Moreover, the relationship between credit and formality is stronger in high-formality countries.
Dabla-Norris, Gradstein, and Inchauste (2008)	Private credit over deposit money at banks and other financial institutions as a share of GDP.	Percent of sales not reported to tax authorities.	OLS with clustered standard errors.	The 2005 Business Environment and Enterprise Performance Survey of the World Bank and the European Bank for Reconstruction and Development.	Firms that rate financing as major obstacles to their business have, on average, a 16 percent probability of hiding 50 percent of their sales.
Bose, Capasso, and Wurm (2012)	Liquid liabilities and total domestic credit provided by depository banks, bank overhead costs, net interest margin, lending-deposit rate spread, and level of bank concentration. All as a percentage of GDP.	Percent of sales not reported to tax authorities, dynamic MIMIC (DYMIMIC) method (Schneider 2007) and WEF (World Economic Forum) measure.	FE and GMM (generalized method of moments).	Beck, Demirgüç-Kunt, and Levine (2000) database and the World Bank World Development Indicators (WDI).	Improvement in the depth and efficiency of the banking sector leads to a smaller informal economy.
Elgin and Uras (2013)	Money and quasi money, domestic credit provided by financial corporations to the private sector, domestic credit from the financial sector, and net credit to central government.	DYMIMIC approach (Schneider 2007).	GMM	World Bank (WDI).	A non-linear inverse-U relationship between financial development and shadow economy size.
Capasso and Jappelli (2013)	Probability of being credit-rationed (Guiso, Sapienza, and Zingales 2004).	Irregular job rate Share of income paid in cash.	OLS and instrumental variables estimation.	Bank of Italy's Survey of Households Income and Wealth (SHIW).	Negative and significant effect of financial development on the measure of informal economy. The impact is particularly strong in construction but also in the retail and tourism sectors.

TABLE 6B.1 A summary of empirical studies on financial development and informality (*continued*)

Paper	Measure of financial development (FD).	Measure of the informal economy (IE)	Estimators	Main database	Results
Bittencourt, Gupta, and Stander (2014)	Domestic credit over GDP; interest rate differential between loans and deposits; liquid liabilities as a percentage of real GDP; market capitalisation of all listed companies as a percentage of real GDP.	DYMIMIC approach (Schneider 2010) and Dynamic general equilibrium (DGE) model (Elgin and Öztunali 2012).	FE and GMM	Schneider et al. (2010), Elgin and Öztunali (2012), World Bank WDI, Global Development Finance, and World Governance Indicators (WGI).	Lower (higher) levels of financial development and higher (lower) levels of inflation lead to a higher (lower) size of the shadow economy.
Berdiev and Saunoris (2016)	Money and quasi money (M2) as percentage of GDP; domestic credit provided by financial corporations to the private sector (private credit) as a percentage of GDP; and domestic credit from the financial sector to various sectors and net credit to the central government (financial credit) as percentage of GDP	Dynamic general equilibrium (DGE) model (Elgin and Öztunali 2012).	GMM and panel vector autoregression (VAR) analysis	World Bank WDI and Elgin and Öztunali (2012).	A shock to M2 reduces the size of the shadow economy, and this effect becomes insignificant after eight years. A shock to the shadow economy shrinks financial development.
Bayar and Ozturk (2016)	Domestic credit to private sector.	DYMIMIC approach (Schneider, Raczkowski, and Mróz 2015).	Cointegration analysis	Schneider, Raczkowski, and Mróz (2015), World Bank and Heritage Foundation.	Financial development and improvements in institutional quality reduce the size of the shadow economy, in the long run.
Canh and Thanh (2020)	Overall financial development, overall financial institutions, overall financial markets, financial institutions' depth, financial institutions' access, financial institutions' efficiency, financial markets' depth, financial markets' access, and financial markets' efficiency.	DYMIMIC approach (Medina and Schneider 2018).	Dynamic fixed effects—autoregressive distributed lag	Medina and Schneider (2018), Svirydzenka (2016), World Bank WDI and WGI; Heritage Foundation	Non-linear negative relationship between financial development and shadow economy for eight out of the nine financial indicators.
Gharleghi and Jahanshahi (2020)	Liquid liabilities, private credit and stock market capitalisation.	MIMIC and PMM (predictive mean matching) method (Medina and Schneider 2018).	Threshold FE.	World Bank WDI and global financial development.	Financial development has a negative and significant effect on the shadow economy, but only for countries that have a per capita GDP of US$33,600 and higher.

Source: World Bank.

TABLE 6B.2 Data sources of variables used in annex 6A

Variable	Source	No. of EMDEs	Years
Corporate income tax rate	Végh and Vuletin (2015; updated to 2019)	118	1990-2018
Individual income tax rate	Végh and Vuletin (2015; updated to 2019)	111	1990-2019
VAT rate	Végh and Vuletin (2015; updated to 2019)	95	1990-2020
Ease of paying taxes	*Doing Business* (2020)	152	2006-18
Presence and quality of government programs	GEM (2020)	75	2000-18
Commercial and professional infrastructure	GEM (2020)	75	2000-18
Life expectancy at birth	WDI (2020)	153	1990-2018
Mobile cellular subscriptions	WDI (2020)	154	1990-2018
Labor market efficiency	WEF (2020)	115	2007-17
Hiring and firing regulation	Fraser institute (2020)	121	1990-2018
Cost of business start-up procedures (percent of GNI per capita)	*Doing Business* (2020)	152	2003-18
Number of days required to start a business	*Doing Business* (2020)	152	2003-18
Control of corruption	ICRG (2020)	102	1990-2018
Basic school entrepreneurial education	GEM (2020)	75	2000-18
PISA score on reading	WDI (2020)	47	2000-18
Domestic credit to the private sector (percent of GDP)	WDI (2020)	148	2000-18
Bank branches (per 100,000 adults)	World Bank (2019c)	143	2001-17

Source: World Bank.
Note: GEM = Global Entrepreneurship Monitor; GNI = gross national income; ICRG = *International Country Risk Guide*; PISA = Programme for Internatonal Student Assessment; VAT = value added tax; WDI = World Development Indicators; WEF = World Economic Forum.

TABLE 6B.3 Policy indicators and employment informality

Policy	High informality	Low informality	P-value for t-test
Corporate income tax rate	26.4	21.4	0.00
Individual income tax rate	28.3	20.0	0.00
VAT rate	14.0	13.8	0.84
Number of tax payments per year (2010-18)	34.6	24.3	0.00
Number of hours spent on paying taxes per year (2010-18)	311.6	280.4	0.54
Cost of complying with VAT refund (hours)	36.7	15.4	0.00
Number of days needed to obtain VAT refund	41.0	26.3	0.01
Cost of business start-up procedures (percent of GNI pc)	77.6	21.5	0.00
Number of days required to start a business	35.1	27.9	0.04
Labor market regulation index (Fraser Institute)	6.0	6.6	0.01
Labor market efficiency (WEF)	4.1	4.2	0.60
Minimum wage (percent of GDP pc)	6.4	3.3	0.00
Minimum wage (1 = worst, 10 = best)	5.9	6.9	0.02
Hiring and firing (1= worst, 10 = best)	4.8	4.6	0.35
Working hours (1= worst, 10 = best)	8.0	7.6	0.27
Dismissal costs (1= worst, 10 = best)	5.3	6.2	0.11
Tax morale (1 = highest, 10 = lowest)	2.2	2.4	0.22
Governmental support and policies (1 = worst, 4 = best)	2.5	2.6	0.38
Governmental programs (1= worst, 4 = best)	2.4	2.5	0.08
Commercial and professional infrastructure (1 = worst, 4 = best)	2.9	2.9	0.27
Physical and service infrastructure (1= worst, 4= best)	3.5	3.6	0.14
Adequacy of social insurance programs (percent of household income)	27.4	34.1	0.04
Coverage of unemployment benefits (percent of population)	5.0	5.2	0.91
Access to electricity (percent of population)	56	92.3	0.00
Internet users (percent of population)	10.5	26	0.00
Paved road (percent of road)	31.5	61.0	0.00
Mobile cellular subscriptions (per 100 people)	33.8	55.8	0.00
Nurses and midwives (per 1,000 people)	1.4	3.7	0.00
Physicians (per 1,000 people)	0.6	1.5	0.00
Life expectancy (years)	61.9	71.0	0.00
Bureaucracy quality (ICRG)	1.5	2.0	0.00
Control of corruption (ICRG)	2.3	2.6	0.10
Law and order (ICRG)	3.0	3.6	0.00
Years of schooling	8.2	5.3	0.00
Literacy	69.2	91.1	0.00
PISA score (math)	392.8	432.9	0.00
PISA score (reading)	388.1	434.7	0.00
PISA score (science)	398.2	440.8	0.00
Basic school entrep. edu and training (1= worst, 4 = best)	1.9	2.0	0.39
Post school entrep. edu and training (1= worst, 4 = best)	2.8	2.8	0.72
Identify access to finance as a major constraint (percent of firms)	32.3	28.9	0.24

TABLE 6B.3 Policy indicators and employment informality (*continued*)

Policy	High informality	Low informality	P-value for t-test
Percent of firms using banks to finance investments	20.7	30.9	0.00
Proportion of investment financed internally	73.6	66.3	0.00
Commercial bank branches (per 100,000 adults)	10.9	18.5	0.00
ATMs (per 100,000 adults)	21.2	52.2	0.00
Domestic credit to private sector (percent of GDP)	35.0	55.1	0.00
Account ownership (percent of age 15+)	37.2	54.0	0.00
Internal financing (percent of age 15+)	16.6	11.1	0.00
IMF financial development index	0.2	0.3	0.00

Sources: Global Entrepreneurship Monitor; *International Country Risk Guide* (ICRG); KPMG; University of Michigan; Organisation for Economic Co-operation and Development; Végh and Vuletin (2015); World Bank (*Doing Business*, World Development Indicators); World Economic Forum (WEF); World Value Surveys.

Note: Data are from emerging market and development economies (EMDEs) over the period 1990-2018. The group differences between EMDEs with "high informality" and those with "low informality" are tested. "High informality" ("Low informality") are EMDEs with above-median (below-median) employment informality (proxied by self-employment shares in percent of total employment) averaged over the period 1990-2018 (or otherwise specified). "Paved road" is calculated as 100 minus the share of unpaved road in percent of total road. Outliers are dropped in the case of individual tax rates, tax morale, nurses, and dismissal coasts. ATM = automated teller machine; GNI = gross national income; IMF = International Monetary Fund; pc = per capita; PISA = Programme for International Student Assessment; VAT = value added tax. Please see details in the notes to figures 6.2-6.12.

TABLE 6B.4 Regression results from local-projection models: DGE-based informal output in percent of GDP

Dep. var. = DGE-based output informality (percent of official GDP)	(1) t = 1	(2) t = 2	(3) t = 3	(4) t = 4	(5) t = 5
Corporate income tax rate	0.006*	0.011**	0.012**	0.011**	0.010
	(0.003)	(0.005)	(0.006)	(0.006)	(0.007)
Observations	1,289	1,210	1,131	1,053	976
R-squared	0.012	0.014	0.014	0.015	0.019
Number of economies	81	80	79	78	76
Individual income tax rate	0.005*	0.009**	0.014***	0.018***	0.014**
	(0.003)	(0.003)	(0.005)	(0.006)	(0.006)
Observations	1,286	1,206	1,127	1,048	971
R-squared	0.012	0.015	0.023	0.030	0.026
Number of economies	82	80	80	78	72
VAT rate	-0.024	-0.043	-0.041	-0.049	-0.038
	(0.026)	(0.046)	(0.044)	(0.039)	(0.040)
Observations	1,234	1,154	1,075	998	923
R-squared	0.015	0.020	0.018	0.021	0.022
Number of economies	82	80	79	77	73
Ease of paying taxes	-0.002	0.000	-0.002	-0.006*	-0.002
	(0.002)	(0.004)	(0.003)	(0.003)	(0.004)
Observations	684	603	524	445	375
R-squared	0.013	0.008	0.010	0.013	0.017
Number of economies	83	80	80	71	70
Presence and quality of government programs	0.029	0.001	-0.062	-0.055	-0.142**
	(0.037)	(0.045)	(0.064)	(0.072)	(0.065)
Observations	484	450	407	363	319
R-squared	0.002	0.001	0.003	0.002	0.016
Number of economies	61	60	56	51	47

TABLE 6B.4 Regression results from local-projection models: DGE-based informal output in percent of GDP (*continued*)

	(1)	(2)	(3)	(4)	(5)
Dep. var. = DGE-based output informality (percent of official GDP)	**t = 1**	**t = 2**	**t = 3**	**t = 4**	**t = 5**
Commercial and prof. infrastructure	-0.016	-0.091**	-0.090	-0.020	-0.051
	(0.026)	(0.044)	(0.057)	(0.036)	(0.057)
Observations	484	450	407	363	319
R-squared	0.001	0.009	0.007	0.000	0.009
Number of economies	61	60	56	51	47
Life expectancy at birth	0.012	-0.015	-0.060**	-0.108***	-0.151***
	(0.012)	(0.019)	(0.024)	(0.033)	(0.040)
Observations	3,191	3,072	2,952	2,832	2,712
R-squared	0.000	0.000	0.003	0.011	0.022
Number of economies	121	121	121	121	121
Mobile cellular subscriptions (per 100 people)	-0.002***	-0.002**	-0.003*	-0.005*	-0.010**
	(0.000)	(0.001)	(0.002)	(0.003)	(0.004)
Observations	3,144	3,026	2,907	2,788	2,669
R-squared	0.001	0.001	0.002	0.010	0.022
Number of economies	120	120	120	120	120
Labor market efficiency (WEF)	-0.031	-0.071	-0.127	-0.203	-0.239*
	(0.056)	(0.088)	(0.138)	(0.153)	(0.131)
Observations	909	816	721	626	527
R-squared	0.003	0.003	0.003	0.005	0.010
Number of economies	106	105	105	103	98
Hiring and firing regulation (Fraser)	0.005	-0.002	-0.017	-0.028	-0.046*
	(0.008)	(0.012)	(0.017)	(0.024)	(0.027)
Observations	1384	1283	1180	1079	980
R-squared	0.006	0.012	0.014	0.015	0.015
Number of economies	105	104	102	100	100
Cost of business start-up procedures (in percent of GNI per capita)	-0.000	0.001*	0.001*	0.001	0.001**
	(0.000)	(0.000)	(0.001)	(0.000)	(0.000)
Observations	1,496	1,377	1,257	1,137	1,017
R-squared	0.002	0.010	0.008	0.005	0.008
Number of economies	121	121	121	121	112
No. of days required to start a business	0.001	0.004**	0.005**	0.006**	0.003
	(0.001)	(0.002)	(0.002)	(0.002)	(0.003)
Observations	1,478	1,359	1,241	1,124	1,006
R-squared	0.004	0.008	0.006	0.007	0.004
Number of economies	121	121	121	121	112
Control of corruption (ICRG)	0.004	-0.015	-0.057**	-0.105***	-0.114***
	(0.014)	(0.020)	(0.026)	(0.036)	(0.039)
Observations	2,435	2,343	2,250	2,157	2,064
R-squared	0.001	0.001	0.003	0.006	0.006
Number of economies	94	94	94	94	94
Basic school entrep. edu and training	-0.001	-0.062	-0.041	-0.107	-0.173**
	(0.034)	(0.049)	(0.059)	(0.066)	(0.076)
Observations	484	450	407	363	319
R-squared	0.000	0.004	0.002	0.006	0.020
Number of economies	61	60	56	51	47

TABLE 6B.4 Regression results from local-projection models: DGE-based informal output in percent of GDP (continued)

	(1)	(2)	(3)	(4)	(5)
Dep. var. = DGE-based output informality (percent of official GDP)	**t = 1**	**t = 2**	**t = 3**	**t = 4**	**t = 5**
PISA score on reading	-0.003**	-0.005**	-0.004	-0.002	-0.000
	(0.001)	(0.002)	(0.004)	(0.005)	(0.007)
Observations	405	374	344	313	282
R-squared	0.016	0.024	0.021	0.008	0.001
Number of economies	35	34	33	33	33
Domestic credit to the private sector (percent of GDP)	-0.005***	-0.005**	-0.005***	-0.005**	-0.006**
	(0.002)	(0.002)	(0.002)	(0.002)	(0.003)
Observations	2,515	2,402	2,290	2,178	2,067
R-squared	0.006	0.004	0.009	0.021	0.038
Number of economies	121	118	116	116	116
Bank branches (per 100,000 adults)	-0.013***	-0.021***	-0.024***	-0.029**	-0.031**
	(0.004)	(0.008)	(0.009)	(0.012)	(0.012)
Observations	1,435	1,331	1,224	1,111	997
R-squared	0.005	0.006	0.005	0.007	0.012
Number of economies	118	118	118	118	118

Sources: Global Entrepreneurship Monitor; *International Country Risk Guide* (ICRG); KPMG; University of Michigan; Organisation for Economic Co-operation and Development; Végh and Vuletin (2015); World Bank (*Doing Business*, World Development Indicators); World Economic Forum (WEF).

Note: Data for the period 1990-2018 and EMDEs. See annex 6A for details. DGE = dynamic general equilibrium model; EMDEs = emerging market and developing economies; GNI = gross national income; PISA = Programme for International Student Assessment; VAT = value added tax.* p < 0.10, ** p < 0.05, *** p < 0.01.

TABLE 6B.5 Regression results from local-projection models: Self-employment in percent of total employment

	(1)	(2)	(3)	(4)	(5)
Dep. var. = DGE-based output informality (percent of official GDP)	**t = 1**	**t = 2**	**t = 3**	**t = 4**	**t = 5**
Corporate income tax rate	0.005	-0.037	-0.053	-0.074	-0.043
	(0.036)	(0.055)	(0.066)	(0.064)	(0.045)
Observations	1,050	975	901	834	769
R-squared	0.002	0.002	0.002	0.005	0.003
Number of economies	76	75	68	66	65
Individual income tax rate	0.011	0.009	0.004	-0.013	-0.017
	(0.027)	(0.020)	(0.028)	(0.036)	(0.037)
Observations	1,044	968	896	830	765
R-squared	0.002	0.001	0.001	0.003	0.003
Number of economies	77	73	67	66	62
VAT rate	0.013	-0.004	-0.146	0.025	0.102
	(0.119)	(0.116)	(0.129)	(0.142)	(0.111)
Observations	1,008	934	862	795	730
R-squared	0.002	0.000	0.002	0.003	0.003
Number of economies	75	73	68	66	64
Ease of paying taxes	0.029	0.027	-0.009	-0.006	-0.096
	(0.037)	(0.029)	(0.040)	(0.030)	(0.076)
Observations	537	461	389	321	264
R-squared	0.011	0.010	0.014	0.044	0.031
Number of economies	77	73	69	58	55

TABLE 6B.5 Regression results from local-projection models: Self-employment in percent of total employment (*continued*)

	(1)	(2)	(3)	(4)	(5)
Dep. var. = DGE-based output informality (percent of official GDP)	t = 1	t = 2	t = 3	t = 4	t = 5
Presence and quality of government programs	-0.172	-1.219	-0.388	-1.517	-0.912
	(0.364)	(0.745)	(0.963)	(1.159)	(0.884)
Observations	430	390	346	304	266
R-squared	0.001	0.013	0.009	0.018	0.012
Number of economies	53	52	48	43	39
Commercial and professional infrastructure	0.134	-0.506	-0.907	-0.570	0.286
	(0.477)	(0.744)	(0.985)	(0.969)	(0.541)
Observations	430	390	346	304	266
R-squared	0.001	0.006	0.013	0.010	0.009
Number of economies	53	52	48	43	39
Life expectancy at birth	0.005	-0.009	-0.211	-0.229	-0.273
	(0.095)	(0.183)	(0.357)	(0.492)	(0.636)
Observations	2,144	2,030	1,916	1,803	1,693
R-squared	0.001	0.000	0.000	0.000	0.000
Number of economies	115	115	114	111	111
Mobile cellular subscriptions (per 100 people)	-0.003	-0.010	-0.012	-0.003	0.004
	(0.005)	(0.010)	(0.010)	(0.012)	(0.013)
Observations	2,136	2,020	1,905	1,791	1,680
R-squared	0.001	0.001	0.001	0.000	0.000
Number of economies	117	117	116	113	112
Labor market efficiency (WEF)	-0.511	-1.965*	-1.727*	1.492	0.309
	(0.672)	(1.114)	(1.026)	(1.449)	(1.431)
Observations	667	580	494	415	337
R-squared	0.002	0.004	0.005	0.003	0.001
Number of economies	92	91	83	80	73
Hiring and firing regulation (Fraser)	-0.159	0.000	-0.133	-0.185	0.272
	(0.301)	(0.149)	(0.207)	(0.195)	(0.270)
Observations	1,086	995	903	815	731
R-squared	0.001	0.000	0.000	0.001	0.002
Number of economies	93	93	89	85	79
Cost of business start-up procedures (percent of GNI per capita)	-0.021	-0.007	-0.007	0.011	-0.021**
	(0.020)	(0.007)	(0.011)	(0.007)	(0.010)
Observations	1,039	931	825	722	624
R-squared	0.021	0.004	0.008	0.016	0.029
Number of economies	109	107	104	99	91
No. of days required to start a business	-0.021	-0.004	-0.040**	-0.025	-0.036*
	(0.025)	(0.036)	(0.020)	(0.028)	(0.018)
Observations	1,031	924	819	718	620
R-squared	0.002	0.002	0.009	0.012	0.013
Number of economies	109	107	104	99	91
Control of Corruption (ICRG)	-0.178	-0.029	-0.100	0.114	0.311
	(0.221)	(0.318)	(0.306)	(0.409)	(0.479)
Observations	1,708	1,623	1,538	1,454	1,373
R-squared	0.001	0.000	0.000	0.000	0.000
Number of economies	86	86	85	82	82
Basic school entrep. edu and training	-0.280	-0.681	-1.326*	-1.389*	-1.099
	(0.411)	(0.835)	(0.783)	(0.758)	(0.840)
Observations	430	390	346	304	266
R-squared	0.001	0.007	0.017	0.016	0.014
Number of economies	53	52	48	43	39

TABLE 6B.5 Regression results from local-projection models: Self-employment in percent of total employment (*continued*)

	(1)	(2)	(3)	(4)	(5)
Dep. var. = DGE-based output informality (percent of official GDP)	**t = 1**	**t = 2**	**t = 3**	**t = 4**	**t = 5**
PISA score on reading	0.01	0.014	0.014	0.005	0.003
	(0.008)	(0.009)	(0.012)	(0.014)	(0.019)
Observations	395	346	304	273	245
R-squared	0.015	0.016	0.036	0.08	0.043
Number of economies	37	36	35	34	33
Domestic credit to the private sector	-0.015*	-0.008	0.012	0.010	-0.006
(percent of GDP)	(0.008)	(0.013)	(0.020)	(0.013)	(0.014)
Observations	1,711	1,602	1,495	1,389	1,285
R-squared	0.001	0.000	0.001	0.000	0.000
Number of economies	113	111	109	106	105
Bank branches	0.010	0.028	0.032	0.064	0.071
(per 100,000 adults)	(0.048)	(0.066)	(0.056)	(0.072)	(0.074)
Observations	991	891	792	693	598
R-squared	0.002	0.004	0.006	0.007	0.009
Number of economies	104	102	100	96	96

Sources: Global Entrepreneurship Monitor; *International Country Risk Guide* (ICRG); KPMG; University of Michigan; Organisation for Economic Co-operation and Development; Végh and Vuletin (2015); World Bank (*Doing Business*, World Development Indicators); World Economic Forum (WEF).

Note: Data for the period 1990-2018 and EMDEs. See annex 6A for details. DGE = dynamic general equilibrium model; EMDEs = emerging market and developing economies; GNI = gross national income; PISA = Programme for International Student Assessment; VAT = value added tax. * p < 0.10, ** p < 0.05, *** p < 0.01.

TABLE 6B.6 Robustness checks: OLS and quantile regressions between policy measures and DGE-based output informality

Dep. var. = DGE-based output informality (percent of official GDP)		**Quantile regression**		
Explanatory var=	**OLS**	**Tau = 0.25**	**Tau = 0.50**	**Tau = 0.75**
Corporate income tax rate	0.226*	0.361*	0.176	0.221
	(0.130)	(0.216)	(0.162)	(0.182)
Observations	102	102	102	102
(Pseudo) R-squared	0.030	0.026	0.022	0.025
Individual income tax rate	0.218**	0.300***	0.159	0.214
	(0.097)	(0.108)	(0.144)	(0.140)
Observations	92	92	92	92
(Pseudo) R-squared	0.056	0.072	0.021	0.023
VAT rate	0.480**	0.532**	0.589**	0.592
	(0.189)	(0.216)	(0.271)	(0.377)
Observations	85	85	85	85
(Pseudo) R-squared	0.065	0.097	0.051	0.020
Tax payments number per year	0.254***	0.290***	0.250***	0.265***
	(0.057)	(0.071)	(0.071)	(0.071)
Observations	122	122	122	122
(Pseudo) R-squared	0.153	0.114	0.099	0.094
Times spent on tax payment (hours per year)	0.005	0.004	0.001	0.001
	(0.004)	(0.006)	(0.005)	(0.005)

TABLE 6B.6 Robustness checks: OLS and quantile regressions between policy measures and DGE-based output informality (*continued*)

Dep. var. = DGE-based output informality (percent of official GDP)		Quantile regression		
Explanatory var =	OLS	Tau = 0.25	Tau = 0.50	Tau = 0.75
Observations	122	122	122	122
(Pseudo) R-squared	0.017	0.022	0.003	0.000
Time to comply with VAT refund	0.067	0.087	0.030	0.039
	(0.052)	(0.086)	(0.084)	(0.101)
Observations	58	58	58	58
(Pseudo) R-squared	0.023	0.045	0.014	0.003
Time to obtain VAT refund (weeks)	0.037	0.093	0.057	0.076
	(0.064)	(0.097)	(0.091)	(0.113)
Observations	58	58	58	58
(Pseudo) R-squared	0.006	0.036	0.023	0.009
Cheating on taxes	2.688	3.431	3.801	2.107
	(1.627)	(3.225)	(2.382)	(3.628)
Observations	60	60	60	60
(Pseudo) R-squared	0.027	0.023	0.042	0.020
Coverage of unemployment benefits and ALMP	-0.509*	-0.283	-0.731**	-0.662
	(0.261)	(0.453)	(0.347)	(0.424)
Observations	59	59	59	59
(Pseudo) R-squared	0.061	0.028	0.032	0.064
Adequacy of social insurance programs	-0.107*	-0.102	-0.152**	-0.040
	(0.060)	(0.087)	(0.074)	(0.086)
Observations	93	93	93	93
(Pseudo) R-squared	0.030	0.022	0.029	0.003
Access to electricity	-0.112***	-0.155***	-0.124***	-0.029
	(0.022)	(0.044)	(0.029)	(0.039)
Observations	122	122	122	122
(Pseudo) R-squared	0.123	0.114	0.101	0.011
Mobile cellular subscriptions	-0.181***	-0.265***	-0.217***	-0.055
	(0.046)	(0.064)	(0.054)	(0.073)
Observations	121	121	121	121
(Pseudo) R-squared	0.096	0.119	0.096	0.007
Fixed broadband subscriptions	-0.554***	-0.472	-0.855***	-0.338
	(0.181)	(0.297)	(0.222)	(0.277)
Observations	120	120	120	120
(Pseudo) R-squared	0.060	0.051	0.071	0.010
Individuals using the internet	-0.373***	-0.462***	-0.384***	-0.292***
	(0.059)	(0.106)	(0.071)	(0.099)
Observations	121	121	121	121
(Pseudo) R-squared	0.167	0.124	0.154	0.057
Paved road	-0.099***	-0.112**	-0.114***	-0.082**
	(0.031)	(0.052)	(0.037)	(0.037)
Observations	113	113	113	113
(Pseudo) R-squared	0.087	0.037	0.077	0.049

TABLE 6B.6 Robustness checks: OLS and quantile regressions between policy measures and DGE-based output informality (*continued*)

Dep. var.=DGE-based output informality (percent of official GDP)		Quantile regression		
Explanatory var=	OLS	Tau=0.25	Tau=0.50	Tau=0.75
Life expectancy	-0.440***	-0.650***	-0.446***	-0.208
	(0.088)	(0.167)	(0.096)	(0.168)
Observations	122	122	122	122
(Pseudo) R-squared	0.140	0.124	0.127	0.014
Governmental support and policies	-4.395	-3.581	-2.064	-9.491**
	(2.750)	(4.150)	(3.287)	(4.184)
Observations	67	67	67	67
(Pseudo) R-squared	0.040	0.025	0.010	0.048
Governmental programs	-2.449	-2.754	-2.494	-9.192
	(3.429)	(5.181)	(3.963)	(6.068)
Observations	67	67	67	67
(Pseudo) R-squared	0.008	0.008	0.009	0.018
Commercial and professional infrastructure	-0.447	11.103	0.231	-7.960
	(5.081)	(8.123)	(6.682)	(10.032)
Observations	67	67	67	67
(Pseudo) R-squared	0.000	0.017	0.000	0.018
Physical and services infrastructure	-4.913*	-10.333***	-7.245**	-3.501
	(2.916)	(3.597)	(3.147)	(5.325)
Observations	67	67	67	67
(Pseudo) R-squared	0.041	0.085	0.036	0.014
Labor market regulations	-1.318**	-0.801	-1.108	-0.667
	(0.665)	(1.136)	(0.882)	(0.871)
Observations	117	117	117	117
(Pseudo) R-squared	0.029	0.008	0.021	0.005
Labor market efficiency (WEF)	-1.163	-0.919	1.961	0.799
	(2.627)	(4.055)	(2.986)	(3.013)
Observations	108	108	108	108
(Pseudo) R-squared	0.002	0.003	0.005	0.002
Minimum wage (percent of GDP per capita)	-0.007	0.043	-0.058	-0.171
	(0.093)	(0.323)	(0.169)	(0.145)
Observations	90	90	90	90
(Pseudo) R-squared	0.000	0.002	0.003	0.006
Hiring regulations and minimum wage	-1.163***	-1.376**	-1.232**	-0.459
	(0.379)	(0.557)	(0.490)	(0.529)
Observations	117	117	117	117
(Pseudo) R-squared	0.079	0.062	0.041	0.009
Hiring and firing regulations	0.427	0.797	2.083*	2.681**
	(1.287)	(2.146)	(1.200)	(1.240)
Observations	113	113	113	113
(Pseudo) R-squared	0.001	0.003	0.016	0.013
Hours regulations	-0.874	-0.117	-1.175	-0.732
	(0.582)	(1.129)	(0.779)	(0.725)
Observations	117	117	117	117
(Pseudo) R-squared	0.017	0.000	0.024	0.008

TABLE 6B.6 Robustness checks: OLS and quantile regressions between policy measures and DGE-based output informality (*continued*)

Dep. var.=DGE-based output informality (percent of official GDP)		Quantile regression		
Explanatory var=	OLS	Tau=0.25	Tau=0.50	Tau=0.75
Mandated cost of worker dismissal	0.019	-0.015	0.208	0.081
	(0.360)	(0.524)	(0.441)	(0.387)
Observations	117	117	117	117
(Pseudo) R-squared	0.000	0.000	0.000	0.001
Cost of business start-up procedures	0.043***	0.046**	0.047***	0.028*
(in percent of GNI per capita)	(0.011)	(0.019)	(0.012)	(0.015)
Observations	122	122	122	122
(Pseudo) R-squared	0.125	0.097	0.095	0.021
Time required to start a business	0.006	0.016	-0.000	0.009
(days)	(0.012)	(0.037)	(0.028)	(0.025)
Observations	122	122	122	122
(Pseudo) R-squared	0.001	0.004	0.000	0.001
Bureaucracy quality	-6.672***	-6.480**	-6.358***	-6.831***
(ICRG)	(0.935)	(2.862)	(1.419)	(1.991)
Observations	95	95	95	95
(Pseudo) R-squared	0.193	0.122	0.167	0.091
Control of corruption	-7.268***	-6.200*	-8.457***	-7.383***
(ICRG)	(1.491)	(3.534)	(1.944)	(2.445)
Observations	95	95	95	95
(Pseudo) R-squared	0.149	0.077	0.105	0.051
Law and order	-4.951***	-6.801***	-4.842***	-3.981***
(ICRG)	(1.022)	(1.537)	(1.576)	(1.511)
Observations	95	95	95	95
(Pseudo) R-squared	0.185	0.171	0.101	0.043
Years of schooling	-0.780**	-1.383*	-1.022**	-0.539
(interpolated over 5-yr period)	(0.319)	(0.755)	(0.501)	(0.544)
Observations	99	99	99	99
(Pseudo) R-squared	0.034	0.046	0.046	0.005
Literacy rate, adult total	-0.115***	-0.211***	-0.136**	-0.039
(percent of people ages 15 and above)	(0.034)	(0.076)	(0.053)	(0.059)
Observations	119	119	119	119
(Pseudo) R-squared	0.054	0.083	0.062	0.003
PISA: Mean performance on the mathematics scale	-0.050	-0.074	-0.057	0.019
	(0.032)	(0.049)	(0.042)	(0.065)
Observations	44	44	44	44
(Pseudo) R-squared	0.048	0.056	0.054	0.004
PISA: Mean performance on the reading scale	-0.075**	-0.094*	-0.053	-0.016
	(0.029)	(0.047)	(0.042)	(0.072)
Observations	44	44	44	44
(Pseudo) R-squared	0.103	0.112	0.062	0.004

TABLE 6B.6 Robustness checks: OLS and quantile regressions between policy measures and DGE-based output informality (*continued*)

Dep. var.=DGE-based output informality (percent of official GDP)		Quantile regression		
Explanatory var=	OLS	Tau=0.25	Tau=0.50	Tau=0.75
PISA: Mean performance on the science scale	-0.079**	-0.080	-0.058	-0.016
	(0.030)	(0.049)	(0.040)	(0.066)
Observations	44	44	44	44
(Pseudo) R-squared	0.114	0.101	0.072	0.005
Basic school entrepreneurial education and training	-1.376	2.037	-1.656	-1.289
	(3.224)	(5.681)	(4.398)	(6.114)
Observations	68	68	68	68
(Pseudo) R-squared	0.002	0.001	0.006	0.003
Post school entrepreneurial education and training	1.631	5.478	-0.494	-0.964
	(3.096)	(5.836)	(4.124)	(6.222)
Observations	68	68	68	68
(Pseudo) R-squared	0.003	0.011	0.001	0.001
Commercial bank branches (per 100,000 adults)	-0.116	-0.189*	-0.205*	-0.185
	(0.081)	(0.111)	(0.109)	(0.123)
Observations	121	121	121	121
(Pseudo) R-squared	0.017	0.025	0.036	0.007
ATMs (per 100,000 adults)	-0.055*	-0.087*	-0.103**	-0.034
	(0.032)	(0.045)	(0.042)	(0.045)
Observations	120	120	120	120
(Pseudo) R-squared	0.026	0.036	0.033	0.003
Domestic credit to private sector (percent of GDP)	-0.120***	-0.163***	-0.155***	-0.137***
	(0.034)	(0.044)	(0.039)	(0.043)
Observations	120	120	120	120
(Pseudo) R-squared	0.124	0.126	0.086	0.046
Account ownership (percent of age 15+)	-0.184***	-0.234***	-0.211***	-0.203***
	(0.038)	(0.059)	(0.051)	(0.060)
Observations	110	110	110	110
(Pseudo) R-squared	0.146	0.133	0.129	0.058
Internal financing (percent of age 15+)	0.263*	0.222	0.351**	0.428**
	(0.133)	(0.196)	(0.166)	(0.195)
Observations	105	105	105	105
(Pseudo) R-squared	0.034	0.007	0.040	0.023
IMF financial development index	-28.857***	-37.263***	-35.054***	-25.386***
	(6.643)	(8.042)	(6.545)	(8.872)
Observations	119	119	119	119
(Pseudo) R-squared	0.187	0.165	0.158	0.073
Identify access to finance as a major constraint (percent of firms)	0.138**	0.219***	0.164**	0.010
	(0.060)	(0.079)	(0.070)	(0.077)
Observations	109	109	109	109
(Pseudo) R-squared	0.050	0.067	0.060	0.001
Percent of firms using banks to finance investment	-0.197***	-0.163	-0.270***	-0.245***
	(0.064)	(0.115)	(0.072)	(0.087)
Observations	109	109	109	109
(Pseudo) R-squared	0.070	0.037	0.102	0.036

TABLE 6B.6 Robustness checks: OLS and quantile regressions between policy measures and DGE-based output informality (*continued*)

Dep. var. = DGE-based output informality (percent of official GDP)		Quantile regression		
Explanatory var =	OLS	Tau = 0.25	Tau = 0.50	Tau = 0.75
Proportion of investment financed internally	0.115	0.127	0.239***	0.113
	(0.073)	(0.118)	(0.088)	(0.101)
Observations	109	109	109	109
(Pseudo) R-squared	0.019	0.015	0.058	0.016

Sources: Global Entrepreneurship Monitor; *International Country Risk Guide* (ICRG); KPMG; University of Michigan; Organisation for Economic Co-operation and Development; Végh and Vuletin (2015); World Bank (*Doing Business*, World Development Indicators); World Economic Forum (WEF); World Value Surveys.

Note: Data are from EMDEs averaged over the period 1990-2018 (or otherwise specified). All regressions here use the same sample of data as in figures 6.2-6.12; please see details above. The cells show the coefficients of regressing various policy measures (listed in the first column on the left) against the share of informal output (dynamic general equilibrium estimates) in percent of official GDP, with standard errors shown in parentheses. ALMP = active labor market programs; ATM = automated teller machine; DGE = dynamic general equilibrium model; EMDEs = emerging market and developing economies; GNI = gross national income; IMF = International Monetary Fund; OLS = ordinary least squares; PISA = Programme for International Student Assessment; VAT = value added tax. * $p < 0.10$, ** $p < 0.05$, *** $p < 0.01$.

TABLE 6B.7 Robustness checks: OLS and quantile regressions between policy measures and employment informality

Dep. var = Self-employment (percent of total employment)		Quantile regression		
Explanatory var =	OLS	Tau = 0.25	Tau = 0.50	Tau = 0.75
Corporate income tax rate	1.005**	0.872**	1.042***	1.671***
	(0.383)	(0.339)	(0.352)	(0.431)
Observations	96	96	96	96
(Pseudo) R-squared	0.131	0.084	0.090	0.091
Individual income tax rate	0.869***	0.840***	0.958***	1.217***
	(0.167)	(0.211)	(0.222)	(0.327)
Observations	87	87	87	87
(Pseudo) R-squared	0.235	0.176	0.152	0.104
VAT rate	0.610	0.949*	0.094	1.271**
	(0.408)	(0.505)	(0.582)	(0.634)
Observations	84	84	84	84
(Pseudo) R-squared	0.031	0.027	0.001	0.017
Payments number per year	0.576***	0.470***	0.598***	0.615**
	(0.126)	(0.159)	(0.224)	(0.242)
Observations	107	107	107	107
(Pseudo) R-squared	0.149	0.093	0.072	0.075
Time hours per year	0.010	0.027**	0.019	0.006
	(0.011)	(0.011)	(0.013)	(0.017)
Observations	107	107	107	107
(Pseudo) R-squared	0.011	0.017	0.006	0.003
Time to comply with VAT refund	0.367***	0.471***	0.440***	0.210
	(0.089)	(0.116)	(0.140)	(0.203)
Observations	57	57	57	57
(Pseudo) R-squared	0.198	0.180	0.190	0.063

TABLE 6B.7 Robustness checks: OLS and quantile regressions between policy measures and employment informality (*continued*)

Dep. var=Self-employment (percent of total employment)		Quantile regression		
Explanatory var=	OLS	Tau = 0.25	Tau = 0.50	Tau = 0.75
Time to obtain VAT refund (weeks)	0.401***	0.304*	0.538***	0.243
	(0.106)	(0.158)	(0.195)	(0.247)
Observations	57	57	57	57
(Pseudo) R-squared	0.158	0.094	0.135	0.064
Cheating on taxes	-2.961	-5.067	-7.284	-9.456
	(5.663)	(6.863)	(6.395)	(9.700)
Observations	60	60	60	60
(Pseudo) R-squared	0.006	0.010	0.037	0.008
Coverage of unemployment benefits and ALMP	-0.158	-0.130	-0.740	-0.516
	(0.484)	(0.749)	(0.824)	(1.069)
Observations	61	61	61	61
(Pseudo) R-squared	0.001	0.006	0.004	0.005
Adequacy of social insurance programs	-0.409**	-0.549***	-0.407*	-0.617**
	(0.176)	(0.173)	(0.218)	(0.246)
Observations	100	100	100	100
(Pseudo) R-squared	0.083	0.066	0.033	0.055
Access to electricity	-0.646***	-0.777***	-0.681***	-0.600***
	(0.044)	(0.067)	(0.059)	(0.054)
Observations	135	135	135	135
(Pseudo) R-squared	0.604	0.347	0.396	0.449
Mobile cellular subscriptions	-0.736***	-0.699***	-0.906***	-1.035***
	(0.127)	(0.097)	(0.108)	(0.116)
Observations	135	135	135	135
(Pseudo) R-squared	0.392	0.221	0.238	0.302
Fixed broadband subscriptions	-3.270***	-2.765***	-3.454***	-3.802***
	(0.370)	(0.403)	(0.522)	(0.579)
Observations	133	133	133	133
(Pseudo) R-squared	0.409	0.221	0.237	0.291
Individuals using the internet	-1.377***	-1.330***	-1.655***	-1.719***
	(0.252)	(0.168)	(0.159)	(0.166)
Observations	135	135	135	135
(Pseudo) R-squared	0.506	0.297	0.340	0.378
Paved road	-0.481***	-0.380***	-0.558***	-0.585***
	(0.058)	(0.086)	(0.093)	(0.080)
Observations	123	123	123	123
(Pseudo) R-squared	0.331	0.135	0.164	0.250
Life expectancy	-2.212***	-2.253***	-2.532***	-2.241***
	(0.195)	(0.368)	(0.240)	(0.203)
Observations	134	134	134	134
(Pseudo) R-squared	0.513	0.218	0.325	0.412
Governmental support and policies	0.703	3.155	-2.222	9.974
	(6.145)	(8.093)	(7.662)	(12.051)
Observations	67	67	67	67
(Pseudo) R-squared	0.000	0.000	0.004	0.020

TABLE 6B.7 Robustness checks: OLS and quantile regressions between policy measures and employment informality (*continued*)

Dep. Var = Self-employment (percent of total employment)		Quantile regression		
Explanatory var=	OLS	Tau = 0.25	Tau = 0.50	Tau = 0.75
Governmental programs	-6.528	7.571	-9.682	-1.630
	(7.281)	(9.356)	(11.291)	(13.709)
Observations	67	67	67	67
(Pseudo) R-squared	0.013	0.003	0.028	0.002
Commercial and professional infrastructure	-1.596	-6.546	-11.359	9.077
	(9.923)	(14.381)	(15.818)	(22.277)
Observations	67	67	67	67
(Pseudo) R-squared	0.000	0.001	0.015	0.011
Physical and services infrastructure	-14.349**	-17.995**	-11.027	-20.035*
	(5.998)	(7.641)	(8.756)	(11.638)
Observations	67	67	67	67
(Pseudo) R-squared	0.083	0.052	0.036	0.028
Labor market regulations	-5.493***	-7.961***	-6.992***	-2.988
	(1.807)	(1.792)	(2.566)	(3.500)
Observations	118	118	118	118
(Pseudo) R-squared	0.076	0.113	0.033	0.010
Labor market efficiency (WEF)	-5.669	-22.362***	-1.195	7.654
	(5.586)	(6.306)	(9.499)	(10.068)
Observations	111	111	111	111
(Pseudo) R-squared	0.009	0.060	0.000	0.013
Minimum wage (percent of GDP per capita)	2.678***	3.739***	3.729***	2.989**
	(0.825)	(0.800)	(1.065)	(1.220)
Observations	88	88	88	88
(Pseudo) R-squared	0.163	0.125	0.108	0.083
Hiring regulations and minimum wage	-2.897***	-3.965***	-2.796*	-1.898
	(0.915)	(1.118)	(1.633)	(1.922)
Observations	118	118	118	118
(Pseudo) R-squared	0.078	0.082	0.044	0.016
Hiring and firing regulations	1.639	-0.599	3.501	6.065
	(2.441)	(3.891)	(3.476)	(4.971)
Observations	114	114	114	114
(Pseudo) R-squared	0.004	0.001	0.007	0.005
Hours regulations	-1.470	-1.495	-0.930	-1.479
	(1.480)	(2.096)	(2.350)	(2.919)
Observations	118	118	118	118
(Pseudo) R-squared	0.008	0.008	0.004	0.006
Mandated cost of worker dismissal	-1.360*	-3.211***	-1.334	0.528
	(0.767)	(0.967)	(1.236)	(1.684)
Observations	118	118	118	118
(Pseudo) R-squared	0.023	0.063	0.017	0.001
Cost of business start-up procedures (in percent of GNI per capita)	0.212***	0.200***	0.214***	0.293***
	(0.036)	(0.042)	(0.038)	(0.049)
Observations	128	128	128	128
(Pseudo) R-squared	0.311	0.173	0.185	0.181

TABLE 6B.7 Robustness checks: OLS and quantile regressions between policy measures and employment informality (*continued*)

Dep. var=Self-employment (percent of total employment)		Quantile regression		
Explanatory var=	OLS	Tau = 0.25	Tau = 0.50	Tau = 0.75
Time required to start a business	0.002	-0.037	0.086	0.096
(days)	(0.064)	(0.066)	(0.081)	(0.098)
Observations	128	128	128	128
(Pseudo) R-squared	0.000	0.004	0.004	0.005
Bureaucracy quality	-18.151***	-17.404***	-21.895***	-21.096***
(ICRG)	(2.818)	(5.502)	(3.827)	(5.172)
Observations	96	96	96	96
(Pseudo) R-squared	0.261	0.136	0.187	0.209
Corruption	-13.561***	-11.653*	-18.131***	-19.699**
(ICRG)	(3.836)	(6.162)	(6.052)	(8.577)
Observations	96	96	96	96
(Pseudo) R-squared	0.087	0.075	0.059	0.049
Law and order	-12.164***	-12.517***	-13.164***	-15.214***
(ICRG)	(2.471)	(2.503)	(4.010)	(4.700)
Observations	96	96	96	96
(Pseudo) R-squared	0.192	0.177	0.085	0.085
Years of schooling	-7.167***	-7.460***	-7.437***	-7.749***
(interpolated over 5-yr period)	(0.600)	(1.149)	(0.884)	(1.030)
Observations	99	99	99	99
(Pseudo) R-squared	0.492	0.234	0.308	0.372
Literacy rate, adult total	-0.901***	-1.002***	-0.868***	-0.795***
(percent of age 15 +)	(0.063)	(0.116)	(0.109)	(0.142)
Observations	126	126	126	126
(Pseudo) R-squared	0.514	0.287	0.311	0.325
PISA: Mean performance on the mathematics scale	-0.102*	-0.199**	-0.134**	-0.154
	(0.052)	(0.080)	(0.056)	(0.106)
Observations	47	47	47	47
(Pseudo) R-squared	0.077	0.141	0.106	0.046
PISA: Mean performance on the reading scale	-0.136**	-0.172**	-0.161***	-0.126
	(0.056)	(0.081)	(0.056)	(0.105)
Observations	47	47	47	47
(Pseudo) R-squared	0.130	0.136	0.129	0.082
PISA: Mean performance on the science scale	-0.125*	-0.228***	-0.137**	-0.192*
	(0.068)	(0.083)	(0.054)	(0.112)
Observations	47	47	47	47
(Pseudo) R-squared	0.108	0.150	0.136	0.077
Basic school entrepreneurial education and training	-10.050	-8.825	-7.669	-9.750
	(8.002)	(9.540)	(10.866)	(14.816)
Observations	73	73	73	73
(Pseudo) R-squared	0.025	0.012	0.010	0.010
Post school entrepreneurial education and training	-6.402	-1.901	-4.408	-17.024
	(8.904)	(9.332)	(10.969)	(15.196)
Observations	73	73	73	73
(Pseudo) R-squared	0.010	0.001	0.001	0.021

TABLE 6B.7 Robustness checks: OLS and quantile regressions between policy measures and employment informality (*continued*)

Dep. var = Self-employment (percent of total employment)		Quantile regression		
Explanatory var =	**OLS**	**Tau = 0.25**	**Tau = 0.50**	**Tau = 0.75**
Commercial bank branches	-0.746***	-0.391	-0.841***	-1.131***
(per 100,000 adults)	(0.207)	(0.241)	(0.249)	(0.276)
Observations	108	108	108	108
(Pseudo) R-squared	0.147	0.051	0.091	0.135
ATMs	-0.512***	-0.482***	-0.539***	-0.563***
(per 100,000 adults)	(0.071)	(0.095)	(0.092)	(0.100)
Observations	107	107	107	107
(Pseudo) R-squared	0.405	0.185	0.237	0.257
Domestic credit to private sector	-0.345***	-0.243***	-0.258**	-0.455***
(percent of GDP)	(0.078)	(0.078)	(0.113)	(0.116)
Observations	106	106	106	106
(Pseudo) R-squared	0.181	0.080	0.083	0.139
Account ownership	-0.655***	-0.681***	-0.646***	-0.882***
(percent of age 15+)	(0.098)	(0.102)	(0.131)	(0.189)
Observations	99	99	99	99
(Pseudo) R-squared	0.336	0.222	0.194	0.166
Internal financing	1.280***	1.210***	1.760***	1.062**
(percent of age 15+)	(0.252)	(0.390)	(0.378)	(0.469)
Observations	96	96	96	96
(Pseudo) R-squared	0.170	0.087	0.136	0.114
IMF financial development index	-96.053***	-90.486***	-115.068***	-97.609***
	(15.714)	(15.812)	(19.794)	(21.793)
Observations	104	104	104	104
(Pseudo) R-squared	0.341	0.207	0.197	0.210
Identify access to finance as a major constraint (percent of firms)	0.459***	0.214	0.656***	0.585***
	(0.147)	(0.183)	(0.247)	(0.213)
Observations	114	114	114	114
(Pseudo) R-squared	0.084	0.011	0.027	0.109
Percent of firms using banks to finance investments	-0.825***	-0.539***	-0.897***	-1.115***
	(0.137)	(0.186)	(0.258)	(0.233)
Observations	114	114	114	114
(Pseudo) R-squared	0.214	0.100	0.129	0.176
Proportion of investment financed internally	0.731***	0.551**	0.737***	1.066***
	(0.157)	(0.253)	(0.271)	(0.236)
Observations	114	114	114	114
(Pseudo) R-squared	0.149	0.051	0.088	0.153

Sources: Global Entrepreneurship Monitor; *International Country Risk Guide* (ICRG); KPMG; University of Michigan; Organisation for Economic Co-operation and Development; Végh and Vuletin (2015); World Bank (*Doing Business*, World Development Indicators); World Economic Forum (WEF); World Value Surveys.
Note: Data are from EMDEs averaged over the period 1990-2018 (or otherwise specified). All regressions here use the same sample of data as in figures 6.2-6.12; please see details above. The cells show the coefficients of regressing various policy measures (listed in the first column on the left) against the share of informal output (dynamic general equilibrium estimates) in percent of official GDP, with standard errors shown in parentheses. ALMP = active labor market programs; ATM = automated teller machine; EMDEs = emerging market and developing economies; GNI = gross national income; IMF = International Monetary Fund; OLS = ordinary least squares; PISA = Programme for International Student Assessment; VAT = value added tax. * p < 0.10, ** p < 0.05, *** p < 0.01.

References

Alfaro, L., O. Becerra, and M. Eslava. 2020. "EMEs and COVID-19: Shutting Down in a World of Informal and Tiny Firms." NBER Working Paper 27360, National Bureau of Economic Research, Cambridge, MA.

Almeida, R., J. Behrman, and D. Robalino. 2012. *The Right Skills for the Job? Rethinking Training Policies for Workers.* Human Development Perspectives. Washington, DC: World Bank.

Amaral, P. S., and E. Quintin. 2006. "A Competitive Model of the Informal Sector." *Journal of Monetary Economics* 53 (7): 1541-53.

Anand, R., and P. Khera. 2016. "Macroeconomic Impact of Product and Labor Market Reforms on Informality and Unemployment in India." IMF Working Paper 1647, International Monetary Fund, Washington, DC.

Andrews, D., A. Sánchez, and Å. Johansson. 2011. "Towards a Better Understanding of the Informal Economy." OECD Economics Department Working Paper 873, Organisation for Economic Co-operation and Development, Paris.

Antunes, A. R., and T. Cavalcanti. 2007. "Start Up Costs, Limited Enforcement, and the Hidden Economy." *European Economic Review* 51 (1): 203-24.

Auriol, E., and M. Warlters. 2005. "Taxation Base in Developing Countries." *Journal of Public Economics* 89 (4): 625-46.

Awasthi, R., and M. Engelschalk. 2018. "Taxation and the Shadow Economy: How the Tax System Can Stimulate and Enforce the Formalization of Business Activities." Policy Research Working Paper 8391, World Bank, Washington, DC.

Aziz, M., D. Bloom, S. Humair, E. Jimenez, L. Rosenberg, and Z. Sathar. 2014. "Education System Reform in Pakistan: Why, When, and How?" IZA Policy Paper 76, Institute for the Study of Labor, Bonn, Germany.

Bachas, P., L. Gadenne, and A., Jensen. 2020. "Informality, Consumption Taxes and Redistribution." Policy Research Working Paper 9267, World Bank, Washington, DC.

Barro, R. J., and L. W. Lee. 2013. "A New Data Set of Educational Attainment in the World, 1950–2010." *Journal of Development Economics* 104 (September): 184-98.

Bayar, Y., and O., Ozturk. 2016. "Financial Development and Shadow Economy in European Union Transition Economies." *Managing Global Transitions* 14 (2): 157-73.

Beck, T., A. Demirgüç-Kunt, and R. Levine. 2000. "A New Database on the Structure and Development of the Financial Sector." *World Bank Economic Review* 14 (3): 597-605.

Bellon, M., J. Chang, E. Dabla-Norris, S. Khalid, F. Lima, E. Rojas, and P. Villena. 2019. "Digitalization to Improve Tax Compliance: Evidence from VAT e-Invoicing in Peru." IMF Working Paper 19/231, International Monetary Fund, Washington, DC.

Berdiev, A., and J., Saunoris. 2016. "Financial Development and the Shadow Economy: A Panel VAR Analysis." *Economic Modelling* 57 (September): 197-207.

Benjamin, N., and A. Mbaye. 2012. *The Informal Sector in Francophone Africa: Firm Size, Productivity, and Institutions.* Washington, DC: World Bank.

Betcherman, G., N. Melten Daysal, and C. Pagés. 2010. "Do Employment Subsidies Work? Evidence from Regionally Targeted Subsidies in Turkey." *Labour Economics* 17 (4): 710-22.

Birdsall, N., A. de la Torre, and F. Caicedo. 2010. "The Washington Consensus: Assessing a Damaged Brand." Policy Research Working Paper 5316, World Bank, Washington, DC.

Bittencourt, M., R. Gupta, R., and L., Stander. 2014. "Tax Evasion, Financial Development and Inflation: Theory and Empirical Evidence." *Journal of Banking and Finance* 41(1): 194-208.

Blackburn, K., N. Bose, and S. Capasso. 2012. "Tax Evasion, the Underground Economy and Financial Development." *Journal of Economic Behavior and Organization* 83 (2): 243-53.

Bosch, M., E. Goñi-Pacchioni, and W. Maloney. 2012. "Trade Liberalization, Labor Reforms and Formal-Informal Employment Dynamics." *Labour Economics* 19 (5): 653-67.

Bose, N., S. Capasso, and M. Wurm. 2012. "The Impact of Banking Development on the Size of the Shadow Economy." *Journal of Economic Studies* 39 (6): 620-28.

Bruhn, M., and D. McKenzie. 2014. "Entry Regulation and the Formalization of Microenterprises in Developing Countries." *World Bank Research Observer* 29 (2): 186-201.

Burki, A. A., and Q. Abbas. 1991. "Earnings Functions in Pakistan's Urban Informal Sector: A Case Study." *The Pakistan Development Review* 30 (4): 695-706.

Busso, M., J. Camacho, J. Messina, and G. Montenegro. 2020. "Social Protection and Informality in Latin America during the COVID-19 Pandemic." IDB Working Papers 10849, Inter-American Development Bank, Washington, DC.

Canh, N., and S. Thanh. 2020. "Financial Development and the Shadow Economy: A Multi-Dimensional Analysis." *Economic Analysis and Policy* 67 (September): 37-54.

Capasso, S., and T. Jappelli. 2013. "Financial Development and the Underground Economy." *Journal of Development Economics* 101 (March): 167-78.

Capasso, S., S. Monferrà, and G. Sampagnaro. 2015. "The Shadow Economy and Banks' Lending Technology." CSEF Working Papers 422, Centre for Studies in Economics and Finance, University of Naples, Italy.

Card, D., J. Kluve, and A. Weber. 2018. "What Works? A Meta-Analysis of Recent Active Labor Market Program Evaluations." *Journal of the European Economic Association* 16 (3): 894-931.

Caro, P., and A. Sacchi. 2020. "The Heterogeneous Effects of Labor Informality on VAT Revenues: Evidence on a Developed Country." *Journal of Macroeconomics* 63 (March): 103-90.

Carrillo, P., D. Pomeranz, and M. Singhal. 2017. "Dodging the Taxman: Firm Misreporting and Limits to Tax Enforcement." *American Economic Journal: Applied Economics* 9 (2): 144-64.

Chodorow-Reich, G., G. Gopinath, P. Mishra, and A. Narayanan. 2018. "Evidence from India's Demonetization," NBER Working Paper 25370 National Bureau of Economic Research, Cambridge, MA.

Choi, J., and M. Thum. 2005. "Corruption and the Shadow Economy." *International Economic Review* 46 (3): 817-36.

Cnossen, S. 1998. "Global Trends and Issues in Value Added Taxation." *International Tax and Public Finance* 5 (3): 399-428.

Crouzet, N., A. Gupta, and F. Mezzanotti. 2020. "Shocks and Technology Adoption: Evidence from Electronic Payment Systems." Mimeo.

Dabla-Norris, E., M. Gradstein, and G. Inchauste. 2008. "What Causes Firms to Hide Output?" *Journal of Development Economics* 85 (1-2): 1-27.

Daude, C., H. Gutiérrez, and Á. Melguizo, 2012. "What Drives Tax Morale?" OECD Development Centre Working Paper 315, Organisation for Economic Co-operation and Development, Paris.

D'Erasmo, P. 2016. "Access to Credit and the Size of the Formal Sector." *Economía* 16 (2): 143-99.

De Giorgi, G., M. Ploenzke, and A. Rahman. 2018. "Small Firms' Formalisation: The Stick Treatment." *The Journal of Development Studies* 54 (6): 983-1001.

De Paula, Á., and J. Scheinkman. 2010. "Value-Added Taxes, Chain Effects, and Informality." *American Economic Journal: Macroeconomics* 2 (4): 195-221.

De Soto, H. 1989. *The Other Path: The Invisible Revolution in the Third World.* New York: Harper & Row.

DeBacker, J., B. Heim, and A. Tran. 2015. "Importing Corruption Culture from Overseas: Evidence from Corporate Tax Evasion in the United States." *Journal of Financial Economics* 117(1): 122-38.

Dreher, A., and F. Schneider. 2010. "Corruption and the Shadow Economy: An Empirical Analysis." *Public Choice* 144 (1): 215-38.

EBRD (European Bank for Reconstruction and Development). 2018. *Transition Report 2018-19: Work in Transition.* London: European Bank for Reconstruction and Development.

Elgin, C., and O. Öztunali. 2012. "Shadow Economies around the World: Model Based Estimates." Working Papers 2012/05, Bogazici University, Istanbul, Turkey.

Elgin, C., and B. Uras. 2013. "Is Informality A Barrier to Financial Development?" *SERIEs* 4 (3): 309-31.

Emran, S., and J. Stiglitz. 2005. "On Selective Indirect Tax Reform in Developing Countries." *Journal of Public Economics* 89 (4): 599-623.

Fan, H., Y. Liu, N. Qian, and J. Wen. 2020. "The Effects of Computerizing VAT Invoices in China." NBER Working Paper 24414, National Bureau of Economic Research, Cambridge, MA.

Fajnzylber, P., W. Maloney, and G. Montes-Rojas. 2011. "Does Formality Improve Micro-Firm Performance? Evidence from the Brazilian SIMPLES Program." *Journal of Development Economics* 94 (2): 262-76.

Fang, P., A. Kennedy, and D. Resnick. 2020. "Scaling up and Sustaining Social Protection under COVID-19." COVID-19 Policy Response Portal Project Note 3, International Food Policy Research Institute, Washington, DC.

Farazi, S. 2014. "Informal Firms and Financial Inclusion: Status and Determinants." Policy Research Working Paper 6778, World Bank, Washington, DC.

Ferreira-Tiryaki, G. 2008. "The Informal Economy and Business Cycles." *Journal of Applied Economics* 11 (1): 91-117.

Fields, G. S. 1975. "Rural-Urban Migration, Urban Unemployment and Underemployment, and Job-Search Activity in LDCs." *Journal of Development Economics* 2 (2): 165-87.

Franjo, L., N. Pouokam, and F. Turino. 2020. "Financial Frictions and Firm Informality: A General Equilibrium Perspective." IMF Working Paper 20-211, International Monetary Fund, Washington, DC.

Fraser Institute. 2020. *The Human Freedom Index 2020. A Global Measurement of Personal, Civil, and Economic Freedom.* Washington, DC: Cato Institute and Fraser Institute.

Gatti, R., and M. Honorati. 2008. "Informality Among Formal Firms: Firm-Level, Cross-Country Evidence on Tax Compliance and Access to Credit." Policy Research Working Paper 4476, World Bank, Washington, DC.

Gharleghi, B., and A., Jahanshahi. 2020. "The Shadow Economy and Sustainable Development: The Role of Financial Development." *Journal of Public Affairs* 20 (3): 1-7.

Gindling, T., and K. Terrell. 2007. "The Effects of Multiple Minimum Wages throughout the Labor Market: The Case of Costa Rica." *Labor Economics* 14 (3): 485-511.

Goldberg, P. K., and N. Pavcnik. 2003. "The Response of the Informal Sector to Trade Liberalization. *Journal of Development Economics* 72 (2): 463-96.

Guiso, L., P. Sapienza, and L. Zingales. 2004. "Does Local Financial Development Matter?" *Quarterly Journal of Economics* 119 (3): 929-68.

Guo, J., and F. Hung. 2020. "Tax Evasion and Financial Development under Asymmetric Information in Credit Markets." *Journal of Development Economics* 145 (April):102463.

Gupta, S., M. Keen, A. Shah, and G. Verdier. 2017. *Digital Revolutions in Public Finance.* Washington, DC: International Monetary Fund.

Haltiwanger, J., R. Jarmin, and J. Miranda. 2013. "Who Creates Jobs? Small versus Large versus Young." *Review of Economics and Statistics* 95 (2): 347-61.

Harju, J., T. Matikka, and T. Rauhanen. 2019. "Compliance Costs vs. Tax Incentives: Why Do Entrepreneurs Respond to Size-based Regulations?" *Journal of Public Economics* 173 (C): 139-64.

Harris, J., and M. Todaro. 1970. "Migration, Unemployment, and Development: A Two Sector Analysis." *American Economic Review* 60 (1): 126-42.

Hathaway, R. 2005. *Education Reform in Pakistan: Building for the Future. Woodrow Wilson International Center for Scholars.* Washington, DC: Woodrow Wilson International Center for Scholars.

Hohberg, M., and J. Lay. 2015. "The Impact of Minimum Wages on Informal and Formal Labor Market Outcomes: Evidence from Indonesia." *IZA Journal of Labor & Development* 4 (1): 1-25.

Ihrig, J., and K. Moe. 2004. "Lurking in the Shadows: The Informal Sector and Government Policy." *Journal of Development Economics* 73 (2): 541-57.

ICRG (*International Country Risk Guide*). 2020. *International Country Risk Guide.* New York: The PRS Group.

Iriyama, A., R. Kishore, and D. Talukdar. 2016. "Playing Dirty or Building Capability? Corruption and HR Training as Competitive Actions to Threats from Informal and Foreign Firm Rivals." *Strategic Management Journal* 37 (10): 2152-73.

Jessen, J., and J. Kluve. 2021. "The Effectiveness of Interventions to Reduce Informality in Low-and Middle-Income Countries." *World Development* 138 (February): 1-19.

Jordà, Ò. 2005. "Estimation and Inference of Impulse Responses by Local Projections." *American Economic Review* 95 (1): 161-82.

Junquera-Varela R. F., M. Verhoeven, G. P. Shukla, B. Haven, R. Awasthi, and B. Moreno-Dodson. 2017. *Strengthening Domestic Resource Mobilization: Moving from Theory to Practice in Low- and Middle-Income Countries.* Washington, DC: World Bank.

Kanbur, R., and M. Keen. 2014. "Thresholds, Informality, and Partitions of Compliance." *International Tax and Public Finance* 21(4): 536-59.

Keen, M. 2008. "VAT, Tariffs, and Withholding: Border Taxes and Informality in Developing Countries." *Journal of Public Economics* 92 (10): 1892-1906.

Kim, Y., N. Loayza, and C. Meza-Cuadra, 2016. "Productivity as the Key to Economic Growth and Development," Research and Policy Briefs 108092, World Bank, Washington, DC.

Koh, W., G. Kindberg-Hanlon, Y. Okawa, T. Kaskin, E. Vashakmadze, D. Vorisek, and L. S. Ye. Forthcoming. "Informality in Emerging Markets and Developing Economies: Regional Dimensions and Policy Options." Mimeo, World Bank, Washington, DC.

Kopczuk, W. 2005. "Tax Bases, Tax Rates and the Elasticity of Reported Income." *Journal of Public Economics* 89(11-12): 2093-119.

Kuddo, A. 2018. "Labor Regulations Throughout the World: An Overview." Jobs Working Paper 16, World Bank, Washington DC.

Kugler, A. 2004. "The Effect of Job Security Provision Regulations on Labor Market Flexibility: Evidence from the Colombian Labor Market Reform." In *Law and Employment: Lessons from Latin America and the Caribbean*, edited by J. Heckman and C. Pagés, 183-228. Chicago: University of Chicago Press.

Kugler A., M. Kugler, and L. Herrera-Prada, 2017. "Do Payroll Tax Breaks Stimulate Formality? Evidence from Colombia's Reform." *Economía* 18 (1): 3-40.

Lahiri, A. 2020. "The Great Indian Demonetization." *Journal of Economic Perspectives* 34 (1): 55-74.

Lemos, S. 2009. "Minimum Wage Effects in a Developing Country." *Labour Economics* 16 (2): 224-37.

Loayza, N. 2016. "Informality in the Process of Development and Growth." *The World Economy* 39 (12): 1856-916.

Loayza, N. 2018. "Informality: Why Is It So Widespread and How Can It Be Reduced?" Research & Policy Brief 20, World Bank, Kuala Lumpur, Malaysia.

Loayza, N., and S. Pennings. 2020. "Macroeconomic Policy in the Time of Covid-19: A Primer for Developing Countries." Research & Policy Brief 28, World Bank, Kuala Lumpur.

Loayza, N., L. Servén, and N. Sugawara. 2010. "Informality in Latin America and the Caribbean." In *Business Regulation and Economic Performance*, edited by N. Loayza and L. Servén. Washington, DC: World Bank.

Luttmer, E., and M. Singhal. 2014. "Tax Morale." *Journal of Economic Perspectives* 28 (4): 149-68.

Maloney, W. 2004. "Informality Revisited." *World Development* 32 (7): 1159-78.

Maloney, W, and J. Nuñez Mendez. 2004. "Measuring the Impact of Minimum Wages: Evidence from Latin America." In *Lessons from Latin America and the Caribbean*, edited by C. Pagés and J. Heckman. Chicago: University of Chicago Press.

Manning, A. 2021. "The Elusive Employment Effect of the Minimum Wage." *Journal of Economic Perspectives* 35 (1): 3-26.

Marusic, A., W. Nielsen, T. Ghossein, and S. Solf. 2020. *Re-thinking the Approach to Informal Businesses: Typologies, Evidence and Future Exploration. Finance, Competitiveness and Innovation in Focus.* Washington, DC: World Bank.

McCaig, B., and N. Pavcnik. 2015. "Informal Employment in a Growing and Globalizing Low-Income Country." *American Economic Review* 105 (5): 545-50.

Medina, L., and F. Schneider. 2018. "Shadow Economies Around the World: What Did We Learn Over the Last 20 Years?" IMF Working Paper 18/17, International Monetary Fund, Washington, DC.

Morales, L., and C. Medina. 2016. "Assessing the Effect of Payroll Taxes on Formal Employment: The Case of the 2012 Tax Reform in Colombia." Borradores de Economia 971, Banco de la Republica de Colombia, Bogota.

Munkacsi, Z., and M. Saxegaard. 2017. "Structural Reform Packages, Sequencing, and the Informal Economy." IMF Working Paper 17/125, International Monetary Fund, Washington, DC.

Naim, M. 1999. "Fads and Fashion in Economic Reforms: Washington Consensus or Washington Confusion?" Paper prepared for the IMF Conference on Second Generation Reforms, International Monetary Fund, Washington, DC.

Naritomi, J. 2019. "Consumers as Tax Auditors." *American Economic Review* 109 (9): 3031-72.

Nguimkeu, P. 2015. "An Estimated Model of Informality with Constrained Entrepreneurship." Working Paper, Georgia State University, Atlanta.

Nguimkeu, P., and C. Okou. 2019. "Increasing Informal Sector Productivity." In *The Future of Work in Africa: Harnessing the Potential of Digital Technologies for All*, edited by J. Choi, M. A. Dutz, and Z. Usman, 121-162. Washington, DC: World Bank.

OECD (Organization for Economic Co-operation and Development). 2019. *Tax Morale: What Drives People and Businesses to Pay Tax?* Paris: OECD.

OECD (Organization for Economic Co-operation and Development). 2020. "Distributional Risks Associated with Non-standard Work: Stylised Facts and Policy Considerations". Tackling coronavirus series. Paris: OECD.

Oviedo, A., M. Thomas, and K. Karakurum-Özdemir. 2009. "Economic Informality: Causes, Costs, and Policies—A Literature Survey." Working Paper 167, World Bank, Washington, DC.

Perry, G. E., W. F. Maloney, O. S. Arias, P. Fajnzylber, A. D. Mason, and J. Saavedra-Chanduvi. 2007. *Informality: Exit and Exclusion*. Washington, DC: World Bank.

Piggott, J., and J. Whalley. 2001. "VAT Base Broadening, Self Supply, and the Informal Sector." *American Economic Review* 91 (4): 1084-94.

Prichard, W., A. Custers, R. Dom, S. Davenport, and M. Roscitt. 2019. "Innovations in Tax Compliance: Conceptual Framework." Policy Research Working Paper 9032, World Bank, Washington, DC.

Quintin, E. 2008. "Contract Enforcement and the Size of the Informal Economy." *Economic Theory* 37 (3): 395-416.

Rocha, R., G. Ulyssea, and R. Rachter. 2018. "Do Lower Taxes Reduce Informality? Evidence from Brazil." *Journal of Development Economics* 134 (September): 28-49.

Roubini, N., and X. Sala-i-Martin. 1992. "Financial Repression and Economic Growth." *Journal of Development Economics* 39 (1): 5-30.

Roubini, N., and X. Sala-i-Martin. 1995. "A Growth Model of Inflation, Tax Evasion, and Financial Repression." *Journal of Monetary Economics* 35: 275-301.

Schneider, F. 2007. "Shadow Economies and Corruption All Over the World: New Estimates for 145 Countries." *Economics—The Open-Access, Open-Assessment E-Journal* 1(2007-9): 1-66.

Schneider, F., A. Buehn, and C. E. Montenegro. 2010. "Shadow Economies All over the World: New Estimates for 162 Countries from 1999 to 2007." Policy Research Working Paper 5356, World Bank, Washington, DC.

Schneider, F., K. Raczkowski, and B. Mróz. 2015. "Shadow Economy and Tax Evasion in the EU." *Journal of Money Laundering Control* 18 (1): 34-51.

Slemrod, J. 2019. "Tax Compliance and Enforcement." *Journal of Economic Literature* 57 (4): 904-54.

Straub, S. 2005. "Informal Sector: The Credit Market Channel." *Journal of Development Economics* 78 (2): 299-321.

Sung, M. J., R. Awasthi, and H. Lee. 2017. "Can Tax Incentives for Electronic Payments Reduce the Shadow Economy? Korea's Attempt to Reduce Underreporting in Retail Businesses." Policy Research Working Paper 7936, World Bank, Washington, DC.

Svirydzenka, K. 2016. "Introducing a New Broad-based Index of Financial Development." IMF Working Paper 16/5, International Monetary Fund, Washington, DC.

Teulings, C. N., and N. Zubanov. 2014. "Is Economic Recovery a Myth? Robust Estimation of Impulse Responses." *Journal of Applied Econometrics* 29 (3): 497-514. Ulyssea, G. 2010. "Regulation of Entry, Labor Market Institutions and the Informal Sector. *Journal of Development Economics* 91 (1): 87-99.

Ulyssea, G. 2010. "Regulation of Entry, Labor Market Institutions and the Informal Sector." *Journal of Development Economics* 91: 87-99.

Ulyssea, G. 2018. "Firms, Informality, and Development: Theory and Evidence from Brazil." *The American Economic Review* 108 (8): 2015-47.

Ulyssea, G. 2020. "Informality: Causes and Consequences for Development." *Annual Review of Economics* 12 (1): 527-46.

Urzua, S., and F. Saltiel. Forthcoming. "The Effect of the Minimum Wage on Employment in Brazil." *Economic Development and Structural Change.*

Végh, C., and G. Vuletin. 2015. "How Is Tax Policy Conducted over the Business Cycle?" *American Economic Journal: Economic Policy* 7 (3): 327-70.

Verner, D., and M. Verner. 2005. "Economic Impacts of Professional Training in the Informal Sector of Cote d'Ivoire: Evaluation of the PAFPA." Policy Research Working Paper 3668, World Bank, Washington, DC.

Waseem, M. 2018. "Taxes, Informality and Income Shifting: Evidence from A Rrecent Pakistani Tax Reform." *Journal of Public Economics* 157 (C): 41-77.

WEF (World Economic Forum). 2020. *Global Competitiveness Report Special Edition 2020: How Countries are Performing on the Road to Recovery.* World Economic Forum, Geneva.

Williams, C., and F. Schneider. 2016. *Measuring the Global Shadow Economy: The Prevalence of Informal Work and Labour.* Cheltenham, UK: Edward Elgar Publishing.

Williamson, J. 2000. "What Should the World Bank Think about the Washington Consensus?" *World Bank Research Observer* 15 (2): 251-64.

World Bank. 2009. *Doing Business 2009.* Washington DC: World Bank.

World Bank. 2010. *Doing Business 2010: Reforming through Difficult Times.* Washington DC: World Bank.

World Bank. 2011. *Doing Business 2011: Making a Difference for Entrepreneurs*. Washington DC: World Bank.

World Bank. 2012. *Doing Business 2012: Doing Business in a More Transparent World*. Washington DC: World Bank.

World Bank. 2013. *Risk and Opportunity—World Development Report 2014*. Washington, DC: World Bank.

World Bank. 2014. *World Development Report 2014: Risks and Opportunities*. Washington, DC: World Bank.

World Bank. 2016. *World Development Report 2016: Digital Dividends*. Washington, DC: World Bank.

World Bank. 2017. *The Global Findex Database 2017: Measuring Financial Inclusion and the Fintech Revolution*. Washington, DC: World Bank.

World Bank. 2018a. *Global Economic Prospects: Broad-Based Upturn, but for How Long?* January. Washington, DC: World Bank.

World Bank. 2018b. *Risk Sharing for a Diverse and Diversifying World of Work*. Washington, DC: World Bank.

World Bank. 2018c. *World Development Report 2018: Learning to Realize Education's Promise*. Washington, DC: World Bank.

World Bank. 2019a. *World Development Report 2019: The Changing Nature of Work*. Washington, DC: World Bank.

World Bank. 2019b. *Global Economic Prospects: Darkening Skies*. January. Washington, DC: World Bank.

World Bank. 2019c. *Global Financial Development Report 2019/2020: Bank Regulation and Supervision a Decade after the Global Financial Crisis*. Washington, DC: World Bank.

World Bank. 2020a. *Doing Business* database. Washington DC: World Bank.

World Bank. 2020b. *Global Economic Prospects*. June. Washington DC: World Bank.

World Bank. 2020c. *World Development Indicators 2020*. Washington, DC: World Bank.

World Bank. 2021. *Global Economic Prospects*. January. Washington, DC: World Bank.

World Bank and PwC. 2019. *Paying Taxes 2020*. Washington, DC: World Bank.